Money and Financial Markets

Money and Financial Markets

By
Niti Bhasin
Associate Professor, Department of Commerce,
Delhi School of Economics (DSE),
University of Delhi, Delhi

New Century Publications
New Delhi, India

New Century Publications,
4800/24, Bharat Ram Road,
Ansari Road, Daryaganj,
New Delhi – 110 002 (India)

Tel.: 011- 4358 7398, 4101 7798, 2324 7798
E-mail: info@newcenturypublications.com • ncpublications2000@gmail.com

www.newcenturypublications.com

Editorial office:
4832/24, Ansari Road, Daryaganj,
New Delhi – 110 002

Tel.: 011- 4356 0919

First Published: **2020**

ISBN: **978-81-7708-505-1**

Published by New Century Publications and printed at Milan Enterprises, New Delhi

Designs: Patch Creative Unit, New Delhi

PRINTED IN INDIA

About the Book

Money is the pivot around which an economy revolves. A modern economy, characterized by acute specialisation and exchange, is unthinkable without money, financial intermediaries, financial markets and financial instruments.

In recent years, there has been a gradual switchover from the use of paper-based payment mediums to those based on electronics. E-money is one such new product which has appeared on Indian horizon recently. Crypto currency is another instrument which is a type of digital token that relies on cryptography for chaining together digital signatures of token transfers, peer-to-peer networking and decentralization.

Similarly, complex financial products, such as derivatives, have proliferated in the financial markets. These products have become highly popular with banks and financial institutions as they allow them to hedge their risks and manage their regulatory and economic capital more efficiently.

This book provides a comprehensive description of the theory and functioning of modern monetary and financial systems with reference to India.

It is spread over 33 chapters which have been organized into 5 theme parts.

Part I (chapters 1 to 2) is titled An Introduction to Money. Apart from explaining the meaning, kinds and functions of money (including e-money, digital money, virtual currency and crypto currency), it also discusses the theories of money supply determination.

Part II (chapters 3 to 17) is titled Financial Institutions, Markets, Instruments and Innovations. It deals with discussion on financial system, financial institutions, financial markets and their integration, asymmetric information, adverse selection, moral hazard, financial crisis, money market in India, capital market in India, modernization of stock exchanges, depository system, and financial derivatives.

Part III (chapters 18 to 21) is titled Interest Rates. It covers determination of interest rates, causes of interest rate differentials, theories of term structure of interest rates, and interest rates in India.

Part IV (chapters 22 to 26) is titled Banking System. It focuses on functions of a commercial bank, balance sheet and portfolio management of a bank, structure and changing role of banks in India, banking sector reforms in India since 1991, and digital technology in the banking sector.

Part V (chapters 27 to 33) is titled Central Banking and Monetary Policy. It delves into functions of central bank, balance sheet of central bank, instruments of monetary control, monetary management in an open economy, Reserve Bank of India, monetary policy of India, and inflation targeting in India.

About the Author

Dr. Niti Bhasin is presently Associate Professor in the Department of Commerce, Delhi School of Economics (DSE), University of Delhi, Delhi and has teaching and research experience of about 19 years. A gold medallist in the M. Com. examination of 2000 of University of Delhi, she holds M.Phil. and Ph.D. degrees from the Department of Commerce, University of Delhi. She has published research papers in refereed academic journals including *Multinational Business Review* (Emerald), *Journal of International Trade and Economic Development* (Taylor and Francis), and *Global Business Review* (Sage).

She has been invited to deliver keynote address and share her views at various forums including Mahidol University (Bangkok); National Defence College, Ministry of Defence, New Delhi; PHD Chamber of Commerce and Industry; and Department of Economic Affairs, Ministry of Finance, Government of India.

She has attended and presented papers at various international conferences/seminars including World Finance Conference (Brazil) and Henley Business School, University of Reading (UK). She is the recipient of Best Business Academic of the Year Award (2011) by Indian Commerce Association. Before joining the Department of Commerce, Delhi School of Economics, she taught for about 4 years at Shri Ram College of Commerce (SRCC), University of Delhi, Delhi. Her areas of specialisation include international business, foreign investment, finance and taxation.

Contents

About the Book..v
About the Author..vi
Preface..xiv-xvi
Explanation of Select Terms Related to Money and Financial Markets............xvii-xxii
Abbreviations/Acronyms..xxiii-xxiv

Part I: An Introduction to Money

1. Meaning, Kinds and Functions of Money 1-10

1.1 Meaning of Money
1.2 Metallic Money, Paper Money and Fiduciary Money
1.3 Electronic Money (E-Money)
1.4 Digital Money (or Digital Currency)
1.5 Virtual Currency
1.6 Crypto Currency
1.7 Functions of Money

2. Theories of Money Supply Determination 11-18

2.1 What is Money Supply?
2.2 Why is Money Supply Important?
2.3 Relationship between Money and Prices: The Equation of Exchange
2.4 Four Measures of Money Supply
2.5 Determinants of Money Supply
2.6 Fiscal Deficits and Monetary Expansion
2.7 Money Supply in Open Economy
2.8 Measures of Money Supply in India

Part II: Financial Institutions, Markets, Instruments and Innovations

3. Financial System and Financial Institutions 19-26

3.1 Meaning, Importance and Functions of Financial System
3.2 Role of Government in Financial Development
3.3 Determinants of Access to Financial Services
3.4 Regulation and Supervision of Financial System
3.5 Financial Neutrality versus Financial Activism
3.6 Financial Volatility versus Financial Stability
3.7 Financial Globalisation

4. Classification, Regulation and Supervision of Financial Institutions in India 27-31

4.1 Classification of Financial Institutions in India
4.2 Regulation and Supervision of Financial Institutions in India

5. Financial Institutions in India at a Glance 32-36

5.1 Commercial Banks
5.2 Regional Rural Banks (RRBs)
5.3 Urban Co-operative Banks (UCBs)
5.4 Rural Co-operative Credit Institutions
5.5 Development Finance Institutions (DFIs)
5.6 Non-banking Financial Companies (NBFCs)
5.7 Mutual Funds
5.8 Pension Funds
5.9 Insurance Organisations

6. Role of Financial Markets 37-42

6.1 Importance of Financial Markets
6.2 Types of Financial Markets
6.3 Regulation and Supervision of Financial Markets in India
6.4 Financial Markets and Monetary Policy of the RBI
6.5 Reforms in the Financial Markets

7. Integration of Financial Markets 43-56

7.1 Integration of Financial Markets: Conceptual Framework
7.2 Need for Integration of Domestic Financial Markets
7.3 Measures Taken for Integration of Financial Markets in India
7.4 Segment-wise Integration
7.5 Regional Financial Integration (Asia)
7.6 International Financial Integration

8. Asymmetric Information, Adverse Selection and Moral Hazard 57-60

8.1 Asymmetric Information
8.2 Adverse Selection
8.3 Moral Hazard

9. Financial Crisis 61-64

9.1 Types of Financial Crisis
9.2 Asian Financial Crisis, 1997
9.3 Financial (Sub-prime) Crisis, 2007-08

10. Money Market 65-80

10.1 Meaning and Functions of Money Market
10.2 Reserve Bank of India (RBI) and the Money Market
10.3 Evolution of Money Market in India
10.4 Developments in the Money Market since 1991
10.5 Component-wise Analysis of Money Market in India
10.6 Report of the Technical Group on Money Market
10.7 Areas of Concern

11. Capital Market Evolution and Reforms in India 81-88

11.1 Meaning and Importance of Capital Market
11.2 Capital Market in the Pre-reforms (i.e. Pre-1991) Period
11.3 Capital Market Reforms since 1991
11.4 Introduction of Free Pricing
11.5 Strengthening of Disclosure Norms
11.6 Transparency and Efficiency
11.7 Shortening of Settlement Cycle
11.8 Growth of Service Providers
11.9 Protection of Investors
11.10 Issues and Concerns

12. Legal Framework for Capital Market in India 89-103

12.1 Securities and Exchange Board of India (SEBI) Act, 1992
12.2 Securities Contracts (Regulation) Act (SCRA), 1956
12.3 Depositories Act, 1996 and Depositories and Participants Regulations, 2018
12.4 Companies Act, 2013: Main Provisions
12.5 Limited Liability Partnership (LLP) Act, 2008
12.6 Insolvency and Bankruptcy Code (IBC), 2016

13. Modernisation of Stock Exchanges 104-111

13.1 Stock Market
13.2 Trading Infrastructure in Stock Exchanges
13.3 Bombay Stock Exchange (BSE) Ltd.
13.4 National Stock Exchange (NSE) of India Ltd.
13.5 Demutualisation and Corporatisation of Stock Exchanges

14. Depository System, Dematerialization (Demat) and Rematerialization (Remat) 112-115

14.1 Depository System
14.2 Depositories Act, 1996 and Depositories and Participants Regulations, 2018

14.3 Dematerialization (Demat)
14.4 Rematerialization (Remat)
14.5 National Securities Depository Ltd. (NSDL)
14.6 National Securities Clearing Corporation Ltd. (NSCCL)

15. Emergence and Popularity of Financial Derivatives 116-124
15.1 Emergence of Complex Financial Products
15.2 Meaning of Derivatives
15.3 Reasons for the Popularity of Derivatives
15.4 Variants (or Types) of Derivative Contracts
15.5 Participants in the Derivatives Market
15.6 Economic Role of Derivatives
15.7 History of Derivatives
15.8 International Experience of Derivatives

16. Forwards, Futures and Options 125-138
16.1 Forwards/Forward Contracts
16.2 Futures/Future Contracts
16.3 Options
16.4 Currency Futures
16.5 Forward Markets Commission (FMC)

17. Derivative Instruments in India 139-152
17.1 L.C. Gupta Committee on Derivatives Trading in India
17.2 Amendment of Securities Contract Regulation Act (SCRA)
17.3 Measures to Protect the Rights of Investors in the Derivatives Market
17.4 Recent Developments in the Derivatives Market
17.5 Credit Derivatives
17.6 Credit Derivatives in India
17.7 Traders and Trading System of Derivatives

Part III: Interest Rates

18. Determination of Interest Rates 153-159
18.1 Significance of Interest Rate
18.2 Types of Rate of Interest
18.3 Loanable Fund Theory of the Rate of Interest
18.4 Liquidity Preference Theory of the Rate of Interest

19. Causes of Interest Rate Differentials 160-164
19.1 How Are Interest Rates Determined?
19.2 What is an Interest Rate Differential?

19.3 Causes of Differences in Interest Rates
19.4 Types of Credit: Based on Repayment and Interest Options

20. Theories of Term Structure of Interest Rates **165-168**
20.1 What is Term Structure of Interest Rates?
20.2 Shapes and Uses of Yield Curve
20.3 Three Theories to Explain Yield Curve

21. Interest Rates in India **169-176**
21.1 Interest Rate Policy: Pre-reforms Period (Before 1991)
21.2 Interest Rate Policy: Post-reforms Period (i.e. since 1991)
21.3 Current Interest Rate Policy of RBI
21.4 Competitive Financial Saving Rates

Part IV: Banking System

22. Meaning, Importance and Functions of a Commercial Bank **177-182**
22.1 Meaning and Importance of Commercial Banks
22.2 Functions of a Commercial Bank
22.3 Deposits and Loans

23. Balance Sheet and Portfolio Management of a Bank **183-186**
23.1 Balance Sheet of a Bank
23.2 Portfolio Management

24. Structure and Changing Role of Banks in India **187-197**
24.1 Post-Independence History and Developments
24.2 Classification of Commercial Banks in India
24.3 Legal Framework for Banking Sector in India
24.4 Ownership and Governance of Commercial Banks in India
24.5 Deposit Insurance System

25. Banking Sector Reforms in India Since 1991 **198-205**
25.1 Backdrop of Banking Sector Reforms
25.2 Objectives of Banking Sector Reforms
25.3 Contents of Banking Sector Reforms
25.4 Challenges for the Banking Sector

26. Digital Technology in Banking Sector **206-212**
26.1 Digitization in Banking Sector
26.2 Benefits of Digital Payments
26.3 Card-based Electronic Payment Systems

26.4 Non-card Electronic Payment Systems
26.5 Cyber Security Concerns

Part V: Central Banking and Monetary Policy

27. History, Objectives and Functions of Central Bank **213-221**
27.1 History of Central Banks
27.2 Changing Objectives of Central Banks
27.3 Functions of a Central Bank

28. Balance Sheet of Central Bank **222-226**
28.1 Significance of the Balance Sheet of Central Bank
28.2 Frequency and Format of Balance Sheet
28.3 Components of the Balance Sheet
28.4 Balance Sheet of the Reserve Bank of India (RBI)

29. Instruments of Monetary Control **227-230**
29.1 Enhanced Need for Monetary Control
29.2 Bank Rate Policy
29.3 Cash Reserve Ratio (CRR)
29.4 Open Market Operations
29.5 Moral Suasions
29.6 Macro Prudential Policy
29.7 Additional Tools of Monetary Management in India

30. Monetary Management in an Open Economy **231-235**
30.1 Closed versus Open Economy
30.2 Monetary Transmission Mechanism in the Open Economy
30.3 Recent Challenges in Monetary Management
30.4 India's Monetary Management in the Globalized World

31. Reserve Bank of India **236-244**
31.1 Establishment and Early History of RBI
31.2 Pre-Independence Activities of RBI
31.3 Functions of Reserve Bank of India (RBI)
31.4 Changing Role of RBI in the Financial Sector
31.5 RBI's Vision Documents for Payments

32. Monetary Policy of India **245-256**
32.1 Meaning of Monetary Policy
32.2 Objectives of Monetary Policy
32.3 Monetary Policy Framework

32.4 Monetary Policy Process
32.5 Monetary Transmission Mechanism
32.6 Operating Procedures of Monetary Policy
32.7 Constituents of Monetary Reforms
32.8 Instruments of Monetary Policy
32.9 Monetary Policy Assessment

33. Inflation Targeting in India **257-262**
33.1 What is Inflation (Price Rise)?
33.2 Measurement and Reporting of Inflation
33.3 Price Stability as an Objective of Monetary Policy in India
33.4 What is Inflation Targeting?
33.5 Origin of Inflation Targeting
33.6 Need for Inflation Targeting
33.7 Fixing of Inflation Target
33.8 Monetary Policy Committee (MPC)

Bibliography **263-266**
Index **267-274**

Preface

Money is the life blood of an economy. Money has the same importance in economics as *vote* in a democracy. A modern economy is unthinkable without money. Money performs a variety of functions. It acts, among others, as a medium of exchange, standard of value, measure of deferred payments, and store of value

Financial intermediaries, financial markets and financial instruments are at the heart of an economic system. A financial system helps to mobilize the financial surpluses of an economy and transfer them to areas of financial deficit. It is the linchpin of any development strategy. The financial system promotes savings by providing a wide variety of financial assets to the general public. Savings collected from the household sector are pooled together and allocated to various sectors of the economy for raising production levels. If the allocation of credit is judicious and socially equitable, it can help achieve the twin objectives of growth and social justice.

India has a long and chequered history of financial intermediation, particularly commercial banking. The core function of financial institutions is to facilitate smooth and efficient allocation of resources from savers to the ultimate users. In the context of relatively under-developed capital market and with little internal resources, firms or economic entities depend largely on financial institutions for their fund requirements. In terms of sources of credit, they can broadly be categorized as institutional and non-institutional. For example, the major institutional sources of credit in India are commercial banks, development finance institutions (DFIs) and non-banking financial companies (NBFCs) including housing finance companies (HFCs). The non-institutional or unorganized sources of credit include moneylenders and indigenous bankers.

Financial markets are a mechanism which allows people to buy and sell financial securities and other fungible items of value. Fungible means interchangeable or exchangeable items (like goods, services, currencies) as contrasted with non-fungible items such as human beings. Thus, financial markets include capital market (trading in shares and bonds etc.), commodity market (trading in gold and silver etc.), foreign exchange market (trading in different currencies) and other such markets.

Well-functioning financial markets enable efficient use of market-based instruments of monetary policy by improving interest rate signals in the economy. Apart from enhancing the efficiency of monetary policy, deep and organized financial markets promote mobilization of domestic savings and improve the allocative efficiency of financial intermediation, and foster the necessary conditions to emerge as an international or a regional financial centre. Strong domestic financial markets also act as a buffer against external disturbances and help in absorbing shocks to the domestic banking system during crises. Further, they provide incentives for development of hedging instruments, and lower macroeconomic volatility and financial instability. Efficient financial markets also have several indirect benefits such as rapid accumulation of physical and human capital, more stable investment financing, and faster technological progress.

Developed and well-integrated financial markets are critical for sustaining high growth, effective conduct of monetary policy, developing a diversified financial system, financial integration and ensuring financial stability. The question therefore is not whether developed financial markets are needed, but how to go about in developing them fully. Financial markets presently deal with complex and sophisticated products. Introduction of such products would require clear regulatory frameworks, appropriate institutions and development of human resource skills. The speed for further changes in the financial markets would thus depend on how quickly a system is able to meet these requirements.

The need for developed financial markets also arises in the context of increasing integration of domestic financial markets with international financial markets. The concept of globalization is no longer restricted to its traditional sense—variety of cross-border transactions in goods and services—but also extends to international capital flows, driven by rapid and widespread diffusion of technology. In fact, most of the literature in recent years on globalization has centred around financial integration due to the emergence of worldwide financial markets and the possibility of better access to external financing for a variety of domestic entities.

The maturity and sophistication of financial system depends upon the prevalence of a variety of financial instruments to suit the varied investment requirements of heterogeneous investors so as to enable it to mobilize savings from as wide section of the investing public as possible. Since early 1990s, the Indian financial system has witnessed tremendous growth in financial product innovation by financial institutions.

In recent years, complex financial products, such as derivatives, have proliferated in developed countries. These products have become highly popular with banks and financial institutions as they allow them to hedge their risks and manage their regulatory and economic capital more efficiently.

The emergence of the market for derivative products, most notably forwards, futures and options, can be traced back to the willingness of risk-averse economic agents to guard themselves against uncertainties arising out of fluctuations in asset prices. By their very nature, the financial markets are marked by a very high degree of volatility. Through the use of derivative products, it is possible to partially or fully transfer price risks by locking-in asset prices. As instruments of risk management, derivatives generally do not influence the fluctuations in the underlying asset prices. However, by locking-in asset prices, derivative products minimize the impact of fluctuations in asset prices on the profitability and cash flow situation of risk-averse investors.

Central banks occupy a pivotal position in the institutional fabric of an economy. The functions of a modern central bank are vastly different from what was expected from the early central banks founded in Europe in the 17th century. The evolution of central banking in the Indian context has its own specificity. The RBI, while discharging its statutory responsibilities, has played a crucial role in the nation building process, particularly in the development of the financial sector. In fact, institution building constitutes a distinguishing feature of central banking in India.

Monetary policy refers to the use of monetary instruments under the control of the central bank to regulate magnitudes such as interest rates, money supply and availability of credit with a view to achieving the ultimate objective of economic policy. In India, the Reserve Bank of India (RBI) is vested with the responsibility of conducting monetary policy. This responsibility is explicitly mandated under the Reserve Bank of India Act, 1934. The conduct of monetary policy has been changing in response to the process of financial liberalisation.

The operating procedure of monetary policy changed dramatically with the opening up of the Indian economy in the 1990s. It was driven by the following: (a) the need for a market-oriented policy mix of open market operations and interest rate signals consistent with the process of price discovery; (b) the need to manage capital flows following the opening up and (c) the need for swift policy reactions to maintain orderly conditions in the financial markets.

The primary objective of monetary policy of RBI is to maintain price stability while keeping in mind the objective of growth. Price stability is a necessary precondition to sustainable growth.

The efficacy of monetary policy depends on the magnitude and the speed with which policy rate changes are transmitted to the ultimate objectives of monetary policy, viz., inflation and growth. With the deepening of financial systems and growing sophistication of financial markets, most monetary authorities use interest rate as the key instrument to achieve the ultimate objectives of monetary policy. Adjustments in the policy interest rate, for instance, directly impact short-term money market rates which then transmit the monetary policy impulses across financial markets and maturity spectrum, including banks' deposit and lending rates. These, in turn, influence consumption, saving and investment decisions of firms and households, which ultimately influence aggregate demand, and hence, output and inflation. The interest rate channel of transmission is the leading channel of transmission in several countries, including many emerging market economies.

In short, the study of money, financial institutions, financial markets and financial instruments is a pre-requisite to understand the functioning of a modern globally-integrated economy.

New Delhi
June 2020

Niti Bhasin

Explanation of Select Terms Related to Money and Financial Markets

Annuity: It is a fixed sum of money paid to an annuitant yearly, usually for the remaining part of his life. It is a form of pension which provides a regular annual income. An annuity may be purchased by making a lump sum cash payment.

Arbitrageurs: They are in business to take advantage of a discrepancy between prices in two different markets. If, for example, they see the futures price of an asset getting out of line with the cash price, they will take offsetting positions in the two markets to lock-in a profit. Arbitragers are traders and market-makers who deal in buying and selling derivatives contracts hoping to profit from price-differentials between different markets. A market maker is one who provides two-way quotes for a given product and thereby runs a position in that product.

Asymmetric Information: Asymmetric information (also known as information failure) occurs when one party to an economic transaction possesses greater material knowledge than the other party. Almost all economic transactions involve information asymmetries.

Balance Sheet: Balance sheet of a business entity (e.g. a bank) is a statement of its liabilities and assets at a point of time. It reflects the policies, size and soundness of the operations of the business. The liabilities indicate the sources of its funds. The assets show the nature of its investments. For example, the liabilities of a bank include paid-up capital and reserves, deposits, borrowings and bills payable. Similarly, assets of a bank include, *inter alia*, cash in hand, money at call/short notice, investment in securities and loans and advances.

Bank Rate: As lender of the last resort, the central bank helps the commercial banks in temporary need of cash when other sources of raising cash are exhausted. An increase in the bank rate would discourage commercial banks to borrow from the central bank and a corresponding increase in the lending rate of commercial banks to general public would decrease public borrowings from the banks.

Bond: A bond is a promise to pay a stated sum of money as interest each year and to repay the face value of bond at some future redemption date. Some bonds, called *perpetuities*, pay a fixed sum of interest each year forever but never repay the principal, i.e. they have no redemption date.

Book-building: It is a process by which demand for the securities proposed to be issued is built-up and the price for securities is assessed for determination of the quantum of such securities to be issued.

Call Money Market: This is the most important component of the organised money market located in metropolitan cities of a country. It deals in credit for very short period of time, less than 15 days, even 1 or 2 days. The main participants in this market are the commercial banks who are surplus/short of funds temporarily. It is also called *inter-bank call money market*.

Capital Market: Capital market is a market for long-term funds. Capital market channelises household savings to the corporate sector and allocates funds to firms. In this process, it allows both firms and households to share risks associated with business. Moreover, capital market enables the valuation of firms on an almost continuous basis and plays an important role in the governance of the corporate sector.

Cash Reserve Ratio (CRR): In most countries, commercial banks are required statutorily to hold cash reserves with the central bank. A low CRR requirement allows banks to lend more of their deposits. It is expansionary because it creates credit. A high CRR requirement is contractionary. It gives banks less money to lend.

Central Bank: Central bank of a country is usually a government owned and operated institution that controls the banking system and money supply in the economy. It is responsible for: (a) issuing currency, (b) managing money supply, (c) administering rate of interest, (d) monitoring borrowing and lending policies of commercial banks, (e) undertaking governmental banking activities and (f) maintaining foreign exchange reserves, external value of money and a country's balance of payments.

Commercial Bank: A commercial bank is a financial intermediary which accepts deposits of money from the public and lends them with a view to make profits. A post office may accept deposits but it cannot be called a bank because it does not perform the other essential function of a bank, i.e. lending money. Through mobilization of resources and their better allocation, commercial banks play an important role in the development process of underdeveloped countries.

Crypto Currency: A crypto currency is a type of digital token that relies on cryptography for chaining together digital signatures of token transfers, peer-to-peer networking and decentralization. In some cases, a proof-of-work scheme is used to create and manage the currency.

Derivatives: Derivative instruments comprise financial products which have grown up around securities, currency and commodity trading and whose price is a function of some other underlying security, currency rate or other commodity. The term is usually used to include swaps, futures, options, forwards and a wide range of financially engineered instruments which are hybrids of other financial products.

Digital Currency (or Digital Money): According to the Bank for International Settlements, digital currency is an asset represented in digital form and having some monetary characteristics. Digital currency can be denominated to a sovereign currency and issued by the issuer responsible to redeem digital money for cash. In that case, digital currency represents electronic money (e-money). Digital currency denominated in its own units of value or with decentralized or automatic issuance will be considered as a virtual currency.

E-Money: E-money may be broadly defined as an electronic store of monetary value on a technical device used for making payments to undertakings other than the issuer without necessarily involving bank accounts in the transaction, but acting as a prepaid bearer instrument.

Financial Intermediaries: Financial intermediaries are an integral part of a modern industrial economy. They are institutions, such as commercial banks, which act as middlemen between the lenders and the borrowers. Financial intermediaries are beneficial both to lenders and borrowers. Lenders stand to gain because they can invest their funds at low risk and greater liquidity with financial institutions. The main advantage to borrowers is availability of adequate credit at reasonable rate of interest.

Financial Market: It is a market in which financial assets of various kinds like shares, debentures and bills are dealt with. A financial market consists of: (a) money market which deals in short-term credit and (b) capital market which provides medium-term and long-term credit.

Financial System: It refers to the whole gamut of institutional arrangements which help to mobilise financial surpluses of an economy and transfer them to areas of financial deficit. Financial system of a country rests on three pillars: (a) financial institutions or financial intermediaries, (b) financial markets and (c) financial assets. Financial system is the linchpin of a modern industrial economy.

Financial Year: It is the year of account for financial purposes, often not coinciding with the calendar year. For example, in India the financial year (or fiscal year) runs from April 1 to March 31 of the following year. In USA, the fiscal year runs from July 1 to June 30.

Forwards/Forward Contracts: A forward contract is a customised contract between two entities, where settlement takes place on a specific date in the future at today's pre-agreed price. A forward contract is an agreement to buy or sell an asset on a specified date for specified price.

Future Trading: It refers to commodity or currency trading done on contract for future delivery. The purpose is to insure against risks of price changes, exchange rate changes etc. or to make a profit by speculating on the price trends.

Futures/Future Contracts: Future contracts are special types of forward contracts in the sense that the former are standardised exchange-traded contracts. Future contract markets are designed to solve the problems that exist in forward markets. A future contract is an agreement between two parties to buy or sell an asset at a certain time in future, at a certain price. However, unlike forward contracts, future contracts are standardized and stock exchange-traded.

Hedgers: Hedgers face risk associated with the price of an asset. They use future or option markets to reduce or eliminate this risk. In other words, hedgers are those who wish to protect their existing exposures and essentially are safety-driven.

Hedging: It is a method to guard against fluctuations in the prices of commodities (particularly raw materials) scheduled for future delivery by dealing in futures market. *Buying hedge* and *selling hedge* are the two basic types of hedge operations.

High-powered Money: It is composed of cash in the hands of the public, bank reserves and clearing balances held by the commercial banks with the central bank.

Inflation Targeting: Inflation targeting is a monetary policy strategy used by central banks for maintaining price level at a certain level or within a range. It indicates the primacy of price stability as the key objective of monetary policy. The argument for price stability stems from the fact that rising prices create uncertainties in decision making, adversely affecting savings and encouraging speculative investments. Inflation targeting brings in more predictability and transparency in deciding monetary policy.

Liquidity of an Asset: Liquidity of an asset means how easily it can be converted into cash and at what loss of its capital value. If an asset cannot be converted into cash easily (i.e. at short notice) or at minimum loss of its value, it is less liquid.

Liquidity Preference Theory of the Rate of Interest: According to British economist John Maynard Keynes (1883-1946), rate of interest is a reward for parting with liquidity for a specified period of time. Rate of interest, he believed, is a purely monetary phenomenon determined by the demand for and supply of money (liquidity). The supply of money is given by the government, and it is an exogenous (or autonomous) factor and accepted as it is. However, the demand for money (or preference for liquidity) varies and hence plays active role in the determination of the rate of interest.

Loanable Fund Theory of the Rate of Interest: Loanable fund theory is attributed to Swedish economist Knut Wicksell (1851-1926) and the British economist Dennis Robertson (1890-1963). According to this theory, the rate of interest is determined by the demand for and the supply of loanable funds in an economy. The demand for loans originates from three types of borrowers, viz. producers, consumers and government. Supply of loans comes from the current savings of households as well as business firms.

Marginal Standing Facility (MSF): MSF is a facility under which scheduled commercial banks can borrow additional amount of overnight money from the RBI by dipping into their SLR portfolio up to a limit (currently two percent of their net demand and time liabilities deposits) at a penal rate of interest, currently 50 basis points (half percent) above the repo rate. This provides a safety valve against unanticipated liquidity shocks to the banking system.

Model Listing Agreement: Listing agreement is an agreement entered between a stock exchange and the company seeking listing of securities on the exchange. It contains various requirements and disclosure obligations that companies must follow to remain as listed entities.

Monetary Policy: Monetary policy refers to the expansion or contraction of money and credit supply in an economy. Since monetary policy includes the regulation of both the volume and allocation of credit therefore credit policy is a part of the overall monetary policy. Monetary policy operates through changes in the stock of money and changes in the cost and availability of credit.

Money Market: It is a market for short-term funds with a maturity of up to one year and includes financial instruments that are close substitutes for money. The main instruments comprising the money market are call money/notice money, certificates of deposit, commercial bills, commercial paper and inter-corporate funds.

Moral Hazard: In economics, moral hazard occurs when someone increases his exposure to risk when insured, especially when a person takes more risks because someone else bears the cost of those risks. A moral hazard may occur where the actions of one party may change to the detriment of another after a financial transaction has taken place. A party makes a decision about how much risk to take, while another party bears the costs if things go badly, and the party isolated from risk behaves differently from how it would if it were fully exposed to the risk.

Open Market Operations: The central bank can enter the money market for the purpose of purchase or sale of government securities on its own account. Every open market purchase by the central bank increases primary money by equal amount while every sale decreases it. As regards their advantages, open market operations are highly flexible, easily reversible in time, their effect on money supply is immediate, and they do not carry *announcement effects* as in the case of changes in the bank rate.

Options: Options are fundamentally different from forward and future contracts. An option gives the holder of the option the right to do something. The holder does not have to necessarily exercise this right. In contrast, in a forward or future contract, the two parties commit themselves to doing something.

Portfolio: It refers to the list of investments in shares, debentures, bonds etc. that a person or an institution has made.

Repo Rate: Repo rate is the rate at which RBI lends money to the banks against the collateral of government and other approved securities. Repo rate, along with other instruments of monetary policy, is used to balance growth (more spending) and inflation.

Reverse Repo Rate: It is the (fixed) interest rate at which the RBI absorbs short-term liquidity, generally on an overnight basis, from banks against the collateral of government and other approved securities under the Liquidity Adjustment Facility (LAF). The RBI also conducts variable interest rate reverse repo auctions, as necessary.

RuPay: RuPay is an Indian domestic card payment scheme conceived and launched by National Corporation of India (NPCI). It aims to fulfil RBI's vision to offer a domestic, open-loop, multilateral system which will allow all Indian banks and financial institutions in India to participate in electronic payments. RuPay, the word itself has a sense of nationality in it. RuPay is the coinage of two terms Rupee and payment.

Speculative Bubbles and Crashes: A speculative bubble exists in the event of large, sustained overpricing of some class of assets. One factor that frequently contributes to a bubble is the presence of buyers who purchase an asset based solely on the expectation that they can later resell it at a higher price, rather than calculating the income it will generate in the future. If there is a bubble, there is also a risk of a *crash* in asset prices. Market participants will go on buying only as long as they expect others to buy, and when many decide to sell the price will fall. However, it is difficult to predict whether an asset's price actually equals its fundamental value, so it is hard to detect bubbles reliably.

Speculators: They bet on future movements in the price of an asset. Future and option contracts can give them an extra leverage; that is, they can increase both the potential gains and potential losses in a speculative venture. Speculators are willing risk takers who are expectation-driven.

Stock Market: A stock (or share) market deals mainly in corporate securities like shares and debentures. It is an important component of the capital market of the financial system.

Venture Capital: It is a term used for investment made in those lines where risk element is very high, especially in new lines of production, new markets or new processes.

Virtual Currency: According to the European Central Bank, virtual currency is a digital representation of value, not issued by a central bank, credit institution or e-money institution, which, in some circumstances, can be used as an alternative to money. Virtual currency is a type of unregulated, digital money, which is issued and usually controlled by its developers, and used and accepted among the members of a specific virtual community.

Yield Curve: Yield curve depicts the interest rates of similar quality bonds at different maturities. Generally, yields increase in line with maturity, giving rise to an upward-sloping, or normal, yield curve. The yield curve is primarily used to illustrate the term structure of interest rates for standard government-issued securities. This is important as it is a measure of the debt market's feeling about risk.

Zero-tax Company: Income tax laws usually provide for a host of deductions and incentives to promote socio-economic objectives of state policy. It is likely that a profit-making company may arrange its affairs in such a way that the cumulative effect of all deductions is to reduce its income declared in the tax return to zero. To deal with such situations, some countries have introduced minimum alternative tax.

Abbreviations/Acronyms

ADB	Asian Development Bank
ADRs	American depository receipts
AEPS	Aadhaar-enabled Payment System
ATM	Automated Teller Machine
BCs	Business Correspondents
BHIM	Bharat Interface for Money
BOLT	BSE Online Trading
BSE	Bombay Stock Exchange
CAC	Capital Account Convertibility
CBLO	Collateralised Borrowing and Lending Obligations
CDs	Certificates of Deposit
CIBIL	Credit Information Bureau (India) Ltd.
CP	Commercial Paper
CPI	Consumer Price Index
CRR	Cash Reserve Ratio
Demat	Dematerialisation
DFIs	Development Finance Institutions
DPs	Depository Participants
ECBs	External commercial borrowings
E-commerce	Electronic Commerce
EFT	Electronic Funds Transfer
E-money	Electronic Money
FCCBs	Foreign Currency Convertible Bonds
FDI	Foreign Direct Investment
FIIs	Foreign Institutional Investors
FIMMDA	Fixed Income Money Market and Derivatives Association
GDRs	Global Depository Receipts
IBBI	Insolvency and Bankruptcy Board of India
IBC	Insolvency and Bankruptcy Code, 2016
IDRs	Indian Depository Receipts
IMF	International Monetary Fund
IMPS	Immediate Payment Services
IRDA	Insurance Regulatory and Development Authority
IT	Information Technology
KYC	Know Your Customer
LAF	Liquidity Adjustment Facility
LLP	Limited Liability Partnership Act, 2008
MFs	Mutual Funds
MIFOR	Mumbai Inter-Bank Forward Offered Rate
MPC	Monetary Policy Committee

MSF	Marginal Standing Facility
NBFCs	Non-banking Financial Companies
NEAT	National Stock Exchange for Automated Trading
NEFT	National Electronic Funds Transfer
NPAs	Non-Performing Assets
NPCI	National Payments Corporation of India
NSCCL	National Securities Clearing Corporation Ltd.
NSDL	National Securities Depository Ltd.
NSE	National Stock Exchange
NSSF	National Small Savings Fund
OMOs	Open Market Operations
OTC	Over-the-Counter
PSBs	Public Sector Banks
RBI	Reserve Bank of India
Remat	Rematerialisation
RRBs	Regional Rural Banks
RTGS	Real Time Gross Settlement
SCRA	Securities Contracts (Regulation) Act, 1956
SEBI	Securities and Exchange Board of India
SENSEX	Sensitive Index
SLR	Statutory Liquidity Ratio
UCBs	Urban Co-operative Banks
UIDAI	Unique Identification Authority of India
USSD	Unstructured Supplementary Service Data
UTI	Unit Trust of India
VAT	Value-added Tax
WMA	Ways and Means Advances
WPI	Wholesale Price Index
WTO	World Trade Organization
YTM	Yield-to-Maturity

Part I
An Introduction to Money

1

Meaning, Kinds and Functions of Money

Money is the pivot around which an economy revolves. A modern economy, characterized by acute specialization, is unthinkable without money. Money has the same importance in economics as *vote* in a democracy.

1.1 Meaning of Money

Under a system of simple commodity production, exchange of goods was accomplished largely through barter. The main difficulty of the barter system was the double coincidence of wants. In a modern economy, characterised by acute specialisation and exchange, barter system would just be impossible. It is, therefore, necessary to accept some thing as a medium of exchange. Any generally accepted thing which serves as a medium of exchange is called money. Historically, a variety of things have served as money including goats, coins, paper currency and demand deposits of banks.

1.2 Metallic Money, Paper Money and Fiduciary Money

1.2.1 Metallic Money: Coins are example of metallic money. Their intrinsic value is less than their face value and therefore they are not full-bodied but only token money. Since coins have an inherent value therefore they can be called commodity money. The intrinsic value of a coin is equal to the value of the metal contained in it. Even if it is not a legal tender it can buy goods equal to the value of the metal.

1.2.2 Paper Money: In modern times, paper currency has replaced metallic money. Paper money is accepted by the people readily in all kinds of transactions. This is so because government makes it legal tender. In other words, it circulates by command (fiat) and therefore is called *fiat money*. Legal tender is any official medium of payment recognized by law that can be used to pay for public or private debt especially pay taxes to Government. Value of the paper of the currency note of ₹ 2,000 is almost negligible, but this paper, after being declared as legal tender, can buy goods worth ₹ 2,000. Paper money does not have any intrinsic value. Its value comes from Government order. Presently, world over all government use fiat money.

1.2.3 Fiduciary Money: Deposit money denotes bank deposits against which cheques can be drawn. Normally, demand deposits are taken into account for this purpose. Deposit money is not a legal tender like currency notes. Because it circulates by trust commanded by its issuers therefore it is called *fiduciary money*.

1.3 Electronic Money (E-Money)

In recent years, there has been a gradual switchover from the use of paper-based payments media to those based on electronics. While the basic characteristics of these new instruments are by and large similar to those of paper-based instruments, the former present a different set of challenges to policy makers. E-money is one such new product which has appeared on Indian horizon recently.

1.3.1 Definition and Kinds of E-Money: E-money may be broadly defined as an electronic store of monetary value on a technical device used for making payments to undertakings other than the issuer without necessarily involving bank accounts in the transaction, but acting as a prepaid bearer instrument. E-money can be classified into the following two broad categories:

1. Pre-paid stored value card (also called electronic purse).
2. Pre-paid software-based product that uses computer networks such as internet (also referred to as digital cash or network money).

The stored value card scheme typically uses a microprocessor chip embedded in a plastic card while software based scheme typically uses specialised software installed in a personal computer. The stored value card could be of three types:

1. Single-purpose card.
2. Closed-system or limited-purpose card.
3. General-purpose or multi-purpose card.

The single-purpose card generally with a magnetic chip recording the amount of fund therein is designed to facilitate only one type of transaction, e.g. telephone calls, public transportation, laundry, parking facilities etc. In this case the distinguishing point is that the issuer and the service provider (acceptor) are identical for the cards. These cards are expected to substitute coins and currency notes. [1]

Closed-system or limited-purpose card is generally used in a small number of well-identified points of sale within a well-identified location such as corporate/university campus. [2]

Multi-purpose card can perform a variety of functions with several vendors, viz. credit card, debit card, stored value card, identification card, repository of personal medical information etc. The importance of these cards is especially underscored with respect to regulatory oversight, restrictions on issuers and their implications for monetary policy. These cards may reduce demand for current accounts in the bank for likely reduction in transaction costs, and prudent portfolio management.

It is important to distinguish here the so-called *access* products, e.g. credit card and debit card from e-money. The former typically require a telephone or a personal computer with appropriate software to access the customer account before transferring the value while under e-money, the amount of value is already embedded and it may be increased or reduced without necessarily involving a personal bank account. In a sense, e-money can be construed as an electronic form of traveller's cheques (TCs). In both cases, the user pays for the instrument upfront.

1.3.2 Benefits of E-money: Use and spread of e-money depends upon the incentives of issuers, merchants and consumers. For issuers, the principal motivation arises from revenues to be earned from investment of outstanding balances (i.e. float income), savings of costs from reduced handling of cash and incentive of offering fee-based service to consumers and merchants besides the larger security emanating from audit trail of transactions and improved management information system.

For merchants, the trade-off would be between reduction in cost of handling physical cash vis-à-vis cost of putting in place necessary infrastructure.

For consumers, the use of e-money would depend upon the perceived security and privacy of e-money and ease with which e-money could be used which would again depend upon willingness of merchants to accept e-money. In other words, apart from security, privacy and ease, network effects are also important for wider use of e-money.

An economy like India, where cash transactions are very high, could benefit from using e-money through cost savings from printing and minting of smaller denomination notes and coins and eliminating the cost of handling, storing, transporting and insuring currency. These should also improve operational efficiency of the financial sector as also extension of banking to the urban poor and rural communities besides facilitating E-governance initiatives of governments. However, such benefits should be weighed against the need to build up the costly infrastructure to operate nationwide cashless retail payment system.

1.3.3 Implications of E-money for the Central Bank: Before analysing the likely implications, it is instructive to note that e-money can be issued in three alternate ways. Each of these three ways may have different implications for conduct of monetary policy.

1. E-money can be issued in exchange of cash (i.e. 100 percent backing of central bank money). Under that circumstance, there may be only marginal change in total money supply in the economy provided there is no significant change in velocity of circulation of money.
2. E-money can also be issued on credit against interest payment.
3. E-money could also be issued as a separate form of currency independent of central bank money by entities other than the central bank. In that case, e-money would compete against the central bank money as a medium of exchange. However, such a scenario in which public gets e-money from an entity in exchange for something other than the central bank money seems remote now.

Currency notes and coins generally form an overwhelming part of the balance sheet of any central bank. If e-money is extensively used and in the process, replaces substantially central bank's money, central bank's balance sheet would *shrink* while that of the issuing authority of e-money would *expand* in relative terms.

With large scale use of e-money, it is apprehended that central bank's balance sheet may shrink to such an extent relative to that of the banking sector that it may be unable to perform its liquidity absorption function [in effect, open market operations (OMO)] on account of non-availability of adequate volume of assets. Under that circumstance, extensive e-monetisation in the economy could jeopardise the conduct of monetary policy of the central bank. It may, however, be noted that the central bank would not have any problem in liquidity injection because central bank money is still the only legal tender in the economy.

Apart from constraining its liquidity management function, relative shrinkage in balance sheet may also have implications regarding loss of *seigniorage* revenue for the central bank. This is because currency notes and coins are the interest-free liability of the central bank towards public (i.e. public have in effect lent to the central bank such amount free of interest) which are then used by the central bank to purchase interest bearing assets. Thus, interest earned on these assets constitutes its seigniorage revenue. Therefore, if the central bank's operating costs are high which are more likely in an environment where central bank is required to intervene more, it may even incur losses on account of seigniorage revenue foregone. This may also have adverse implications for governments with chronic budget deficits as they would be deprived of the transfer of surplus to its treasury from the profitable central bank.

A distinguishing characteristic of e-money is that unlike innovations in other retail payments media—which facilitate more efficient access to traditional form of central bank money—e-money could have the potential to become an independent medium of exchange. In that eventuality, two extreme views are being offered. On the one hand, one group perceives that in a highly technologically-advanced networked world, private entities may not require central bank money for settlement and, therefore, there may not be any central bank in future. Some of them also question whether private money is more efficient than central bank money from social welfare viewpoint and if so under what circumstance private money can replace central bank money altogether. On the other hand, there is another group of academicians and practitioners who strongly believe that central banks would continue to be as effective as ever though they may be required to respond differently in the changed environment.

1.3.4 E-Money in India: In India, where cash transactions are high in number, the use of E-money can be beneficial in terms of reduced miscellaneous costs, viz. cost of printing and minting of smaller denomination notes and coins and transportation and storage costs. However, certain additional costs for setting up of network infrastructure to operate nationwide are also associated with it. The RBI has been partnering a multi-application smart card project, under the aegis of the Ministry of Communications and Information Technology, Government of India, to run a pilot project on the use of multi-application smart cards in the country. Various issues relating to technology, security, regulatory and supervisory concerns and legal implications have been examined to make the use of smart cards a viable proposition after the conclusion of the pilot project. The project is aimed at combining applications relating to banking, insurance, postal services, identification, etc in a single card.

The Reserve Bank of India had constituted a Working Group on Electronic Money (Chairman: Zaire J. Camas) in January 2002 which submitted its Report in July 2002. The Group identified certain areas of concern from the point of view of the central bank in the context of more widespread use of e-money. Some of the suggestions made by the Group included: (a) multi-purpose e-money to be issued only by authorised banks on a credit basis which should be strictly regulated and closely monitored, (b) redeemability should be ensured in order to preserve the unit of account function of money as well as to control money supply in the economy and (c) reporting of e-money statistics should be ensured for the purposes of monetary policy and protection against criminal abuse such as money laundering.

1.4 Digital Money (or Digital Currency)

Most of the traditional money supply is bank money held on computers. This is also considered digital currency. One could argue that our increasingly cashless society means that all currencies are becoming digital (sometimes referred to as *electronic money*), but they are not presented to us as such.

Digital money (or *digital currency*) can be defined as an Internet-based form of currency or medium of exchange which is distinct from physical currency (banknotes and coins), but allows for instantaneous transactions and borderless transfer-of-ownership. Both virtual currencies and crypto currencies are types of digital currencies, but the converse is incorrect. Like traditional money these currencies may be used to buy physical goods and services but could also be restricted to certain communities such as for example for use inside an on-line game or social network.

According to the Bank for International Settlements', "Digital Currencies" report of November 2015, digital currency is an asset represented in digital form and having some monetary characteristics. Digital currency can be denominated to a sovereign currency and issued by the issuer responsible to redeem digital money for cash. In that case, digital currency represents electronic money (e-money). Digital currency denominated in its own units of value or with decentralized or automatic issuance will be considered as a virtual currency.

1.5 Virtual Currency

According to the European Central Banks', "Virtual Currency Schemes: A Further Analysis" report of February 2015, virtual currency is a digital representation of value, not issued by a central bank, credit institution or e-money institution, which, in some circumstances, can be used as an alternative to money. In the previous report of October 2012, the virtual currency was defined as a type of unregulated, digital money, which is issued and usually controlled by its developers, and used and accepted among the members of a specific virtual community.

The US Department of Treasury in 2013 defined virtual currency more tersely as "a medium of exchange that operates like a currency in some environments, but does not have all the attributes of real currency". According to these definitions, virtual currency does not have the status of a legal tender.

1.6 Crypto Currency

A crypto currency is a type of digital token that relies on cryptography for chaining together digital signatures of token transfers, peer-to-peer networking and decentralization. In some cases, a proof-of-work scheme is used to create and manage the currency.

1.6.1 What is Crypto Currency? Crypto currency is a class of privately issued digital means of payment that depends predominantly on cryptography and distributed ledger technology (DLT) such as the block chain. A block chain is a continuous ledger in which transactions are stored as blocks and linked using cryptography. Crypto currency is often allotted through initial coin offerings (ICOs), which are used as a means of raising capital through crowd-funding. Crypto currency typically has some monetary characteristics, but is not a liability of any entity and is not backed by any authority. Its value is driven by users' confidence in it. This, coupled with limited supply, makes its value highly volatile and, therefore, not a reliable medium of exchange or store of value.

1.6.2 Dangers Posed by Crypto Currency: Though crypto currency may not currently pose systemic risks, its increasing popularity leading to price bubbles raises serious concerns for consumer and investor protection, and market integrity.

The crypto currency eco-system may affect the existing payment and settlement system which could, in turn, influence the transmission of monetary policy. Furthermore, being stored in digital/electronic media—electronic wallets—it is prone to hacking and operational risk, a few instances of which have already been observed globally. There is no established framework for recourse to customer problems and disputes resolution as payments by crypto currencies take place on a peer-to-peer basis without an authorised central agency which regulates such payments. There exists a high possibility of its usage for illicit activities, including tax avoidance.

The absence of information on counterparties in such peer-to-peer anonymous or pseudonymous systems could subject users to unintentional breaches of anti-money laundering laws as well as laws for combating the financing of terrorism. A globally coordinated approach is necessary to prevent abuses and to strictly limit interconnections with regulated financial institutions.

1.6.3 Remedial Measures: On a global level, regulatory responses to crypto currency have ranged from a complete *clamp down* in some jurisdictions to a comparatively *light touch regulatory approach*. The Securities and Exchange Commission (SEC) and the Commodity Futures Trading Commission (CFTC) have emerged as the primary regulators of crypto currencies in the United States, where these assets like most other jurisdictions, do not enjoy the legal tender status. Asian countries have experienced oversized concentration of crypto players. Thus, Japan and South Korea account for the biggest shares of crypto asset markets in the world. In the case of Bit coins, half of transactions worldwide are carried out in Japan. In September 2017, Japan approved transactions by its exchanges in crypto currencies. China's exchanges hosted disproportionately large volumes of global Bit coin trading until their ban recently.

In India, the Government and the Reserve Bank of India (RBI) are keeping a close watch on crypto currency and have issued pre-emptive cautionary warnings. In early April 2018, RBI barred its regulated entities from dealing in or providing services to any individual or business entities dealing with or settling in virtual currencies. Regulated entities which already provide such services were asked to exit the relationship within 3 months.

Developments on this front need to be monitored as some trading may shift from exchanges to peer-to-peer mode, which may also involve increased usage of cash. Possibilities of migration of crypto exchange houses to dark pools/cash and to offshore locations, thus raising concerns on money laundering as well as financing of terrorism.

Rapid changes in the landscape of the payments industry, along with factors such as emergence of private digital tokens and the rising costs of managing fiat paper/metallic money, have led central banks around the world to explore the option of introducing fiat digital currencies. In India, an inter-departmental group has been constituted by RBI to study and provide guidance on the desirability and feasibility to introduce a central bank digital currency.

In his Budget Speech to the Parliament on February 1, 2018, Finance Minister Shri Arun Jaitley observed, "Distributed ledger system or the block chain technology allows organization of any chain of records or transactions without the need of intermediaries. The Government does not consider crypto-currencies legal tender or coin and will take all measures to eliminate use of these crypto assets in financing illegitimate activities or as part of the payment system. The Government will explore use of block chain technology proactively for ushering in digital economy". [3]

In July 2018, RBI banned all banks, non-banking financial companies (NBFCs) and other financial institutions from crypto transactions.

Though crypto currency is not a legal tender yet it is not illegal for Indians to buy, own or sell bitcoins. Unlike regular currency which has government backing, crypto currency one can hold at once own risk. In October 2018, crypto currency exchange Unocoin launched an ATM (or a kiosk) in Bengaluru for Indians to buy and sell bitcoins. However, it was soon closed by the authorities for being illegal and without approval.

1.7 Functions of Money

Money performs a variety of functions.

1.7.1 Medium of Exchange: The first and the most important function of money is to act as a medium of exchange. As a matter of fact, money is defined in terms of this unique function. Other functions of money are more or less derived from this function. By using money as a medium of exchange, a society can get rid of the difficulties of barter system. By the use of money, exchange becomes easy and this promotes specialisation which has its own advantages in a modern society.

1.7.2 Standard of Value: Money serves as a unit of account or standard of value. Money is used to express and compare the values of goods and services which enter the market. Values of goods and services when expressed in terms of money are called prices. With the help of these prices, the ratio of exchange between any two commodities can easily be determined. As a measure of value, money helps us to know almost instantly how much sugar is worth how much butter.

Unfortunately, money as a standard of value is not fixed but a variable one. This is so because the value of money, i.e. the purchasing power of money itself changes from time to time in view of the changes in the general level of prices. The same ten rupee note purchases different quantities of sugar at different times. It is like measuring cloth with a rubber meter the length of which varies with stretching efforts. This instability in money as a standard of value can cause great turmoil in the economy. It is interesting to note that in measuring weight, length and time man has devised invariable units, namely kilogram, metre and minute which are fixed over time and across regions. However, a fixed measure of value is yet to be achieved.

1.7.3 Measure of Deferred Payments: Money serves as a measure of deferred or future payments. These deferred payments pertain to debts and interest thereon, insurance premiums and future instalments of goods purchased at present. The agreements of deferred payments are in terms of money the value of which is subject to fluctuations. Therefore, money is an imperfect standard of deferred payments also. This attribute has serious repercussions for debtors and creditors.

1.7.4 Store of Value: Money also serves as a store of value. People find it easy to hold some of their wealth in money form rather than in terms of commodities. Value can, of course, be stored in terms of other assets but they are not as readily acceptable means of payment as money. However, variations in the value of money cause disturbances in its role as a store of value as in the case of its function as a measure of value and as a standard of deferred payments.

Endnotes

1. It is important to note that the European Central Bank (ECB) has exempted these single-purpose pre-paid cards from the purview of their policy initiatives on e-money because of their smaller denominations as well as limited risk exposure for customers and the financial system as a whole.
2. European Central Bank (ECB) has recommended that these cards be subject to lighter regulations and be issued by credit institutions.
3. Government of India, Ministry of Finance, Budget Papers 2018-19, *Speech of the Finance Minister*, para 112.

2

Theories of Money Supply Determination

2.1 What is Money Supply?

Money supply refers to the stock of money held by the public in an economy. In other words, it is the stock of money available to public for use in connection with the economic activities of the country. Total stock of money in existence is different (and greater) than the stock of money held by the public. Money supply is a stock concept to be measured at a point of time.

Money supply always refers to the amount of money held by the public, i.e. households, firms and institutions other than government, central bank and commercial banks. The rationale for considering money supply as held by the public is to separate the producers (or supplier) of money [Central Government and Reserve Bank of India (RBI) in the case of India] from holders (or demanders) of money.

2.2 Why is Money Supply Important?

Money supply and changes in it are important because they affect prices, wages, rate of interest and other crucial variables in the economy. Growth of money supply is a crucial factor not only for economic development but also for the achievement of price stability in the economy. Developing economies have to face the problem of inadequacy of monetary resources in the initial stages of development and it can be solved through monetary expansion.

Monetary expansion, through budgetary deficits, can lead to inflation (price rise) in the economy. A mild inflation (say 3 to 4 percent per year) arising out of the expansion of money may stimulate investment by raising profit expectations. However, a significant rate of inflation (say 10 percent or more) can be harmful for the smooth functioning of the economy. Hence, rate of inflation must remain within safe limits. With this objective in view, central banks around the world (including RBI) follow the policy of *controlled expansion of money supply*.

In short, management of money supply is an economy is essential to ensure growth with price stability.

2.3 Relationship between Money and Prices: The Equation of Exchange

Price level is determined by the relationship between money and the goods which it is used to buy. Money in an economy consists partly of currency and partly of bank deposits. The currency and bank deposits that actually circulate are used over and over again in the course of a specified period (say one year). Every time they are used they enter into a price. Therefore, the total amount of purchasing power which enters into the price level depends on the flow (rather than the stock) of money. The flow can be considered in terms of the stock if the latter is multiplied by its velocity of circulation which is defined as the average number of times a unit of money changes hands during the course of one year. If M is the stock of money and V its velocity of circulation, then the flow of money will be MV.

On the other hand, there are goods and services that are exchanged against money. In fact, every time there is a business transaction in which any commodity or service is offered in exchange for money, a price emerges that enters into the price level. Furthermore, if a given commodity passes through several hands, a price is established at each such transfer. In other words, this commodity enters into the price level several times. Hence, the commodity side of the price level consists of the total number of units exchanged in a given period of time (one year). These units can be represented by the letter T, i.e. total number of unit transactions, or the total volume of trade.

Algebraically, average price in all these transactions must be equal to the total flow of money divided by the number of goods exchanged. If we represent this average price by P, then we have the simple algebraic formula: $P = MV/T$. This formula is known as the equation of exchange.

It is clear from this equation that the value of P must depend upon the ratio between the numerator and the denominator. Or, to put it differently, the general level of prices must depend upon the ratio between the flow of money (MV) and the flow of goods (T). When more money is spent relatively to the goods flowing into the markets, prices can be expected to rise. Conversely, if the flow of money is reduced, goods remaining unchanged, prices can be expected to fall. Similarly, if the flow of goods increases in relation to the flow of money, prices will fall, and if flow of goods decreases, money in circulation remaining unchanged, prices will rise. Equation of exchange is one version of the quantity theory of money.

2.4 Four Measures of Money Supply

There is no unique definition of money supply. Since various things serve as money in an economy, there are various measures of money supply depending on what is included and excluded from a particular definition.

Several definitions of money supply have been given and therefore various measures of money supply based on them have been estimated.

Firstly, different components of money supply have been distinguished on the basis of the different functions that money performs. For example, currency, demand deposits and debit/credit cards are used by the people primarily as a medium of exchange for buying goods and services and making other transactions. They are money because they are used as a medium of exchange and are generally referred to as M_1. Another measure of money supply is M_3 which includes both M_1 and time deposits held by the public in the banks. Time deposits are money that people hold as store of value. If time deposits component of money supply measure M_3, which serves as a store of value is increasing rapidly, it can be inferred that people are planning to save more and accordingly consume less.

Secondly, monetary aggregates are categorized based on the liquidity of instruments. Liquidity means how easily money can be converted to cash. Thus, high liquidity means cash and money in saving account. Fixed deposit in a bank is example of low liquidity. Government bond is example of lower liquidity.

Therefore, for the sake of monetary analysis and policy formulation, a single measure of money supply is not only inadequate but may be misleading too. Hence various measures of money supply are prepared to meet the needs of monetary analysis and policy formulation.

As in other countries, RBI has adopted four concepts of money supply in its analysis of the quantum of and variations in money supply. The four standard measures of money stock, viz. M_1, M_2, M_3 and M_4 and their components are presented in Table 2.1. These measures indicate the monetary liability of the *money creating* sectors to the *money using* sectors within the country referred to as the *public*.

Table 2.1: Money Supply Measures

M_1 (or narrow money)	Currency with the public + demand deposits with the banking system + other deposits with the RBI
M_2	M_1 + post office savings deposits
M_3 (or broad money)	M_1 + time deposits with the banking system
M_4	M_3 + total post office deposits

Note: Banks cover commercial and co-operative banks.
Source: Reserve Bank of India, *Comprehensive Guide for Current Statistics of the RBI Monthly Bulletin*, June 2017.

2.4.1 Money Supply M_1 (or Narrow Money): This measure is the most liquid measure of money supply as the money included in it can be easily used as a medium of exchange, i.e. as a means of making payments. It is composed of the following elements:

M1 = C + DD + OD where

C = Currency with the public.

DD = Demand deposits with the banking system.

OD = Other deposits with the RBI.

- **Currency with the Public:** Currency with the public is arrived at after deducting cash with banks from total currency in circulation. Currency in circulation comprises notes, rupee and small coins.
- **Demand Deposits with Banking System:** These represent demand deposits with all the commercial and co-operative banks (including co-operative societies).
- **Other Deposits with RBI:** Other deposits with the RBI for the purpose of monetary compilation include deposits from foreign central banks, multilateral institutions, financial institutions, balances in depositor education and awareness (DEA) fund, and sundry deposits.

2.4.2 Money Supply M_2: M_2 is a broader concept of money supply than M_1. In addition to the three items of M_1, the concept of money supply M_2 includes savings deposits with the post office savings banks. Thus,

$M_2 = M_1$ + Savings deposits with the post office savings banks.

The reason why money supply M_2 has been distinguished from M_1 is that saving deposits with post office (not chequable accounts) are not as liquid as demand deposits with commercial and co-operative banks. However, saving deposits with post offices are more liquid than time deposits with the banks.

2.4.3 Money Supply M_3 (or Broad Money): M_3 is a broad concept of money supply. In addition to the items of money supply included in measure M_1, in money supply M_3 time deposits with the banks are also included. Thus,

$M_3= M_1$+ Time deposits with the banking system.

Time deposits are generally considered to serve as store of value and represent savings of the people and are not liquid as they cannot be withdrawn through drawing cheque on the bank.

2.4.4 Money Supply M_4: The measure M_4 of money supply includes not only all the items of M_3 but also the total deposits with the post office. Thus,

$M_4 = M_3$ + Total deposits with post office.

In India, total deposits with post office comprise savings bank deposits, time deposits, recurring deposits and other deposits including post office cumulative time deposits.

2.5 Determinants of Money Supply

Money supply is determined by a host of endogenous and exogenous factors. Some of these factors are explained below:

2.5.1 Cash Reserve Ratio (CRR): CRR is the average daily balance that a bank is required to maintain with the RBI as a share of such percent of its net demand and time liabilities (NDTL) that the RBI may notify from time-to-time in the Gazette of India. Increase/decrease in CRR is used by the RBI as an instrument of monetary control, particularly to mop up excess increases in the supply of money.

2.5.2 Statutory Liquidity Ratio (SLR): Apart from the CRR, banks in India are also subject to statutory liquidity requirement. SLR is the share of NDTL that a bank is required to maintain in safe and liquid assets, such as, unencumbered government securities, cash and gold. Changes in SLR often influence the availability of resources in the banking system for lending to the private sector. The underlying philosophy of this provision is to allocate total bank credit between the government and the rest of the economy.

2.5.3 Open Market Operations (OMOs): OMOs are conducted by the RBI via outright sale/purchase of government securities to/from the market with the primary aim of modulating rupee liquidity conditions in the market. OMOs are an effective quantitative policy tool in the armoury of the RBI, but are constrained by the stock of government securities available with it at a point in time.

2.5.4 Public Desire to Hold Currency: Public desire to hold cash relative to deposits in commercial banks also determines the supply on money.

2.5.5 High Powered Money and Money Multiplier (or Money-multiplier Theory of Money Supply): High-powered money (also called *base money*) is the highly liquid component of money stock in the economy and plays a crucial role in the determination of other monetary aggregates.

The high-powered money which is denoted by H consists of the currency (notes and coins) issued by the Government of India and the RBI. A part of the currency issued is held by the public, which is designated as C_p and a part is held by the banks as reserves which is designate as R. A part of these currency reserves of the banks is held by them in their own cash vaults and a part is deposited with the RBI in the reserve accounts which the banks hold with RBI. Accordingly, the high-powered money can be obtained as sum of currency held by the public and the part held by the banks as reserves. Thus,

$H = C_p + R$

Again, Government of India and RBI are producers of the high-powered money and the commercial banks do not have any role in producing this high-powered money (H). However, commercial banks are producers of demand deposits which are also used as money like currency.

The amount of high-powered money is fixed by RBI by its past actions. Thus, changes in high-powered money are the result of decisions of RBI which owns and controls it.

The money multiplier which may be denoted by m is the ratio of total money supply (M_1) to the stock of high-powered money (H), i.e. $m = M_1/H$. The size of money multiplier depends on the preference of the public to hold currency relative to deposits, and banks' desired cash reserves ratio to deposits.

It follows from above that if there is increase in currency held by the public which is a part of the high-powered money with demand deposits remaining unchanged, there will be a direct increase in the money supply in the economy because this constitutes a part of the money supply.

Money multiplier is the degree to which money supply is expanded as a result of the increase in high-powered money. If we know the value of money multiplier we can predict how much money will change when there is a change in the amount of high-powered money. Change in the high-powered money is decided and controlled by RBI, the money multiplier determines the extent to which decision by RBI regarding the change in high-powered money will bring about change in the total money supply in the economy.

Theory of determination of money supply explains how a given supply of high-powered money leads to multiple expansion in money supply through the working of money multiplier. Money multiplier does not show much variation in the long-run. However, it can change significantly in the short-run, causing large variations in money supply. This unpredictable variation in money multiplier in the short-run affecting money supply in the economy prevents the central bank of a country from controlling exactly and precisely the money supply in the economy.

2.6 Fiscal Deficits and Monetary Expansion

Fiscal deficits are not only inflationary, but also put pressure on real interest rates and crowd out private investment. There is a vicious circle between inflation and budget deficits: higher deficits cause higher inflation through excessive money financing and then, the higher inflation feeds back into higher deficits by reducing the real value of tax collections. Budget deficits turn out to be especially inflationary when the central bank is not independent and the financial markets are not developed enough to contain inflationary expectations. The very existence of large fiscal deficits puts continuous pressure on inflationary expectations. While the conventional view is that fiscal deficits lead to excessive monetary expansion and hence inflation, a more recent view— the fiscal theory of the price level— argues that fiscal imbalances lead to an increase in inflation and it is the money supply which adjusts subsequently to higher prices.

The inflationary consequences of the fiscal dominance of monetary policy brought into sharp focus the need to reduce fiscal imbalances, *per se,* as well as the draft of resources by the government on the central bank.

This need for monetary and fiscal coordination naturally raises the issue of its nature. A key issue in this context is whether this coordination should be rule-based or discretionary. Frameworks based on clear mandates and rules are usually considered preferable to *ad hoc* discretionary coordination, which could be clouded by problems of implementation and incentive distortions caused by electoral cycles. Furthermore, uncertainty and imperfect information about the current state of the economy as well as future outlook make it difficult to agree and implement a case-by-case discretionary approach to coordination. On all these grounds, there is an explicit preference for frameworks based on clear mandates/rules. In most countries, these take two forms: (a) central bank independence and (b) fiscal responsibility legislation as, for example, Fiscal Responsibility and Budget Management (FRBM) Act, 2003 of India.

An ideal fiscal rule should be well-defined, transparent, simple, flexible, adequate relative to the final goal, enforceable, consistent and supported by structural reforms if needed. The form of fiscal responsibility legislation has varied from country to country, depending upon factors such as the historical background, social set-up, nature of financial market evolution and objectives of macro-economic policies. Some countries have set transparency requirements for their governments while others follow expenditure rules and deficit and debt rules.

The efficacy of the fiscal rules remains a matter of debate. First, the frameworks may be circumvented by creative accounting (for example, modifying accounting practices and changing the nominal timing or other classification of taxes and expenditure). A second issue of contention is that fiscal rules might increase business cycle fluctuations. Two opposing factors are at work here. On the one hand, fiscal rules restrict unbridled government spending and this checks the excessive build-up of deficits and public debt which imparts stability to the economy. On the other hand, fiscal rules may restrict the government's ability to take countercyclical policy measures and hence, contribute to increased business cycle volatility. Ultimately, it is, therefore, an empirical exercise as to which of these two effects dominates. Fiscal rules are inflexible and inhibit counter-cyclical fiscal policy and thus lead to more volatile business cycles. In contrast, such rules do not have any affect on output volatility as fiscal rules may limit destabilising politically motivated and biased policies. Overall, fiscal policy rules are likely to be effective if they are accompanied by strong commitments and increased transparency.

The inflationary consequences of the monetisation of fiscal deficits are now well-recognised. As a result, there is a widespread consensus in favour of central bank independence, backed by some form of fiscal discipline. Such clear-cut rules are an essential pre-requisite to contain inflation and stabilise inflation expectations.

2.7 Money Supply in Open Economy

The transactions of an open economy also affect the growth of money supply in it. In the open economy there is free flow of goods and services through trade with foreign countries. Besides, in the open economy there are flows of capital between countries. The impact of transactions of an open economy on the money supply can be better understood from national income identity of an open economy.

When in an open economy, with flexible exchange rate regime, there is deficit in the overall balance of payments (i.e. on both current and capital accounts), it means that capital inflows are insufficient to bridge the gap in the balance of payments. This has to be met with the use of foreign exchange reserves held by the central bank (RBI in the case of India).

When RBI pays foreign exchange to finance the deficit in overall balance of payments, it gets rupees in return. [1] Thus, rupee currency flows into the RBI. As a result, money supply (rupee currency) in the economy decreases.

Conversely, there can be a surplus in the overall balance of payment (i.e. capital inflows exceed the deficit in current account). The large capital inflows can occur due to heavy foreign investments. These large capital inflows will cause appreciation of Indian rupee. To prevent the high appreciation of the Indian rupee, RBI can purchase foreign currency (generally US dollar) from the foreign exchange market. When RBI purchases dollars from the foreign exchange market, it pays rupees to the sellers of foreign exchange. The supply of money (rupee) in the market increases. More accurately, the supply of high-powered money increases.

2.8 Measures of Money Supply in India

The total supply of money and changes in it profoundly affect prices, wages, rate of interest and other crucial variables in the economy. Measurement of money supply though important is not easy because there is no unique definition of money supply. Since various things serve as money in an economy, there are various measures of money supply depending on what we include and exclude from a particular definition. Supply of money at a point of time is a stock concept while changes in the stock per year or per month are a flow concept.

Total stock of money in existence is different (and greater) than the stock of money held by the public. The term *public* includes all economic units (households, business enterprises etc.) except Central and State Governments, RBI and commercial banks.

When we refer to stock of money, it always means stock of money held by the public. The purpose of this distinction is to separate the suppliers (or producers) of money from the holders (or demanders) of it.

Since Independence in 1947, money supply in India has increased substantially. It is indicative of the growing monetisation of the economy. The composition of money supply has also undergone drastic changes. The share of currency in money supply has declined and that of bank deposits increased, particularly after the expansion of banking facilities to all corners of the country. Various components of money stock for the year 2018-19 are given in Table 2.2.

Table 2.2: Components of Money Stock, 2018-19

(₹ crore)

1. Currency in circulation	21,36,770
2. Cash with banks	84,536
3. Currency with public (1-2)	20,52,234
4. *Other* deposits with the RBI	31,742
5. *Bankers'* deposits with RBI	6,01,969
6. Demand deposits with banks	16,26,309
7. Time deposits with banks	1,17,20,589
8. Reserve money (1+4+5)	27,70,481
9. Narrow money (3+4+6)	37,10,285
10. Broad money (7+9)	1,54,30,874

Source: Reserve Bank of India, *Handbook of Statistics on Indian Economy, 2018-19*, Table 40 (excerpted).

Endnote

1. Balance of payments (BoP) is a financial statement of a country showing the flows of goods, services and funds between its residents and those of rest of the world during a given period of time. BoP statistics systematically summarise, for a specific period, the economic transactions of an economy with the rest of the world. BoP is based on double entry book-keeping system.

   A country's BoP is influenced by all the factors that affect international trade. These include factor endowments and productivity, trade policy, exchange rates, foreign currency reserves, inflation and demand.

   There may be deficit or surplus in BOP depending upon the situation. A sustained deficit in the balance of payments could have adverse effects for a country. It is essentially going into debt (much like a household would).

Part II
Financial Institutions, Markets, Instruments and Innovations

3

Financial System and Financial Institutions

Finance is the lifeblood of a modern economy. A financial system helps to mobilise the financial surpluses of an economy and transfer them to areas of financial deficit. It is the linchpin of any development strategy. The financial system promotes savings by providing a wide variety of financial assets to the general public. Savings collected from the household sector are pooled together and allocated to various sectors of the economy for raising production levels. If the allocation of credit is judicious and socially equitable, it can help achieve the twin objectives of growth and social justice.

3.1 Meaning, Importance and Functions of Financial System

Financial sector of an economy is a multi-faceted term. It refers to the whole gamut of legal and institutional arrangements, financial intermediaries, markets and instruments with both domestic and external dimensions.

A well-functioning financial system is a pre-requisite for the pursuit of economic growth with stability. The core function of a financial system is to facilitate smooth and efficient allocation of resources from savers to the ultimate users. The financial infrastructure contributes to the effective functioning of institutions and markets and thereby to stability. Hence, it serves as the foundation for adequate access to financial services and sustained financial development.

In the context of relatively under-developed capital market and with little internal resources, firms or economic entities depend largely on financial intermediaries for their fund requirements. In terms of sources of credit, they could be broadly categorised as institutional and non-institutional. For example, the major institutional sources of credit in India are commercial banks, development finance institutions (DFIs) and non-banking financial companies (NBFCs) including housing finance companies (HFCs). The non-institutional or unorganised sources of credit include moneylenders, indigenous bankers and sellers for trade credit. However, information about unorganised sector is limited and not readily available.

The relationship between finance and development has been a crucial subject of public policy for long. As early as in the 19th century, a number of economists stressed the importance of financial development for the growth of an economy. The banking system was recognised to have important ramifications for the level and growth rate of national income via the identification and funding of productive investments. This, in turn, was expected to induce a more efficient allocation of capital and foster growth. A contrary view also prevailed at the same time suggesting that economic growth would create demand for financial services. This meant that financial development would follow growth more or less automatically. In other words, financial development could be considered as a by-product of economic development.

Following are some of the functions performed by a financial system:

1. It facilitates trading and hedging of risks. Risk mitigation reduces uncertainty and enables resources to flow towards most profitable projects. Such a situation raises the efficiency of investments and the rate of growth.
2. By acting as an efficient conduit for allocating resources, the financial system enables improvement in technical progress. Technological innovations take place when entrepreneurs exploit the best chances of successfully imitating technologies in their production processes and introducing new products.
3. To the extent that financial development leads to the creation of financial infrastructure and enables better and more efficient provision of goods and services, costs of transactions would be lower, with positive spill over on economic growth.

The role and importance of the financial sector in the process of economic growth has evolved over time along with the changing paradigms. Till the late 1960s, the role of financial intermediaries in general, and banks in particular, in the process of economic growth of a country was largely ignored.

3.2 Role of Government in Financial Development

An important aspect of the process of financial development has been the role of the government. In many developing economies the governments traditionally played a significant role in fostering financial development. In the context of developing countries, this role is all the more important because financial systems in these countries are characterised by nascent accounting frameworks and inadequate legal mechanisms.

Several developing countries, therefore, undertook programmes for reforming their financial systems. In the initial stages of the development process, the financial sector in developing countries was characterised by directed credit allocation, interest rate restrictions and lending criteria based on social needs etc. These policies retarded the nature of financial intermediation in developing countries and the recognition of the same paved the way for financial sector reforms. Since the late 1970s and the 1980s, financial sector reforms encompassing deregulation of interest rates, revamping of directed credit and measures to promote competition in the financial services became an integral part of the overall structural adjustment programmes in many developing economies.

The interface between financial system and economic development revolves around on a wide range of issues, the following being more prominent.

1. Extant of state ownership of financial entities vis-à-vis private sector ownership.
2. Corporate governance in banks and other segments of the financial system.
3. Transparency of policies and practices of monetary and financial agencies.
4. Prudential requirements of market participants.
5. Maintenance of best practices in accounting and auditing.
6. Comprehensive and efficient regulation and supervision of the financial system.
7. Collection, processing and dissemination of information in order to meet the market needs.

The commonality among these concerns has given rise to a wide recognition and acceptance of having a set of international standards and best practices that every country should strive to foster and implement.

3.3 Determinants of Access to Financial Services

In the literature on finance, a number of factors have been mentioned which affect the access to financial services. Some important factors among these are as under:

1. **Level of Income:** Financial status of people is always important in gaining access to financial services. Extremely poor people find it difficult to access financial services even when the services are tailored for them.
2. **Type of Occupation:** Many banks have not developed the capacity to evaluate loan applications of small borrowers and unorganised enterprises and hence tend to deny loan requests by them.
3. **Legal Identity:** Lack of legal identities like identity cards, birth certificates or written records often exclude ethnic minorities, economic and political refugees and migrant workers from accessing financial services.
4. **Attractiveness of the Product:** Benefits of financial products offered and how their availability is marketed are crucial in accessing financial services.
5. **Terms and Conditions:** Terms and conditions attached to products such as minimum balance requirements and conditions relating to the use of accounts often dissuade people from using such products/services. Generally, transaction is free as long as the account has sufficient funds to cover the cost of transactions made. However, there is a range of other charges that have a disproportionate effect on people with low income.
6. **Socio-cultural Barriers:** Lack of financial literacy (basic accounting skills) and cultural and religious barriers to banking often constrain demand for financial services. Access to credit is often limited for women who do not have, or cannot hold title to assets such as land and property or must seek male guarantees to borrow.
7. **Living Conditions:** Factors like density of population, rural and remote areas, mobility of the population (i.e. highly mobile people with no fixed or formal address), insurgency in a location etc. also affect access to financial services.
8. **Age Factor:** Financial service providers usually target the middle of the economically active population, often overlooking older or younger customers.

3.4 Regulation and Supervision of Financial System

An efficient and robust regulatory structure is an essential pre-requisite for the stability of the financial system. The implications of increased cross-sectoral and cross-border conglomeration of financial companies highlight the need for increased focus on co-ordination and information sharing among regulators. The emergence of the holding company structure and its legal implications has given rise to concerns about their regulation and supervision. The recent international financial turbulence has shown that there is no single fail-proof method of financial regulation and that an ideal system would have elements of both principles-based and rules-based regulation.

The recent global financial crisis has highlighted the importance of liquidity management for institutions. In this context, it is imperative to have an adequate liquidity infrastructure in place. In the Indian context, active liquidity management has been an integral part of the Reserve Bank of India's monetary operations and it is being achieved through various instruments. However, the use of monetary policy requires to be further honed in order to deal with the impact of external capital flows.

3.5 Financial Neutrality versus Financial Activism

The views on neutrality of financial intermediaries to economic growth, however, came under attack during the late 1960s. It was pointed out that there exists a strong positive correlation between financial development and economic growth of a country. Financial experts started emphasising the negative impact of *financial repression*, under which the government determined the quantum, allocation and price of credit, on the growth process. They argued that credit is not just another input and instead, credit is the engine of growth.

The world of finance has changed markedly over the last 30 years or so. The change has been brought about by a number of events and circumstances. The growing dissatisfaction with the working of the fixed exchange rate system during the 1960s led many countries, especially of the industrialised world, to adopt a floating exchange rate system by the early 1970s. There was also a growing realisation that for achieving sustained growth with stability, it would be necessary to have freer trade, liberalised external capital movements, and a relatively flexible use of domestic monetary policy. With trade being subject to multilateral negotiations, industrialised countries and some of the emerging market economies took steps to liberalise capital movements across countries since about the middle of the 1970s. Simultaneously, efforts were made to remove distortions in the domestic financial sector through elimination or containment of reserve requirements and interest rate regulations. These initiatives coincided with the rapid technological improvements in electronic payments and communication systems. The interaction among these factors helped the process of internationalisation of financial markets.

Under the impact of economic liberalisation, the industrialised countries, as a group, improved their relative economic position in the world economy, and posted high growth rates in the 1980s and thereafter. This experience has confirmed the release of growth impulses following financial liberalisation.

Developing countries, on their part, have been adopting, since the early 1980s, market-oriented strategies of financial development, partly supported by international financial institutions, and partly to avail of the large pool of resources available in international financial markets. They either dismantled or sharply contained *financial repression* and undertook financial reforms with a view to enhancing allocative efficiency and competitiveness. Financial development required the deepening and widening of the existing financial markets as well as the introduction of new products and instruments to cater to the needs of savers and investors.

Financial development depends on market-based regulatory framework and incentives (disincentives) that promote market discipline. If market discipline is not well-understood or not complied with, there would arise possibilities of inefficiencies and/or volatilities in asset prices and capital movements. Financial stability, therefore, is a pre-requisite for sustained financial development which in turn would impact growth rate positively.

3.6 Financial Volatility versus Financial Stability

The process of deregulation and globalisation of financial markets gained momentum in the 1990s, and expanded the choices for investors, and helped to improve the prospects of reducing the costs of financial transactions and improving operational and allocative efficiency of the financial system. A number of developing countries, especially in Asia, that moved early on to the path of economic liberalisation had experienced large capital inflows through the 1980s and the first half of the 1990s. Large capital inflows, however, carry the risk of financial sector vulnerability, where the use of such flows is not administered by application of appropriate mix of macroeconomic measures. The currency and financial crises in Mexico and Thailand, followed by Korea and Indonesia, provide many insights about the problems that would arise when exchange rates are inflexible, and banking and financial systems are weak.

The experience of the crisis-affected countries highlights the need for setting in place regulatory and supervisory frameworks to ensure the safety and stability of financial systems. Their experience also underscores the premise that financial development is only a necessary condition for sustainable growth, and by no means a sufficient condition. In view of the costs of financial crises falling on the sovereign governments, financial stability has come to occupy a centre-stage in formulating public policy for economic development.

3.7 Financial Globalisation

No major economy in the world today can be viewed in isolation from the rest of the world. Given the size and the growing magnitude of interaction—in terms of trade, services, and capital flows—and the greater openness to globalisation, India is in a different economic milieu today than it was two decades ago. India is virtually part of the world of globalised finance and is learning to walk, negotiating the strong currents, both positive and negative, generated by the forces of financial globalisation.

The 1990s witnessed a paradigm shift towards market-oriented economic policies and a careful dismantling of obstacles in its wake. This has helped the smaller, emerging economies gain access to world markets, emergent technologies and collaborations. This has also given them a window to the developed world and helped them understand the significant role of globalisation as an instrument, which could be utilised not just to achieve economic efficiency, but also eradicate poverty.

Globalisation has also resulted in the creation of a new business framework. More changes can be expected in the business scenario specifically in terms of openness, adaptiveness and responsiveness. The most important dimensions of economic globalisation are: (a) breaking down of national barriers; (b) international spread of trade, financial and production activities, and (c) growing power of transnational corporations and international financial institutions in these processes. While economic globalisation is a very uneven process, with increased trade and investment being focused in a few countries, almost all countries are greatly affected by this process.

A major feature of globalisation is the growing concentration and monopolisation of economic resources and power by transnational corporations and by global financial firms and funds. This process has been termed transnationalisation, in which fewer and fewer transnational corporations are gaining a large and rapidly increasing proportion of world economic resources, production and market shares. Where a multinational company used to dominate the market of a single product, a big transnational company (TNC) now typically produces or trades in an increasing multitude of products, services and sectors. Through mergers and acquisitions, fewer and fewer of these TNCs now control a larger and larger share of the global market, whether in commodities, manufactures or services.

4

Classification, Regulation and Supervision of Financial Institutions in India

Financial institutions in India have transited since the mid-1990s from an environment of an administered regime to a system dominated by market-determined interest and exchange rates, and migration of the central bank from direct and quantitative to price-based instruments of monetary policy and operations. However, increased globalisation has resulted in further expansion and sophistication of the financial sector, which has posed new challenges to regulation and supervision, particularly of the banking system. In this context, the capabilities of the existing regulatory and supervisory structures also need to be assessed by benchmarking them against the best international practices.

Emphasizing the need for an efficient financial intermediation, the Twelfth Five Year Plan (2012-17) observed, "While availability of savings in the aggregate is an important part of macroeconomic balance, it is also important to have an efficient financial system that can channel savings to the most productive uses, and also ensure inclusiveness. The past two decades have seen far-reaching change in the character and structure of the country's banking system and the capital markets. These changes have addressed the management of credit risk, provisioning against delinquent loans and a greater focus on fee-based income. The interest rate regime that used to be highly regulated was systematically replaced by a commercially determined framework that helped price-in credit quality, duration and diversification of risk. The kind of loan products available and the servicing of these for the commercial sector have also become more efficient. Retail banking, that is, personal loans for buying homes and other durable assets, and payment and settlement facilities, have become an important and rapidly growing component of banking. Lending to small borrowers typified by the self-help group (SHG) and micro finance has come some distance towards making financial inclusion meaningful.

These changes have also changed the behaviour of corporate borrowers. In many ways, financial risk was not meaningful in the years before 1991. It changed subsequently, and with it the incentives to maintain a clean credit record and a lower leverage. Dismantling of the production licensing system, lower import tariffs and the end of quantitative restrictions on imports made competition a reality in India, that is, both domestic competition and competition vis-à-vis the global producers. Finally, the decline in the ownership functions of government and quasi-governmental agencies, and the enhanced role of capital markets in raising finance has given new importance to the interests of shareholders, especially minority shareholders. Associated with this is the challenge of corporate control, which now has to face up to proactive mergers, acquisition and sale". [1]

4.1 Classification of Financial Institutions in India

Financial institutions in India can be classified as given in Table 4.1.

Table 4.1: Classification of Financial Institutions in India

1. Reserve Bank of India (RBI)
2. Commercial Banks
2.1 Scheduled Commercial Banks
2.1.1 Public Sector Banks: (a) State Bank group, (b) nationalised banks and (c) other public sector banks
2.1.2 Private Sector Banks: (a) old private banks and (b) new private banks
2.1.3 Foreign banks
2.1.4 Regional rural banks
2.2 Non-scheduled commercial banks (local area banks)
2.3 Payment banks
3. Co-operative Banks
3.1 Urban co-operative banks
3.1.1 Scheduled
3.1.2 Non-scheduled
3.2 Rural co-operative banks
3.2.1 Short-term structure: (a) State co-operative banks (SCBs) and (b) District central co-operative banks (DCCBs)
3.2.2 Primary agricultural credit societies (PACS)
3.2.3 Long-term structure: (a) State co-operative agriculture and rural development banks (SCARDBs) and (b) Primary co-operative agriculture and rural development banks (PCARDBs)
4. State Financial Corporations (SFCs)
5. Development Finance Institutions (DFIs)
6. Non-banking Financial Companies (NBFCs)
6.1 NBFCs (Deposit-taking)
6.2 NBFCs (Non-deposit-taking)
6.3 Residuary non-banking companies (RNBCs)
6.4 Primary dealers
6.5 Housing finance companies
7. Mutual Funds
7.1 Bank-sponsored
7.2 Institution-sponsored 7.2.1 Indian 7.2.2 Foreign
7.3 Joint ventures (predominantly Indian)
7.4 Joint ventures (predominantly foreign)

8. Pension Funds
9. Insurance Institutions
9.1 Life insurance 9.1.1 Public 9.1.2 Private
9.2 Non-life insurance 9.2.1 Public 9.2.2 Private 9.2.3 Others [Deposit Insurance and Credit Guarantee Corporation (DICGC) and Reinsurance Corporation of India Ltd.]
10. Other Institutions
Other institutions established to meet specific financing needs include Power Finance Corporation (PFC) and Rural Electrification Corporation (REC) (financial assistance to the power sector) and Indian Railway Finance Corporation (IRFC), which is the capital market financing arm of Indian Railways. These institutions have been notified as public financial institutions (PFIs) under the Companies Act, 1956 and enjoy less stringent compliance and regulatory norms. In addition, at the state-level, there exists the North Eastern Development Finance Corporation (NEDFC) extending credit to industry and agricultural concerns in the North Eastern region, and Technical Consultancy Organisations, providing technical inputs for feasibility studies on viability of projects. Besides, the State Industrial Development Corporations (SIDCs), registered under the Companies Act, 1956 also provide credit to industries at the state level.
11. Financial Institutions (1 to 10)
12. Banking Sector (1+2+3)

4.2 Regulation and Supervision of Financial Institutions in India

Financial institutions in India are regulated and supervised by various authorities and legislations (Table 4.2).

Table 4.2: Regulation and Supervision of Financial Institutions in India

Institutions	Regulator(s)	Act(s)
Commercial banks	- Reserve Bank of India (RBI)	- Banking Regulation Act, 1949 - Reserve Bank of India Act, 1934 - State Bank of India Act, 1955 - State Bank of India (Subsidiary) Banks Act, 1959 - Banking Companies (Acquisition and Transfer of Undertaking) Acts, 1970 and 1980 - Deposit Insurance and Credit Guarantee Co-operation (DICGC) Act, 1961

Urban co-operative banks	- RBI - Registrar of Co-operative Societies	- Banking Regulation Act, 1949 - Co-operative Societies Act of various State Governments - Multi-State Co-operative Societies Act, 2002 - DICGC Act, 1961
Regional rural banks (RRBs)	- RBI - National Bank for Agriculture and Rural Development (NABARD)	- Banking Regulation Act, 1949 - DICGC Act, 1961 - Regional Rural Banks Act, 1976 - Reserve Bank of India, Act, 1934
State co-operative banks/district central co-operative banks	- RBI - Registrar of Co-operative Societies - NABARD	- Banking Regulation Act, 1949 - Co-operative Societies Act of various State Governments - DICGC Act, 1961
Development finance institutions (DFIs)/Non-banking financial companies (NBFCs)	- RBI - Ministry of Corporate Affairs	- Reserve Bank of India, Act, 1934 - Companies Act, 1956
Housing finance companies	- National Housing Bank (NHB) - Ministry of Corporate Affairs	- Reserve Bank of India, Act, 1934 - National Housing Bank Act, 1987 Companies Act, 1956
Mutual funds	- Securities and Exchange Board of India (SEBI)	- Securities and Exchange Board of India (SEBI) Act, 1992
Insurance companies	- Insurance Regulatory and Development Authority (IRDA)	- Insurance Regulatory and Development Authority (IRDA) Act, 1999

Commercial banks are the dominant institutions in the Indian financial landscape. According to Committee on Financial Sector Assessment, "Though public sector banks (PSBs) account for around 70 percent of commercial banking assets, competition in the banking sector has increased in recent years with the emergence of private players as also with greater private shareholding of PSBs. Listing of PSBs on stock exchanges and increased private shareholding have also added to competition. The new private banks which accounted for 2.6 percent of the commercial banking sector in March 1997 have developed rapidly and accounted for nearly 17 percent of the commercial banking assets by end-March 2008. Together with cooperative banks, the banking sector accounts for nearly 70 per cent of the total assets of Indian financial institutions". [2]

Endnotes

1. Government of India, Planning Commission, *Twelfth Five Year Plan* (2012-17), Volume I, Chapter 2, paras 2.78 and 2.79.
2. Reserve Bank of India, *Committee on Financial Sector Assessment* (Chairman: Rakesh Mohan), March 2009, Volume II, p. 64.

5

Financial Institutions in India at a Glance

Financial institutions (intermediaries) in India consist of commercial banks, regional rural banks (RRBs), urban co-operative banks (UCBs), rural co-operative credit institutions, development finance institutions (DFIs), non-banking financial companies (NBFCs), mutual funds, pension funds, and insurance organisations. These institutions, which provide a meeting ground for the savers and the investors, form the core of India's financial sector. Through mobilisation of resources and their better allocation, financial intermediaries play an important role in the development process of underdeveloped countries.

Financial institutions in India have transited since the mid-1990s from an environment of an administered regime to a system dominated by market-determined interest and exchange rates, and migration of the central bank from direct and quantitative to price-based instruments of monetary policy and operations. However, increased globalisation has resulted in further expansion and sophistication of the financial sector, which has posed new challenges to regulation and supervision, particularly of the banking system. In this context, the capabilities of the existing regulatory and supervisory structures also need to be assessed by benchmarking them against the best international practices.

5.1 Commercial Banks

Commercial banks are the dominant institutions in the Indian financial landscape. Commercial banks in India can be classified as follows:

1. Scheduled and non-scheduled banks.
2. Indian and foreign banks.
3. Public sector and private sector banks.

Until the early 1990s, the banking sector suffered from lack of competition, low capital base, low productivity and high intermediation cost. Commenting on the performance of the nationalised banks, the Reserve Bank of India observed, "After the nationalisation of large banks in 1969 and 1980, the Government-owned banks have dominated the banking sector. The role of technology was minimal and the quality of service was not given adequate importance. Banks also did not follow proper risk management systems and the prudential standards were weak. All these resulted in poor asset quality and low profitability". [1]

Prior to reforms, the Indian Government determined the quantum, allocation and the price of credit, a situation referred to as *financial repression* by some experts. It was in this backdrop, that wide-ranging banking sector reforms in India were introduced as an integral part of the economic reforms initiated in the early 1990s.

For details, see chapter 25 of this book.

5.2 Regional Rural Banks (RRBs)

Regional rural banks (RRBs) form an important segment of the rural financial sector. They were conceived as institutions that combine the local feel and familiarity of the co-operatives with the business capabilities of commercial banks. This sector has an exclusive role in improving financial inclusion and catering to vital sectors like agriculture and allied economic activities. Public policy, therefore, aims at keeping this sector viable and strong through various forms of active intervention.

The renewed emphasis on agricultural and rural development by the Government of India would lead to a growing demand for different types of financial services in the rural areas, as financial needs of the rural economy becomes diversified. The present structure of rural credit may not be able to cater to the same. RRBs would be called upon to play a greater role in providing such services due to their rural character and feel. RRBs have to take over a larger share of credit disbursements calling for much larger resource mobilization, as also greater efforts for their institutional strengthening.

5.3 Urban Co-operative Banks (UCBs)

The co-operative banking system forms an integral part of the Indian financial system. It comprises urban cooperative banks and rural co-operative credit institutions. Urban co-operative banks have a single-tier structure whereas rural co-operatives have a two- or three-tier structure.

The single tier urban co-operative banks (UCBs)—also referred to as primary cooperative banks—play an important role in meeting the growing credit needs of urban and semi-urban areas of the country. The UCBs, which grew rapidly in the early 1990s, showed certain weaknesses arising out of lack of sound corporate governance, unethical lending, comparatively high levels of non-performing loans and their inability to operate in a liberalised environment. Accordingly, some of the weak UCBs have been either liquidated or merged with other banks.

The financial reforms process initiated in 1991 has tried to achieve regulatory convergence among various financial intermediaries in view of their systemic importance. Therefore, the basic objectives and instruments of reforms for co-operative banks have been the same as for state co-operative banks (SCBs). However, given the special characteristics of co-operative banks, they have been extended certain dispensations in terms of pace and sequencing of reforms.

5.4 Rural Co-operative Credit Institutions

Historically, rural co-operative credit institutions (or simply rural co-operatives) have played an important role in providing institutional credit to the agricultural and rural sectors. The structure of rural co-operative banks is not uniform across all the States of the country. Some States have a unitary structure with the State level banks operating through their own branches, while others have a mixed structure incorporating both unitary and federal systems.

The rural credit co-operative system has served as an important instrument of credit delivery in rural and agricultural areas. The separate structure of rural co-operative sector for long-term and short-term loans has enabled these institutions to develop as specialised institutions for rural credit delivery. At the same time, their federal structure has helped in providing support structure for the guidance and critical financing for the lower structure.

5.5 Development Finance Institutions (DFIs)

Development finance institutions (DFIs) or simply financial institutions were set up in India at various points of time starting from the late 1940s to cater to the medium to long-term financing requirements of industry as the capital market in India had not developed sufficiently. After Independence in 1947, the national government adopted the path of planned economic development and launched the First Five Year Plan in 1951. This strategy of development provided the critical inducement for establishment of DFIs at both all-India and state-levels. In order to perform their role, DFIs were extended funds of the RBI and government guaranteed bonds, which constituted major sources of their funds. Funds from these sources were not only available at concessional rates, but also on a long-term basis with their maturity period ranging from 10-15 years. On the asset side, their operations were marked by near absence of competition.

A large variety of financial institutions have come into existence over the years to perform various types of financial activities. While some of them operate at all-India level, others are state level institutions. Besides providing direct loans (including rupee loans, foreign currency loans), financial institutions also extend financial assistance by way of underwriting and direct subscription and by issuing guarantees. Recently, some DFIs have started extending short-term/working capital finance, although term-lending continues to be their primary activity.

5.6 Non-banking Financial Companies (NBFCs)

In the multi-tier financial system of India, NBFCs stand apart for more than one reason. Though these companies essentially do the job of financial intermediation, they are still not fully comparable with the other segments of the financial system. This is so in view of the wide variations in the profile of the players in this sector in terms of their nature of activity—lending, investment, lease, hire purchase, chit fund, pure deposit mobilisation, fee based activity etc.—the volume of activity, the sources of funding they rely on (public deposits and non-public deposits), method of raising resources, deployment pattern etc. This has naturally resulted in the creation of multifarious categories of NBFCs and therefore, diverse regulatory dispensation by RBI.

Although NBFCs in India have existed for a long time, they shot into prominence in the second half of the 1980s and in the first-half of the 1990s, as deposits raised by them grew rapidly. NBFCs were historically subjected to a relatively lower degree of regulation *vis-à-vis* banks. Prior to reforms in this sector, operations of NBFCs were characterized by several distinctive features *viz.*, no entry barriers, limited fixed assets and no holding of inventories-all of which led to a proliferation of NBFCs. Primarily engaged in the area of retail banking, they face competition from banks and financial institutions. With the increasing services sector activity in India, the NBFCs have been playing a critical role in providing credit. NBFCs have extensive networks with some of them accepting public deposits.

5.7 Mutual Funds

Mutual funds are very popular all over the world and they play an important role in the financial system of many countries. Mutual funds are an ideal medium for investment by small investors in the stock market. Mutual funds pool together the investments of small investors for participation in the stock market. Being institutional investors, mutual funds can afford market analysis generally not available to individual investors. Furthermore, mutual funds can diversify the portfolio in a better way as compared with individual investors due to the expertise and availability of funds.

In general, the mutual fund regulatory framework in India is much more extensive and developed than in many other countries. Indian mutual funds are unit trusts, formed under the Indian Trusts Act of 1882. Their operation is governed by mutual fund regulations, totalling 78, promulgated by SEBI in exercise of the powers conferred by Section 30, read with clause (c) of sub-section (2) of Section 11 of the Securities and Exchange Board of India, Act 1992. The first set of mutual fund regulations was originally promulgated in 1996, and has since been amended from time to time. In order to remove any difficulties in the application or interpretation of these regulations, Regulation 77 of the mutual funds regulations additionally authorises SEBI to issue "clarifications and guidelines in the form of notes or circulars which shall be binding upon the sponsor, mutual funds, trustees, asset management companies and custodians".

5.8 Pension Funds

Pension sector reforms were initiated in India to establish a robust and sustainable social security arrangement in the country seeing that only about 12-13 percent of the total workforce was covered by any formal social security system. The New Pension System (NPS) was introduced by the Government from January 1, 2004 for new entrants to the Central Government service, except the Armed Forces, and was extended to the general public from May 1, 2009 on a voluntary basis. The features of the NPS design are self-sustainability, portability and scalability. Based on individual choice, it is envisaged as a low-cost and efficient pension system backed by sound regulation. As a pure "defined contribution" product with no defined benefit element, returns are totally market- related. The NPS provides various investment options and choices to individuals to switch over from one option to another or from one fund manager to another, subject to certain regulatory restrictions.

Pension Fund Regulatory and Development Authority (PFRDA), set up as a regulatory body for the pension sector, is engaged in consolidating the initiatives taken so far regarding the full NPS architecture and expanding the reach of the NPS distribution network. The full NPS architecture comprising a central recordkeeping agency (CRA), pension fund managers (PFMs), trustee bank, custodian and NPS Trust has been put in place and is fully operational.

NSDL g-Governance Infrastructure Ltd. and Karvy Computershare Private Ltd. have been selected as the CRA. The PFRDA has also appointed 7 pension funds for the government and private sector, namely UTI Retirement Solutions Limited, SBI Pension Funds Pvt. Ltd., ICICI Prudential Pension Fund Management Co. Ltd., LIC Pension Fund Ltd., Birla Sun Life Pension Management Ltd., Kotak Mahindra Pension Fund Ltd. and HDFC Pension Management Co. Ltd. as pension funds under the NPS.

5.9 Insurance Organisations

Insurance has been an important part of the Indian financial system. Until recently, insurance services were provided by the public sector i.e. life insurance by the Life Insurance Corporation of India (LIC) since the mid-1950s, and general insurance by the General Insurance Corporation (GIC) and its four subsidiaries since the 1970s. The insurance industry was opened up to the private sector in August 2000. The primary objective of liberalisation in the insurance sector was to deepen insurance penetration by enlarging consumer choices through product innovation. The increased competition has led to rapid product innovations for catering to the diverse requirements of the various segments of the population. Besides statutory commitments in respect of weaker sections of society, competitive pressures are pushing life insurers to adopt innovative marketing strategies to extend insurance penetration, especially targeting lower income groups. Insurance industry in India is broadly classified into: (a) life insurance, and (b) non-life insurance business.

The Indian insurance industry has witnessed a sea-change since opening up to private players in 1999. The liberalisation has transformed the industry's outlook towards the vast Indian market. The spurt in the number of players has led to innovation in product development and distribution channels, thus treating the Indian customer to a whole new range of insurance products, each suited to match unique requirements of different societal segments.

The ultimate objective of reforms is to increase insurance-density and insurance penetration levels by designing more tailor-made products for customers, both individuals and institutions. Overall, the reach of the sector has increased since opening up with a wider choice available to the policy holder. Simultaneously, the increase in resource mobilisation has resulted in the investment in the infrastructure and social sectors.

The supervisory control of insurance companies is exercised by Insurance Regulatory and Development Authority (IRDA) and these powers flow from Insurance Act, 1938 as well as from IRDA Act, 1999. IRDA Act 1999 states: "Subject to the provisions of this Act and any other law for the time being in force, the Authority shall have the duty to regulate, promote and ensure orderly growth of insurance business and reinsurance business".

Endnote

1. Reserve Bank of India, Report on Currency and Finance, 2001-02, p. VI-1.

6

Role of Financial Markets

Financial market is a mechanism which allows people to buy and sell financial securities and other fungible items of value. Fungible means interchangeable or exchangeable items (like goods, services, currencies) as contrasted with non-fungible items such as human beings. Thus, financial market can mean capital market (trading in shares and bonds etc.), commodity market (trading in gold and silver etc.), foreign exchange market (trading in different currencies) and other such markets.

6.1 Importance of Financial Markets

A well-functioning financial market enables efficient use of market-based instruments of monetary policy by improving interest rate signals in the economy. Apart from enhancing the efficiency of monetary policy, deep and well-functioning financial markets promote mobilisation of domestic savings and improve the allocative efficiency of financial intermediation, and foster the necessary conditions to emerge as an international or a regional financial centre. Strong domestic financial markets also act as a buffer against external disturbances and help in absorbing shocks to the domestic banking system during crises. Further, they provide incentives for development of hedging instruments, and lower macroeconomic volatility and financial instability. Efficient financial markets also have several indirect benefits such as rapid accumulation of physical and human capital, more stable investment financing, and faster technological progress.

Developed and well-integrated financial markets are critical for sustaining high growth, for the effective conduct of monetary policy, for developing a diversified financial system, financial integration and ensuring financial stability. The question therefore is not whether developed financial markets are needed, but how to go about in developing them fully. Financial markets presently deal with complex and sophisticated products. Introduction of such products would require clear regulatory frameworks, appropriate institutions and development of human resource skills. The speed for further changes in the financial markets would thus depend on how quickly are we able to meet these requirements.

The need for developed financial markets also arises in the context of increasing integration of domestic financial markets with international financial markets. The concept of globalisation is no longer restricted to its traditional sense—variety of cross-border transactions in goods and services—but also extends to international capital flows, driven by rapid and widespread diffusion of technology. In fact, most of the literature in recent years on globalisation has centred around financial integration due to the emergence of worldwide financial markets and the possibility of better access to external financing for a variety of domestic entities.

Financial market development is a complex and time-consuming process. There are no short cuts for developing well-functioning markets with depth and liquidity. Some of the preconditions for financial market reform are the following.

1. Macroeconomic stability.
2. Sound and efficient financial institutions and structure.
3. Prudential regulation and supervision.
4. Strong creditor rights.
5. Contract enforcement.

6.2 Types of Financial Markets

The financial markets can broadly be divided into money market and capital market.

6.2.1 Money Market: Money market is a market for debt securities that pay off in the short term usually less than one year, for example the market for 90-days treasury bills. This market encompasses the trading and issuance of short term non equity debt instruments including treasury bills, commercial papers, bankers acceptance, certificates of deposits etc.

6.2.2 Capital Market: Capital market is a market for long-term debt and equity shares. In this market, the capital funds comprising of both equity and debt are issued and traded. This also includes private placement sources of debt and equity as well as organized markets like stock exchanges. Capital market can be further divided into primary and secondary markets.

In the primary market securities are offered to public for subscription for the purpose of raising capital or fund. Secondary market is an equity trading venue in which already existing/pre-issued securities are traded among investors.

Secondary market refers to a market where securities are traded after being initially offered to the public in the primary market and/or listed on the stock exchange. Majority of the trading is done in the secondary market. Secondary market comprises of equity markets and the debt markets.

For the general investor, the secondary market provides an efficient platform for trading of his securities. For the management of the company, secondary equity markets serve as a monitoring and control conduit by facilitating value-enhancing control activities, enabling implementation of incentive-based management contracts, and aggregating information (via price discovery) that guides management decisions.

6.3 Regulation and Supervision of Financial Markets in India

Financial markets in India have evidenced significant development since the financial sector reforms initiated in the 1990s. The development of these markets has been done in a calibrated, sequenced manner and in step with those in other markets in the real economy. The emphasis has been on strengthening price discovery, easing restrictions on flows or transactions, lowering transaction costs, and enhancing liquidity.

Benefiting from a series of policy initiatives over time, greater domestic market integration has also been witnessed.

The equity, government securities, foreign exchange and money markets along with their corresponding derivatives segments have developed into reasonably deep and liquid markets and there has been significant increase in domestic market integration over the years. However, the credit derivative market is yet to take off in any significant manner. As regards corporate bonds, though the primary market has seen an increase in issuance, the secondary market has not developed commensurately.

Financial markets in India are regulated and supervised by the Reserve Bank of India (RBI) and the Securities and Exchange Board of India (SEBI). Financial markets under the purview of the RBI include the following:

1. Money market and derivatives.
2. Foreign exchange market and derivatives.
3. Government securities market and interest rate derivatives.
4. Credit markets and derivatives.

Financial markets under the control and supervision of SEBI are as under:

1. Equity market and derivatives.
2. Corporate bond market.

6.4 Financial Markets and Monetary Policy of the RBI

From the point of view of RBI, developed financial markets are critical for effective transmission of monetary policy impulses to the rest of the economy. Monetary transmission cannot take place without efficient price discovery, particularly with respect to interest rates and exchange rates. The transmission process for policy actions by RBI involves two stages. In the first stage, policy actions are transmitted to financial markets. The second stage of the transmission mechanism involves the propagation of monetary policy impulses from the financial system to the real economy and aggregate prices. A successful implementation of policy requires a reasonably accurate assessment of how rapidly the effects of policy actions are transmitted through the financial system to the real economy, affecting aggregate spending decisions of households and firms, and from there to aggregate demand and inflation.

As a debt manager to the Government, the development of a deep and liquid market for government securities is of critical importance to the RBI as it results in better price discovery and cost effective Government borrowing. The government securities market also provides an effective transmission mechanism for monetary policy, facilitates the introduction and pricing of hedging products and serves as a benchmark for pricing other debt instruments. Although the government securities market has developed considerably over the years, more needs to be done for it to become fully developed.

6.5 Reforms in the Financial Markets

Financial markets in India have existed for a long time. However, they remained relatively underdeveloped for a variety of reasons. India introduced financial sector reforms as a part of structural reforms in the early 1990s. Several measures have been taken by regulatory authorities to develop and strengthen India's financial system in order to make it compatible with best international practices.

Reforms in the financial markets encompassed all segments—money market, credit market, government securities market, foreign exchange market, equity market and corporate debt market. The development of financial markets in India has been pursued to bring about a transformation in the structure, efficiency and stability of markets as also to facilitate integration of markets. The emphasis has been on strengthening price discovery, easing of restrictions on flows or transactions, lowering of transaction costs, and enhancing liquidity. Development of these markets has been done in a calibrated, sequenced and careful manner in step with those in other markets in the real economy. The sequencing has also been informed by the need to develop market infrastructure, technology and capabilities of market participants and financial institutions in a consistent manner. In a low income economy like India, the cost of downside risk is very high, so the objective of maintaining financial stability has to be constantly kept in view while developing financial markets.

The objectives of developing financial markets are as under:

1. To encourage competitive forces.
2. To facilitate the use of a variety of instruments.
3. To promote the growth of different kinds of institutions offering a wide range of financial instruments and services to potential savers and investors.
4. To protect the interests of savers by reducing their risks.
5. To promote the development of instruments that help in risk management.

For regulating financial markets, regulators are guided by various considerations in the larger interest of society. Broadly, the objective of regulation is to protect the interests of depositors and investors (safety and conduct of business), promote financial inclusion, ensure monetary and financial stability and achieve sustained economic progress.

During the post-reforms period, the structure of financial markets has witnessed a remarkable change in terms of financial instruments traded in various segments of the financial market and market participants.

Reforms in the financial markets have encompassed all segments. The development of financial markets in India has been pursued to bring about a transformation in the structure, efficiency and stability of the markets as also to facilitate their integration. The emphasis has been on strengthening price discovery, easing restrictions on flows or transactions, lowering transaction costs, and enhancing liquidity. During the post-reform period, the structure of financial markets has witnessed a significant change in terms of financial instruments traded in various segments of the financial market and market participants. The development of these markets has been done in a calibrated, sequenced and careful manner in step with those in other markets in the real economy. Sequencing has also been informed by the need to develop market infrastructure, technology and the capabilities of market participants and financial institutions in a consistent manner.

The gradual removal of structural bottlenecks in the Indian financial markets and a shift away from the erstwhile administered rates has led to greater domestic market integration. This has also benefited from a series of other policy initiatives over time which included enabling market-determined price discovery through interest rate deregulation; expansion and diversification of the investor base; introduction of a variety of instruments of varying features and tenor; and improvement in market infrastructure. Some of the markets which show strong co-movement are money and government securities markets, exchange rate and stock markets, and foreign exchange forward and money markets.

The need to further develop financial markets has also been underlined by the two high-powered committees, *viz.* Committee on Fuller Capital Account Convertibility (FCAC) [1] and the High Powered Expert Committee on Making Mumbai an International Financial Centre. [2] The Committee on Fuller Capital Account Convertibility in its Report submitted in July 2006 indicated that in order to make a move towards fuller capital account convertibility, it needs to be ensured that different financial market segments are not only well-developed but also that they are well-integrated. Otherwise, shocks to one or more market segments would not get transmitted to other segments efficiently so that the entire financial system is able to absorb the shocks with minimal damage.

To sum up, financial markets in India have seen considerable development since financial sector reforms were initiated in the 1990s. Given the imperatives of the prevailing context, the initial nudge had to be provided through specific policy instruments and actions, but over a period of time these markets have acquired a dynamic of their own. The process of transition in respect of all financial market segments has been largely disruption-free, accommodating the unique features of the existing system while trying to align with the best international practices.

Indian financial markets can be broadly categorised into the money market, government securities market, equity market, corporate bond market, credit market and foreign exchange market. While equity, government securities, foreign exchange and money markets along with their corresponding derivatives segments have developed into reasonably deep and liquid markets, credit derivatives markets are yet to take off in any significant manner. As regards corporate bonds, while primary issuances have been significant, though concentrated in terms of issuers to public sector financial institutions, these have largely been on a private placement basis and the secondary market has not developed commensurately.

In an emerging market like India, where the cost of downside risk is very high, the objective of maintaining financial stability has always been kept in view while developing financial markets. Financial intermediaries like banks have also gained from better determination of interest rates in financial markets by pricing their own products better. Moreover, their own risk management has also improved through the availability of different varieties of financial instruments. The access of real sector entities to finance has also been assisted by the appropriate development of the financial market and the availability of transparent information on benchmark interest rates and prevailing exchange rates. Though several reform measures have recently been initiated to develop the financial markets in India, resulting in various segments of the financial market being better developed and integrated, the financial markets need to develop further in line with the evolving financial and economic scenario.

These developments have facilitated the growth of deeper and more efficient domestic markets, facilitating a more effective channel for transmission of monetary and financial policy impulses. India's experience once again demonstrates that the development of financial markets is an arduous and time-consuming task that requires conscious policy actions and effective implementation. Financial markets have to be created, nurtured and monitored on a continuous basis, as they attain maturation.

Endnotes

1. Reserve Bank of India, *Report of the Committee on Fuller Capital Account Convertibility* (Chairman: S.S. Tarapore), 2006.
2. Government of India, *High Powered Expert Committee Report on Making Mumbai an International Financial Centre*, April 2007.

7

Integration of Financial Markets

Integrated financial markets are a key element in the transmission process and hence for the smooth conduct of monetary policy. Financial integration also leads to a better diversification of risks and makes a positive contribution to financial stability by improving the capacity of economies to absorb shocks. On the other hand, fully integrated financial markets also pave the way for shocks to propagate more quickly among market participants, which could necessitate appropriate safeguards. To mitigate the risks and maximise benefits from financial integration, it is imperative that the financial markets are developed further. Enhanced co-operation among various regulatory authorities is also important for ensuring effective corrective action in an increasingly integrated environment. Further, it is necessary to establish further linkages amongst the various components of financial infrastructure—the trading, payment, clearing, settlement and custodian systems.

Financial markets in India have come a long way and are getting increasingly integrated domestically and globally. Reform measures in terms of free pricing, removal of barriers to flows and broad-based participation have yielded results in terms of fairly high degree of integration of the money market, the government securities market and the foreign exchange market, although in varying degrees. The money market and the foreign exchange market are reasonably well integrated, which is reflected in the high correlation coefficients between various money market rates and forward premia. The inter-linkage between the domestic money and international markets has also increased as is reflected in the increasing importance of interest rate differentials in the determination of forward premia. In general, the interest rate differential between the domestic money and international markets motivates market participants to shift funds between the markets. Thus, interest arbitrage links the domestic and international money markets and the forward markets.

7.1 Integration of Financial Markets: Conceptual Framework

7.1.1 Meaning: Integration of financial markets is a process of unifying markets and enabling convergence of risk-adjusted returns on the assets of similar maturity across the markets. The process of integration is facilitated by an unimpeded access of participants to various market segments. Financial markets all over the world have witnessed growing integration within as well as across boundaries, spurred by deregulation, globalisation and advances in information technology. Central banks in various parts of the world have made concerted efforts to develop financial markets, especially after the experience of several financial crises in the 1990s.

Expectedly, financial markets tend to be better integrated in developed countries. At the same time, deregulation in developing countries has led to removal of restrictions on pricing of various financial assets, which is one of the pre-requisites for market integration.

Financial market integration encompasses a complex interplay of various factors such as policy initiatives, structure and growth of financial intermediaries, organic linkages among market participants and the preference of savers and investors for financial instruments. The study of integration of financial markets must keep in view the heterogeneity of markets, dimensions of integration, measurement issues and perceived benefits and risks of integration.

Financial market integration at the theoretical level has been postulated in several ways. The most popular economic principles of financial integration include the law of one price, term structure of interest rates, parity conditions such as purchasing power parity, covered and uncovered interest parity conditions, capital asset price model and arbitrage price theory.

7.1.2 Heterogeneous Nature of Financial Markets: Various financial market segments are not uniform as they trade in a variety of instruments which differ in terms of risk and liquidity. Financial markets are heterogeneous due to following reasons:

1. Some market segments are national, whereas others are international in nature, depending on where financial transactions occur among participants within a country's geographic boundary or across the border. Generally, money and credit market segments involving participation of banks and other financial institutions operating within a country's boundary are national in character. Conversely, foreign exchange markets dealing with cross-border transactions and stock markets with cross-listings of securities and participation of foreign institutional investors are international in nature.
2. Financial markets differ in terms of depth and liquidity. For instance, money market instruments are more liquid, while bonds in the capital markets are less liquid.
3. Financial markets differ in terms of economic nature of instruments catering to various needs of economic agents. For instance, a distinction can be made between saving, investment, credit and derivative instruments.
4. Financial markets are differentiated in terms of risk profile of instruments such as government bonds, which do not involve default and credit risks, and corporate bonds, which are relatively more risky in nature. Integration of market segments, thus, reflects an investor's attitude towards risk and the trade-off between risk and return on assets.
5. Market participants in different financial markets could be different such as banks, non-bank financial institutions, including mutual funds, insurance companies, mortgage institutions and specialised long-term financial institutions.

7.1.3 Dimensions of Financial Market Integration: Broadly, financial market integration occurs in three dimensions, nationally, regionally and globally. From an alternative perspective, financial market integration could take place horizontally and vertically. In the horizontal integration, inter-linkages occur among domestic financial market segments, while vertical integration occurs between domestic markets and regional/international financial markets.

A. Domestic Financial Integration: It entails horizontal linkages of various segments, reflecting portfolio diversification by savers, investors and intermediaries. Under horizontal integration, market interest rates typically revolve around a basic reference rate, which is defined as the price of a short-term low-risk financial instrument in a competitive and liquid market. Domestic markets may be closely integrated because intermediaries operate simultaneously in various market segments; for instance, commercial banks operate in both the saving (deposit) and loan markets.

B. Regional Financial Integration: It occurs due to ties between a given region and the major financial centre serving that region. Economic integration might be easier to achieve at a regional level due to network externalities and the tendency of market makers to concentrate in certain geographical centres. Furthermore, regional financial integration can be an important means of developing local financial markets, for instance, through peer pressure to strengthen institutions and upgrade local practices.

C. Global Financial Integration: It refers to the opening up of domestic markets and institutions to the free cross-border flow of capital and financial services by removing barriers such as capital controls and withholding taxes. A deeper dimension of global integration entails removing obstacles to movement of people, technology and market participants across border. Global integration is promoted through harmonisation of national standards and laws, either through the adoption of commonly agreed minimum standards or the mutual recognition of standards.

7.1.4 Measures of Financial Integration: Indicators of financial integration can be classified into *de jure* and *de facto* measures.

The existence of legal restrictions on trade and capital flows across border as well as market segments is the most frequently used *de jure* indicators. However, these indicators have several shortcomings as restrictions may not be binding, or they are not respected. They may not cover a specific aspect of all possible impediments to financial integration.

De facto indicators of financial integration are usually based either on prices or quantities. The commonly used price-based measures for gauging price equalisation and convergence of market segments include cross-market spreads, correlation among various interest rates, tests of common trend in the term structure of interest rates and volatility transmission. Interest rate spreads between the official short-term rate and a benchmark short-term market instrument on the one hand, and various other market interest rates on the other, are used for measuring price convergence and effectiveness of policy. Price-related measures also include covered and uncovered interest rate parity as well as asset price correlations between countries. There are, however, serious practical problems in using prices to measure regional or global financial integration, particularly in developing countries. This is because prices may move together because of a common external factor or because of similar macroeconomic fundamentals and not because of market integration. Moreover, prices may be affected by differences in currency, credit and liquidity risks, implying different price movements even if there is a substantial degree of financial integration.

7.1.5 Benefits and Risks of Financial Integration: Though financial integration provides several benefits, it also involves various risks. The benefits and costs of financial market integration depend on the degree of domestic financial market integration, international financial integration and financial development. Evaluating the benefits and risks of financial market integration is a complex issue, particularly in an economy with open capital account.

A. Benefits: The benefits of global integration depend on size, composition, and quality of capital flows. Global financial integration involves direct and indirect or collateral benefits. Analytical arguments supporting financial openness revolve around main considerations such as the benefits of international risk sharing for consumption smoothing, the positive impact of capital flows on domestic investment and growth, enhanced macroeconomic discipline and increased efficiency as well as greater stability of the domestic financial system associated with financial openness. International financial integration could positively affect total factor productivity. Financial openness may increase the depth and breadth of domestic financial markets and lead to an increase in the degree of efficiency of the financial intermediation process by lowering costs and excessive profits associated with monopolistic and cartelised markets, thereby lowering the cost of investment and improving the resource allocation.

B. Risks: Financial market integration also poses some risks and entails costs. A major risk is that of contagion, which was evident in the case of East Asian crisis and the recent global financial turmoil. Increased domestic and international integration accentuates the risk of contagion as problems in one market segment are likely to be transmitted to other markets with the potential to cause systemic instability.

In the context of globalisation, potential costs include: (a) high degree of concentration of capital flows, (b) misallocation of flows which may hamper their growth effects and exacerbate domestic distortions; (c) loss of macroeconomic stability, (d) pro-cyclical nature of short-term capital flows and the risk of abrupt reversals, (e) a high degree of volatility of capital flows which relates in part to herding and contagion effects, and (f) risks associated with foreign bank penetration.

Direct investment tends to be less volatile than other forms of capital flows. Volatility of capital flows translates into exchange rate instability (under flexible exchange rate) or large fluctuations in official reserves (under a pegged exchange rate regime). Nominal exchange rate volatility may hamper expansion of exports if appropriate hedging techniques are not available to exporters. Large capital inflows can also lead to rapid monetary expansion, inflationary pressures, real exchange rate appreciation and widening of current account deficits.

The nature of optimal integration is highly country-specific and contextual. Financial integration needs to be approached cautiously, preferably within the framework of a plausible roadmap that is drawn up embodying the country-specific context and institutional features. On balance, there appears to be a greater advantage in well-managed and appropriate integration into the global process, which implies not large-scale but more effective interventions by the authorities.

7.2 Need for Integration of Domestic Financial Markets

Integration of financial markets assumes importance due to the following reasons:

1. Efficient and integrated financial markets constitute an important vehicle for promoting domestic savings, investment and consequently economic growth.
2. Financial market integration, by enhancing competition and efficiency of intermediaries in their operations and allocation of resources, contributes to financial stability.
3. Integrated markets serve as a conduit for authorities to transmit important price signals.
4. Integrated financial markets induce market discipline and informational efficiency.
5. Market integration promotes the adoption of modern technology and payment systems to achieve cost effective financial intermediation services.
6. Integrated markets lead to innovations and cost effective intermediation, thereby improving access to financial services for members of the public, institutions and companies alike.
7. Financial market integration fosters the necessary condition for financial sector of a country to emerge as an international or a regional financial centre.

An important objective of reforms in India has been to integrate the various segments of the financial market for bringing about a transformation in the structure of markets, reducing arbitrage opportunities, achieving higher level of efficiency in market operation of intermediaries and increasing efficacy of monetary policy in the economy. Efficient allocation of funds across the financial sector and uniformity in the pricing of various financial products through greater inter-linkages of financial markets has been the basic emphasis of monetary policy.

In the domestic sphere, integration of markets has been pursued through the following measures:

1. Strengthening competition.
2. Financial deepening with innovative instruments.
3. Easing of restrictions on flows or transactions.
4. Lowering of transaction costs.
5. Enhancing liquidity.

Financial markets in India have also increasingly integrated with the global financial system as a result of calibrated and gradual capital account liberalisation in keeping with the underlying macroeconomic developments, the state of readiness of the domestic financial system and the dynamics of international financial markets.

Until the early 1990s, India's financial sector was tightly controlled. Interest rates in all market segments were administered. The flow of funds between various market segments was restricted by extensive micro-regulations. There were also restrictions on participants operating in different market segments. Banks remained captive subscribers to government securities under statutory arrangements. The secondary market of government securities was dormant. In the equity market, new equity issues were governed by several complex regulations and restrictions. The secondary market trading of such equities lacked transparency and depth. The foreign exchange market remained extremely shallow as most transactions were governed by inflexible and low limits under exchange regulation and prior approval requirements. The exchange rate was linked to a basket of currencies. Although the financial sector grew considerably in the regulated environment, it could not achieve the desired level of efficiency. Compartmentalisation of activities of different types of financial intermediaries eliminated the scope for competition among existing financial intermediaries.

Financial markets reform initiated in the early 1990s focused on removal of structural bottlenecks, introduction of new players/instruments, free pricing of financial assets, relaxation of quantitative restrictions, improvement in trading, clearing and settlement practices and greater transparency. Other policy initiatives in the money, the foreign exchange, the government securities and the equity markets were aimed at strengthening institutions, greater transparency, encouraging good market practices, effective payment and settlement mechanism, rationalised tax structures and enabling legislative framework. Dismantling of various price and non-price controls in the financial system has facilitated the integration of financial markets.

Broadly, India's domestic financial market comprises the money market, the credit market, the government securities market, the equity market, the corporate debt market and the foreign exchange market. The channels of integration among various market segments differ. For instance, the Indian money and the foreign exchange markets are intrinsically linked in view of the presence of commercial banks and the short-term nature of both markets. The linkage is established through various channels such as banks borrowing in overseas markets, providing hedging facilities to corporates, accepting foreign currency deposits and acting as conduit for making payments for overseas merchant transactions. The linkage between the call money and the government securities markets exists, as at times, large positions in government securities are funded through short-term borrowings. The foreign exchange market and the equity markets are linked through the operations of foreign institutional investors. The emerging linkages among the money, the government securities and the foreign exchange markets have at times necessitated the use of short-term monetary measures by the RBI for meeting demand-supply mismatches to curb volatility.

7.3 Measures Taken for Integration of Financial Markets in India

Broadly, integration of financial markets in India has been facilitated by various measures in the form of free pricing, widening of participation base in markets, introduction of new instruments and improvements in payment and settlement infrastructure.

7.3.1 Free Pricing: Free pricing in financial markets has been facilitated by various measures. These have included, *inter alia,* the following:

1. Freedom to banks to decide interest rate on deposits and credit.
2. Replacement of administered interest rates on government securities by an auction system.
3. Abolition of the system of *ad hoc* Treasury Bills in April 1997 and its replacement by the system of ways and means advances (WMAs) with effect from April 1, 1997.
4. Shift in the exchange rate regime from a single-currency fixed-exchange rate system

to a market-determined floating exchange rate regime.

5. Gradual liberalisation of the capital account.
6. Freedom to banks to determine interest rates (subject to a ceiling) and maturity period of foreign currency non-resident (FCNR) deposits (not exceeding three years).
7. Use derivative products for hedging risk.
8. In 1992, the Capital Issues (Control) Act, 1947 was repealed and with this ended all controls related to raising of resources from the market. Since then the issuers of securities can raise capital from the market without requiring any consent from any authority, either for making the issue or for pricing it.

7.3.2 Widening Participation: This has been achieved with the adoption of following measures:

1. Enhanced presence of foreign banks in line with India's commitment to the World Trade Organization (WTO) under GATS, strengthened domestic and international markets inter-linkages, apart from increasing competition.
2. Participation in the call market was gradually widened by including non-banks such as financial institutions, non-banking financial companies, primary/satellite dealers, mutual funds and corporates (through primary dealers). The process of transformation of the call money market into a pure inter-bank market which commenced from May 2001, was completed in August 2005.
3. Foreign institutional investors (FIIs) have been allowed to participate in the Indian equity market and set up 100 percent debt funds to invest in government (Central and State) dated securities in both the primary and secondary markets. This provided a major thrust to the integration of domestic markets with international markets.
4. Linkage between the domestic foreign exchange market and the overseas market (vertical integration) has been facilitated by allowing banks/authorised dealers (ADs) to borrow and invest funds abroad (subject to certain limits), and to lend in foreign currency to companies in India for any productive purpose, giving them the choice to economise on interest cost and exchange risk. Exporters also have the ability to substitute rupee credit for foreign currency credit.
5. Indian companies have been permitted to raise resources from abroad through American/global depository receipts (ADRs/GDRs), foreign currency convertible bonds (FCCBs) and external commercial borrowings (ECBs), thus, facilitating integration of domestic capital market with international capital market. The RBI allowed two-way fungibility of ADRs/GDRs in February 2002.
6. Corporates have been allowed to undertake active hedging operations by resorting to cancellation and rebooking of forward contracts, booking forward contracts based on past performance, using foreign currency options and forwards, and accessing foreign currency-rupee swap to manage longer-term exposures arising out of external commercial borrowings.
7. Integration of the credit market and the equity market has been strengthened by application of capital adequacy norms and allowing public sector banks to raise capital from the equity market up to 49 percent of their paid-up capital.

7.3.3 New Instruments: These have included the following:

1. Repurchase agreement (repo) has introduced as a tool of short-term liquidity adjustment. The liquidity adjustment facility (LAF) is open to banks and primary dealers. The LAF has emerged as a tool for both liquidity management and also signalling device for interest rates in the overnight market. Several new financial instruments such as inter-bank participation certificates (1988), certificates of deposit (June 1989), commercial paper (January 1990) and repos (December 1992) have been introduced. Collateralised borrowing and lending obligation (CBLO) and market repos have also emerged as money market instruments.
2. New auction-based instruments were introduced for 364-day, 182-day, 91-day and 14-day Treasury Bills, the zero coupon bond and government of India dated securities. In the long-term segment, floating rate bonds (FRBs) benchmarked to the 364-day Treasury Bills yields and a 10-year loan with embedded call and put options exercisable on or after 5 years from the date of issue have been introduced.
3. Derivative products—such as forward rate agreements and interest rate swaps—were introduced in July 1999 to enable banks, FIs and PDs to hedge interest rate risks. A rupee-foreign currency swap market has been developed. ADs in the foreign exchange market have been permitted to use cross-currency options, interest rate and currency swaps, caps/collars and forward rate agreements (FRAs) in the international foreign exchange market, thereby facilitating the deepening of the market and enabling participants to diversify their risk.

7.3.4 Institutional Measures: These have included the following:

1. Institutions such as Discount and Finance House of India (DFHI), Securities Trading Corporation of India (STCI) and PDs have been allowed to participate in more than one market, thus strengthening the market inter-linkages.
2. The Clearing Corporation of India Ltd. (CCIL) was set up to act as a central counter-party to all trades involving foreign exchange, government securities and other debt instruments routed through it and to guarantee their settlement.

7.3.5 Technology, Payment and Settlement Infrastructure: Measures taken in this regard have included the following:

1. The delivery-versus-payment (DvP) system, the negotiated dealing system (NDS) and subsequently, the advanced negotiated dealing system-order matching (NDS-OM) trading module and the real time gross settlement system (RTGS) have brought about immense benefits in facilitating transactions and improving the settlement process, which have helped in the integration of markets.
2. In the equity market, the floor-based open outcry trading system has been replaced by electronic trading system in all the stock exchanges.

Various segments of financial markets have become better integrated in the reform period, especially from the mid-1990s. As reforms in the financial markets progressed, linkages amongst various segments of market and between domestic and international markets improved.

7.4 Segment-wise Integration

7.4.1 Integration of the Government Securities Market: The existence of a well-developed government securities market is a pre-requisite for a market-based monetary policy and for facilitating financial market integration. The government securities market is also required to develop a domestic rupee yield curve, which could provide a credible benchmark for pricing of securities in other markets. The government securities market is increasingly getting integrated with other market segments as is reflected in the close co-movement of interest rates.

7.4.2 Integration of the Credit Market: The integration of the credit market with other money market segments has become more pronounced in recent years. Sustained credit demand has led to higher demand for funds, exerting some pressure on liquidity. This has been reflected in the decline in investment of banks in government securities and higher activity in all the money market segments such as inter-bank call money, collateralised borrowing and lending obligation (CBLO) and market repo rates.

7.4.3 Integration of the Foreign Exchange Market: The degree of integration of the foreign exchange market with other markets is largely determined by the degree of openness. At the cornerstone of the international finance, integration through foreign exchange market is characterised with the purchasing power parity (PPP) doctrine. According to the PPP, in the absence of restrictions on cross border movements of goods and services and assuming no transactions costs, commodity prices expressed in any single currency should be the same all over the world. In other words, the path of the nominal exchange rate should be guided by the developments in the domestic prices of goods and services vis-à-vis prices of the major trading partners.

7.4.4 Stock Market Integration: The equity market has relatively low and negative correlation with other market segments. The low correlation of the equity market with risk free instruments is indicative of greater volatility of stock returns and the existence of large equity risk premium. The large risk premium occurs when equity price movements cannot be rationalised with standard inter-temporal optimisation models of macroeconomic fundamentals such as consumption and savings. This can be on account of different participants in the equity and other financial markets. For instance, the common participation by banks in the money, the government, the foreign exchange and the credit markets ensures fairly high correlation among these segments. The exposure of banks to the capital market remains limited on account of restrictions due to prudential regulation.

7.5 Regional Financial Integration (Asia)

After the South East Asian crisis of 1997, the geographic scope of cooperation initiatives is expanding across sub-regions of Asia. Asian economies have embarked on various initiatives for regional monetary and financial cooperation.

7.5.1 SEANZA and SEACEN [1]: SEANZA and SEACEN are the oldest initiatives in central bank cooperation in Asia. The SEANZA, formed in 1956, promotes cooperation among central banks by conducting intensive training courses for higher central banking executive positions with the objective to build up knowledge of central banking and foster technical cooperation among central banks in the SEANZA region. The SEACEN provides a forum for member central bank governors to be familiar with each other and to gain deeper understanding of the economic conditions of the individual SEACEN countries. It initiates and facilitates co-operation in research and training relating to the policy and operational aspects of central banking, i.e., monetary policy, banking supervision and payments and settlement systems.

7.5.2 Asian Clearing Union (ACU): ACU—an arrangement of central banking cooperation—is successfully functioning since 1974 for multilateral settlement of payments for promoting trade and monetary cooperation among the member countries. [2] Since 1989, the ACU has also included a currency swap arrangement among its operational objectives.

7.5.3 EMEAP: A more explicit central banking cooperation has been existing in the form of EMEAP since 1991. [3] The ongoing work of EMEAP seeks to further strengthen policy analysis and advice within the region and encourage co-operation with respect to operational and institutional central banking issues. EMEAP central banks have actively coordinated on issues relating to financial markets, banking supervision and payment and settlement systems. The Asian Bond Fund (ABF) initiative of the EMEAP Group has been one of the major initiatives aimed at broadening and deepening the domestic and regional bond markets in Asia. The initiative has been in the form of ABF1 and ABF2. In the near term, the ABF2 Initiative is expected to help raise investor awareness and interest in Asian bonds by providing innovative, low-cost and efficient products in the form of passively managed bond funds. More and more similar kinds of index-driven private bond funds are rapidly emerging in Asia. At present, India does not contribute in the ABF. The informal meeting organised by Asia Cooperation Dialogue (ACD) is, however, attended by participant central banks including India, to discuss promotion of supply of Asian Bonds. The Government of India has given a commitment on participation in the ABF2 to the tune of US$ 1 billion.

7.5.4 SAARCFINANCE: SAARCFINANCE, established in September 1998 is a regional network of the SAARC Central Bank Governors and Finance Secretaries which aims at strengthening the SAARC with specific emphasis on international finance and monetary issues. [4] India has been very actively participating in SAARCFINANCE activities.

7.5.5 ASEAN+3: The countries of ASEAN—Brunei Darussalam, Cambodia, Indonesia, Lao PDR, Malaysia, Myanmar, the Philippines, Singapore, Thailand and Vietnam—and India have entered into a Framework Agreement on comprehensive economic cooperation. The ASEAN has embarked on a process to expand economic cooperation with its neighbours in the north, namely China, Japan and South Korea (ASEAN+3). As far as India's association with ASEAN community is concerned, currently India is not a full-fledged part of the ASEAN network but holds a regular summit with the ASEAN. However, in the years ahead, it is envisaged that ASEAN+3+3 network [5] would help India to share and cooperate on various financial issues as the present network of ASEAN+3 has been consistently engaging in economic policy dialogue of unprecedented scope and depth.

7.5.6 Chiang Mai Initiative: Another instance of central banking cooperation in Asia exists in the form of reciprocal currency or swap arrangements under the Chiang Mai Initiative. [6] The ASEAN Swap Arrangement (ASA) was created primarily to provide liquidity support to countries experiencing balance of payments difficulties. The Finance Ministers of ASEAN+3 announced this initiative in May 2000 with the intention to cooperate in four major areas, *viz.* monitoring capital flows, regional surveillance, swap networks and training personnel.

The clearest evidence of Asian countries' desire to forge closer economic relationships is the proliferation of free trade agreements (FTAs). By 2006, there were more than 30 FTAs under negotiation in East Asia alone. Increasingly, these agreements are also deeper, extending to areas beyond just tariff reduction. An example is the recently signed India-Singapore comprehensive economic cooperation agreement, which covers not only trade in goods, but also services, investments and cooperation in technology, education, air services and human resources.

Regional integration in Asia has improved significantly due to liberalisation measures, formation of several regional cooperation agreements and stronger economic activity in the region. The sharp increase in intra-regional trade indicates that regional economies are better integrated. Regional financial integration is manifested in the price co-movements in the stock, the money and the bond markets. Stock markets in the Asian region are better correlated than the bond and the money markets.

7.6 International Financial Integration

In the wake of globalization, capital has become more mobile across national boundaries as nations are increasingly relying on savings of other nations to supplement the domestic savings. Technological developments in electronic payment and communication systems have substantially reduced the arbitrage opportunities across financial centres, thereby aiding the cross border mobility of funds. Changes in the operating framework of monetary policy, with a shift in emphasis from quantitative controls to price-based instruments such as the short-term policy interest rate, brought about changes in the term structure of interest rates. This has contributed to the integration of various financial market segments. Harmonisation of prudential regulations in line with international best practices, by enabling competitive pricing of products, has also strengthened the market integration process.

Development of financial markets is required for the purpose of not only realising the hidden saving potential and effective monetary policy, but also for expanding the role and participation of a country in the process of globalization, regional and international integration. With growing openness, global factors come to play a greater role in domestic policy formulation, leading to greater financial market integration.

A key feature of global financial integration since early 1980s is the shift in the composition of capital flows to developing and emerging market economies. Private sector flows have outpaced official flows due to increasing liberalisation. Moreover, a shift has occurred in terms of components, from the dominance of debt flows in the 1970s and the 1980s to foreign direct investment (FDI) and portfolio flows since the 1990s. FDI flows have been determined by several push and pull factors, including strong global growth, soft interest rates in home countries, lessening of risks in developing countries, greater business and consumer confidence, rising corporate profitability, large scale corporate restructuring, sharp recovery of asset prices and rising commodity prices. Trade and FDI openness has encouraged domestic institutional and governance reforms promoting trade and investment further. The hope of better risk sharing, more efficient allocation of capital, more productive investment and ultimately higher standards of living for all have also propelled the drive for stronger regional connections of financial systems across the world. In terms of overall financial flows, Asia has benefited from the surge in net capital flows to emerging markets in recent years.

Greater international financial market integration exposes domestic markets to certain risks and contagion. For instance, global financial imbalances, growing sophistication of financial market participants and the proliferation of complex and highly leveraged financial instruments, including credit derivatives and structured products such as collateralised debt obligations, can heighten volatility in the financial markets. Thus, with growing international integration, there would be a need to be vigilant about the risk profile of financial intermediaries and their vulnerability to abrupt market price shocks. This underlines the need for appropriate risk management strategies as also greater coordination and information sharing among central banks to prevent the transmission of adverse developments abroad to the domestic economy and markets.

With growing financial globalisation, it is important for India to develop financial markets to manage the risks associated with large capital flows. The Report of the Committee on Fuller Capital Account Convertibility, 2006 (Chairman: S.S. Tarapore) observed that in order to make a move towards the fuller capital account convertibility, it needs to be ensured that different market segments are not only well-developed but also that they are well-integrated.

As a result of policy measures undertaken since the early 1990s, India's trade and financial integration has grown with the global economy. The increasing openness of the Indian economy to the external sector in recent years characterises its expanding economic relationships with the rest of Asia. In recent years, the Asian economies are emerging as major trading partners of India.

In tandem with trade openness, India's capital account has witnessed a structural transformation since the early 1990s, with a shift in the composition from official flows to market-oriented private sector flows. From 1950 to 1980, trade balance was financed by capital account balance comprising mainly the official flows. During the 1980s, the dependence on official flows moderated sharply with private debt flows in the form of external commercial borrowing and non-resident Indian (NRI) deposits emerging as the key components of the capital account.

Following the shift in emphasis from debt to non-debt flows in the reform period, foreign investment comprising direct investment and portfolio flows emerged as predominant component of capital account.

To sum up, since early 1990s, there has been a rapid increase in the pace of globalisation, led by growing participation of developing and emerging economies. Financial integration has outpaced trade integration. Cross-border flows of real and financial capital have increased sharply, reflecting the decline in the degree of home bias in capital markets.

The domestic credit market is also getting increasingly integrated with the international capital market as large and creditworthy borrowers have been raising large resources by way of external commercial borrowings. Such corporates are, therefore, less constrained by domestic credit conditions. Raising of resources by banks, the major players in the credit market, by way of external commercial borrowings, *albeit* within limits, has also integrated the domestic and international credit markets. The money market and the government securities market are also integrated as changes in money market rates are quickly transmitted to government securities yields. The linkage between the money market and the credit market also exists even as some stickiness has been observed in the lending interest rate structure. The inter-linkages between the credit market and the bond market are also growing through asset securitisation by banks.

However, the inter-linkages between the equity market on the one hand, and the money, the foreign exchange and the government securities markets on the other, are still weak. The term money market and the private corporate debt market are missing links in the Indian financial markets. There is not much activity in the public issue segment of the corporate debt market, despite availability of good infrastructure, a vibrant equity market and a reasonably developed government securities market. In the corporate debt market, the issuers prefer the private placement segment, which lacks transparency and deprives the retail investor from participating in the debt market.

Regional integration has served as a major catalyst to the global integration process since early 1990s. East and Southeast Asian economies, in particular, have achieved substantial integration. Apart from Asia's growing integration with the rest of the world, increasing integration within Asia also reflects the growing intra-regional trade and financial flows. The stock markets in Asia are more integrated than the money and the bond markets. In the region, Japan, Hong Kong and Singapore serve as the nodal centres for other stock markets. India's trade and financial links with Asia are also growing amidst recent initiatives taken to promote regional cooperation. Emerging Asia has become the *growth centre* of the world due to shifting of production base to the region. This is likely to stimulate greater financial integration in the region.

At the regional level, India's trade links with Asia are growing at a rapid pace, spurred by trade links with China and Southeast Asian countries. Also, India's financial integration with the Asian region has occurred through the linkage of regional stock markets and through modest correlation of bond and money markets.

A key feature of global financial integration since early 1980s has reflected in the shift in the composition of capital flows to developing and emerging market economies, especially from official to private flows. India's financial integration within the region and with the international financial markets is likely to increase in future in view of its robust growth prospects. However, if benefits are to be maximised from a more integrated economy, efforts are needed towards a greater sophistication of financial markets and financial market instruments that allow risks to be shared more broadly and capital to flow into the most productive sectors.

India's integration with the world economy has increased significantly in terms of trade openness and financial integration. Tariff liberalisation and removal of non-tariff barriers have contributed to India's trade integration at global and regional levels. India's capital account has witnessed a structural transformation during the reform period with cross-border non-debt creating private capital flows, emerging as a major component. India is now a major destination for global portfolio equity flows suggesting growing confidence of foreign investors in the Indian economy and financial markets.

Integration among various market segments has grown, especially in the recent period. Growing integration among various financial market segments has been accompanied by lower volatility of interest rates. Financial market integration reflects a dynamic interaction among various parameters such as liquidity, safety and risk, foreign exchange market development, private sector activity, and macroeconomic fundamentals. Alternatively, financial integration exhibits interaction among financial intermediaries, the Government, the private sector and the external sector.

Endnotes

1. The SEANZA refers to South East Asia, New Zealand and Australia. The SEACEN refers to South East Asia Central Banks.
2. At present, its membership includes eight members including India, Islamic Republic of Iran, Nepal, Pakistan and Sri Lanka being the founder members (Myanmar, Bangladesh and Bhutan joined later).
3. Members are the central banks of Australia, China, Hong Kong, Indonesia, Japan, Korea, Malaysia, New Zealand, the Philippines, Singapore and Thailand.
4. SAARCFINANCE members are India, Pakistan, Sri Lanka, Bangladesh, Bhutan, Maldives and Nepal. It is a permanent body, which got formal recognition of SAARC at the 11th SAARC Summit, held in Kathmandu, Nepal in January 2002.
5. India, Australia and New Zealand are included in ASEAN+3+3.
6. Under this Initiative, the total resources available are currently estimated to be around US$ 75 billion (up from less than US$ 40 billion in May 2005), reflecting the renegotiation of most Bilateral Swap Agreements (BSAs).

8

Asymmetric Information, Adverse Selection and Moral Hazard

8.1 Asymmetric Information

Asymmetric information (also known as information failure) occurs when one party to an economic transaction possesses greater material knowledge than the other party. Almost all economic transactions involve information asymmetries.

The insurance market is a typical example of how asymmetric information affects the economy and causes market failure. The property market is another example in which the seller has more information than the potential buyer.

Asymmetric information means that one party (property developer) has more information than the other (property buyer) when making decisions and transactions. The imperfect information causes an imbalance of power. Accurate information is essential for sound economic decisions. When a market experiences an imbalance it can lead to market failure.

Asymmetric information gives either the buyer or seller a better opportunity to make a profit from the purchase or sale.

The concept of asymmetric information centres around a situation in which there is unequal knowledge between each party to a transaction, that one party has better information than the other the party. This type of asymmetry creates an imbalance in a transaction.

Asymmetric information can lead to either adverse selection or moral hazard. Hence, the following two basic models describe information asymmetry:

1. Adverse selection.
2. Moral hazard.

Adverse selection occurs when there is a lack of symmetric information prior to a deal between a buyer and a seller. Moral hazard occurs when there is asymmetric information between two parties and a change in the behaviour of one party after a deal is struck.

8.2 Adverse Selection

Adverse selection occurs when there is a lack of symmetric information prior to a deal between a buyer and a seller. Asymmetric information, also called information failure, happens when one party to a transaction has greater material knowledge than the other party.

In the case of insurance, adverse selection is the tendency of those in dangerous jobs or high-risk lifestyles to purchase products like life insurance. In these cases, it is the buyer who actually has more knowledge (e.g. about his health).

Adverse selection for insurers occurs when an applicant manages to obtain coverage at lower premiums than the insurance company would charge if it were aware of the actual risk regarding the applicant, usually as a result of the applicant withholding relevant information or providing false information.

Adverse selection is a term commonly used in economics, insurance, and risk management that describes a situation where market participation is affected by asymmetric information. When buyers and sellers have different information, it is known as a state of asymmetric information. Traders with better private information about the quality of a product will selectively participate in trades which benefit them the most, at the expense of the other trader. Insiders have more information about stocks/shares than laymen.

The party without the information is worried about an unfair (or rigged) trade, which occurs when the party who has all the information uses it to their advantage. The fear of rigged trade can prompt the worried party to withdraw from the interaction, diminishing the volume of trade in the market. This can cause a knock-on effect and the unravelling of the market. An additional implication of this potential for market collapse is that it can work as an entry deterrence that leads to high margins without additional entry.

Buyers sometimes have better information about how much benefit they can extract from a service. For example, an all-you-can-eat buffet restaurant that sets one price for all customers risks being adversely selected against by high appetite and hence, the least profitable customers. The restaurant has no way of knowing whether a given customer has a high or low appetite. The customer is the only one who knows if they have a high or low appetite. In this case the high appetite customers are more likely to use the information they have and to go to the restaurant.

In this case, the seller suffering from adverse selection can protect himself by screening customers or by identifying credible signals of appetite. Some examples of this phenomenon occur in signalling games and screening games.

An example where the buyer is adversely selected against is in financial markets. A company is more likely to offer stock when managers privately know that the current stock price exceeds the fundamental value of the firm. Uninformed investors rationally demand a premium to participate in the equity offer. While this example functions as a good hypothetical example of the buyer being adversely selected against, in reality the market can know that the managers are selling stocks (perhaps in required company reports). The market price of stocks will then reflect the information that managers are selling stocks.

Economists argue that the inefficiency results from information asymmetry. If insurance companies could perfectly observe the actions of their clients, they could deny coverage to clients choosing risky actions (like smoking in bed or not wearing helmets), allowing them to provide thorough protection against risk (fire or accidents) without encouraging risky behaviour. However, since insurance companies cannot perfectly observe their clients' actions, they are discouraged from providing the amount of protection that would be provided in a world with perfect information.

8.2.1 Adverse Selection in Capital Market: When raising capital, some types of securities are more prone to adverse selection than others. An equity offering for a company that reliably generates earnings at a good price will be bought up before an unknown company's offering, leaving the market filled with less desirable offerings that were unwanted by other investors. Assuming that managers have inside information about the firm, outsiders are most prone to adverse selection in equity offers. This is because managers may offer stock when they know the offer price exceeds their private assessments of the company's value. It also arises in banking and finance. If a financial institution knows it is protected by a lender of last resort, it may make riskier investments than it would in the absence of the protection.

8.3 Moral Hazard

In economics, moral hazard occurs when someone increases his exposure to risk when insured, especially when a person takes more risks because someone else bears the cost of those risks. A moral hazard may occur where the actions of one party may change to the detriment of another after a financial transaction has taken place. A party makes a decision about how much risk to take, while another party bears the costs if things go badly, and the party isolated from risk behaves differently from how it would if it were fully exposed to the risk.

Among the early contributors to the contract-theoretic literature on moral hazard were Oliver Hart and Sanford J. Grossman.

Moral hazard occurs when a party will take a risk because the cost of the risk is not felt by that party. Moral hazard is a situation in which one party to an agreement engages in risky behaviour or fails to act in good faith because it knows the other party bears the consequences of that behaviour. Government bailout is a common example of moral hazard in the business world.

Moral hazard also arises in a principal-agent problem, where one party, called an agent, acts on behalf of another party, called the principal. The agent usually has more information about his or her actions or intentions than the principal does, because the principal usually cannot completely monitor the agent. The agent may have an incentive to act inappropriately (from the viewpoint of the principal) if the interests of the agent and the principal are not aligned.

8.3.1 Moral Hazards in Financial Transactions: With respect to the worldwide financial crisis (sub-prime loans) of 2008, many may have suspected that the borrowers would not be able to maintain their payments in the long run and that, for this reason, the loans were not going to be worth much. Still, because there were many buyers of these loans (or of pools of these loans) willing to take on that risk, the originators did not concern themselves with the potential long-term consequences of making the loans. After selling the loans, the originators bore none of the risk so there was little to no incentive for the originators to investigate the long-term value of the loans.

Moral hazard can also occur with borrowers. Borrowers may not act prudently (in the view of the lender) when they invest or spend funds recklessly. For example, credit card companies often limit the amount borrowers can spend with their cards because without such limits, borrowers may spend borrowed funds recklessly, leading to default.

8.3.2 Moral Hazard in Insurance Industry: The concept of moral hazard comes originally from the insurance industry. Insurance companies worried that protecting their clients from risks (like fire, or car accidents) might encourage those clients to behave in riskier ways like smoking in bed or driving recklessly. This problem may inefficiently discourage those companies from protecting their clients as much as the clients would like to be protected. A person with insurance against automobile theft may be less cautious about locking his car because the negative consequences of vehicle theft are now the responsibility of the insurance company. A party makes a decision about how much risk to take, while another party bears the costs if things go badly, and the party insulated from risk behaves differently from how it would if it were fully exposed to the risk.

In insurance markets, moral hazard occurs when the behaviour of the insured party changes in a way that raises costs for the insurer since the insured party no longer bears the full costs of that behaviour. Because individuals no longer bear the cost of medical services, they have an added incentive to ask for pricier and more elaborate medical service, which would otherwise not be necessary. In those instances, individuals have an incentive to over consume, simply because they no longer bear the full cost of medical services. A further example has been identified in flood risk management in which it is proposed that the possession of insurance undermines efforts to encourage people to integrate flood protection and resilience measures in properties exposed to flooding.

Sometimes moral hazard is so severe that it makes insurance policies impossible. Coinsurance, co-payments, and deductibles reduce the risk of moral hazard by increasing the out-of-pocket spending of consumers, which decreases their incentive to consume. Thus, the insured have a financial incentive to avoid making a claim.

In short, moral hazard can occur under a type of information asymmetry where the risk-taking party to a transaction knows more about its intentions than the party paying the consequences of the risk. More broadly, moral hazard can occur when the party with more information about its actions or intentions has a tendency or incentive to behave inappropriately from the perspective of the party with less information.

9

Financial Crisis

A financial crisis is any of a broad variety of situations in which some financial assets suddenly lose a large part of their nominal value. In the 19th and early 20th centuries, many financial crises were associated with banking panics.

Other situations that are often called financial crises include stock market crashes and the bursting of other financial bubbles, currency crises, and sovereign defaults. Financial crises directly result in a loss of paper wealth but do not necessarily result in significant changes in the real economy.

Many economists have offered theories about how financial crises develop and how they could be prevented. There is no consensus, however, and financial crises continue to occur from time-to-time.

9.1 Types of Financial Crisis

9.1.1 Banking Crisis: When a bank suffers a sudden rush of withdrawals by depositors, this is called a *bank run*. Since banks lend out most of the cash they receive in deposits, it is difficult for them to quickly pay back all deposits if these are suddenly demanded. Thus, a run renders the bank insolvent, causing customers to lose their deposits, to the extent that they are not covered by deposit insurance. Banking crises generally occur after periods of risky lending and resulting loan defaults. This was the reason for worldwide financial crisis (also called sub-prime crisis) of 2008.

9.1.2 Currency Crisis: A currency crisis is normally considered as part of a financial crisis. In general, a currency crisis can be defined as a situation when the participants in an exchange market come to recognize that a significant fall in the external value of a currency (say Indian rupee) is imminent to happen. Hence, currency crisis is also called devaluation crisis.

9.1.3 Speculative Bubbles and Crashes: A speculative bubble exists in the event of large, sustained overpricing of some class of assets. One factor that frequently contributes to a bubble is the presence of buyers who purchase an asset based solely on the expectation that they can later resell it at a higher price, rather than calculating the income it will generate in the future. If there is a bubble, there is also a risk of a *crash* in asset prices. Market participants will go on buying only as long as they expect others to buy, and when many decide to sell the price will fall. However, it is difficult to predict whether an asset's price actually equals its fundamental value, so it is hard to detect bubbles reliably.

9.1.4 International Financial Crisis: When a country that maintains a fixed exchange rate is suddenly forced to devalue its currency due to accruing an unsustainable current account deficit, this is called a *currency crisis* or *balance of payments crisis*.

When a country fails to pay back its sovereign debt, this is called a *sovereign default*. While devaluation and default could both be voluntary decisions of the government, they are often perceived to be the involuntary results of a change in investor sentiment that leads to a sudden stop in capital inflows or a sudden increase in capital flight.

9.2 Asian Financial Crisis, 1997

It was a period of financial crisis that gripped much of East Asia and Southeast Asia beginning in July 1997 and raised fears of a worldwide economic meltdown due to financial contagion.

The crisis started in Thailand with the financial collapse of Baht (Thai currency) after the Thai government was forced to float the Baht due to lack of foreign currency to support its currency peg to the U.S. dollar. Capital flight ensued, beginning an international chain reaction. At the time, Thailand had acquired a burden of foreign debt that made the country effectively bankrupt even before the collapse of its currency. As the crisis spread, most of Southeast Asia and Japan saw slumping currencies, devalued stock markets and other asset prices, and a precipitous rise in private debt.

Indonesia, South Korea, and Thailand were the countries most affected by the crisis. Hong Kong, Laos, Malaysia and Philippines were also hurt by the slump. Brunei, China, Singapore, Taiwan, and Vietnam were less affected, although all suffered from a loss of demand and confidence throughout the region. Japan was also affected, though less significantly.

Although most of the governments of Asia had seemingly sound fiscal policies, the International Monetary Fund (IMF) stepped in to initiate a US$ 40 billion programme to stabilize the currencies of South Korea, Thailand, and Indonesia, the economies which were particularly hard hit by the crisis.

However, efforts to stem a global economic crisis did little to stabilize the domestic situation in Indonesia. After 30 years in power, Indonesian President Suharto was forced to step down on May 21, 1998 in the wake of widespread rioting that followed sharp price increases caused by a drastic devaluation of the rupiah.

By 1999, analysts saw signs that the economies of Asia were beginning to recover. After the crisis, economies in the region worked towards financial stability and better financial supervision.

9.3 Financial (Sub-prime) Crisis, 2007-08

The financial turmoil (nick-named global financial tsunami, global financial flu etc.) which surfaced in August 2007 in the US financial system as a result of defaults of sub-prime mortgage loans blew into an unprecedented financial crisis engulfing international money, credit, equity and foreign exchange markets. What started off as a sub-prime crisis in the US housing mortgage sector turned successively into a global banking crisis, global financial crisis and then in a global economic crisis (recession). It was billed by experts as the worst since the Great Depression of late 1920s and early 1930s that originated in the advanced economies and rapidly engulfed the whole world. [1]

The sub-prime crisis was preceded by an extended phase of buoyant world economy characterized by output expansion, burgeoning world trade, favourable financial and economic conditions, liquidity overhang and low interest rates. Economists termed it as a period of *great moderation*.

The *great moderation* soon turned into *great dismay* when global financial turmoil—simmering since August 2007—began unleashing its full fury in September 2008 with a series of failures of major financial institutions.

Excess liquidity in the system encouraged banks and financial institutions, particularly in the US, to lend to sub-prime borrowers. There was a gradual build-up of toxic debt which was aided by shoddy financial engineering in the form of slicing-dicing and re-bundling of mortgage-backed securities. When the global interest rates started hardening, a large chunk of borrowers began defaulting setting off a crisis in the money market that subsequently spread to other financial markets.

Though adversely affected by global meltdown, Indian economy showed considerable absorption capacity and resilience. Soon after the start of the crisis, net portfolio flows to India turned negative as foreign institutional investors (FIIs) rushed to sell equity stakes in a bid to replenish overseas cash balances. This had a knock-on effect on the stock market which nosedived to record levels. Supply and demand imbalance in the foreign exchange market led to depreciation of rupee vis-à-vis other currencies. The current account was affected mainly after September 2008 through slowdown in exports. Despite setbacks, however, the balance-of-payments situation of the country remained comfortable.

India remained relatively immune from the fallout of the crisis due to several reasons including prudential, supervisory and regulatory framework of the Reserve Bank of India (RBI). Moral suasions on the part of Government of India, RBI and Securities and Exchange Board of India (SEBI) also worked. More importantly, the Indian banking system showed remarkable market discipline, docility, and sincerity of purpose as against the financial gimmicks and dubious practices (repacking of loans, ninja loans etc.) of the financial institutions in the US.

The Indian approach focused on gradual, phased and calibrated opening of the domestic financial and external sectors, taking into cognizance reforms in the other sectors of the economy. Financial markets contributed to efficient channelling of domestic savings into productive uses and—by financing the overwhelming part of domestic investment—were supporting domestic growth. These characteristics of India's external and financial sector management coupled with ample forex reserves reduced the susceptibility of the Indian economy to global turbulence.

Most of the crises over the past few decades have had their roots in developing and emerging countries, often resulting from abrupt reversals in capital flows, and from loose domestic monetary and fiscal policies. In contrast, the sub-prime crisis has had its roots in the US.

Although emerging market economies, including India, do not have direct or significant exposure to stressed financial instruments or troubled financial institutions, yet they are not immune to the adverse effects of the financial crisis.

Endnote

1. In the early years of 1930s, USA and other capitalist countries of the world suffered a business depression of extraordinary severity. The demand for goods fell sharply and so also the prices. Many business firms failed and million of workers were rendered unemployed. These events revealed that something was seriously wrong with the working of a capitalist system. Out of the turmoil of depression came a book that had a profound effect on the thinking of economists. It was titled *The General Theory of Employment, Interest and Money* (1936) authored by British economist John Maynard Keynes (1883-1946). This work was immediately recognised as a revolutionary landmark in the history of economic ideas.

10

Money Market

10.1 Meaning and Functions of Money Market

Money market is the most important segment of the financial system as it provides the fulcrum for equilibrating short-term demand for and supply of funds, thereby facilitating the conduct of monetary policy. It is a market for short-term funds with a maturity of up to one year and includes financial instruments that are close substitutes for money. [1] The main instruments comprising the money market are: (a) call money/notice money, (b) certificates of deposit (CDs), (c) treasury bills (abolished with effect from April 1997), (d) repurchase agreements (repos), (e) commercial bills, (f) commercial paper (CPs), and (g) inter-corporate funds.

While inter-bank money markets and central bank lending via repo operations or discounting, provide liquidity for banks, private non-bank money market instruments, such as commercial bills and commercial paper provide liquidity to the commercial sector. Unlike in developed economies where money markets are promoted by financial intermediaries out of efficiency considerations, in India, as in many other developing countries, the evolution of the money market and its structure has been integrated into the overall deregulation process of the financial sector.

The money market is generally expected to perform three broad functions.

1. It provides an equilibrating mechanism to even out demand for and supply of short-term funds.
2. It also presents a focal point for central bank intervention for influencing liquidity and general level of interest rates in the economy.
3. It provides reasonable access to providers and users of short-term funds to fulfil their borrowing and investment requirements at an efficient market clearing price.

10.2 Reserve Bank of India (RBI) and the Money Market

The RBI is the most important constituent of the money market. Owing to its implications for conducting monetary policy, the money market falls under the direct purview of regulation of the RBI. The primary objective of the RBI's operations in the money market has been to ensure that short-term interest rates and liquidity are maintained at levels which are consistent with the overall monetary policy objectives, viz. maintaining price stability, ensuring adequate flow of credit to the productive sectors of the economy and maintaining orderly conditions in the financial markets. Liquidity and interest rates in the system are influenced by the RBI through the use of various instruments at its disposal which, *inter alia*, include the following.

1. Variations in cash reserve ratio.

2. Standing facilities/refinance schemes.
3. Repo and reverse repo transactions.
4. Changes in the Bank Rate.
5. Open market operations.
6. Foreign exchange swap operations.

Recognising the important role of the market in the monetary policy process, the RBI has taken active interest in continuously refining the money market instruments in order to have greater control over the liquidity in the system and for creating an efficient mechanism to impart interest rate signals.

10.3 Evolution of Money Market in India

10.3.1 Pre-Independence Period: Money market prior to Independence was characterised by paucity of instruments, lack of depth and dichotomy in the market structure. The inter-bank call money market was the core of the Indian money market. Before the establishment of the RBI in 1935, the money market consisted of two fairly distinct sectors, *viz.* the organised and unorganised sectors. While the organised sector consisted of the Imperial Bank of India—a quasi-central bank till 1935, the Indian joint-stock banks and the exchange banks, the indigenous bankers such as the shroffs, money lenders, chit funds etc. formed the unorganised part. Co-operative credit institutions occupied an intermediate position between the two sectors.

The Imperial Bank, the foremost commercial bank of the country and a few of the leading Indian joint-stock banks discounted *hundis* (internal bills of exchange). This was the main credit instrument of the unorganised sector which provided the only link between the two sectors. Owing to the absence of a proper central bank, the money market was characterised by sharp imbalances between the supply and demand for funds, wide fluctuations in interest rates during the busy and slack seasons and marked regional variations in interest rates. The Imperial Bank could not, however, lend stability to the money market as it had to borrow from the Government at high rates of interest. Nevertheless, the bank rendered assistance to the money market by using the large Government balances at its disposal, which constituted its major investible resources.

The Bank Rate was the prime lending rate at which the Imperial Bank generally advanced money against Government securities. This rate was determined by the Committee of the Central Board of the Imperial Bank and depended on the demand for money which in turn was determined almost entirely by the requirements of trade, particularly foreign trade, in staple commodities such as foodgrains, raw cotton, raw jute and jute manufactures. The rates of interest on loans, including the Bank Rate, fluctuated according to the ebb and flow of this trade. The Imperial Bank would usually not reduce the Bank Rate when its cash to liabilities ratio (an indication of liquidity) was found to be low. Apart from the Bank Rate, the Imperial Bank also periodically announced a *hundi* rate, which was generally equal to or slightly higher than the Bank Rate. Through the rates which the Imperial Bank charged on its advances and the discount of *hundis,* and by its willingness or refusal to extend financial assistance, it could profoundly influence the provision of credit as well as money market rates.

After the formation of the RBI in 1935, the organised market comprised the RBI, the Imperial Bank, foreign banks and the Indian joint stock banks. *Quasi*-Government bodies and large-sized joint stock companies also participated in the money market as lenders, the money lent by them being usually termed as *house money*. Financial intermediaries such as call loan brokers, general finance and stock brokers also functioned in the market. Although the magnitude of funds dealt within the call market was not large in relation to the deposit resources of banks, it was the most sensitive segment of the money market. The Imperial Bank did not participate in the call money market, but other banks obtained loans and advances from it. Subsequently, however, banks increasingly shifted their demand for accommodation to the RBI. Besides the call money market, there was no other significant segment in the market.

With the establishment of the RBI in April 1935, the task of determining the Bank Rate was taken over by it from the Imperial Bank. It was on July 4, 1935, i.e. the day before the scheduled banks were to lodge their statutory deposits with the RBI, that the Bank Rate of 3.5 percent was officially announced for the first time by the RBI. It was the standard rate at which the RBI was prepared to buy or re-discount bills of exchange or other eligible commercial papers. Subsequently, the official rate of the Imperial Bank was re-designated as the Imperial Bank advance rate (as distinct from the Imperial Bank *hundi* rate), which was to be the rate for advances against Government securities and the benchmark for the calculation of interest on other advances on which a fluctuating rate of interest was charged.

10.3.2 Post-Independence Period: At the time of Independence in 1947, money market structure in India was loose though not entirely uncoordinated. The indigenous bankers enjoyed rediscount facilities from the Imperial Bank and other commercial banks which, in turn, had access to the RBI. Recourse on the part of the indigenous money market to the resources of the organised market took place usually during the busy season when the crops were being harvested and moved from the producer to the wholesaler.

Though the RBI was empowered, under the statute, to use the usual instruments of monetary policy, the choice of the instruments of monetary control that could be used was limited by the structural characteristics of the money market. An important aspect of the money market in India was the seasonality in the demand for money and credit which broadly followed the course of the agricultural season. The incidence of closing of accounts of the Government at the end of the financial year in March also added to the element of seasonality in the money market.

The introduction of Bill Market Scheme by the RBI on January 16, 1952 was a landmark in the growth of money market in India. [2] Under the scheme, the RBI made advances to scheduled banks in the form of demand loans against their promissory notes supported by 90 days usance bills or promissory notes of their constituents. It was primarily a scheme for providing accommodation to banks. The scheme, however, did not succeed in developing a market in genuine bills.

In order to serve the economy in general and the rural sector in particular, the All-

India Rural Credit Survey Committee recommended the creation of the state-partnered and state-sponsored bank by taking over the Imperial Bank of India, and integrating with it, the former state-owned or state-associate banks. An Act was, accordingly, passed in the Parliament in May 1955 and the State Bank of India was constituted on July 1, 1955.

A new scheme called the Bills Rediscounting Scheme was introduced with several new features in November 1970 under which the RBI rediscounted genuine trade bills at the Bank Rate or at a rate specified by it, at its discretion. Over the years the rediscounting facility was made restrictive and made available on a discretionary basis. The other instrument in the money market was participation certificates (introduced in 1970). Both of these were, however, not significant.

Prior to financial sector reforms initiated in early 1990s, money market in India was characterised by poor liquidity, the paucity of instruments and limited number of participants. The major features of the Indian money market were the following.

1. Restricted market with a narrow base and limited number of participants—banks and two all India financial institutions. The entry into the market was tightly regulated. Moreover, the market was lopsided with a few large lenders and a large number of borrowers. The market lacked participants who could make for an active market by alternating between lending and borrowing.
2. The overall size of the market was also very small relative to the size of the economy—overall transactions barely formed 3 to 4 percent of the bank deposits.
3. The market was also characterised by paucity of instruments and dealings were generally confined to overnight call and short notice (up to 14 days), inter-bank deposits/loans, Repo market and bills rediscounting.
4. The interest rates in the market were also tightly regulated and controlled (by a voluntary agreement between the participants through the Indian Banks' Association (IBA) intermediation). However, during periods of tight liquidity, the prescribed rates were not strictly adhered to, and more often breached.

Owing to the above features, the unorganised money market used to meet the sectoral financing gaps (i.e. the requirements of unsatisfied borrowers in the organised financial system). Interest rates in the unorganised sector were higher than those in the organised sector and were more market-related.

The Committee to Review the Working of the Monetary System in India (Chairman: Sukhamoy Chakravarty), 1985 first underlined the need to develop money market instruments in India, while the Working Group on the Money Market (Chairman: N. Vaghul), 1987 laid the blueprint for the institution of money markets. Based on the recommendations of the Chakravarty Committee and the Vaghul Working Group, the RBI has gradually developed money market in India through the following measures.

First, interest rate ceilings on inter-bank call/notice money (10 percent), inter-bank term money (10.5-11.5 percent), rediscounting of commercial bills (12.5 percent) and inter-bank participation without risk (12.5 percent) were withdrawn effective May 1, 1989.

Secondly, several financial innovations in terms of money market instruments, such as auctions of Treasury Bills (beginning with the introduction of 182-day Treasury Bills effective November 1986), certificates of deposit (June, 1989), commercial paper (January 1990) and RBI repo (December 1992) were introduced.

Thirdly, barriers to entry were gradually eased by: (a) increasing the number of players (beginning with the Discount and Finance House of India (DFHI) in April 1988 followed by primary and satellite dealers and money market mutual funds), (b) relaxing both issuance restrictions and subscription norms in respect of money market instruments and allowing determination of yields based on demand and supply of such paper, and (c) enabling market evaluation of associated risks, by withdrawing regulatory restrictions such as bank guarantees in respect of CPs.

Fourthly, the development of markets for short-term funds at market determined interest rates has been fostered by a gradual switch from a cash credit system to a loan-based system, shifting the onus of cash management from banks to borrowers and phasing out the 4.6 percent 91-day tap Treasury bills, which in the past provided an avenue for investing short-term funds.

Finally, institutional development has been carried out to facilitate inter-linkages between the money market and the foreign exchange market, especially after a market-based exchange rate system was put in place in March 1993.

10.4 Developments in the Money Market since 1991

The money market in India witnessed significant progress particularly from the mid-1990s, in terms of refinements in money market instruments, introduction of new instruments and supplementary measures to add depth and liquidity to the market.

During the 1990s, the participation in the call money market was widened to cover primary and satellite dealers and corporates (through primary dealers) besides other participants. While banks and primary dealers are permitted to lend and borrow in the market, other entities can participate only as lenders. Following the recommendations of the Committee on Banking Sector Reforms (Chairman: M. Narasimham), 1998 and the RBI's Internal Working Group to Examine the Development of Call Money Market (1997), steps were initiated to reform the call money market and make it a pure inter-bank market, in a phased manner starting in 1999. With the development of the repo market since the late 1990s, the call money market has gradually been transformed into a pure inter-bank market including primary dealers. This process, which was initiated in 1999, was completed in August 2005.

A significant development in the Indian money market has been the introduction of Rupee derivatives, i.e. interest rate swaps (IRS)/forward rate agreements (FRA) in 1999 to further deepen the money market and enable market participants to hedge their risks. In addition to several other measures taken since its introduction, with effect from May 20, 2005, market participants were advised to use only domestic Rupee benchmarks for interest rate derivatives. Market participants were, however, given a transition period of six months for using Mumbai inter-bank forward offered rate (MIFOR) as a benchmark, subject to review. However, on request from the Fixed Income Money Market and Derivatives Association (FIMMDA), market participants have been allowed to use

MIFOR swaps in respect of transactions having underlying permissible forex exposures, for market making purpose, subject to appropriate limit as may be approved by the RBI.

Following the recommendations of the Technical Group on Money Market (May 2005), the focus and policy thrust of the RBI in the money market has been towards encouraging the growth of collateralised market, ensuring transparency and better price discovery, providing avenues for better risk management and strengthening monetary operations.

Trading in money market instruments can take place on a trading platform or in the OTC market. Electronic platforms are available for deals in the call, notice and term money market transactions, market repo and collateralised borrowing and lending obligation (CBLO). OTC deals are done for commercial paper (CP) and certificate of deposit (CD), as well as for call/notice/term money markets. Settlement is done over the real time gross settlement system—either as a gross settlement or as a multilateral netted batch. CP and CD deals, which are mostly in the form of private placements, are done OTC.

The RBI's regulatory powers over money market securities was strengthened under Clause 45(W) of the RBI Amendment Act, 2006, wherein the RBI was given specific powers to 'regulate the financial system of the country to its advantage, determine the policy relating to interest rates or interest rate products, and give directions on that behalf to all agencies or any of them, dealing in securities, money market instruments, foreign exchange, derivatives, or other instruments of like nature as the Bank may specify from time to time'.

10.5 Component-wise Analysis of Money Market in India

10.5.1 Call/Notice Money Market: The call money market is an important segment of the money market where uncollateralized borrowing and lending of funds take place on overnight basis. Presently, participants in the call money market in India include scheduled commercial banks (excluding regional rural banks), cooperative banks (other than land development banks), and primary dealers, both as borrowers and lenders. Prudential limits in respect of both outstanding borrowing and lending transactions in the call money market for each of these entities are specified by the RBI.

Money market in India comprises mainly of the call money market. Although other money market segments, viz. commercial bills market and inter-corporate deposits market have been in existence for a long time, there has not been much activity in these segments. Therefore, for assessing the impact of reforms on the money market, the focus is mainly on the call money market. The impact of reforms is assessed in terms of behaviour of the call money market and the market growth related parameters, including those instruments which were introduced in the 1990s.

Call money market deals in overnight funds. Notice money market deals in funds for 2 to 14 days. The call/notice money market serves the purpose of equilibrating the short-term liquidity position of banks and other participants. In order to modulate short-term liquidity under diverse market conditions, the Government introduced a full-fledged liquidity adjustment facility (LAF) on June 5, 2000. Under this scheme, the RBI can adjust market liquidity on a daily basis through repo/reverse repo auctions of varying frequencies. This has emerged as an effective instrument to facilitate overnight call rate movement, resulting in stability and orderly market conditions.

The overnight inter-bank call money market, in which banks trade positions to maintain cash reserves, is the key segment of the money market in India. It is basically an over the counter (OTC) market without the intermediation of brokers. Participation has been gradually widened to include other financial institutions, primary/satellite dealers, mutual funds and other participants in the bills rediscounting market and corporates (through primary dealers) besides banks, LIC and UTI. While banks and primary dealers are allowed two-way operations, other non-bank entities can only participate as lenders. As per the announced policies, once the repo market develops, the call money market would be made into a pure inter-bank market, including primary dealers.

On the supply side, the call money market is influenced by liquidity conditions mainly governed by deposit mobilisation, capital flows and the RBI's operations affecting banks' reserve requirements. On the demand side, it is influenced by tax outflows, government borrowing programme, non-food credit off-take and seasonal fluctuations, such as large currency withdrawals during the festival season. In times of easy liquidity, call rates tend to hover around the RBI's repo rate, which provides a ready avenue for parking short-term surplus funds. During periods of tight liquidity, call rates tend to move up towards the Bank Rate and more recently the RBI's reverse repo rate as the RBI modulates liquidity in pursuit of monetary stability. Besides, there are other influences such as: (a) reserve requirement prescriptions (and stipulations regarding average reserve maintenance), (b) investment policy of non-bank participants in the call market which are among the large suppliers of funds in the call market, and (c) asymmetries of the call money market, with few lenders and chronic borrowers.

The turnover in the call/notice money market depends on the amount of surplus funds available with some participants and the requirements of funds by some other participants. Over the years, the number of participants in the market has gradually increased to include banks and primary dealers both as lenders and borrowers, and select mutual funds, insurance companies, development financial institutions and corporates through primary dealers (as lenders).

The call money market, the dominant market, was strictly an inter-bank market till 1971 when the UTI and LIC were allowed to operate in the market. While commercial and cooperative banks participated as both lenders and borrowers, LIC and UTI, institutions with a sizeable short-term float funds, were permitted to lend in order to augment the supply of funds in the market. The overnight call/term money had traditionally facilitated banks in maintaining reserve requirements. Thus, in the 1970s and 1980s, call money market in India remained basically "an over the counter (OTC) market" as brokers were not permitted in the market.

Prior to December 1973, the call market rates were freely determined by the market but as the rates touched a high of 25 to 30 percent and remained at that level, the Indian Banks' Association (IBA) intervened and brought some order in the market as it was felt that high interest rate over long periods would distort the entire banking system operations and would also militate against the basic objectives of planned credit allocation under an administered structure of lending rates. A ceiling of 15 percent on call money rate was fixed by the IBA in December 1973; the ceiling was, however, reduced in phases to 8.5 percent by March 1978. The resurgence of inflationary pressures and the sharp upward movement in administered interest rates in 1979-80 necessitated increase in the ceiling on call rates to 10 percent in April 1980.

In the initial phase of money market reforms in the late 1980s, considerable volatility was noticed in the call rate, resulting primarily from a free call money market, while interest rates in other segments of the money market remained regulated. As a result, any fluctuation in the liquidity conditions impinged on the call money market.

The call money market during the 1990s witnessed orderly conditions barring a few episodes of volatility. The call rates first came under pressure in May 1992 when they touched a peak of 35.3 percent, essentially reflecting liquidity tightness due to high levels of statutory pre-emptions and withdrawal of all reliance facilities except for export credit refinance. After witnessing tranquil conditions during July 1992 until December 1994, the call money market came under pressure again during 1995-96. The call rate touched a peak of around 35 percent in November 1995, largely mirroring turbulence in the foreign exchange market. To stabilise the market, the RBI injected liquidity through reverse repos, enhanced banks' refinance facilities against government securities and reduced the CRR. The call rate softened to a single digit level thereafter till December 1997. However, the call rate hardened again and touched a high of around 29 percent, in January 1998, reflecting the mopping up of money market liquidity by the RBI to ease the pressure in the foreign exchange market. During 1999-2000, the inter-bank call money rates ruled steady within a narrow range, except for a few bouts of volatility, primarily attributable to the unanticipated demand for reserves by commercial banks.

Thus, for a few episodes of volatility, conditions in the call money market remained stable in the 1990s. The full-fledged liquidity adjustment facility (LAF), which was introduced on June 5, 2000, with a view to modulating short-term liquidity under diverse market conditions, emerged as an effective instrument to provide a corridor for the overnight call rate movement. The LAF combined with strategic open market operations (OMOs), has since been used to signal the monetary stance by removing shortfalls and excesses of liquidity in the system so as to keep short-term interest rates reasonably stable.

Over the years, a few banks tended to be overtly exposed to the call/notice money market. Such banks relied excessively on the call money market for carrying out banking operations and long-term asset creation. The Committee on Banking Sector Reforms (Chairman: M. Narasimham), 1998 recommended that there must be clearly defined prudent limits beyond which banks should not be allowed to rely on the call/notice money market and that access to this market should essentially be for meeting unforeseen mismatches and not as regular means of financing lending operations of banks. With progressive regulations, asset liability management system was put in place, which kept the mismatches in cash flows in the 1-28 days bucket under check.

As part of streamlining the LAF and improving the transmission channel of monetary policy, the phasing out of non-bank participants from the call money market commenced from May 2001. Furthermore, recognising that building up of substantial exposure to the call/notice money market relative to the balance-sheet size by some participants on a continuous basis has the potential not only for default and the consequent systemic instability, but also for impeding other segments of the money market, participants are now operating within limits on both lending and borrowing operations. Thus, the call/notice money market is evolving as a pure inter-bank market with ALM discipline for participants and prudential limits for borrowing and lending.

With the establishment of the Clearing Corporation of India Ltd. (CCIL) and the enhanced liquidity in the repo market both in government and non-government securities, it is envisaged that eventually both the call market and the repo market, combined with other money market instruments, would constitute an integrated market for equilibrating short-term funds for both, banks and non-banks.

10.5.2 Commercial Paper (CP): CP was introduced as a money market instrument in January 1990. The purpose was to enable the companies to diversify their sourcing of short-term borrowings. It also provided investors with an additional instrument for investment.

CP is issued by non-banking companies and all-India financial institutions (AIFIs) as an unsecured promissory note or in a dematerialised form at a rate of discount not tied to any transaction. It is privately placed with investors through the agency of banks. Banks act as both principals (i.e. as counter parties in purchases and sales) and agents in dealership and placement.

Conditions relating to issuing of CPs have been relaxed gradually with a view to broad-basing the market. For instance, the maturity period has been changed from 91 days to 6 months from the earlier 15 days up to 1 year. The minimum size of CPs has also been reduced from ₹ 1 crore to ₹ 5 lakh. The issuer base has been widened by allowing PDs, SDs and AIFIs, apart from corporates, to issue CPs to access short-term funds.

The limit for issuance of CP, which was initially carved out of the maximum permissible bank finance (MPBF), was later linked to the cash credit component of MPBF. With the cash credit component gradually shrinking and, thereby, restricting the development of CP, the issuance limit was delinked from the cash credit limit in October 1997. Initially, banks were required to restore the cash credit limit on the maturity of the paper, guaranteeing the issuer funds at the point of redemption. This *stand-by* facility was withdrawn in October 1994 to impart a measure of independence to CP as a money market instrument.

The pricing of CP usually lies between the scheduled commercial banks' lending rate and some representative money market rate. The Indian CP market is driven by the demand for CP by scheduled commercial banks, which in turn is governed by bank liquidity. Banks' investments in CP, despite a positive interest rate differential between the bank loan rate and the CP rate, may be explained by two factors, viz.: (i) the higher transaction costs of bank loans, and (ii) the relative profitability of CP as an attractive short-term instrument to park funds during times of high liquidity.

As inter-bank call rates are typically lower than the CP rates, some banks also fund CP by borrowing from the call money market and thus book profit through arbitrage between the two money markets. Most of the CPs seem to have been issued by the manufacturing companies for a maturity period of approximately 3 months or less, mainly due to the fact that investors do not wish to lock funds for long periods of time.

Secondary activity is subdued in most CP markets on account of the investors' preference to hold the instrument due to higher risk-adjusted returns relative to those of other instruments. However, mutual funds find the secondary market relatively remunerative, since stamp duty for the issuer will be higher in case the buyer is a mutual fund rather than a bank. Hence, there is a tendency to route a CP through an institution (usually a bank), which attracts lower stamp duty in the primary market, to a mutual fund in the secondary market.

The Indian CP market is driven by swings in bank liquidity. Banks prefer investing in CPs especially in times of easy liquidity as they can park funds at interest rates higher than call rates and at the same time avoid higher transaction costs associated with bank loans. The effective discount rate of CP usually lies between representative money market rate and the bank lending rate. On the other hand, companies are able to raise funds through CPs at a lower rate than the lending rates of banks under easy liquidity conditions.

Further measures to spur the CP market have included conversion of CP into a stand-alone product in October 2000, trading of CPs in dematerialised form (which helped to lower transaction costs) and reduction in stamp duty effective March 1, 2004.

10.5.3 Certificates of Deposit (CDs): CDs were introduced in 1989 as a money market instrument to mobilise large value deposits. Such deposits were freed from interest rate regulations in 1992. Banks can now have the option to meet their liquidity needs through these certificates issued at a premium during tight liquidity conditions.

CDs are essentially securitised short-term time deposits issued by banks during periods of tight liquidity, at relatively high interest rates (in comparison with term deposits). But the transaction cost of CDs is often lower as compared with that of retail deposits. When credit picks up, placing pressure on banks' liquidity, banks try to meet their liquidity gap by issuing CDs, often at a premium. The required amounts are mobilised in larger amounts through CDs, often for short periods in order to avoid interest liability overhang in the subsequent months when credit demand slackens. As banks offer higher interest rates on CDs, subscribers find it profitable to hold CDs till maturity. As a result, the secondary market for CDs has been slow to develop.

The steady increase of CDs has been on account of several factors.

1. Revised guidelines by the RBI on investments by banks in non-SLR debt securities.
2. Reduction in stamp duty on CDs effective March 1, 2004.
3. Withdrawal of tax deduction at source.
4. Disallowing premature closure of deposits under CDs.
5. Greater opportunity for secondary market trading.

On the demand side, the Securities and Exchange Board of India (SEBI) placing a bar on mutual funds (MFs) from parking funds in bank deposits coupled with improved funds position with MFs provided an impetus to the CD market. An encouraging development in the CD market is that some of the top-rated banks have been getting their

CDs rated for better access to the market even when such rating is not mandatory under the extant guidelines.

10.5.4 Repos: Repo (repurchase agreement) is a money market instrument, which enables collaboralised short-term borrowing and lending through sale/purchase operations in debt instruments. Under a repo transaction, a holder of securities sells them to an investor with an agreement to repurchase at a pre-determined date and rate. In the case of a repo, the forward clean price of the bonds is set in advance at a level which is different from the spot clean price by adjusting the difference between repo interest and coupon earned on the security. Repo is also called a ready forward transaction as it is a means of funding by selling a security held on a spot (ready) basis and repurchasing the same on a forward basis. Reverse repo is a mirror image of repo as in the case of former, securities are acquired with a simultaneous commitment to resell.

In India, banks often entered into buy back arrangements in respect of Government and other approved securities and PSU bonds among themselves and with their large public sector and corporate clients until April 15, 1987 when the RBI issued certain guidelines prohibiting buy back arrangements in respect of corporate securities and bonds issued by public sector undertakings. From December 1, 1987 the units of Unit Trust of India were not eligible as approved security for the purpose of entering into repo transactions. In order to ward off any undesirable developments following the detection of large scale misuse of repos, banks were prohibited from entering into buy back arrangements in Government and other approved securities with non-bank clients, while they could enter into buy-back arrangements with other banks (inter-bank) with effect from April 4, 1988.

The repo market suffered a major setback due to the securities irregularities of 1992. The Janakiraman Committee, set up in the wake of the securities market irregularities reported that there existed a thriving market for repos and virtually all wholesale participants of the money market and not only banks, used repo transactions widely, despite there being an explicit prohibition on their use. After the detection of the irregularities, the RBI imposed a ban on ready forward deals and banks were prohibited from undertaking repos in Government dated securities and approved/trustee securities from June 22, 1992. Repos in Treasury Bills were, however, exempted from prohibition. Double ready forward deals, including those in Treasury Bills were also strictly prohibited and the ban was extended to financial institutions as well.

Justice Variava's judgement was of great significance in the context of development of the repo market in India as it held that all repo transactions undertaken by banks and other institutions were illegal and void as they were prohibited under Section 16 of the Securities Contract Regulation Act (SCRA), 1956 and Government's notification dated June 27, 1969. In order to legally facilitate the repo transactions, the RBI had to take up the issue with the Government to exempt banks and such of those entities deemed necessary by the RBI, from the prohibition contained in the notification. Amending the Notification which prohibited forward transactions in securities, the Government issued notifications by virtue of which banking companies, co-operative banks, primary dealers (by name) and satellite dealers (by name) were permitted to undertake ready forward transactions in specified securities, provided the transactions were settled through SGL Accounts maintained at the Public Debt Office, Mumbai. Further, non-bank entities as notified by the Central Government were permitted to undertake reverse repos only.

Following the recommendations of the Committee on Banking Sector Reforms (Chairman: M. Narasimham), 1998, an interim liquidity adjustment facility (ILAF) was introduced initially in April 1999. This later translated into a full-fledged LAF, put in place on June 5, 2000. Under this arrangement, the RBI was able to adjust market liquidity on a daily basis through repo/reverse repo auctions of varying frequencies under the LAF. Though the interest rates in the repo/reverse repo auctions usually emerge out of the bids, the RBI occasionally conducts fixed rate auctions to send signals to the market. Hence, the interest rates emerging out of the repo and reverse repo auctions provide a corridor for call money and other short-term interest rates. The LAF has gradually emerged as the principal operating instrument of monetary policy, replacing all other windows of liquidity support to the market.

In view of the irregularities in securities transactions, repos were initially allowed in Central Government Treasury bills and dated securities, created by converting some of the Treasury bills. In order to activate the repos market, essentially to be an equilibrating force between the money market and the Government securities market, the RBI gradually extended the repos facility to all Central Government dated securities and Treasury Bills of all maturities. Recently, while the State Government securities were made eligible for repos, the RBI also allowed all non-banking entities, maintaining SGL and current accounts with its Mumbai office, to undertake repos (including reverse repos). Furthermore, it has been decided to make PSU bonds and private corporate securities eligible for repos to broaden the repos market.

Repo/reverse repo operations are also undertaken by the RBI as part of its open market operations. The RBI initially conducted repo operations for a period of 14 days. Since November 1996, the RBI has been conducting 3-4 day repo auctions, synchronizing with working day and week-end liquidity conditions, in order to modulate short-term liquidity. With the introduction of liquidity adjustment facility (LAF) from June 5, 2000, the RBI has been injecting liquidity into the system through repos on a daily basis. These operations are conducted on all working days except on Saturdays, through uniform price auctions and are restricted to scheduled commercial banks and PDs.

To develop and widen the repos market, the RBI introduced regulatory safeguards such as delivery versus payments (DvP) system in April 1999. The operationalisation of negotiated dealing system (NDS) and the Clearing Corporation of India Ltd. (CCIL) provided a further boost to this market.

The turnover in the repo market has shown an increasing trend on account of various factors such as limits placed on eligible market participants relating to call/notice money transactions, introduction of DvP III, permitting rollover of repo and market repo rate ruling below the call rate during certain periods. Effective February 23, 2003, based on the advice of the Technical Advisory Committee (TAC) on Money and Government Securities Markets, repo eligibility was extended to select category of non-SGL account holders with adequate safeguards to ensure delivery *versus* payment and transparency. Also effective May 11, 2005, participation in market repo facility has been extended to non-scheduled urban cooperative banks and companies having gilt accounts with scheduled commercial banks, subject to certain eligibility criteria and safeguards.

Being a money market instrument, regulation of the repo market falls under the RBI's jurisdiction. Accordingly, the RBI is concerned with use of repo as an instrument by banks or non-bank entities and issues relating to type of eligible instruments for undertaking repo and eligibility of participants to undertake such transactions. It has been issuing instructions in this regard to banks, in consultation with the Central Government.

10.5.5 Collateralised Borrowing and Lending Obligation (CBLO): It a money market instrument as approved by the RBI. It is a product developed by CCIL for the benefit of entities who have either been phased out from the inter-bank call money market or have been given restricted participation in terms of ceiling on call borrowing and lending transactions and who do not have access to the call money market. CBLO is a discounted instrument available in electronic book entry form for a maturity period ranging from one day to ninety days (can be made available up to one year as per guidelines of RBI).

CBLO is explained as under:

1. An obligation by the borrower to return the money borrowed, at a specified future date.
2. An authority to the lender to receive money lent, at a specified future date with an option/privilege to transfer the authority to another person for value received.
3. An underlying charge on securities held in custody (with CCIL) for the amount borrowed/lent.

10.6 Report of the Technical Group on Money Market

To review the recent developments and current status of money market in the context of evolving monetary policy framework, fiscal scenario, regulatory regime and extent of financial integration, domestic as well as external, a Technical Group on Money Market was constituted. The Group in its Report submitted in May 2005 made several recommendations for furthering the development of the money Market.

The Group recommended that the policy thrust should be to encourage collateralised market, develop the rupee yield curve, ensure transparency and better price discovery, provide avenues for better risk management and strengthen monetary operations. The main recommendations of the Group are set out below.

1. Transactions in the call/notice money market should be conducted on an electronic negotiated quote driven platform.
2. Banks and PDs with appropriate risk management systems in place and balance sheet structure may be allowed more flexibility to borrow in the call/notice money market.
3. Upon accomplishing the call/notice money market into a pure inter-bank one, larger freedom in lending in the call/notice market should be afforded to banks and PDs.
4. Consequent upon coming into effect of the Fiscal Responsibility and Budget Management (FRBM) Act, 2003, there would be a need to broad-base the pool of

securities to act as collateral for repo and CBLO markets.

5. The possibility of conducting repo transactions on an electronic, anonymous order driven trading system be explored.
6. Term money market transactions should be compulsorily reported on NDS platform to improve transparency. Term money market transactions on an electronic, negotiated quote driven platform should be introduced.
7. The maturity period of CDs be reduced to 7 days in line with that of CPs and fixed deposits.
8. Asset-backed CPs be introduced in the Indian market.
9. Appropriate amendment to the Reserve Bank of India Act, 1934 be carried out to provide legal clarity to the OTC derivatives.
10. Regulatory issues pertaining to new instruments such as MIBOR-linked short-term papers need to be addressed for an orderly development of the market.
11. Late hour intra-day LAF as and when warranted in future be explored.

10.6.1 Follow-up Action: Certain recommendations of the Group were accepted for implementation and several measures were initiated in the Annual Policy Statement of the RBI announced in April 2005.

In consonance with the declared policy of phased withdrawal of non-bank participants, barring PDs from the call/notice money market, effective the fortnight beginning June 11, 2005, non-bank participants were allowed to lend, on an average, in a reporting fortnight, up to 10 percent of their average daily lending in the call/notice money market during 2000-01. Effective August 6, 2005 non-bank participants were completely phased out from the call/notice money market. In order to prevent imprudent leveraging of funds, effective April 30, 2005, the benchmark for fixing prudential limits on exposures to the call/notice money market in the case of scheduled commercial banks was linked to their capital funds.

Further steps were taken to broaden the scope of negotiated dealing system (NDS) platform with a view to enhancing transparency and price discovery as also to foster greater market integrity. From April 30, 2005, all NDS members were required to report their term money deals on NDS platform. Further, a screen-based negotiated quote-driven system for all dealings in call/notice and term money market transactions was proposed in the Annual Policy Statement of the RBI for 2005-06. An electronic trading platform for conduct of market repo operations in Government securities, in addition to the existing voice based system, was also proposed. Further, it was proposed to facilitate automated value-free transfer of securities between market participants and the Clearing Corporation of India Ltd. (CCIL) for development of the CBLO segment.

With a view to augmenting the instruments available to banks to manage their liquidity, the minimum maturity period of CDs was reduced from 15 days to 7 days with effect from April 28, 2005. Earlier, in the Mid-term Review of Annual Policy Statement for 2004-05, the minimum maturity period of CP was reduced from 15 days to 7 days with effect from October 26, 2004, in order to provide an option to issuers to raise short-term resources through CP as also an avenue to investors in the form of quality short-term papers.

In order to enhance transparency and facilitate wider dissemination, information on CP issuance, such as issue date, maturity date, issue amount, was made available on the website of the RBI with effect from July 1, 2005.

With a view to harmonising the stamp duty applicable on issuance of CP and bringing the Indian CP market closer to international standard, the Union Budget for 2005-06 proposed to rationalise the stamp duty and apply it uniformly regardless of the initial class of investor.

10.7 Areas of Concern

Although significant progress has been made through initiation of various reforms, there are several issues, which need to be addressed. While the overnight market is reasonably developed, the term-money market is yet to develop necessitating large rollover of short-term funds in the overnight market. This is mainly on account of the inability of participants to form appropriate interest rate expectations in the medium-term due to which there is a tendency on their part to look themselves into a short-term period. Furthermore, overwhelming preference of corporates for *cash* credit rather than for *loan* credit generally forces banks to deploy a large amount in the call/notice money market rather than in the term money market.

Another issue relates to the avenues available to deploy short-term funds to non-bank corporates. A critical issue in transforming the call/notice money market into a pure inter-bank market is the availability of some other avenue for short-term funds for non-bank participants. The commercial bill market continues to be limited, especially as few participants are willing to bear the concomitant risk of default. Thus, the repo trade at this stage offers a quick medium for developing a market for short-term funds especially as the transactions are collateralised in the case of non-banks. While the RBI has taken several steps to develop a repo market for non-bank participants, a vibrant repo market is, however, yet to develop. There is also a need to develop uniform accounting and documentation procedures in this regard.

To sum up, the money market is an important channel for monetary policy transmission and has generally conformed to being a liquid market. The gradual shift towards a collateralised inter-bank market, policy directions towards reductions in statutory reserve requirements, the introduction of new instruments such as CBLO, implementation of RTGS, significant transformation of monetary operations framework towards market-based arrangements and facilitating trading through NDS-CALL are some of the factors that have contributed to the development of a relatively vibrant and liquid money market. However, the inability of market participants to take a medium-to long-term perspective on interest rates and liquidity, coupled with the absence of a credible long-term benchmark, is a major hurdle for further market development and needs to be addressed.

Money market in India, which traditionally consisted largely of call/notice money market, now comprises many other instruments such as CPs, CDs, repos and FRAs/IRS. Various reform measures have helped in improving the depth and efficiency of money market operations. The operationalisation of the LAF has provided an informal corridor for overnight call money borrowing rate, which has further imparted stability and flexibility in the interest rate structure and to the market. The other money market instruments such as CPs and CDs have also been developed through alignment in maturity (with deposit instruments like term deposits) and easing of issuance norms. With proper development of other money market segments, non-banks have been able to smoothly switch over from the call/notice money market to other segments.

The RBI's approach has been to foster balanced development of different segments of the money market, introduce new instruments and make the existing instruments more flexible, reduce dependence of participants on uncollateralised exposures, facilitate price discovery in the short-end and upgrade the payment system infrastructure. Accordingly, the RBI's strategy has focused on developing pure call/notice money market, instituting full-fledged liquidity adjustment facility, developing infrastructure, promoting transparency, and initiating various measures pertaining to instruments for non-bank participants. Following the various initiatives taken by the RBI over the years, the depth and liquidity in the money market has increased significantly.

Historically, the call money market has constituted the core of the money market in India. However, the collateralized segments, viz., market repo and CBLO, have come into prominence recently. The market structure is broad-based with the participation of banks, primary dealers, insurance companies, mutual funds, provident funds, and corporates. Such a broad participation has contributed to an active interest across market segments.

Endnotes

1. There is no demarcated distinction between the short-term money market and the long-term capital market, and in fact there are integral links between the two markets as the array of instruments in the two markets invariably forms a continuum.
2. Rediscounting bills were among the most important instruments of credit control and the Indian Central Banking Enquiry Committee (1931) had recommended early establishment of a market in commercial bills. No steps could, however, be taken by the RBI in this direction until the beginning of 1952 because of the War and the difficulties arising out of the partition of the country.

11

Capital Market Evolution and Reforms in India

11.1 Meaning and Importance of Capital Market

Capital market is a market for long-term funds. The distinction between capital market and money market is not watertight. Broadly speaking, capital market focuses on financing of fixed investment (machinery and equipment) while money market provides working capital finance (raw material etc.).

Capital market channelises household savings to the corporate sector and allocates funds to firms. In this process, it allows both firms and households to share risks associated with business. Moreover, capital market enables the valuation of firms on an almost continuous basis and plays an important role in the governance of the corporate sector.

An efficient capital market is an important constituent of a sound financial system. In India, efforts have been made in recent years to set up an effective regulatory framework covering major participants in the capital market. Similarly, the technology of trading and settlements in the stock exchanges has been upgraded. Internet-based trading in securities has been permitted. Foreign institutional investors (FIIs) and pension funds were allowed to enter the Indian stock market from 1993 onwards. The market has undergone a major transformation in terms of its structure, products, practices, spread, institutional framework and other important aspects like transparency, integrity and efficiency since then. The size of the market has also grown manifold.

The capital market fosters economic growth in following ways:

1. It augments the quantum of savings and capital formation in the economy.
2. It allocates capital efficiently thereby raising the productivity of investment.
3. It enhances the efficiency of a financial system as diverse competitors vie with each other for financial resources.
4. It adds to the financial deepening of the economy by enlarging the financial sector and promoting the use of innovative, sophisticated and cost-effective financial instruments, which ultimately reduce the cost of capital.
5. Well-functioning capital markets also impose discipline on firms to perform.
6. Equity and debt markets stress on the banking sector by diversifying credit risk across the economy.

11.2 Capital Market in the Pre-reforms (i.e. Pre-1991) Period

Historically, different kinds of financial intermediaries have existed in the Indian financial system. At the time of Independence in 1947, working capital requirements of corporates were financed mainly by commercial banks. As the capital market was underdeveloped, a number of development finance institutions (DFIs) were set up at the all-India and the State levels to meet the long-term fund requirements of companies.

Prior to the onset of financial sector reforms in 1991, the capital market structure in India was subject to several controls and opaque procedures. The objective of control over capital issues was to channel the limited capital resources available for investment in the country into desired areas. Apart from this main objective, capital issues control was put to several other uses, these being the following:

1. Regulation of bonus issues.
2. Regulation of terms and conditions of foreign capital participation in Indian companies and the regulation of the terms and conditions of dilution or repatriation of foreign equity.
3. Regulation of capital re-organisation plans of companies, including mergers and amalgamations.
4. Regulation of the capital structure of companies, as well as the terms and conditions of additional issues.
5. Regulation of the volume and timing of the private issue of capital.

Moreover, the trading and settlement system was outdated and not in tune with international practices. Raising of capital from the market was regulated by the Capital Issues (Control) Act, 1947 which was administered by the Controller of Capital Issues (CCIs) in the Ministry of Finance, Government of India. The scheme of controls under the Act required all the companies to obtain prior consent for issues of capital to the public. Pricing as well as the features of the capital structure (such as debt-equity ratios), were controlled by the Government. Similarly, the Securities Contracts (Regulation) Act, 1956 was administered by the Directorate of Stock Exchanges also in the Ministry of Finance. It empowered the Government to recognise/derecognise stock exchanges, stipulate rules and by-laws for their functioning, compel listing of securities by public companies etc. Such a system of regulation and control was fragmented and inadequate in the context of liberalisation wave sweeping across the world. Urgent measures were needed to relax controls and modernise the functioning of capital market.

11.3 Capital Market Reforms since 1991

The Indian equity market has witnessed a series of reforms since the early 1990s. The reforms have been implemented in a gradual and sequential manner, based on international best practices and modified to suit the needs of the country. The reform measures were aimed at the following:

1. Creating growth-enabling institutions.
2. Boosting competitive conditions in the equity market through improved price discovery mechanism.
3. Putting in place an appropriate regulatory framework.
4. Reducing the transaction costs.
5. Reducing information asymmetry, thereby boosting the investor confidence.

These measures were expected to increase the role of the equity market in resource mobilisation by enhancing the access of corporate sector to large resources through a variety of marketable securities. Institutional development was at the core of the reform process.

Reforms in the capital market have had a multi-dimensional impact. The significance of the capital market has improved in providing a mechanism for allocation of resources as is reflected in increase in its share in the sources of finance for the corporates. Various indicators such as reduced volatility are pointers in the direction of increase in the safety of the market. The safety of the market has also been considerably enhanced by adoption of risk management practices and the setting up of settlement guarantee funds and investor protection funds. The integrity and transparency of the market has also gone up with the wider availability of information regarding the performance of corporates. The trading and settlement framework in the Indian stock exchanges now compares favourably with the best international practices. Liquidity in the market has improved considerably.

11.4 Introduction of Free Pricing

Raising of capital from the securities market before 1992 was regulated under the Capital Issues (Control) Act, 1947. Firms were required to obtain approval from the Controller of Capital Issues (CCI) for raising resources in the market. New companies were allowed to issue shares only at par. Only the existing companies with substantial reserves could issue shares at a premium, which was based on some prescribed formula. In 1992, the Capital Issues (Control) Act, 1947 was repealed and with this ended all controls related to raising of resources from the market. Since then the issuers of securities can raise capital from the market without requiring any consent from any authority, either for making the issue or for pricing it. Restrictions on rights and bonus issues have also been removed. New as well as established companies are now able to price their issues according to their assessment of market conditions.

However, issuers of capital are required to meet the guidelines of SEBI on disclosure and investor protection. Companies issuing capital are required to make sufficient disclosures, including justification of the issue price and also material disclosure about the risk factors in their offer prospectus. These guidelines have served as an important measure for protecting the interest of investors and promoting the development of primary market along sound lines.

It may be recalled that in the early 1990s, the liberalisation of the industrial sector and free pricing of capital issues led to an increased number of companies tapping the primary capital market to mobilise resources. Several corporates charged a high premium not justified by their fundamentals. Also, several companies vanished after raising resources from the capital market. SEBI, therefore, strengthened the norms for public issues while retaining the freedom of the issuers to enter the new issues market and to freely price their issues. The disclosure standards were also strengthened for companies coming out with public issues for improving the levels of investor protection. Strict disclosure norms and entry point restrictions prescribed by SEBI made it difficult for most new companies without an established track record to access the public issues market. Whereas this helped to improve the quality of paper coming into the market, it contributed to a decline in the number of issues and the amount mobilised from the market.

11.5 Strengthening of Disclosure Norms

The central goal of securities markets is to obtain a widely-dispersed ownership and trading in securities. There is conflict of interest between the management team, which controls the firm, and the shareholders, who run the firm. Many policy efforts in recent years have been devoted towards improving incentives to managers to maximise the interests of shareholders.

Improvements in disclosure are a central tool for containing the conflicts of interest between the managers and shareholders. In order to foster improvements in disclosure, SEBI set up a system named electronic data information filing and retrieval (EDIFAR) in July 2002. This system offers a mechanism through which firms would electronically file mandatory disclosures to SEBI, and these documents would be available to individuals over the internet, with a near-zero delay. It is envisaged that in the future, disclosure would take place through company websites, exchange websites, and EDIFAR.

For strengthening the process of information flow from the listed companies, several measures have been introduced: (a) while sufficient disclosures are mandatory for the companies at the stage of public issues, the listed companies are also required under the listing agreement to make disclosures on a continued basis, (b) for ensuring quick flow of information to the public, the decision pertaining to dividend, bonus and right announcements or any material event are now required to be disclosed to the public within 15 minutes of the conclusion of the board meeting in which the disclosures are taken, and (c) accounting practices were streamlined with norms introduced for segment reporting, related to party transactions and consolidated balance sheets.

There is a substantial scale of securities issuance taking place through the private placement route. The private placement route has become a mechanism where securities can be placed with a few wholesale buyers of securities, without incurring the overheads of the public issue. SEBI is working on devising clear institutional mechanisms through which some public disclosure is made about these issues, while preserving the rights of issuers to not use the public issue route if it is considered to involve excessive overhead costs.

Without seeking to control the freedom of the issuers to enter the market and freely price their issues, the norms for public issues were made stringent in April 1996 to prevent fraudulent companies from accessing the market. Issuers of capital are now required to disclose information on various aspects such as track record of profitability, risk factors etc. As a result, there has been an improvement in the standards of disclosure in the offer documents for the public and rights issues and easier accessibility of information to the investors. The improvement in disclosure standards has enhanced transparency, thereby improving the level of investor protection.

11.6 Transparency and Efficiency

The National Stock Exchange (NSE) introduced screen-based trading at its inception in 1992 which was followed by other stock exchanges. Screen-based trading makes online, electronic, anonymous and order-driven transactions possible. It is a transparent system which provides equal access to all investors, irrespective of their geographical locations.

The move to an electronic trading system has resulted in transparency in trades, better price discovery and lower transaction costs. The efficiency of the market has improved through faster execution of trades. The operational efficiency of the stock market has also been strengthened through improvements in the clearing and settlement practices and the risk management process. Almost the entire delivery of securities now takes place in dematerialised form. Over the past few years or so, there has been no instance of postponement or clubbing of settlements at two main stock exchanges (BSE and NSE) despite defaults by brokers. The cases of bad deliveries are close to nil. Insider trading has been made a criminal offence. Non-transparent products like *badla* have been banned.

The setting up of trade/settlement guarantee funds in most of the exchanges has considerably reduced settlement risks for investors. Corporate governance practices and disclosure norms have led to transparency in information flows, which in turn have improved the price discovery process.

In order to bring greater transparency to the debt market, and to move away from bilateral negotiation towards anonymous order-matching, trading in government bonds began on stock exchanges on January 16, 2003. This has involved exploiting the identical process flow used for trading in equities. Trade takes place by anonymous order matching for all orders across the country, risk management is done by the clearing corporation, and settlement takes place at the depository. Under this system, government bonds appear in the depository statement of an investor alongside corporate equities and bonds. This system has several strengths.

1. Anonymous trading avoids the supervisory and regulatory difficulties of the telephone market, where counterparties are aware of identities and can engage in trades at off-market prices.
2. This market design offers symmetric market access from locations all over India and over the internet, as opposed to the telephone market, which favours entities in south Bombay.
3. It exploits information technology to guarantees that orders are matched against the best price available in the country. This is in contrast with the telephone market, where traders can search for counterparties, but are not sure of having found the best counterparty.
4. It is fully transparent in that orders and trades are visible in real time. This is in contrast with the telephone market, where orders are not visible, and the transparency of trades is limited and delayed.
5. It exploits the information technology of the depositories of the equity market (NSDL and CDSL), which have the full range of functionality required for investors such as a wide network of IT-enabled depository participants, internet access, strong computer security, access to data about the beneficial owner down to the end-investor.

Issuers also have the option of raising resources through fixed price mechanism or the book building process. [1] Book building was introduced to improve the transparency in pricing of the scrips and determine proper market price for shares.

11.7 Shortening of Settlement Cycle

Capital, unlike labour, is perpetually recycled, and the shorter the cycle, the more efficient is the use of such capital.

Following the enactment of the Depository Act, 1996, two depositories were set up: Central Depository Services Ltd. (CDSL) and National Securities Depository Limited (NSDL). The CDSL and NSDL have been successful in the dematerialisation of securities almost to the full extent. Presently, the transfer of ownership is mostly done through book-entry form. This has greatly improved the speed, accuracy and security of the settlement system. Prior to these arrangements, the settlement cycle was as high as 14 days for specified scrips and 30 days for others. The settlement risk was very high because of unforeseen happenings between the transaction and the settlement. To begin with, the settlement cycle was reduced to a week. Thereafter, rolling settlement was introduced on a T+5 basis in July 2001. From December 2001, all scrips which had established connectivity with the above-mentioned Depositories were moved to rolling settlement. The settlement cycle was further reduced to T+3 in April 2002 and to T+2 in April 2003.

11.8 Growth of Service Providers

Besides strengthening the institutional design of the markets, the reforms have also brought about an increase in the number of service providers who add value to the market. The most significant development in this respect has been the setting up of credit rating agencies. By assigning ratings to debt instruments and by continuous monitoring and dissemination of the ratings, they help in improving the quality of information. At present, six credit rating agencies are operating in India. Besides, two other service providers, *viz*. registrars to issue and share transfer agents, have also grown in number, which help in spreading the services easily and at competitive prices.

11.9 Protection of Investors

Though stock market should be governed by macroeconomic fundamentals of the economy, it is not always so. Manipulations and machinations by speculators, brokers, insiders and rumour-mongers also play a part.

11.9.1 Investor Protection Fund: The stock exchanges have put in place a system for redressal of investor grievances for matters relating to trading members and companies. They ensure that critical and price-sensitive information reaching the exchange is made available to all classes of investor at the same point of time. Further, to protect the interests of investors, the Investor Protection Fund (IPF) has also been set up by the stock exchanges. The exchanges maintain an IPF to take care of investor claims, which may arise out of non-settlement of obligations by the trading member, who has been declared a defaulter, in respect of trades executed on the exchange. Measures of investor protection that have been put in place over the reform period have led to increased confidence among investors. [2] To improve the availability of information to investors, all listed companies are required to publish unaudited financial results on a quarterly basis.

A continuing increase in the savings rate of households suggests that there is no supply constraint in terms of financial resources that could be channelled into the equity market. After the exuberance of the stock market in the mid-1990s and its decline thereafter, a large number of individual investors took flight to safety in bank deposits, safe retirement instruments and insurance. Households in India have increasingly tended to prefer savings in the form of safe and contractual instruments as opposed to capital market based instruments. Although retail investors have started showing some increased interest in the equity market in recent years, there is a need to increase their participation further.

11.9.2 Investor Protection in Derivatives Market:

A. Guiding Principles of Derivatives Market: L.C. Gupta Committee on Derivatives Trading in India recommended the following four guiding principles of derivatives market in India:

1. Fairness and transparency.
2. Safeguard for clients' money.
3. Competent and honest service.
4. Market integrity.

For details, see section 17.1.1 of chapter 17 of this book.

B. Measures to Protect the Rights of Investors in the Derivatives Market: See section 17.3 of chapter 17 of this book.

11.9.3 Financial Literacy: Financial literacy is the possession of a set of skills and knowledge which allow an individual to make informed and effective decisions with all of his financial resources. Understanding basic financial concepts allows people to know how to navigate in the financial system.

National Stock Exchange (NSE) of India is keen to ensure that the people of India are empowered to take sound financial decisions and invest wisely. NSE has also worked with a missionary zeal to educate investors about the opportunities in the market, the precautions they should take and their rights and obligations.

For details, see section 13.4.5 of chapter 13 of this book.

11.10 Issues and Concerns

The role of equity market in capital formation continues to be limited. The private corporate debt market is active mainly in the form of private placements, while the public issue market for corporate debt is yet to pick up. It is the primary equity and debt markets that link the issuers of securities and investors and provide resources for capital formation. A growing economy requires risk capital and long-term resources in the form of debt for enabling the corporates to choose an appropriate mix of debt and equity. Long-term resources are also important for financing infrastructure projects. Therefore, in order to sustain India's high growth path, the capital market needs to play a major role. The significance of a well-functioning domestic capital market has also increased as banks need to raise necessary capital from the market to sustain their growing operations.

A major issue which will influence India's securities markets in the future is the challenge of globalisation. RBI has increasingly moved in the direction of giving access to international diversification to institutional investors and individual investors in India. Financial intermediaries and exchanges in India will also experience global competition. There is a need for fully integrating a global perspective into the plans of firms, exchanges, regulators and policy makers.

The Indian capital market has become modern in terms of market infrastructure and trading and settlement practices. The capital market has also become a much safer place than it was before the reform process began. The secondary capital market in India has also become deep and liquid. There has also been a reduction in transaction costs and significant improvement in efficiency and transparency. However, the role of the domestic capital market in capital formation in the country, both directly and indirectly through mutual funds, continues to be less significant.

Post-liberalization, the Indian stock market witnessed a number of scams due to which small investors are reluctant to enter the market. History has witnessed how regulators remained mute spectators, allowing brokers to trap investors. If the government wants investors back in the capital market, it needs to strengthen the regulators, make them efficient, accountable and investor-friendly. In the current scenario of volatile stock market, which is now a fact of life in the globalised economy, investors have to be on their toes and take proactive decisions. They cannot be docile investors, either be active or be out of business. They should not take the market as a place for speculators and punters.

In civilized societies, the law and legal system are supposed to protect the interests of those who lend and not those who fail to repay.

To sum up, the capital market has been an important source of funding for larger companies and the opening of the economy to portfolio flows from Foreign Institutional Investors (FIIs). In recent years, it has produced a buoyant capital market where companies have raised significant funds through new issues. However, this mechanism has been used mainly by the larger companies to raise funds. There are no effective institutions that can channel equity funding to smaller companies and start-ups. In a knowledge economy, there is need to encourage the growth of venture capital funds and angel investors.

Endnotes

1. Book-building is a process by which demand for the securities proposed to be issued is built-up and the price for securities is assessed for determination of the quantum of such securities to be issued.
2. The World Bank in its survey of *Doing Business* has worked out an investor protection index, which measures the strength of minority shareholders against directors' misuse of corporate assets for his/ her personal gain. The index is the average of the disclosure index, director liability index, and shareholder suits index. The index ranges from 1 to 10, with higher values indicating better investor protection. Based on this index, India fares better than a large number of economies, including even some of the developed ones such as France and Germany.

12

Legal Framework for Capital Market in India

12.1 Securities and Exchange Board of India (SEBI) Act, 1992

The Securities and Exchange Board of India (SEBI) was constituted on April 12, 1988 as a non-statutory body through an Administrative Resolution of the Government for dealing with all matters relating to development and regulation of the securities market and investor protection and to advise the government on all these matters. SEBI was given statutory status and powers through an Ordinance promulgated on January 30, 1992. SEBI was established as a statutory body on February 21, 1992. The Ordinance was replaced by Securities and Exchange Board of India Act, 1992 on April 4, 1992.

In 1992, the Capital Issues (Control) Act, 1947 was repealed and the office of the Controller of Capital Issues (CCIs) was abolished. With this ended all controls related to raising of funds from the market. The move was aimed at enhancing the efficiency, safety, integrity and transparency of the market. Presently, issuers of capital are required to meet the guidelines of SEBI on disclosures and protection of investors.

In short, though SEBI was originally set up in 1988, it did not have any legal status to control securities market transactions. Legal Status was granted to SEBI in 1992 to help it curb malpractices in securities market like rigging of stock prices, insider trading, pricing of new issues without any basis, etc.

12.1.1 Objectives of SEBI: SEBI has emerged as an autonomous and independent statutory body. Its legally mandated objectives are the following:

1. Development of the securities market.
2. Regulation of the securities market activities.
3. Protection of the interests of investors in securities.
4. Prevention of malpractices.
5. Code of conduct for intermediaries.
6. Matters connected therewith and incidental thereto.

SEBI prohibits fraudulent and unfair trade practices, including insider trading. It also regulates substantial acquisition of shares and takeovers. In order to ensure protection of investors and to safeguard the integrity of the markets, there is a comprehensive surveillance system. Stock exchanges are the primary targets for detection of market manipulation, price rigging and other regulatory breaches regarding capital market functioning.

12.1.2 Functions of SEBI: SEBI performs the following functions:

A. Protective Functions:

1. Preventing price rigging.
2. Curbing insider trading.
3. Checking fraudulent and unfair trade practices.
4. Developing and monitoring investor grievance redressal mechanism.

5. Initiating punitive action against erring entities.

B. Developmental Functions:

1. Certification for intermediaries.
2. Technology adoption for faster business.
3. Investment products.

C. Regulatory Functions:

1. Registration of intermediaries.
2. Framing rules for intermediary operations.
3. Regulation of mutual funds.

12.1.3 Powers of SEBI: SEBI regulates and supervises the securities market through its various regulations, guidelines and schemes issued from time-to-time.

Powers and functions of SEBI—as the securities market regulator—have been laid down in the SEBI Act, 1992. SEBI also exercises powers under the Securities Contracts (Regulation) Act, 1956, the Depositories Act, 1996 and certain provisions of the Companies Act, 1956. It regulates the securities markets, securities market institutions and market intermediaries such as the stock exchanges, depositories, mutual funds and other asset management companies, securities dealers and brokers, merchant bankers, credit rating agencies and venture capital funds.

The statutory powers and functions of SEBI were strengthened through the promulgation of the Securities Laws (Amendment) Ordinance on January 25, 1995, which was subsequently replaced by an Act of Parliament.

The SEBI is equipped with the following powers:

1. Powers to register and regulate, inspect, enquire and investigate and undertake audits, and to cancel registration (though in this last case this applies to the mutual fund rather than the AMC); also to prohibit issue of an offer document including prospectus or advertisement.
2. Powers to summon and enforce attendance and examine on oath, inspect registers and documents, discover and enforce disclosure of books of account and other documents.
3. Powers to restrain from business, suspend, search, impound and retain proceeds, access bank data and attach bank accounts, prevent alienation of assets and issue cease and desist orders.
4. Powers to require compensation to be paid to investors.

SEBI has the power to impose penalties for violation of the Act and Regulations made under the Act. The Act empowers SEBI to investigate, adjudicate, hold enquiry and prosecute. There are also general powers to pass directions against listed companies in the interest of investors or the orderly development of securities market.

SEBI has around 650 staff and regional offices in five cities, viz. Mumbai, New Delhi, Chennai, Kolkata and Ahmedabad.

The experience of SEBI during episodes of market misconduct revealed many limitations in the legal provisions of the SEBI Act. In addition, the growing importance of the securities markets in the economy has placed new demands upon SEBI. On

October 28, 2002, an ordinance was promulgated which sought to strengthen SEBI. This ordinance involved organisational strengthening of SEBI, giving SEBI more powers for investigations and penalties, and making clearer concepts like insider trading and market manipulations.

The regulatory ambit has been widened in tune with the emerging needs and developments in the equity markets. Apart from stock exchanges, various intermediaries such as mutual funds, stock brokers and sub-brokers, merchant bankers, portfolio managers, registrars to an issue, share transfer agents, underwriters, debentures trustees, bankers to an issue, custodian of securities, venture capital funds and issuers have been brought under the SEBI's regulatory purview.

12.1.4 Model Listing Agreement: Listing agreement is an agreement entered between a stock exchange and the company seeking listing of securities on the exchange. It contains various requirements and disclosure obligations that companies must follow to remain as listed entities.

The Model Listing Agreement has been stipulated by SEBI and is reviewed and amended by SEBI from time-to-time.

Clause 49 of the Listing Agreement of SEBI requires the companies, who are listed, to comply with certain provisions relating to board of directors, audit committee, subsidiary companies, disclosures, report on corporate governance and compliance.

Stock exchanges are primarily responsible for ensuring compliance of various requirements under Listing Agreement.

Securities Contracts (Regulation) Act (SCRA), 1956 stipulates penalties up to ₹ 25 crore for non-compliance of listing conditions pursuant to adjudication by an adjudicating officer appointed by SEBI.

12.1.5 Appeals against SEBI Judgements: Those who appeal against SEBI judgements are heard by the Securities Appellate Tribunal (SAT) and can also go to the Supreme Court if they do not accept the Tribunal's judgement. The SAT has three members, one of whom is required to be the presiding officer who is a sitting or retired judge of the Supreme Court or High Court. The two other members must be of ability, integrity and standing with experience of corporate law, securities law, finance, economics or accountancy.

12.1.6 Merger of Forward Markets Commission with SEBI: Forward Markets Commission for the purpose of regulating commodity futures market was merged with SEBI in September 2015.

12.2 Securities Contracts (Regulation) Act (SCRA), 1956

SCRA regulates transactions in securities. The Act deals with recognition of stock exchanges by Central Government (whose powers in this case are delegated to SEBI), powers to suspend the business of stock exchange or supersede its governing board. It provides for regulation of contracts and options in securities. There are also provisions relating to listing of securities and right to appeal to Securities Appellate Tribunal in case of refusal by exchange to list securities of listed companies. Under the Act, there are provisions for adjudication proceedings to be conducted by adjudicating officer appointed by SEBI and imposition of monetary penalties for various violations. SEBI also has powers to issue directions against entities such as stock exchanges, listed companies etc. There are also provisions for initiation of prosecution proceedings under the Act.

Central Government has also issued Securities Contracts (Regulation) Rules, 1957 which, *inter alia*, contain qualifications for persons to be members of stock exchange, books of accounts to be maintained by members, listing conditions etc.

Stock exchanges in India are regulated and controlled by the Securities Contracts (Regulation) Act, 1956. The objects clause describes the Act as "An Act to prevent undesirable transactions in securities by regulating the business of dealing therein, by providing for certain other matters connected therewith".

12.2.1 Meaning of Securities and Government Securities: Under Section 2 of the Securities Contracts (Regulation) Act, 1956, securities include the following:

1. Shares, scrips, stocks, bonds, debentures, debenture stocks, or other marketable securities of a like nature in or of any incorporated company or other body corporate.
2. Government securities.
3. Such other instruments as may be declared by the Central Govt. to be securities.
4. Rights or interests in securities.

Government Securities mean securities created and issued—whether before or after the commencement of the Securities Contracts (Regulations) Act, 1956—by the Central Government or a State Government for the purpose of raising a public loan and having one of the forms specified in Section 2(2) of the Public Debt Act, 1944 (since replaced by the Government Securities Act, 2006).

12.2.2 Meaning and Recognition of Stock Exchange: According to the Act, stock exchange means any body of individuals, whether incorporated or not, constituted for the purpose of assisting, regulating or controlling the business of buying, selling or dealing in securities. Any stock exchange, which is desirous of being recognised for the purposes of this Act may make an application in the prescribed manner to the Government (Section 3). The Central Government may grant recognition to a stock exchange if it is satisfied, after making such inquiry as may be necessary in this behalf and after obtaining such further information, if any, as it may require (Section 4).

If the Central Government is of the opinion that the recognition granted to a stock exchange under the provisions of this Act should, in the interest of the trade or in the public interest, be withdrawn, the Central Government may serve on the governing body of the stock exchange a written notice that the Central Government is considering the withdrawal of the recognition for the reasons stated in the notice and after giving an opportunity to the governing body to be heard in the matter, the Central Government may withdraw, by notification in the Official Gazette, the recognition granted to the stock exchange (Section 5).

12.2.3 Amendment of Securities Contract Regulation Act (SCRA): In pursuance of the recommendations of the L.C. Gupta Committee, SCRA was amended in December 1999 to include derivatives within the ambit of *securities* and the regulatory framework was developed for governing derivatives trading. The Act also made it clear that derivatives shall be legal and valid only if such contracts are traded on a recognised stock exchange, thus precluding OTC derivatives. The government also rescinded in March 2000, the three-decade old notification, which prohibited forward trading in securities.

Derivatives trading commenced in India in June 2000 after SEBI granted the final approval to this effect in May 2000. SEBI permitted the derivatives segments of two stock exchanges NSE and BSE, and their clearing house/corporation to commence trading and settlement in approved derivative contracts. To begin with, SEBI approved trading in index future contracts based on S&P CNX Nifty and BSE-30 (Sensex) index. This was followed by approval for trading in options which commenced in June 2001 and the trading in options on individual securities commenced in July 2001. Future contracts on individual stocks were launched in November 2001. Trading and settlement in derivative contracts is done in accordance with the rules, by-laws, and regulations of the respective exchanges and their clearing house/corporation duly approved by SEBI and notified in the official gazette.

12.3 Depositories Act, 1996 and Depositories and Participants Regulations, 2018

Depository Act, 1996 provides for regulation of depositories in securities markets. The Act, *inter alia*, deals with rights and obligations of depositories, depository participants, issuers and beneficial owners. A depository needs certificate from SEBI for commencement of business. Under the Act, SEBI has got powers to call for information and enquiry, give directions, levy penalties and adjudicate. Presently there are two depositories, viz. National Securities Depository Ltd. and Central Depository Securities Ltd.

12.3.1 Depositories Act, 1996:

A. Objectives of the Act: The Act provides for the establishment of depositories in securities with the objective of ensuring free transferability of securities with speed, accuracy and security in the following manner:

1. Making securities of public limited companies freely transferable subject to certain exceptions.
2. Dematerialising the securities in the depository mode.
3. Providing for maintenance of ownership records in a book entry form.

In order to streamline the settlement process, the Act envisages the transfer of ownership of securities electronically by book entry without making the securities move from person to person. The Act has made the securities of all public limited companies freely transferable, restricting the company's right to use discretion in effecting the transfer of securities, and the transfer deed and other procedural requirements under the Companies Act have been dispensed with.

B. Benefits to Investors: These are as under:

1. **Speedy Transfer of Shares:** With the development of National Stock Exchange and the linking up of regional stock exchanges across the country purchase and sale of securities can be conveniently conducted between persons situated far away from each other.
2. **Avoidance of Trading Risks:** Depository system take care of large number of risks

involved in traditional trading involving physical transfer of shares.

3. **Dematerialisation and Rematerialisation:** An investor holding share certificate can get it converted into electronic holding. Again if at some future date the investor wants to convert his electronic holding into share certificate, he is allowed such conversion which is called rematerialisation.
4. **Indemnification of Certain Losses:** Interest of owner of securities under depository mode is protected as the depository takes the responsibility of indemnifying owner for any loss caused due to negligence of the depository or depository participants.
5. **Low Brokerage Cost:** Brokerage cost in the case of dematerialisation is much lower than the cost as regards physical transfer of shares.

C. Right and Obligations of Depositories, Participants, Issuers and Beneficial Owners: These are as follows:

1. Agreement between Depository and Participants: A depository shall enter into an agreement with participant as its agent.
2. Services of Depository: Any person, through a participant, may enter into an agreement, in such form as may be specified by the bye-laws, with any depository for availing its services.
3. Registration of Transfer of Services with Depository: Every depository shall, on receipt of intimate from a participant, registrar the transfer of security in the name of the transferee. If a beneficial owner or a transferee of any security seeks to have custody of such security, the depository shall inform the issuer accordingly.
4. Options to Receive Security Certificate or Hold Securities with Depository: Every person subscribing to securities offered by an issuer shall have the option either to receive the security certificates or hold securities with a depository. Where a person opts to hold a security with a depository, the issuer shall intimate such depository the details of allotment of the security, and on receipt of such information the depository shall enter in its records the name of the allottee as the beneficial owner of that security.
5. Securities in Depositories to be in Fungible Form: All securities held by a depository shall be dematerialized and shall be in a fungible form.
6. Rights of Depositories and Beneficial Owner: Notwithstanding anything contained in any other law for the time being in force, a depository shall be deemed to be the registered owner for the purposes of effecting transfer of ownership of security on behalf of a beneficial owner. The depository as a registered owner shall not have any voting rights or any other rights in respect of securities held by it. The beneficial owner shall be entitled to all rights and benefits and be subjected to all the liabilities in respect of his securities held by a depository.

D. Other Provisions of the Act: These are as under:

1. A stock broker, in his dealings with the clients and the general investing public, must faithfully execute the orders for buying and selling of securities at the best available market price and not refuse to deal with a small investor merely on the ground of the volume of business involved.
2. A stock broker has to issue, without delay to his client, a contract note for all

transactions in the specified form.

3. A stock broker must not disclose or discuss with any other person information of a confidential nature of the client which he comes to know in this business relationship.
4. A stock broker must not encourage sales or purchase of securities with the objective of generating brokerage or commission.
5. A stock broker should not deal or transact business knowingly, directly or indirectly, or execute an order for a client who has failed to carry out his commitments in relation to securities with another stock broker.
6. A stock broker who deals with a client must disclose whether he is acting as a principal or as an agent. He must ensure at the same time that no conflict of interest arises between him and the client.
7. A stock broker should have adequate trained staff and arrangements to render fair, prompt and competent services to the clients.

12.3.2 Securities and Exchange Board of India (Depositories and Participants) Regulations, 2018: SEBI notified the Securities and Exchange Board of India (Depositories and Participants) Regulations, 2018 on October 3, 2018 which gained immediate effect. The Securities and Exchange Board of India (Depositories and Participants) Regulations, 1996 (Old Regulation) stood repealed upon commencement of the new regulations.

A. Highlights of the New Regulation: These are as under:

1. Depositories to declare specific type of securities eligible for dematerialization.
2. Issuers to enter into agreements with depositories to enable the investors to dematerialize securities held by them.
3. There shall be continuous communication between the depositories, participants, issuers, issuers' agents.
4. A mechanism to be developed by depositories for protection of interest of the investors.
5. The interests of the beneficial owners against risks are to be protected by the depositories by applying adequate measures or through insurance.
6. There shall be co-operation between the depositories and the beneficial owners, issuers, issuer's agent, custodians of securities, clearing organizations for having an effective, prompt and accurate clearance and settlement of securities.
7. Participants to execute an agreement with beneficial owners as per the specified manner by the depositories before acting as a participant on his behalf.
8. Every beneficial owner is entitled to have statement of accounts from the participants as per the specified format as may be agreed between them.
9. Participants to submit periodic returns to the SEBI and their respective depositories as per the format specified by SEBI.
10. Participants to ensure safety and security of records and data submitted to them by the investors, issuers etc.
11. Issuers whose securities are eligible for dematerialization to have agreements with the depositories.

12. Depositories to establish an Investor Protection Fund.
13. The procedure of dematerialization of eligible securities has been established under the New Regulation.
14. Issuers or its agents to reconcile the records of dematerialized shares.
15. SEBI has the power to appoint an auditor to inspect or investigate, into the books of account, records, documents, infrastructures, systems and procedures or affairs of a depository, a participant, a beneficial owner, an issuer or its agent.
16. SEBI has the absolute authority to take any action against any issuer or its agent, whoever contravenes any provisions of the New Regulation.

12.4 Companies Act, 2013: Main Provisions

The Companies Act, 1956 was in need of a substantial revamp for quite some time, to make it more contemporary and relevant to corporates, regulators and other stakeholders in India. Therefore, it was replaced by Companies Act, 2013.

12.4.1 Types of Companies:

1. **One-person Company:** The 2013 Act introduces a new type of entity to the existing list i.e. apart from forming a public or private limited company, the 2013 Act enables the formation of a new entity a 'one-person company' (OPC). An OPC means a company with only one person as its member [Section 3(1) of 2013 Act].
2. **Private Company:** The 2013 Act introduces a change in the definition for a private company, *inter alia*, the new requirement increases the limit of the number of members from 50 to 200 [Section 2(68) of 2013 Act].
3. **Small Company:** A small company has been defined as a company, other than a public company.

- Paid-up share capital of which does not exceed ₹ 50 lakh or such higher amount as may be prescribed which shall not be more than ₹ 5 crore.
- Turnover of which as per its last profit-and-loss account does not exceed ₹ 2 crore or such higher amount as may be prescribed which shall not be more than ₹ 20 crore:

As set out in the 2013 Act, this section will not be applicable to the following: (a) a holding company or a subsidiary company, (b) a company registered under section 8 and (c) a company or body corporate governed by any special Act [Section 2(85) of 2013 Act].

4. **Dormant Company:** The 2013 Act states that a company can be classified as dormant when it is formed and registered under this 2013 Act for a future project or to hold an asset or intellectual property and has no significant accounting transaction. Such a company or an inactive one may apply to the ROC in such manner as may be prescribed for obtaining the status of a dormant company [Section 455 of 2013 Act].

12.4.2 Mergers and Acquisitions: The 2013 Act features some new provisions in the area of mergers and acquisitions, apart from making certain changes from the existing provisions. While the changes are aimed at simplifying and rationalising the procedures involved, the new provisions are also aimed at ensuring higher accountability for the company and majority shareholders and increasing flexibility for corporates. The

2013 Act has streamlined as well as introduced concepts such as reverse mergers (merger of foreign companies with Indian companies) and squeeze-out provisions, which are significant. The 2013 Act has also introduced the requirement for valuations in several cases, including mergers and acquisitions, by registered valuers.

12.4.3 Prohibition of Association or Partnership of Persons Exceeding Certain Number: The 2013 Act puts a restriction on the number of partners that can be admitted to a partnership at 100. To be specific, the 2013 Act states that no association or partnership consisting of more than the given number of persons as may be prescribed shall be formed for the purpose of carrying on any business that has for its object the acquisition of gain by the association or partnership or by the individual members thereof, unless it is registered as a company under this 1956 Act or is formed under any other law for the time being in force.

As an exception, the aforesaid restriction would not apply to the following: (a) A Hindu undivided family carrying on any business and (b) an association or partnership, if it is formed by professionals who are governed by special acts like the Chartered Accountants Act etc. [Section 464 of 2013 Act].

12.4.4 Insider Trading and Prohibition on Forward Dealings: The 2013 Act for the first time defines insider trading and price-sensitive information and prohibits any person including the director or key managerial person from entering into insider trading [Section 195 of 2013 Act]. Further, the Act also prohibits directors and key managerial personnel from forward dealings in the company or its holding, subsidiary or associate company [Section 194 of 2013 Act].

12.4.5 Corporate Governance: The 2013 Act intends to improve corporate governance by requiring disclosure of nature of concern or interest of every director, manager, any other key managerial personnel and relatives of such a director, manager or any other key managerial personnel and reduction in threshold of disclosure from 20 percent to 2 percent. The term 'key managerial personnel' has now been defined in the 2013 Act and means the chief executive officer, managing director, manager, company secretary, whole-time director, chief financial officer and any such other officer as may be prescribed.

12.4.6 Accounts and Audit: The 2013 Act has introduced certain significant amendments in this chapter. It has also introduced several additional requirements such as preparation of consolidated financial statements, additional reporting requirements for the directors in their report such as the development and implementation of the risk management policy, disclosures in respect of voting rights not exercised directly by the employees in respect of shares to which the scheme relates, etc., in comparison with the requirements of the 1956 Act.

The 2013 Act features extensive changes within the area of audit and auditors with a view to enhance audit effectiveness and accountability of the auditors. These changes undoubtedly, have a considerable impact on the audit profession. However, it needs to be noted that these changes will also have a considerable impact on the company in terms of time, efforts and expectations involved. Apart from introducing new concepts such as rotation of audit firms and class action suits, the 2013 Act also increases the auditor's liability substantially in comparison with the 1956 Act.

Unlike the appointment process at each annual general meeting under the 1956 Act, the auditor will now be appointed for a period of 5 years, with a requirement to ratify such an appointment at each annual general meeting [Section 139(1) of 2013 Act].

12.4.7 Dividend: The 2013 Act proposes to introduce significant changes to the existing provisions of the 1956 Act in respect of declaration of dividend. The changes are likely to affect the existing practices followed by companies with regard to the declaration of dividend.

The existing provisions of the 1956 Act in relation to the transfer of a specified percentage of profit to reserve is no longer applicable and thus, companies will be free to transfer any or no amount to its reserves.

12.4.8 Revival and Rehabilitation of Sick Companies: Chapter XIX of the 2013 Act lays down the provisions for the revival and rehabilitation of sick companies. The chapter describes the circumstances which determine the declaration of a company as a sick company, and also includes the rehabilitation process of the same. Although it aims to provide comprehensive provisions for the revival and rehabilitation of sick companies, the fact that several provisions such as particulars, documents as well as content of the draft scheme in respect of application for revival and rehabilitation, etc. have been left to substantive enactment, leaves scope for interpretation.

The coverage of this chapter is no longer restricted to industrial companies, and the determination of the net worth would not be relevant for assessing whether a company is a sick company.

12.4.9 Corporate Social Responsibility: The 2013 Act makes an effort to introduce the culture of corporate social responsibility (CSR) in Indian corporates by requiring companies to formulate a corporate social responsibility policy and at least incur a given minimum expenditure on social activities.

12.5 Limited Liability Partnership (LLP) Act, 2008

LLP Act, 2008 provides for a flexible governance structure to be determined by the partners themselves by mutual agreement, easy compliance requirements in comparison to companies, combined with limitation of liability to the extent of the partner's contribution.

The salient features of the LLP Act, 2008 are as under:

1. LLP shall be a body corporate and a legal entity separate from its partners. It will have perpetual succession. Indian Partnership Act, 1932 shall not be applicable to LLPs, since LLP shall be in the form of a body corporate.
2. An LLP has to be incorporated with a minimum of two persons. The Act does not restrict the benefit of LLP structure to certain classes of professionals only and would be available for use by any enterprise which fulfils the requirements of the Act.
3. The LLP will be an alternative corporate business vehicle that would give the benefits of limited liability but would allow its members the flexibility of organizing their internal structure as a partnership based on an agreement.

4. On registration, LLP shall be capable of: (a) suing and being sued and (b) acquiring, owning, holding and developing or disposing off property.
5. A person may cease to be a partner of a LLP in accordance with an agreement with the other partners or in absence of agreement with the other partners, by giving a notice in writing of not less than 30 days of his intention to resign as partner.
6. In the event of an act carried out by a LLP, or any of its partners, with intend to defraud creditors of the LLP or any other person or for any fraudulent purpose, the liability of the LLP and partners, who acted with intend to defraud creditors or for any fraudulent purpose shall be unlimited for all or any of the debts or other liabilities of the LLP.
7. A contribution of a partner may consist of tangible, movable or immovable or intangible property or other benefits to the LLP including money, promissory notes, other agreements to contribute cash or property, and contracts for services performed or to be performed.
8. While the LLP will be a separate legal entity, liable to the full extent of its assets, the liability of the partners would be limited to their agreed contribution in the LLP. Further, no partner would be liable on account of the independent or unauthorized actions of other partners, thus allowing individual partners to be shielded from joint liability created by another partner's wrongful business decisions or misconduct.
9. An LLP shall be under obligation to maintain annual accounts reflecting true and fair view of its state of affairs.
10. Provisions have been made in the Act for corporate actions like mergers, amalgamations etc.
11. There is a provision of voluntary winding up as well as winding up by the Tribunal.
12. There are provisions for inter conversion of LLP into private company etc.

The LLP Act should pave the way for greater corporatisation of the small and medium enterprises, thereby enhancing their access to equity and funds from the market.

12.6 Insolvency and Bankruptcy Code (IBC), 2016

There can be many reasons why an enterprise needs to close down—voluntary or forced by circumstances. The ease of closing down business is crucial for a good entrepreneurship ecosystem.

12.6.1 Need for Entrepreneur-friendly Bankruptcy Laws: With globalisation and competition, the possibility of a large number of manufacturing enterprises not getting business, and having to close, has to be particularly catered to. The experimental character of entrepreneurship and the risks involved need to be understood so that an entrepreneur gets another chance in which he/she may do better. The business environment can be strengthened by reducing the bankruptcy stigma and facilitating re-starts. Unfortunately, a great deal of emphasis is placed on stigmatizing failure. The underlying message is that if an entrepreneur has failed once, he would not be given a second chance. A policy change is needed here. Unless there has been wilful default, surreptitious draining of resources etc., a failed entrepreneur may have actually learnt from his mistakes and become a good investment bet.

At a broader level, the bankruptcy laws should be designed to help viable companies in distress, and make closing and re-starting easier. Enterprises need insolvency procedures which recognise that viable businesses can suffer from temporary problems, e.g. an economy-wide recession. Such procedures should facilitate the necessary internal reorganisation and restructuring of debt. A key objective of the bankruptcy laws should be to help viable companies survive while safeguarding the interests of the creditors. This requires being able to distinguish quickly and at low cost between firms to restructure and firms to close.

The policies and institutions of an economy should provide adequate freedom to every person to enable him to pursue his economic interests meaningfully. Inclusive economies provide such freedom to pursue vocation, create a level playing field for good ideas to replace obsolete ones, and encourage scarce resources to pursue the most productive avenues. Such economies unleash and realize full potential of every person and thereby develop faster.

Business plans entail informed risk taking to compete and succeed. Either incumbents are displaced by new businesses or new businesses fail to carve out a competitive space for themselves. Either way, failure of some businesses is integral to a market economy. When a business fails, it needs to be resolved at the earliest and expeditiously. Any undue delay in commencement or conclusion of resolution may lead to exodus of key stakeholders and aggravate the failure, sometimes beyond repair. If the resolution is not possible, an orderly exit mechanism should allow stakeholders to recover their dues from liquidation proceeds of the business and free-up resources for reallocation.

In many countries reforms have taken place that allow insolvency of businesses to be dealt with in a comprehensive manner that enables revival or rescue before liquidation and winding up. Insolvency is treated as a commercial phenomenon requiring to be dealt with in accordance with commercial principles in a framework of fairness and equity. There is an independent institutionalized process of providing a grace period for businesses to deal with distress. This is intended to enable a revival plan if the business is inherently viable, puts all creditors on hold pending revival, gets business out of holding period if it revives or takes action on winding up if the business is non-revivable. Both personal as well as business insolvency are dealt with on the basis of similar principles with ease of filing for bankruptcy and securing of certain protection from creditor action once this is done.

12.6.2 Situation Prior to IBC, 2016: Unlike limited liability entities, where the liability of the shareholder is limited to the extent of the contribution made or due from him, in proprietorships or partnerships there is no separation of personal and business liability. When a business fails, not only do the assets of the business but the entrepreneur's personal assets also get attached to pay off business dues. Further, all guarantors of the small entrepreneur get personally involved and in the eventuality of failure they also get implicated.

Prior to the implementation of IBC, 2016, insolvency of business entities was governed by a host of outdated legislations. The focus in these laws was not revival followed by structured exit in case of failure, but on recovery of outstanding dues through a court-driven process. The relevant courts under the statutes were district courts which took their own time adjudicating the petitions and were apt to enforce the processes of seizing debtor's estates, appointing receivers and punitive remedies against the debtor including imprisonment rather than enabling any revival or turnaround. Indeed adjudicatory order on an insolvency petition under these statutes laid the entrepreneur open to action including arrest and detention in a civil prison as if business failure was a criminal act.

The existing legal framework for insolvency and bankruptcy was spread across multiple statutes and was found to be inadequate resulting in undue delays in resolution and thus rendering it ineffective, at times. In an economy growing at a rapid pace not only the credit delivery mechanism but also the economic culture surrounding it needs to be as per best global practice. Thus there was need for an effective statutory framework to deal with insolvency and bankruptcy to facilitate development of credit markets in the country, encourage entrepreneurship, improving ease of doing business, facilitate investments, create more employment opportunities leading to higher economic growth and development.

A closure of an enterprise required, inter-alia, legal compliances related to labour laws, taxation laws, power utility, water utility, municipal body, creditors, financial institutions etc. Even when the laws were clear enough on the requirements to be fulfilled, the implementation of the same was problematic for micro, small and medium enterprise (MSMEs).

There was no mechanism that rescued failed firms or released resources from failed firms to alternate firms. The resources did not move seamlessly from less competitive firms to more competitive firms continuously. This deterred optimal utilization of resources and dampened entrepreneurship.

The promoters stayed in control of the company even after default. The creditors were ineffectual in recovering their dues.

There was, thus, a need to streamline the procedures, reduce discretion and intermediation.

12.6.3 Bankruptcy Law Reforms Committee (BLRC): BLRC (Chairman: T.K. Viswanathan) was set up on August 22, 2014 for providing an entrepreneur-friendly legal bankruptcy framework, as announced in the Budget Speech of the Finance Minister for the year 2014-15. BLRC submitted its Report and Draft Bill to the Finance Minister on November 4, 2015. Based on this, a Draft Bill, namely The Insolvency and Bankruptcy Code, 2015 was introduced in the Lok Sabha on December 21, 2015.

12.6.4 Insolvency and Bankruptcy Code (IBC), 2016: IBC, 2016 is the bankruptcy law of India which consolidated the existing framework by creating a single law for insolvency and bankruptcy.

IBC, 2016 is a one-stop solution for resolving insolvencies. A strong insolvency framework—where the cost and time incurred are minimal in attaining liquidation—was long overdue in India. IBC, 2016 is intended to protect the interests of small investors and make the process of doing business a less cumbersome process.

Insolvency and Bankruptcy Code, 2015 was introduced in the Lok Sabha on

December 21, 2015 by Finance Minister Shri Arun Jaitley. It was referred to a Joint Committee of Parliament on December 23, 2015, which recommended it on April 28, 2016. The Code was passed by the Lok Sabha on May 5, 2016 and by the Rajya Sabha on May 11, 2016.

The Code received assent from President Shri Pranab Mukherjee on May 28, 2016 and was notified in The Gazette of India on May 28, 2016. It became effective in December 2016.

It repealed the Presidency Towns Insolvency Act, 1909 and Sick Industrial Companies (Special Provisions) Repeal Act, 2003, among others.

A. Key Features: These are as under:

1. **Insolvency Resolution**: IBC, 2016 outlines separate insolvency resolution processes for individuals, companies and partnership firms. The process may be initiated by either the debtor or the creditors. A maximum time limit, for completion of the insolvency resolution process, has been set for corporates and individuals. For companies, the process will have to be completed in 180 days, which may be extended by 90 days, if a majority of the creditors agree. For start-ups (other than partnership firms), small companies and other companies (with asset less than ₹ 1 crore), resolution process would be completed within 90 days of initiation of request which may be extended by 45 days.
2. **Insolvency Regulator**: Insolvency and Bankruptcy Board of India (IBBI) has been established under IBC, 2016 to oversee the insolvency proceedings in the country and regulate the entities registered under it. IBBI will have 10 members, including representatives from the Ministries of Finance and Law, and the Reserve Bank of India.
3. **Insolvency Professionals**: The insolvency process will be managed by licensed professionals. These professionals will also control the assets of the debtor during the insolvency process.
4. **Bankruptcy and Insolvency Adjudicator**: IBC, 2016 proposes two separate tribunals to oversee the process of insolvency resolution, for individuals and companies: (a) National Company Law Tribunal for companies and limited liability partnership firms and (b) Debt Recovery Tribunal for individuals and partnerships.
5. **Procedure:** A plea for insolvency is submitted to the adjudicating authority (NCLT in case of corporate debtors) by financial or operation creditors or the corporate debtor itself. The maximum time allowed to either accept or reject the plea is 14 days. If the plea is accepted, the tribunal has to appoint an insolvency resolution professional (IRP) to draft a resolution plan within 180 days (extendable by 90 days), following which the corporate insolvency resolution process (CIRP) is initiated by the court. For the said period, the board of directors of the company stands suspended, and the promoters do not have a say in the management of the company. The IRP, if required, can seek the support of the company's management for day-to-day operations. If the CIRP fails in reviving the company the liquidation process is initiated.

12.6.5 Amendments: IBC, 2016 was amended in 2017 to prohibit certain persons from submitting a resolution plan in case of defaults, and to prohibit the sale of property of a defaulter to such persons during liquidation.

12.6.6 Insolvency and Bankruptcy Board of India (IBBI): IBBI was set up on October 1, 2016 under the Insolvency and Bankruptcy Code, 2016. It has regulatory oversight over the insolvency professionals, insolvency professional agencies and information utilities. It writes and enforces rules for transactions, namely corporate insolvency resolution, corporate liquidation, individual insolvency resolution and individual bankruptcy under IBC, 2016. It is a key pillar of the ecosystem responsible for implementation of IBC, 2016.

In short, IBC, 2016 consolidates and amends the laws relating to reorganization and insolvency resolution of corporate persons, partnership firms and individuals in a time bound manner for maximization of the value of assets of such persons, to promote entrepreneurship, availability of credit and balance the interests of all the stakeholders.

IBC, 2016 enables a firm to get in and get out of business with ease, keep striving for resurrection and new pursuits, undeterred by honest business failures. It reduces incidence of failure in two ways. First, the inevitable consequence of default in terms of insolvency proceedings prompts behavioural changes on the part of debtor to try hard to prevent business failure. Second, it reduces failure by setting in motion a process that rehabilitates failing but viable businesses. If rehabilitation is not possible, IBC, 2016 facilitates closure of businesses with the least cost and disruptions. It thus addresses business failures by reducing the chances of failure, rescuing failing businesses where possible and releasing resources from businesses, where rehabilitation is not possible and thereby promotes entrepreneurship. It improves availability of credit by: (a) preventing default, (b) recovering default from future earnings of the firm, post resolution and (c) recovering default from sale of liquidation assets.

It enables the optimum utilization of resources, all the time, either by: (a) preventing use of resources below the optimum potential, (b) ensuring efficient resource use within the firm through resolution of insolvency or (c) releasing unutilized or under-utilized resources for efficient uses through closure of the firm.

By liberating the resources stuck up in inefficient and defunct firms for continuous recycling, the IBC, 2016, has completed the circle of freedom to enter, started by economic reforms since 1991, with freedom to exit.

13

Modernisation of Stock Exchanges

13.1 Stock Market

A stock (or share) market deals mainly in corporate securities. The securities are chiefly in the form of equity shares and debentures. The purpose of these securities is to raise long-term funds for companies engaged in production. The function of the stock market is two-fold: (a) to arrange for the raising of new capital (primary market function), and (b) to provide liquidity to existing securities (secondary market function).

The new capital is raised by the issue of shares and debentures. The corporate enterprises raising new capital may be new companies or existing companies planning expansion of their operations. Sometimes, existing private firms go public, i.e. become public limited companies.

The stock market helps the floatation of new issues by providing a variety of services like underwriting, distribution, and listing of the issue. Underwriting means guaranteeing the purchase of a fixed amount of new issues by the underwriter. The new issues of capital may be a public issue or a rights issue or both in certain proportions. It may be in the form of equity shares or debentures. Debentures, in turn, may be fully convertible, partly convertible, or non-convertible into shares. A public issue implies that the general public is invited to subscribe to the new issue. A rights issue is restricted for subscription by existing shareholders.

Stock market provides facilities for secondary market, i.e. transaction in existing securities. People desirous of converting their cash into securities can go to the stock exchange and buy securities with the help of brokers there. Similarly, securities can be converted into cash by selling them in the market. Transactions in the secondary market reflect the investment climate in the economy. A well-developed stock market helps to access external capital which allows financially constrained domestic firms to expand. It is argued that countries with developed stock markets tend to grow faster.

A list of important stock exchanges in India is given in Table 13.1.

13.1.1 Limitations of Stock Market: It is argued that stock market expansion is not a necessary indication of a country's financial development and stock market development may not help in achieving quicker industrialisation and faster long-term economic growth because of following reasons:

1. Due to inherent volatility and arbitrariness of the stock market, the resulting pricing process is a poor guide to efficient investment allocation.
2. In the wake of unfavourable economic shocks, the interactions between the stock and currency markets may exacerbate macroeconomic instability and reduce long-term economic growth.
3. Stock market development is likely to undermine the financial inclusion role of

existing banking systems in developing countries like India.

Table 13.1: List of Important Stock Exchanges in India
(As on January 17, 2020)

S. No.	Name of the Stock Exchange	S. No.	Name of the Stock Exchange
1.	Bombay Stock Exchange (BSE) Ltd.	11.	Gauhati Stock Exchange*
2.	Calcutta Stock Exchange Ltd.	12.	Hyderabad Stock Exchange*
3.	Indian Commodity Exchange Ltd.	13.	Jaipur Stock Exchange*
4.	Multi Commodity Exchange of India Ltd.	14.	Ludhiana Stock Exchange*
5.	National Commodity and Derivatives Exchange Ltd.	15.	Madhya Pradesh Stock Exchange*
6.	National Stock Exchange (NSE) of India Ltd.	16.	Madras Stock Exchange*
7.	Ahmedabad Stock Exchange*	17.	OTC Exchange of India*
8.	Bangalore Stock Exchange*	18.	Pune Stock Exchange*
9.	Coimbatore Stock Exchange *	19.	Uttar Pradesh Stock Exchange*
10.	Delhi Stock Exchange*	20.	Vadodra Stock Exchange*

* These stock exchanges have been granted exit by SEBI vide different orders.

13.2 Trading Infrastructure in Stock Exchanges

There are 6 permanent stock exchanges in India (S. Nos. 1 to 6 in table above), including the old established Bombay Stock Exchange (BSE) and the National Stock Exchange (NSE) that was set up as a model exchange to provide nation-wide services to investors. The Bombay Stock Exchange (BSE) was set up in 1875 as 'The Native Share and Stock Brokers Association'.

Equity trading is most active in the two major competing stock exchanges, viz. NSE and the BSE. Trading infrastructure in the stock exchanges is anonymous and order-driven, with all orders from market participants being matched based on strike price/time priority.

The Indian capital market is significant in terms of its degree of development, its volume of trading and of the quality of its automated trading and settlement.

The capital markets—though they have suffered from periodic scandals and problems in the past—look much closer in quality to those of developed markets than those in the majority of emerging markets. The range and quality of available securities is evidenced by the substantial flows of foreign institutional investors.

13.3 Bombay Stock Exchange (BSE) Ltd.

BSE is a stock exchange located on Dalal Street, Mumbai. It was the 10th largest stock exchange in the world by market capitalisation as in September 2019.

Established in 1875, BSE Ltd. (formerly known as Bombay Stock Exchange Ltd.), is India's second oldest stock exchange (Oldest being the Calcutta Stock Exchange located at Lyons Range, Kolkata) and one of India's leading exchange groups.

In August 31, 1957, the BSE became the first stock exchange to be recognized by the Indian Government under the Securities Contracts Regulation Act. In 1980 the exchange moved to the Phiroze Jeejeebhoy Towers at Dalal Street, Fort area. In 1986 it developed the BSE SENSEX index, giving the BSE a means to measure overall performance of the exchange. In 2000, the BSE used this index to open its derivatives market, trading SENSEX futures contracts. The development of SENSEX options along with equity derivatives followed in 2001 and 2002, expanding the BSE's trading platform.

BSE has facilitated the growth of the Indian corporate sector by providing it an efficient capital-raising platform. BSE is a corporatized and demutualised entity, with a broad cardholder-base which includes two leading global exchanges, Deutsche Bourse, Fuse and Singapore Exchange as strategic partners. BSE provides an efficient and transparent market for trading in equity, debt instruments, derivatives, mutual funds. It also has a platform for trading in equities of small-and-medium enterprises (SMEs). More than 5,000 companies are listed on BSE making it world's top most exchange in terms of listed members.

BSE also provides a host of other services to capital market participants including risk management, clearing, settlement, market data services and education. It has a global reach with customers around the world and a nation-wide presence.

BSE systems and processes are designed to safeguard market integrity, drive the growth of the Indian capital market and stimulate innovation and competition across all market segments. BSE is the first exchange in India and second in the world to obtain an ISO 9001: 2000 certification. It is also the first exchange in the country and second in the world to receive Information Security Management System Standard BS 7799-2-2002 certification for its On-Line Trading System (BOLT).

It operates one of the most respected capital market educational institutes in the country (the BSE Institute Ltd.). BSE also provides depository services through its Central Depository Services Ltd. (CDSL) arm.

BSE's popular equity index—the S&P BSE SENSEX (formerly SENSEX)—is India's most widely tracked stock market benchmark index. It is traded internationally on the EUREX as well as leading exchanges of the BRCS nations (Brazil, Russia, China and South Africa). On February 19, 2013, BSE entered into Strategic Partnership with S&P DOW JONES INDICES and the SENSEX was renamed as S&P BSE SENSEX.

Historically an open outcry floor trading exchange, the BSE switched to an electronic trading system in 1995. This automated, screen-based trading platform is called BSE on-line trading (BOLT). The BSE has also introduced the world's first centralized exchange-based internet trading system, BSEWEBx.co.in to enable investors anywhere in the world to trade on the BSE platform.

13.4 National Stock Exchange (NSE) of India Ltd.

It is located in Mumbai, India. NSE was established in the mid-1990s as a demutualised electronic exchange. NSE provides a modern, fully automated screen-based trading system, with over two lakh trading terminals, through which investors in every nook and corner of India can trade. NSE has played a critical role in reforming the Indian securities market and in bringing unparalleled transparency, efficiency and market integrity.

Though a number of other exchanges exist, NSE and the Bombay Stock Exchange (BSE) are the two most significant stock exchanges in India, and between them are responsible for the vast majority of share transactions. NSE's flagship index, the CNX NIFTY 50, is used extensively by investors in India and around the world to take exposure to the Indian equities market.

NSE was started by a clutch of leading Indian financial institutions. It offers trading, clearing and settlement services in equity, debt and equity derivatives. It is India's largest exchange, globally in cash market trades, in currency trading and index options. NSE has diversified shareholding. There are many domestic and global institutions and companies that hold stake in the exchange.

NSC was incorporated in 1992 and recognised as a stock exchange in 1993, at a time when P.V. Narasimha Rao was the Prime Minister of India and Dr. Manmohan Singh was the Finance Minister. It was set up to bring in transparency in the markets. Promoted by leading financial institutions, essentially led by IDBI at the behest of the Government of India, it was incorporated in November 1992 as a tax-paying company. In April 1993, it was recognised as a stock exchange under the Securities Contracts (Regulation) Act, 1956. NSE commenced operations in the Wholesale Debt Market (WDM) segment in June 1994. The capital market (equities) segment of the NSE commenced operations in November 1994, while operations in the derivatives segment commenced in June 2000.

NSE changed the way the Indian markets functioned, in the early 1990s, by replacing floor-based trading with nationwide screen-based electronic trading, which took trading to the doorstep of the investor. The exchange was mainly set up to bring in transparency in the markets. Instead of trading membership being confined to a group of brokers, the NSE ensured that anyone who was qualified, experienced and met minimum financial requirements was allowed to trade.

In this context, the NSE was ahead of its times, when it separated ownership and management in the exchange under SEBI's supervision. The price information which could earlier be accessed only by a handful of people can now be seen by a client in a remote location with the same ease. The paper-based settlement has been replaced by electronic depository-based accounts and settlement of trades. A robust risk management system is in place, so that settlement guarantees could protect investors against broker defaults.

NSE was also instrumental in creating the National Securities Depository Limited (NSDL) which allows investors to securely hold and transfer their shares and bonds electronically. It also allows investors to hold and trade in as few as one share or bond. This not only makes holding financial instruments convenient, but more importantly eliminates the need for paper certificates and greatly reduces the incidents of forged or fake certificates and fraudulent transactions that had plagued the Indian stock market. NSDL's security, combined with the transparency, lower transaction prices and efficiency that the NSE offers, has greatly increased the attractiveness of the Indian stock market to domestic and international investors.

Currently, NSE has the following major segments of the capital market:

1. **Equities:** Equities, indices, mutual funds, exchange traded funds, initial public

offerings, and security lending and borrowing scheme.

2. **Derivatives:** Equity derivatives (including Global Indices like S&P 500, Dow Jones and FTSE), currency derivatives, and interest rate futures.
3. **Debt:** Corporate bonds.

13.4.1 Equity Derivatives: NSE commenced trading in derivatives with the launch of index futures on June 12, 2000. The futures and options segment of NSE has made a mark for itself globally. In the futures and options segment, trading in CNX Nifty Index, CNX IT Index, Bank Nifty Index, Nifty Midcap 50 index and single stock futures are available. Trading in Mini Nifty Futures and Options and Long-term Options on CNX Nifty are also available.

On August 29, 2011, NSE launched derivative contracts on the world's most followed equity indices, the S&P 500 and the Dow Jones Industrial Average. NSE is the first Indian exchange to launch global indices. This is also the first time in the world that futures contracts on the S&P 500 index were introduced and listed on an exchange outside of their home country, USA. The new contracts include futures on both the DJIA and the S&P 500, and options on the S&P 500.

On May 3, 2012, NSE launched derivative contracts (futures and options) on FTSE 100, the widely tracked index of the UK equity stock market. This was the first of its kind of an index of the UK equity stock market launched in India. FTSE 100 includes 100 largest UK listed blue chip companies.

On January 10, 2013, NSE signed a letter of intent with the Japan Exchange Group, Inc. (JPX) on preparing for the launch of CNX Nifty Index futures, a representative stock price index of India, on the Osaka Securities Exchange Co., Ltd. (OSE), a subsidiary of JPX. Moving forward, both parties will make preparations for the listing of yen-denominated CNX Nifty Index futures by March 2014. Retail and institutional investors in Japan will be able to take a view on the Indian markets in their own currency and in their own time zone. Investors will therefore not face any currency risk, because they will not have to invest in dollar denominated or rupee denominated contracts.

13.4.2 Currency Derivatives: In August 2008, currency derivatives were introduced in India by NSE with the launch of currency futures in US$ and INR. It also added currency futures in Euros, Pounds and Yen.

13.4.3 Interest Rate Futures: Interest rate futures were introduced for the first time in India by NSE on August 31, 2009, exactly one year after the launch of currency futures. NSE became the first stock exchange to get an approval for interest rate futures, as recommended by the SEBI-RBI committee.

13.4.4 Debt Market: On May 13, 2013, NSE launched India's first dedicated debt platform to provide a liquid and transparent trading platform for debt related products. The debt segment provides an opportunity to retail investors to invest in corporate bonds on a liquid and transparent exchange platform. It also helps institutions who are holders of corporate bonds. It is an ideal platform to buy and sell at optimum prices and help corporates to get adequate demand, when they are issuing the bonds.

13.4.5 Financial Literacy: Financial literacy is the possession of a set of skills and knowledge which allow an individual to make informed and effective decisions with all of his financial resources. Understanding basic financial concepts allows people to know how to navigate in the financial system.

A. Importance of Financial Literacy: People with appropriate financial literacy training make better financial decisions and manage money better that those without such training. Financial literacy focuses on the ability to manage personal finance matters in an efficient manner, and it includes the knowledge of making appropriate decisions about personal finance such as investing, insurance, real estate, budgeting, retirement and tax planning. Financial literacy also involves the proficiency of financial principles and concepts such as financial planning, compound interest, managing debt, profitable savings techniques and the time value of money.

The main steps to achieving financial literacy include learning the skills to create a budget, the ability to track spending, learning the techniques to pay off debt and effectively planning for retirement. These steps can also include counselling from a financial expert. Education about the topic involves understanding how money works, creating and achieving financial goals and managing internal and external financial challenges.

There are many advantages of financial literacy. Financial literacy helps individuals to become self-sufficient so that they can achieve financial stability. Those who understand the subject should be able to answer several questions about purchases, such as whether an item is required, whether it is affordable, and whether it an asset or a liability.

This skill can help a person develop a financial road map to identify what he earns, what he spends and what he owes. This topic also affects small business owners, who greatly contribute to economic growth and stability.

The lack of financial literacy can lead to owing large amounts of debt and making poor financial decisions. Similarly, financial illiteracy may lead to making poor financial choices that can have negative consequences on the financial well-being of an individual.

Financial illiteracy affects all ages and all socio-economic levels. Financial illiteracy causes many people to become victims of predatory lending, sub-prime mortgages, and fraud and high interest rates, potentially resulting in bad credit, bankruptcy or foreclosure.

B. Measures Taken for Financial Literacy: NSE is keen to ensure that the people of India are empowered to take sound financial decisions and invest wisely. It has collaborated, among others, with several universities like Gokhale Institute of Politics and Economics, Pune; Bharati Vidyapeeth Deemed University, Pune; Guru Gobind Singh Indraprastha University, Delhi; Ravenshaw University of Cuttack and Punjabi University, Patiala, to offer MBA and BBA courses. NSE has also provided mock market simulation software called NSE Learn to Trade (NLT) to develop investment, trading and portfolio management skills among the students. The simulation software is very similar to the software currently being used by the market professionals and helps students to learn how to trade in the markets.

The exchange has also worked with a missionary zeal to educate investors about the opportunities in the market, the precautions they should take and their rights and obligations. In order to educate investors and help them invest wisely, NSE conducts nearly 1,500 seminars every year in the metros as well as the smallest towns of India.

NSE also conducts online examination and awards certification, under its Certification in Financial Markets (NCFM) programmes. At present, certifications are available in 46 modules, covering different sectors of financial and capital markets, both at the beginner and advanced levels. The list of various modules can be found at the official site of NSE India. In addition, since August 2009, it offers a short-term course called NSE certified capital market professional (NCCMP). The NCCMP is a 100 hour programme for over 3-4 months, conducted at the colleges, and covers theoretical and practical training in subjects related to the capital markets. NCCMP covers subjects like equity markets, debt markets, derivatives, macroeconomics, technical analysis and fundamental analysis. Successful candidates are awarded joint certification from NSE and the concerned college.

The competition between NSE and BSE is a unique one by international standards, where both exchanges are in the same city and have the same trading hours. All major stocks trade on both exchanges, so the exchanges compete for order flow, and not just listings. The rise of NSE has proved to be a powerful spur to reforms at the BSE. Months after NSE started operations, the BSE also launched electronic trading, and improved rules governing admission of corporate and foreign brokerage firms. Presently, the BSE also uses an open electronic limit order book market, using satellite communications to reach locations outside Bombay.

Associated with the NSE are the National Securities Depositary Ltd. (NSDL) and the National Securities Clearing Corporation Ltd. (NSCCL). The NSDL acts as the registrar for what are now predominantly dematerialized securities and the NSCCL as a clearing house.

The setting up of the NSE as an electronic trading platform set a benchmark of operating efficiency for other stock exchanges in the country. The establishment of NSDL in 1996 and Central Depository Services (India) Ltd. (CSDL) in 1999 has enabled paperless trading in the exchanges. This has also facilitated instantaneous electronic transfer of securities and eliminated the risks to the investors arising from bad deliveries in the market, delays in share transfer, fake and forged shares and loss of scrips. The electronic funds transfer (EFT) facility combined with dematerialisation of shares has created a conducive environment for reducing the settlement cycle in stock markets.

13.5 Demutualisation and Corporatisation of Stock Exchanges

Stock exchanges all over the world were traditionally formed as *mutual* organisations. The trading members not only provided broking services, but also owned, controlled and managed such exchanges for their mutual benefit. Demutualisation refers to the transition process of an exchange from a *mutually-owned* association to a company *owned by shareholders*. In other words, transforming the legal structure of an exchange from a mutual form to a business corporation form is referred to as demutualisation. The above, in effect means that after demutualisation, the ownership, the management and the trading rights at the exchange are segregated from one another.

In a mutual exchange, the three functions of ownership, management and trading are intervened into a single group. Here, the broker members of the exchange are both the owners and the traders on the exchange and they further manage the exchange as well. A demutualised exchange, on the other hand, has all these three functions clearly segregated, i.e. the ownership, management and trading are in separate hands.

In India, NSE was set up as a demutualised corporate body, where ownership, management and trading rights are in the hands of three different sets of groups from its inception. The Stock Exchange, Mumbai—one of the two premier exchanges in the country—has since been corporatised and demutualised and renamed as the Bombay Stock Exchange Ltd. (BSE).

Corporate governance has emerged as an important tool for protection of shareholders. The corporate governance framework in India has evolved over a period of time since the setting up of the Kumar Mangalam Birla Committee by SEBI. India has a reasonably well-designed regulatory framework for the issuance and trading of securities, and disclosures by the issuers with strong focus on corporate governance standards.

To enhance the level of continuous disclosure by the listed companies, SEBI amended the listing agreement to incorporate segment reporting, related party disclosures, consolidated financial results and consolidated financial statements. The listing agreement between the stock exchanges and the companies has been strengthened from time to time to enhance corporate governance standards.

14

Depository System, Dematerialisation (Demat) and Rematerialisation (Remat)

14.1 Depository System

Shares are traditionally held in physical (paper) form. This method has weaknesses like loss/theft of certificates, forged/fake certificates, cumbersome and time consuming procedure for transfer of shares etc. To eliminate these weaknesses, a new system called depository system has been established. A depository is a system which holds shares of an investor in the form of electronic accounts in the same way a bank holds money of a depositor in a savings account.

A depository holds securities in dematerialised form. It maintains ownership records of securities in a book entry form and also effects transfer of ownership through book entry.

Depository system provides the following advantages to an investor:

1. Shares cannot be lost, stolen or mutilated.
2. An investor never needs to doubt the genuineness of his shares i.e. whether they are forged or fake.
3. Share transactions like transfer, transmission etc. can be effected immediately.
4. Transaction costs are usually lower than on the physical segment.
5. There is no risk of bad delivery.
6. Bonus/rights shares allotted to an investor will be immediately credited to his account.
7. An investor receives the statement of accounts of his transactions/holdings periodically.

While the investors have a right to hold securities in either physical or demat form, SEBI has introduced some degree of compulsion in trading and settlement of securities in Demat form. SEBI has mandated compulsory trading and settlement of securities in select securities in dematerialised form. This was initially introduced for institutional investors and was later extended to all investors.

14.2 Depositories Act, 1996 and Depositories and Participants Regulations, 2018

See section 12.3 of chapter 12 of this book.

14.3 Dematerialisation (Demat)

The concept of demat was introduced in Indian capital market in 1996 with the setting up of NSDL. Demat is the process by which the physical certificates of an investor are converted to an equivalent number of securities in electronic form and credited in the investor's account with his depository participant (DP).

When an investor decides to have his shares in electronic form, he should approach a depository participant (DP)—who is an agent of the depository—and open an account. He should then request for the dematerialisation of certificates by filling up a dematerialisation request form (DRF), which is available with the DP and submitting the same along with the physical certificates.

The investor has to ensure that before the certificates are handed over to the DP for demat, they are defaced by marking *Surrendered for Dematerialisation* on the face of the certificates. Before defacing the share certificate, the investor must ensure that it is available for dematerialisation. The investor must therefore check with his depository participant (DP) whether the ISIN (code number for the security in a depository system) has been activated and made available for dematerialisation by the depository. If yes, then the investor may deface the share certificate. Only those certificates can be dematerialised that are already registered in the investor's name and are in the list of securities admitted for dematerialization by National Securities Depository Limited (NSDL).

His DP will arrange to get them sent to and verified by the company, and on confirmation credit his account with an equivalent number of shares. This process is known as dematerialisation (demat). An investor can always reverse this process if he so desires and get his shares reconverted into paper format. This process is known as rematerialisation.

14.3.1 Benefits of Demat: These are the following:

1. Elimination of bad deliveries.
2. Elimination of all risks associated with physical certification.
3. No stamp duty.
4. Immediate transfer and registration of securities.
5. Faster settlement cycle.
6. Faster disbursement of rights, bonus etc.
7. Reduction in brokerage by many brokers for trading in dematerialised securities.
8. Reduction in handling of huge volumes of paper and postal delays.
9. Periodic status report.
10. Elimination of problems relating to change of address of investor, transmission etc.
11. Elimination of problems related to selling securities on behalf of a minor.
12. Ease in portfolio monitoring.

14.4 Rematerialisation (Remat)

If the investor wishes to get back his securities in physical form, all he has to do is to request his DP for rematerialisation of the same. Rematerialisation is the term used for converting electronic holdings back into certificates. An investor's DP will forward his request to NSDL, after verifying that he has the necessary balance. NSDL in turn will intimate the registrar who will print the certificates and dispatch the same to the investor.

14.5 National Securities Depository Ltd. (NSDL)

It was created in 1995. Based in Mumbai, it was the first central securities depository in India. Promoted by institutions of national stature responsible for the economic development of India, it has established a national infrastructure of international standards that handles most of the securities held and settled in dematerialised form in the Indian capital market.

Although India had a vibrant capital market which is more than a century old, the paper-based settlement of trades caused substantial problems such as bad delivery and delayed transfer of title. The enactment of Depositories Act in August 1996 paved the way for establishment of NSDL, the first depository in India. It went on to establish infrastructure based on international standards.

NSDL has the objective of ensuring the safety and soundness of Indian marketplaces by developing settlement solutions that increase efficiency, minimise risk and reduce costs. NSDL plays a quiet but central role in developing products and services that will continue to nurture the growing needs of the financial services industry.

In the depository system, securities are held in depository accounts, which are similar to holding funds in bank accounts. Transfer of ownership of securities is done through simple account transfers. This method does away with all the risks and hassles normally associated with paperwork. Consequently, the cost of transacting in a depository environment is considerably lower as compared to transacting in certificates.

NSDL is promoted by Industrial Development Bank of India Limited (IDBI)—the largest development bank of India, Unit Trust of India (UTI)—the largest mutual fund in India and National Stock Exchange of India Limited (NSE)—the largest stock exchange in India. Some of the prominent banks in the country have taken a stake in NSDL.

14.6 National Securities Clearing Corporation Ltd. (NSCCL)

NSCCL, a wholly-owned subsidiary of NSE, was incorporated in August 1995 and commenced operating as a clearing corporation in April 1996. Clearing and settlement operations of the NSE are managed by NSCCL. It was the first clearing corporation to provide novation/settlement guarantee that revolutionised the entire concept of settlement system in India. It was set up to: (a) bring and sustain confidence in clearing and settlement of securities, (b) promote and maintain short and consistent settlement cycles, (c) provide counterparty risk guarantee, and (d) operate a tight risk containment system.

The settlements of trade in the equities market (both cash and derivative segments) are settled in the BSE by clearing house called BOISL which is a company jointly promoted by BSE (49 percent) and Bank of India (51 percent). BOISL, *inter alia*, handles some of the settlement-related activities of BSE as per instructions and directions of BSE. Responsibility of the clearing house is to handle such settlement activities including co-ordination with the market participants, viz. depositories, clearing banks etc.

However, the overall responsibility of settlement and risk management functions, viz. collection of margins, collateral management etc. pertaining to transactions done on BSE Online Trading (BOLT) System lies with the BSE.

NSCCL undertakes clearing of transactions executed on the National Stock Exchange for Automated Trading (NEAT) system of NSE. It carries out clearing and settlement functions as per the settlement cycles of different sub-segments in the equities segment. The reforms in the securities settlement systems have resulted in following benefits:

1. Reduction and mitigation of systemic, structural and operational risks.
2. Increase speed of transaction, execution and settlement of trade and quicker settlement of transactions with finality.
3. Safety of the settlement process.
4. Reduction of transaction costs and, thereby, making market more efficient and transparent for investors and participants.

To sum up, the improvement in clearing and settlement system has brought a substantial reduction in transaction costs. Several measures were also undertaken to enhance the safety and integrity of the market. These include capital requirements, trading and exposure limits, daily margins comprising mark-to-market margins and VaR based margins. Trade/settlement guarantee fund has also been set up to ensure smooth settlement of transactions in case of default by any member. Another important development of the reform process was the opening up of mutual funds industry to the private sector in 1992, which earlier was the monopoly of the Unit Trust of India (UTI) and mutual funds set up by public sector financial institutions.

Since 1992, foreign institutional investors (FIIs) are permitted to invest in all types of securities, including corporate debt and government securities in stages and subject to limits. Further, the Indian corporate sector was allowed to access international capital markets through American depository receipts (ADRs), global depository receipts (GDRs), foreign currency convertible bonds (FCCBs) and external commercial borrowings (ECBs). Eligible foreign companies have been permitted to raise money from domestic capital markets through issue of Indian depository receipts (IDRs).

Regulations governing substantial acquisition of shares and takeovers of companies have also been put in place. These are aimed at making the takeover process more transparent and to protect the interests of minority shareholders.

To sustain confidence in clearing and settlement of securities, NSE set up the National Securities Clearing Corporation Ltd. (NSCCL) in August, 1995 which carries out the clearing and settlement of the trades executed in the equities and derivatives segments and operates the subsidiary general ledger (SGL) for settlement of trades in government securities. Similarly, the BSE has its own clearing house.

The equity market has witnessed widespread development in infrastructure and its functioning is comparable to international standards. It has seen significant increase in growth and diversity in composition since early 1990s.

15

Emergence and Popularity of Financial Derivatives

15.1 Emergence of Complex Financial Products

In recent years, complex financial products such as asset-backed securities, derivatives, credit-default swaps (CDSs) and collateralised debt obligations (CDOs) have proliferated in developed countries. These products have become highly popular with banks and financial institutions as they allow them to hedge their risks and manage their regulatory and economic capital more efficiently.

Although various structured products have enabled the transfer of risks and enhanced the liquidity of instruments, the recent turmoil in the US sub-prime mortgage market and related developments connected with complex derivatives have also brought to the fore the risks posed by these instruments.

The emergence of the market for derivative products, most notably forwards, futures and options, can be traced back to the willingness of risk-averse economic agents to guard themselves against uncertainties arising out of fluctuations in asset prices. By their very nature, the financial markets are marked by a very high degree of volatility. Through the use of derivative products, it is possible to partially or fully transfer price risks by locking-in asset prices. As instruments of risk management, derivatives generally do not influence the fluctuations in the underlying asset prices. However, by locking-in asset prices, derivative products minimize the impact of fluctuations in asset prices on the profitability and cash flow situation of risk-averse investors.

Derivative products initially emerged as hedging devices against fluctuations in commodity prices and commodity-linked derivatives remained the sole form of such products for a long time. The financial derivatives came into spotlight in post-1970 period due to growing instability in the financial markets. However, since their emergence, financial derivatives have become very popular and by 1990s, they accounted for about two-thirds of total transactions in derivative products. In recent years, the market for financial derivatives has grown tremendously both in terms of variety of instruments available, their complexity and also turnover.

In India also financial products such as mortgage-backed securities (MBS) and asset-backed securities (ABS) are in existence. Besides the securitised products, the Indian forex and rupee derivative markets have also developed significantly over the years.

In respect of forex derivatives involving rupee, residents have access to foreign exchange forward contracts, foreign currency-rupee swap instruments and currency options—both cross currency and foreign currency-rupee. As stated in the Annual Policy Statement for the year 2008-09, the Reserve Bank of India (RBI) announced the introduction of currency futures in the eligible exchanges for which the broad framework was announced in August 2008. In future, some more innovative and complex products might emerge. These products may pose several regulatory and supervisory challenges.

15.2 Meaning of Derivatives

Derivative in mathematics means a variable derived from another variable. The term *derivative* indicates that it has no independent value, i.e. its value is entirely *derived* from the value of the underlying asset. The underlying asset can be security, commodity, bullion, currency, live stock or anything else. In other words, derivative means a forward, future, option or any other hybrid contract of pre-determined fixed duration, linked for the purpose of contract fulfilment to the value of a specified real or financial asset of an index of securities. Similarly, in the financial sense, a derivative is a financial product, which has been derived from a market for another product. Without the underlying product, derivatives do not have any independent existence in the market.

Derivative instruments are defined by the Indian Securities Contracts (Regulation) Act, 1956 to include: (i) a security derived from a debt instrument, share, secured/unsecured loan, risk instrument or contract for differences, or any other form of security, and (ii) a contract that derives its value from the prices/index of prices of underlying securities.

In other words, derivatives are financial instruments/contracts whose value depends upon the value of an underlying. Since their value is essentially derived out of an underlying, they are financial abstractions whose value is derived mathematically from the changes in the value of the underlying.

The International Monetary Fund (IMF) defines derivatives as, "financial instruments that are linked to a specific financial instrument or indicator or commodity and through which specific financial risks can be traded in financial markets in their own right. The value of a financial derivative derives from the price of an underlying item, such as an asset or index. Unlike debt securities, no principal is advanced to be repaid and no investment income accrues".

Derivatives have come into being because of the existence of risks in business. Thus, derivatives are means of managing risks. The parties managing risks in the market are known as *hedgers*. Some people/organizations are in the business of taking risks to earn profits. Such entities represent the *speculators*. The third players in the market, known as the *arbitragers,* take advantage of the market mistakes.

In recent years, derivatives have become increasingly important in the field of finance. While futures and options are now actively traded on many exchanges, forward contracts are popular on the over-the-counter (OTC) market.

15.3 Reasons for the Popularity of Derivatives

Financial derivatives have become popular due to the following reasons:

1. Increased volatility in asset prices in financial markets.
2. Increased integration of national financial markets with the international markets.
3. Marked improvement in communication facilities and sharp decline in their costs.

4. Development of more sophisticated risk management tools, providing economic agents a wider choice of risk management strategies.
5. Innovations in the derivatives markets, which optimally combine the risks and returns over a large number of financial assets, leading to higher returns, reduced risk as well as transaction costs as compared to individual financial assets.

In the class of equity derivatives, futures and options on stock indices have gained more popularity than on individual stocks, especially among institutional investors, who are major users of index-linked derivatives. Even small investors find these useful due to high correlation of the popular indices with various portfolios and ease of use. The lower costs associated with index derivatives vis-à-vis derivative products based on individual securities is another reason for their growing use.

15.4 Variants (or Types) of Derivative Contracts

Derivative contracts have several variants. The most common variants are forwards, futures, options and swaps.

15.4.1 Forwards/Forward Contracts: A forward contract is a customised contract between two entities, where settlement takes place on a specific date in the future at today's pre-agreed price. A forward contract is an agreement to buy or sell an asset on a specified date for specified price. One of the parties to the contract assumes a long position and agrees to buy the underlying asset on a certain specified future date, for a certain specified price. The other party assumes a short position and agrees to sell the asset on the same date for the same price. Other contract details like delivery date, price and quantity are negotiated bilaterally by the parties to the contract.

Forward contracts are normally traded outside stock exchanges. They are popular on the over the counter (OTC) market.

The salient features of forward contracts are as follows:

1. They are bilateral contracts and hence exposed to counter party risk.
2. Each contract is customer designed, and, hence, is unique in terms of contract size, expiration date and the asset type and quality.
3. The contract price is generally not available in public domain.
4. On the expiration date, the contract has to be settled by delivery for the asset.
5. If a party wishes to reverse the contract, it has to compulsorily go to the same counterparty, which often results in a high price being charged.

Forward contracts are very useful in hedging and speculation. A typical hedging application may pertain to an exporter who expects to receive payment in US dollars, 2 months later. He is exposed to the risk of exchange rate fluctuations. By using the currency forward market to sell dollars forward, he can lock-on a rate today and reduce his uncertainty. Likewise, an importer who is required to make a payment in US dollars 2 months hence can reduce his exposure to exchange rate fluctuations by buying dollars forward.

15.4.2 Futures/Future Contracts: Future contracts are special types of forward contracts in the sense that the former are standardised exchange-traded contracts. Future contract markets are designed to solve the problems that exist in forward markets. A future contract is an agreement between two parties to buy or sell an asset at a certain time in future, at a certain price. However, unlike forward contracts, future contracts are standardized and stock exchange-traded. To facilitate liquidity in the future contracts, the exchange specifies certain standard features for the contract. It is a standardized contract with a standard underlying instrument, a standard quantity and quality of the underlying instrument that can be delivered, and a standard timing of such settlement. A future contract may be offset prior to maturity by entering into an equal and opposite transaction. The standardized items in a future contract are the following:

1. Quantity of the underlying.
2. Quality of the underlying.
3. Date/month of delivery.
4. Units of price quotation and minimum price change.
5. Location of settlement.

15.4.3 Options: Options are fundamentally different from forward and future contracts. An option gives the holder of the option the right to do something. The holder does not have to necessarily exercise this right. In contrast, in a forward or future contract, the two parties commit themselves to doing something. Whereas it costs nothing (except margin requirements) to enter into a future contract, the purchase of an option requires an up front payment.

Options are of two types: calls options and put options. Calls options give the buyer the right but not the obligation to buy a given quantity of the underlying asset, at a given price on or before a given future date. Put options give the buyer the right, but not the obligation to sell a given quantity of the underlying asset at a given price on or before a given date.

A. Warrants: Options generally have lives of up to 1 year, the majority of options traded on options exchanges having maximum maturity of 9 months. Longer-dated options are called *warrants* and are generally traded over-the-counter.

B. LEAPS: The acronym LEAPS means Long-term Equity Anticipation Securities. These are options having a maturity of up to 3 years.

C. Baskets: Basket options are options on portfolios of underlying assets. The underlying asset is usually a moving average or a basket of assets. Equity index options are a form of basket options.

15.4.4 Swaps: Swaps are private agreements between two parties to exchange cash flows in the future according to a pre-arranged formula. They can be regarded as portfolios of forward contracts. Following are the two commonly used swaps:

A. Interest Rate Swaps: These entail swapping of only the interest-related cash flows between the parties in the same currency.

B. Currency Swaps: These entail swapping of both principal and interest between the parties, with the cash flows in one direction being in a different currency than those in the opposite direction.

15.4.5 Swaptions: Swaptions are options to buy or sell a swap that will become operative at the expiry of the options. Thus, swaption is an option on a forward swap. Rather than have call options and put options, the swaptions market has receiver swaptions and payer swaptions.

15.5 Participants in the Derivatives Market

The following three broad categories of participants, viz. hedgers, speculators, and arbitrageurs trade in the derivatives market.

15.5.1 Hedgers: Hedgers face risk associated with the price of an asset. They use future or option markets to reduce or eliminate this risk. In other words, hedgers are those who wish to protect their existing exposures and essentially are safety-driven.

15.5.2 Speculators: They bet on future movements in the price of an asset. Future and option contracts can give them an extra leverage; that is, they can increase both the potential gains and potential losses in a speculative venture. Speculators are willing risk takers who are expectation-driven.

15.5.3 Arbitrageurs: They are in business to take advantage of a discrepancy between prices in two different markets. If, for example, they see the futures price of an asset getting out of line with the cash price, they will take offsetting positions in the two markets to lock-in a profit. Arbitragers are traders and market-makers who deal in buying and selling derivatives contracts hoping to profit from price-differentials between different markets. A market maker is one who provides two-way quotes for a given product and thereby runs a position in that product.

15.6 Economic Role of Derivatives

Derivative markets perform three essential economic functions:

1. Risk management.
2. Price discovery.
3. Transactional efficiency.

The first function refers to the ability of traders to offset financial risks through derivatives. The principal benefit of the derivatives market is that it provides the opportunity for risk management through hedging. [1] Derivatives are innovations in risk management not in risk itself.

The second refers to the better allocation of resources in an economy that is created by the wide availability of an equilibrium price which serves as a measure of value.

The third function alludes to increased efficiency of transacting through derivatives. Derivative markets reduce the costs of trading and raising capital, thereby enhancing their risk management and price discovery functions.

Derivatives have played a major role in the development of financial markets and their integration across several economies, especially in developed countries. Derivatives serve to achieve a more complete financial system because previously fixed combinations of the risk properties of loans and financial assets can be bundled and unbundled into new synthetic assets. For instance, structured products or synthetic derivatives could be created by adding elementary assets or underlying assets such as bonds, equities and borrowing and lending instruments with a combination of derivative products such as put and call options. Repackaging risk properties in this way can provide a more perfect match between an investor's risk preferences and the effective risk of the portfolio or cash-flow. Derivatives allow individual risk elements of an asset to be priced and traded individually, thus ensuring an efficient price system in the asset markets.

The economic functions performed by derivatives market can be summarised as under:

1. Derivatives market helps to increase savings and investment in the long-run. Transfer of risk enables market participants to expand their volume of activity.
2. Derivatives trading acts as a catalyst for new entrepreneurial activity. Derivatives have a history of attracting many bright, creative, well educated people with an entrepreneurial attitude.
3. Prices in an organized derivatives market reflect the perception of the market participants about the future and lead the prices of underlying to the perceived future level.
4. Prices of derivatives converge with the prices of the underlying at the expiration of the derivatives contract. In fact, derivatives help in the discovery of the future as well as current prices.
5. Derivatives market helps to transfer risks from those who have them but may not like them to those who have an appetite for them.
6. Derivatives, due to their inherent nature are linked to the underlying cash markets. With the introduction of derivatives, the underlying market witnesses higher trading volumes because of participation by more players who would not otherwise participate for lack of an arrangement to transfer risk.
7. Speculative trades shift to a more controlled environment of derivatives market. In the absence of an organized derivatives market, speculators trade in the underlying cash markets. Margining, monitoring and surveillance of the activities of various participants become extremely difficult in these kinds of mixed markets.

15.7 History of Derivatives

The first future contracts are generally traced to the Yodoya rice market in Osaka, Japan around 1650. These were evidently standardized contracts, which made them much like today's futures, although it is not known if the contracts were marked to market daily and/or had credit guarantees.

Probably the next major event, and the most significant as regards the history of US future markets, was the creation of the Chicago Board of Trade in 1848. Due to its prime location on Lake Michigan, Chicago was developing as a major centre for the storage, sale, and distribution of Midwestern grain. Due to the seasonality of grain, Chicago's storage facilities were unable to accommodate the enormous increase in supply that occurred following the harvest. Similarly, its facilities were underutilized in the spring. Chicago spot prices rose and fell drastically. A group of grain traders created the *to-arrive* contract, which permitted farmers to lock-in the price and deliver the grain later. This allowed the farmer to store the grain either on the farm or at a storage facility nearby and deliver it to Chicago months later. These *to-arrive* contracts proved useful as a device for hedging and speculating on price changes. Farmers and traders soon realized that the sale and delivery of the grain itself was not as important as the ability to transfer the price risk associated with the grain. The grain could always be sold and delivered anywhere else at any time. These contracts were eventually standardized around 1865, and in 1925 the first future clearing house was formed. From that point on, future contracts were pretty much of the form we know them today.

In the early 19th century, famed New York financier Russell Sage began creating synthetic loans using the principle of put-call parity. Sage would buy the stock and a put from his customer and sell the customer a call. By fixing the put, call, and strike prices, Sage was creating a synthetic loan with an interest rate significantly higher than usury laws allowed.

Interestingly, futures/options/derivatives trading was banned numerous times in Europe and Japan and even in the US in the state of Illinois in 1867 though the law was quickly repealed. In 1874, the Chicago Mercantile Exchange predecessor, the Chicago Produce Exchange, was formed. It became the modern day Merc in 1919. Other exchanges had been popping up around the country and continued to do so.

In 1922, the US Federal Government made its first effort to regulate the futures market with the Grain Futures Act. In 1936, options on futures were banned in the US. All the while options, futures and various derivatives continued to be banned from time to time in other countries.

The 1950s marked the era of two significant events in the futures market. In 1955, the US Supreme Court ruled in the case of Corn Products Refining Company that profits from hedging were treated as ordinary income. This ruling stood until it was challenged by the 1988 ruling in the Arkansas Best case. The Best decision denied the deductibility of capital losses against ordinary income and effectively gave hedging a tax disadvantage. Fortunately, this interpretation was overturned in 1993.

In 1972 the Chicago Mercantile Exchange, responding to the now-freely floating international currencies, created the International Monetary Market, which allowed trading in currency futures. These were the first future contracts that were not on physical commodities. In 1975, the Chicago Board of Trade created the first interest rate futures contract, one based on Ginnie Mae (GNMA) mortgages. While the contract met with initial success, it eventually died. In 1975, the Merc responded with the Treasury bill futures contract. This contract was the first successful pure interest rate futures. In 1982, the Kansas City Board of Trade launched the first stock index futures, a contract on the Value Line Index. The Chicago Mercantile Exchange quickly followed with their highly successful contract on the S&P 500 index.

1973 marked the creation of both the Chicago Board Options Exchange and the publication of perhaps the most famous formula in finance, the option pricing model of Fischer Black and Myron Scholes. These events revolutionized the investment world in ways no one could imagine at that time. The Black-Scholes model, as it came to be known, set up a mathematical framework that formed the basis for an explosive revolution in the use of derivatives. In 1983, the Chicago Board Options Exchange decided to create an option on an index of stocks. Though originally known as the CBOE 100 Index, it was soon turned over to Standard and Poor's and became known as the S&P 100, which remains the most actively traded exchange-listed option.

The 1980s marked the beginning of the era of swaps and other over-the-counter (OTC) derivatives. Although OTC options and forwards had previously existed, the generation of corporate financial managers of that decade was the first to come out of business schools with exposure to derivatives. Soon virtually every large corporation, and even some that were not so large, were using derivatives to hedge, and in some cases, speculate on interest rate, exchange rate and commodity risk. New products were rapidly created to hedge the now-recognized wide varieties of risks. As the problems became more complex, Wall Street turned increasingly to the talents of mathematicians and physicists, offering them new and quite different career paths and unheard-of money. The instruments became more complex and were sometimes even referred to as *exotic*.

In 1994, the derivatives world was hit with a series of large losses on derivatives trading announced by some well-known and highly experienced firms, such as Procter and Gamble and Metallgesellschaft. One of America's wealthiest localities, Orange County, California, declared bankruptcy, allegedly due to derivatives trading, but more accurately, due to the use of leverage in a portfolio of short-term Treasury securities. England's venerable Barings Bank declared bankruptcy due to speculative trading in future contracts by a 28 year old clerk in its Singapore office. These and other large losses led to a huge outcry, sometimes against the instruments and sometimes against the firms that sold them. While some minor changes occurred in the way in which derivatives were sold, most firms simply instituted tighter controls and continued to use derivatives.

15.8 International Experience of Derivatives

As we watch efforts going into the creation of India's exchange-traded derivatives industry, comparisons with other countries are useful. In all OECD countries, derivatives are a crucial and vibrant part of the financial system.

The most interesting and important experience is that of China, a fascinating case study of the merits and demerits of a relatively unregulated start of derivatives trading. In the early 1990s, a plethora of unregulated derivatives exchanges came up in China. Many of these exchanges lacked the key institution of the clearing house as counterparty, and most of them featured rampant market manipulation where insiders in the exchange management earned abnormal profits at the expense of outside market participants.

Many observers have cited China's experience with 50 exchanges as an example of how poorly-regulated and hasty growth of derivatives markets may be problematic. However, the other side of the picture is now clear: the experience with these 50 exchanges got the Chinese markets off the ground, and generated the necessary know-how amongst exchange staff, regulators and users. In the end, China has derivatives exchanges which have significant trading volumes on a world scale.

Another important example is that of Mexico, which is in the same time zone as

Chicago: the derivatives exchanges of Chicago have done a thorough job of launching numerous derivative products based on Mexican underlying. This has made the creation of exchanges in Mexico much harder.

Taiwan is another interesting case. Taiwan is like India in terms of enormous delays which have beset the creation of a domestic derivatives exchange. In January 1997, markets in Chicago and Singapore started trading futures on a Taiwanese market index.

Exchanges such as the Chicago Mercantile Exchange (CME), Chicago Board of Trade (CBOT), Chicago Board Options Exchange (CBOE), American Stock Exchange, Sydney Futures Exchange, Hong Kong Futures Exchange and Singapore International Monetary Exchange (SIMEX) have all launched emerging market initiatives, whereby they aim to trade derivatives of underlying from emerging markets.

The US is an example of a clumsy regulatory approach, where an agency named the CFTC regulates futures while the traditional securities markets regulator, the SEC, regulates options on securities. This artificial distinction has no economic rationale, and has served to distort the development of the markets.

What are the problems which bedevil the growth of derivative markets across emerging markets in general? One source of difficulty is poor infrastructure, particularly in clearing and settlement.

In India, a major initiative in clearing for derivatives was National Securities Clearing Corporation (NSCC) which was created by National Stock Exchange (NSE). NSCC was the first effort in clearing where the clearing corporation becomes the *legal counterparty* to both legs of every transaction, and thus eliminates counterparty risk.

To sum up, derivatives is an area where a *unified* picture of the entire securities industry—spanning equity, debt, foreign exchange, commodities and real estate—is enormously useful. The functioning of the derivatives industry emphasizes that a futures is a futures, regardless of the underlying on which the futures is being traded. The great derivatives exchanges of the world simultaneously trade derivatives on all of equity, debt, foreign exchange, commodities and real estate. In this sense, the basic policy issues faced in the derivatives area (market manipulation, strength of the clearing house and competition between exchanges worldwide) are universal to all major markets.

Endnote

1. Hedging is the process of stabilizing the value (including cash flows) of a given portfolio by neutralizing adverse market movements.

16

Forwards, Futures and Options

16.1 Forwards/Forward Contracts

A forward contract is a particularly simple derivative. A deal for the purchase or sale of a commodity, security or other asset can be in the spot or forward markets. A spot or cash market is the most commonly used for trading. A majority of day to day transaction are in the cash market, where we pay cash and get the delivery of the goods. In addition to a cash purchase, another way to acquire or sell assets is by entering into a forward contract. In a forward contract, the buyer agrees to pay cash at a later date when the seller delivers the goods.

A forward contract is an agreement to buy or sell an asset on a specified date for a specified price. One of the parties to the contract assumes a long position and agrees to buy the underlying asset on a certain specified future date for a certain specified price. The other party assumes a short position and agrees to sell the asset on the same date for the same price. Other contract details like delivery date, price and quantity are negotiated bilaterally by the parties to the contract. The forward contracts are normally traded outside the exchanges.

16.1.1 Salient Features of Forward Contracts: These are as under:

1 They are bilateral contracts and hence exposed to counter party risk.
2 Each contract is custom designed, and hence is unique in terms of contract size, expiration date and the asset type and quality.
3 Contract price is generally not available in public domain.
4 On the expiration date, the contract has to be settled by delivery of the asset.
5 If the party wishes to reverse the contract, it has to compulsorily go to the same counterparty, which often results in high prices being charged.

Usually no money changes hands when forward contracts are entered into, but sometimes one or both the parties to a contract may like to ask for some initial, good-faith deposits to insure that the contract is honoured by the other party.

A forward contract is settled at maturity. The holder of the short position delivers the asset to the holder price. A forward contract is worth zero when it is first entered into. Later it can have position or negative value, depending on movements in the price of the asset.

However, forward contracts in certain markets have become much standardised, as in the case of foreign exchange, thereby reducing transaction costs and increasing transaction volumes. This process of standardisation reaches its limit in the organised futures market.

16.1.2 Advantages of Forwards: Forward contracts are very useful in hedging and speculation. A typical hedging application would be that of an exporter who expects to receive payment in dollars 3 months later. He is exposed to the risk of exchange rate fluctuations. By using the currency forward market to sell dollars forward, he can lock-on to a rate today and reduce his uncertainty. Similarly, an importer who is required to make a payment in dollars 2 months hence can reduce his exposure to exchange rate fluctuations by buying dollars forward.

In a forward contract the price at which the underlying commodity or assets will be traded, is decided at the time of entering into the contract. The essential idea of entering into the forward contract is to peg the price and thereby avoid the price risk. Thus, by entering in the forward contract, one is assured of the price at which one can buy/sell goods or other assets. Manufacturers using a certain raw material whose price is subject to variation, can avoid the risk of price moving adversely by entering into a forward contract and plan their operations better. Similarly, by entering into a forward contract, a farmer can ensure the price he can get for his crops and not worry about what price would prevail at the time of maturity of the contract. Of course, at the time of maturity of contract, if the market price of the commodity is greater than the price agreed, then the buyer stands to gain. The opposite would hold when the market price is lower than the agreed price.

If a speculator has information or analysis, which forecasts an upturn in a price, then he can go long on the forward market instead of the cash market. The speculator would go long on the forward, wait for the price to rise, and then take a reversing transaction to book profits. Speculators may well be required to deposit a margin upfront. However, this is generally a relatively small proportion of the value of the assets underlying the forward contract. The use of forward markets supplies leverage to the speculator.

16.1.3 Problems of Forward Contracts: Forward contracts have been in existence for quite some time. The organized commodity exchanges, on which forward contracts are traded, probably started in Japan in the early 18th century, while the establishment of the Chicago Board of Trade (CBOT) in 1848 led to the start of a formal commodity exchange in the US.

A forward contract is evidently a good mean of avoiding price risk, but it entails elements of risk in that a party to the contract may not honour its part of the obligation. Thus, each party is at risk of default. There is another problem. Once a position of buyer and seller takes in a forward contract, an investor cannot retreat except through mutual consent with the party or by entering into an identical contract and taking a position that is the reverse of earlier position. Alternatives are by no means easy. With forward contract entered on a one-to-one basis and with no standardization, the forward contract has virtually no liquidity. This problem of credit risk and no liquidity associated with forward contracts led to the emergence of future contracts. Future contracts are the refined version of forward contracts.

Forward markets world-wide are afflicted by several problems:

1. Lack of centralisation of trading.
2. Illiquidity.
3. Counter party risk.

In the first two of these, the basic problem is that of too much flexibility and generality. The forward market is like a real estate market in that any two consenting adults can form contracts against each other. This often makes them design terms of the deal which are very convenient in that specific situation, but makes the contract non-tradable. Counter party risk arises from the possibility of default by any one party to the transaction. When one of the two sides to the transaction declares bankruptcy, the other suffers. Even when forward markets trade standardised contracts, and hence avoid the problem of illiquidity, still the counterparty risk remains a very serious issue.

16.2 Futures/Future Contracts

Future markets are designed to solve the problems that exist in forward markets. A future contract is an agreement between two parties to buy or sell an asset at a certain time in future at a certain price. However, unlike forward contracts, the future contracts are standardised and exchange traded. To facilitate liquidity in the future contracts, the exchange specifies certain standard features of the contract. It is a standardised contract with standard underlying instrument, a standard quantity and quality of the underlying instrument that can be delivered and a standard timing of such settlement.

A future contract may be offset prior to maturity by entering into an equal and opposite transaction. The standardised items in a future contract are as under:

1. Quantity of the underlying.
2. Quality of the underlying.
3. Date and the month of delivery.
4. Units of price quotation and minimum price change.
5. Location of settlement.

Future contracts are normally traded on an exchange. To make trading possible, the exchange specifies certain standardized features of the contract. As the two parties to the contract do not necessarily know each other the exchange also provides a mechanism, which gives the two parties a guarantee that the contract will be honoured.

16.2.1 Distinction between Futures and Forwards: Forward and future contracts are different in following respects.

A. Standardization: A forward contract is a tailor-made contract between the buyer and the seller where the terms are settled in mutual agreement between the parties. On the other hand, a future contract is standardized in regards to the quality, quantity, place of delivery of the asset etc. Only the price is negotiated. Forwards are popular on the over the counter (OTC) market. Futures are traded on an organised stock exchange. Exchange-traded derivatives tend to be more standardised and offer greater liquidity than OTC contracts, which are negotiated between counterparties and tailored to meet the needs of the parties to the contract. Exchange-traded derivatives also offer centralised limits on individual positions and have formal rules for risk and burden sharing.

B. Liquidity: There is no secondary market for forward contracts while future contracts are traded on organized exchanges. Accordingly, future contracts are usually much more liquid than the forward contracts. Forwards have customised contract terms, and therefore they are less liquid. Futures have standardised contract terms, and hence they are more liquid.

C. Conclusion of Contract: A forward contract is generally concluded with a delivery of the asset in question whereas the future contracts are settled sometimes with delivery of the asset and generally with the payment of the price differences. One who holds a contract can always eliminate his/her obligation by subsequently selling a contract for the same asset and same delivery date, before the conclusion of contract one holds. In the same manner, the seller of a future contract can buy a similar contract and offset his/her position before maturity of the first contract. Each one of these actions is called offsetting a trade.

D. Margins: A forward contract has zero value for both the parties involved so that no collateral is required for entering into such a contract. There are only two parties involved. But in a futures contract, a third party called Clearing Corporation is also involved with which margin is required to be kept by both parties. In other words, forwards require no margin payments. Futures require margin payments.

E. Profit/Loss Settlement: The settlement of a forward contract takes place on the date of maturity so that the profit/loss is booked on maturity only. On the other hand, the future contracts are marked-to-market daily so that the profits or losses are settled daily. In other words, in the case of forwards, settlement happens at the end of the period. Futures follow daily settlement.

Thus, future contracts are a significant improvement over forward contracts as they eliminate counterparty risk and offer more liquidity.

Future contracts represent an improvement over the forward contracts in terms of standardization, performance guarantee and liquidity. A future contract is a standardized contract between two parties where one of the parties commits to sell, and the other to buy, a stipulated quantity of a commodity, currency, security, index or some other specified item at an agreed price on a given date in the future.

Future contracts are traded on commodity exchanges or other future exchanges. People can buy or sell futures like other commodities. When an investor buys a future contract on an organized future exchange, he is in fact assuming the right and obligation of taking the delivery of the specified underlying item on a specified date. Similarly, when an investor sells a contract, to take a short position, one assumes the right and obligation to make the delivery of the underlying asset. There is no risk of non-performance in the case of trading in the future contracts. This is because a clearing house or a clearing corporation is associated with the futures exchange, which plays a pivotal role in the trading of futures. A clearing house takes the opposite in each trade, so that it becomes the buyer to the seller and vice versa. When a party takes a short position in a contract, it is obliged to sell the underlying commodity in question at the stipulated price to the clearing house on maturity of the contract. Similarly, an investor who takes a long position on the contract can seek its performance through the clearing house only.

It is noteworthy that while a clearing house guarantees the performance of the future contracts, the parties in the contracts are required to keep margins with it. The margins are taken to ensure that each party to a contract performs its part. The margins are adjusted on a daily basis to account for the gains or losses, depending upon the situation. This is known as marking-to-market and involves giving a credit to the buyer of the contract, if the price of the contract rises, debiting the seller's account by an equal amount. Similarly, the buyer's balance is reduced when the contract price declines and the seller's account is accordingly updated.

It is not necessary to hold on to a futures contract until maturity and one can easily close out a position. Either of the parties may reverse their position by initiating a reverse trade, so that the original buyer of a contract can sell an identical contract at a later date, cancelling, in effect, the original contract. Thus, the exchange facilitates subsequent selling (buying) of a contract so that a party can offset its position and eliminate the obligation. The fact that the buyer as well as the seller of a contract is free to transfer his interest in the contract to another party makes such contracts highly liquid in nature. In fact, most of the future contracts are cancelled by the parties, by engaging into reverse trades: the buyers cancel a contract by selling another contract, while the seller does so by buying another contract. Only a very small portion of them is held for actual delivery.

16.2.2 History of Futures: Future contracts, especially those which involve agricultural commodities, have been traded for long. In US, for instance, such contracts began on the Chicago Board of Trade (CBOT) in the 1860s. Subsequently, contracts began to trade on commodities involving precious metals like gold, silver etc. However, significant changes have taken place in recent years with the development of financial future contracts. They represent a very significant financial innovation. Such contracts encompass a variety of underlying asset-security, stock indices, and interest rates and so on. The beginnings of financial futures were made with the introduction of foreign currency future contracts on the International Monetary Markets (IMM) in 1972. Subsequently, interest rate futures—where a contract is on an asset whose price is dependent solely on the level of interest rates—were introduced.

An important development took place in the world of future contracts in 1982 when stock index futures were introduced in US, after strong initial opposition to such contracts. A future contract on a stock index has been a revolutionary and novel idea because it represents a contract based not on a readily deliverable physical commodity or currency or other negotiable instrument. It is instead based on the concept of a mathematically measurable index that is determined by the market movements of a pre-determined set of equity stocks. Such contracts are now very widely traded the world over.

16.2.3 Introduction of Futures in India: The first derivative product introduced in the Indian securities market was *index futures* in June 2000. In India, the *stock futures* were first introduced on November 9, 2001.

The Indian capital market has grown quite well since the early 1990s. In the boom period of 1992 and thereafter, even the common man was attracted to the stock market. The stock market was considered a profitable investment opportunity. Before July 2001, various stock exchanges including the Bombay Stock Exchange (BSE), National Stock Exchange (NSE) and Delhi Stock Exchange, provided carry forward facilities through the traditional *badla* system. By means of this system the purchase or sale of a security was not postponed till a particular future date; instead the system only provided for the carry forward of a transaction from one settlement period (seven days) to the next settlement period for the payment of a fee known as *badla* charges.

In the *badla* system, due to limited settlement period and no future price discovery, a speculator could manipulate prices, thus causing loss to small investors and ultimately eroding investors' confidence in the capital market. Hence, the necessity of futures trading in the capital market was emphasized. In the absence of an efficient futures market, there was no price discovery and therefore prices could be moved in any desired direction. Recent developments in the capital market culminated in a ban on *badla* from July 2001.

In the absence of futures trading, certain operators—either on their own or in collusion with corporate management teams—at times manipulated prices in the secondary market, causing irreparable damage to the growth of the market. The small and medium investors, who are the backbone of the market and whose savings come to the market via primary or secondary routes shied away. As the small investors avoided the capital market, the downturn in the secondary market ultimately affected the primary market because people stopped investing in share for fear of loss or liquidity. Introducing futures in major shares along with index futures helped to revive the capital market. This not only provided liquidity and efficiency to the market, but also helped in future price discovery.

16.2.4 Futures and Stock Indices: For understanding stock index futures a thorough knowledge of the composition of indexes is essential. Choosing the right index is important in choosing the right contract for speculation or hedging. For speculation, the volatility of the index is important whereas for hedging the choice of index depends upon the relationship between the stocks being hedged and the characteristics of the index.

Choosing and understanding the right index is important as the movement of stock index futures is quite similar to that of the underlying stock index. Volatility of the future indexes is generally greater than spot stock indexes.

Every time an investor takes a long or short position on a stock, he also has hidden exposure to the Nifty or Sensex. This is so because most often stock values fall in tune with the entire market sentiment and rise when the market as a whole is rising.

Retail investors will find the index derivatives useful due to the high correlation of the index with their portfolio/stock and low cost associated with using index futures for hedging.

16.2.5 Index Futures: A future contract is an agreement between two parties to buy or sell an asset at a certain time in the future at a certain price. Index futures are all future contracts where the underlying is the stock index (Nifty or Sensex) and helps a trader to take a view of the market as a whole.

Index futures permit speculation and if a trader anticipates a major rally in the market, he can simply buy a future contract and hope for a price rise on the future contract when the rally occurs.

16.2.6 Settlements in the Futures Market: All trades in the futures market are cash settled on a T+1 basis and all positions (buy/sell) which are not closed out are marked-to-market. The closing price of the index futures is the daily settlement price and the position is carried to the next day at the settlement price.

The most common way of liquidating an open position is to execute an offsetting future transaction by which the initial transaction is squared up. The initial buyer liquidates his long position by selling identical future contract. In index futures the other way of settlement is cash settled at the final settlement. At the end of the contract period the difference between the contract value and closing index value is paid.

16.3 Options

An option is a contract which gives the buyer the right, but not the obligation, to buy or sell specified quantity of the underlying assets, at a specific (strike) price on or before a specified time (expiration date). The underlying may be a commodity like wheat or rice or financial instrument like equity stock or bonds etc. Options are basically of two types: call options and put options.

16.3.1 Call Options: A call option is an option to buy a stock at a specific price on or before a certain date. In this way, call options are like security deposits. If, for example, Mr. Wilson wants to rent a certain property, and leaves a security deposit for it, the money would be used to insure that he would, in fact, rent that property at the price agreed upon when he returns. If Mr. Wilson never returns, he would lose his security deposit, but he would have no other liability.

Call options usually increase in value as the value of the underlying instrument rises. When you buy a call option, the price you pay for it, called the option premium, secures your right to buy that certain stock at a specified price called the strike price. If you decide not to use the option to buy the stock, and you are not obligated to, your only cost is the *option premium*.

16.3.2 Put Options: Put options are options to sell a stock at a specific price on or before a certain date. In this way, put options are like insurance policies. If you buy a new car, and then buy auto insurance on the car, you pay a premium and are, hence, protected if the asset is damaged in an accident. If this happens, you can use your policy to regain the insured value of the car. In this way, the put option gains in value as the value of the underlying instrument decreases. If all goes well and the insurance is not needed, the insurance company keeps your premium in return for taking on the risk.

With a put option, you can *insure* a stock by fixing a selling price. If something happens which causes the stock price to fall, and thus, *damages* your asset, you can exercise your option and sell it at its *insured* price level. If the price of your stock goes up, and there is no *damage*, then you do not need to use the insurance, and, once again, your only cost is the premium.

Buying put options is buying insurance. To buy a put option on Nifty is to buy insurance which reimburses the full extent to which Nifty drops below the strike price of the put option. This is attractive to many people, and to mutual funds creating *guaranteed return products*. The Nifty index fund industry will find it very useful to make a bundle of a Nifty index fund and a Nifty put option to create a new kind of a Nifty index fund, which gives the investor protection against extreme drops in Nifty.

Selling put options is selling insurance, so anyone who feels like earning revenues by selling insurance can set himself up to do so on the index options market.

Like forwards and futures, options represent another derivative instrument and provide a mechanism by which one can acquire a certain commodity or other asset in order to make profit or cover risk for a price. The options are similar to the future contracts in the sense that they are also standardized but are different from them in many ways. Options, in fact, represent the rights.

An option is the right, but not the obligation, to buy or sell a specified amount (and quality) of a commodity, currency, index, or financial instrument, or to buy or sell a specified number of underlying future contracts, at a specific price on or before a given date in future. Like other contracts, there are two parties to an option contract: the buyer who takes a long position and the seller or writer, who takes a short position. The option contract gives the owner a right to buy/sell a particular commodity or other asset at a specific pre-destined price by a specified date. The price involved is called exercise or strike price and the date involved is known as expiration. It is important to understand that such a contract gives its holder the right, and not the obligation to buy/sell. The option writer, on the other hand, undertakes upon himself the obligation to sell/buy the underlying asset if that suits the option holder. There is a wide variety of underlying assets including agricultural commodities, metals, shares, indices and so on, on which options are written.

Further, like future contracts, options are also tradable on exchanges. The exchange-traded options are standardized contracts and their trading is regulated by the exchanges that ensure the honouring of such contracts. Thus, in case of options as well, a clearing corporation takes the other side in every contract so that the party with the long position has a claim against the clearing corporation and the one with short position is obliged to it. However, buying or selling of future contracts does not require any price to be paid, called premium. The writer of an option receives the premium as a compensation of the risk that he takes upon himself. The premium belongs to the writer and is not adjusted in the price if the holder of the option decides to exercise it. This price is determined on the exchange, like the price of a share, by the forces of demand and supply. Further, like the share prices, the option prices also keep on changing with passage of time as trading takes place.

One difference between future and option trading may be noted. Whereas both parties to a future contract are required to deposit margins to the exchange, only the party with the short position is called upon to pay margin in case of options trading. The party with the long position does not pay anything beyond the premium.

16.3.3 Options in Historical Perspective: Options were traded in the US and UK during the 19th century but confined mainly to the agricultural commodities. Earlier, they were declared illegal in UK in 1733 and remained so until 1860 when the Act declaring them illegal was repealed. In the US, options on equity stocks of the companies were available on the over the counter (OTC) market only, until April 1973. They were not standardized and involved the intra-party risk. In India, options on stocks of companies, though illegal, were traded for many years on a limited scale in the form of *teji* and *mandi*, and related transactions. As such, this trading was a very risky proposition to undertake.

In spite of the long time that has elapsed since the inception of options, they were, until not very long ago, looked down upon as mere speculative tools and associated with corrupt practices. Things changed dramatically in the 1970s when options were transformed from relative obscurity to a systematically traded asset which is an integral part of financial portfolios. In fact, the year 1973 witnessed some major developments. Black and Scholes published a seminal paper explaining the basic principal of options pricing and hedging. In the same year, the Chicago Board Options Exchange (CBOT) was created. It was the first registered securities exchange dedicated to options trading. While trading in options existed for long, it experienced a gigantic growth with the creation of this exchange. The listing of options meant orderly and thicker markets for this kind of securities. Options trading is now undertaken widely in many countries besides the US and UK. In fact, options have become an integral part of the large and developed financial markets.

16.3.4 Advantages of Option Trading:

A. Risk Management: Put options allow investors holding shares to hedge against a possible fall in their value. This can be considered similar to taking out insurance against a fall in the share price.

B. Time to Decide: By taking a call option the purchase price for the shares is locked-in. This gives the call option holder until the expiry day to decide whether or not to exercise the option and buy the shares. Likewise, the taker of a put option has time to decide whether or not to sell the shares.

C. Speculation: The ease of trading in and out of an option position makes it possible to trade options with no intention of ever exercising them. If an investor expects the market to rise, he may decide to buy call options. If expecting a fall, he may decide to buy put options. Either way the holder can sell the option prior to expiry to take a profit or limit a loss. Trading options has a lower cost than shares, as there is no stamp duty payable unless and until options are exercised.

D. Leverage: Leverage provides the potential to make a higher return from a smaller initial outlay than investing directly. However, leverage usually involves more risks than a direct investment in the underlying shares. Trading in options can allow investors to benefit from a change in the price of the share without having to pay the full price of the share.

E. Income Generation: Shareholders can earn extra income over and above dividends by writing call options against their shares. By writing an option they receive the option premium upfront. While they get to keep the option premium, there is a possibility that they could be exercised against and have to deliver their shares to the taker at the exercise price.

F. Strategies: By combining different options, investors can create a wide range of potential profit scenarios.

16.3.5 Distinction between Futures and Options: Options are different from futures in several respects. At a practical level, the option buyer pays for the option in full at the time it is purchased. After this, he only has an upside. There is no possibility of the options position generating any further loss to him—other than the funds already paid for the option. Contrarily, futures are free to enter into but can generate very large losses. This feature makes options attractive to many occasional market participants who do not have time to monitor their futures positions.

More generally, options offer *non-linear payoffs* whereas futures only have *linear payoffs*. By combining futures and options, a wide variety of innovative and useful payoff structures can be created.

16.3.6 Pricing Options: Black-Scholes Formulae: An option buyer has the right but not the obligation to exercise on the seller. The worst that can happen to a buyer is the loss of the premium paid by him. His downside is limited to this premium, but his upside is potentially unlimited. This optionality is precious and has a value, which is expressed in terms of the option price. Just like in other free markets, it is the supply and demand in the secondary market that drives the price of an option.

There are various models which help us get close to the true price of an option. Most of these are variants of the celebrated Black-Scholes model for pricing European options. Today most calculators and spread-sheets come with a built-in Black-Scholes options pricing formula so to price options we do not really need to memorise the formula.

Options have existed—at least in concept—since antiquity. It was not until publication of the Black-Scholes (1973) option pricing formula that a theoretically consistent framework for pricing options became available. That framework was a direct result of work by Robert Merton as well as Fisher Black and Myron Scholes. In 1997, Scholes and Merton won the Nobel Prize in economics for this work. Black had died in 1995, but otherwise would have shared the prize.

The factors affecting the option price are the following:

1. Spot price of the underlying.
2. Exercise price.
3. Risk-free interest rate.
4. Volatility of the underlying.
5. Time to expiration.
6. Dividends on the underlying (stock or index).

Interestingly, before Black and Scholes came up with their option pricing model, there was a widespread belief that the expected growth of the underlying ought to affect the option price. Black and Scholes demonstrate that this is not true. The significance of the Black and Scholes model is that like any good model, it tells us what is important and what is not. It does not promise to produce the exact prices that show up in the market, but certainly does a remarkable job of pricing options within the framework of assumptions of the model. Virtually all option pricing models, even the most complex ones, have much in common with the Black-Scholes model.

Black and Scholes start by specifying a simple and well-known equation that models the way in which stock prices fluctuate. This equation called geometric Brownian

Motion, implies that stock returns will have a lognormal distribution, meaning that the logarithm of the stock's return will follow the normal (bell-shaped) distribution. Black and Scholes then propose that the option's price is determined by only two variables that are allowed to change: time and the underlying stock price. The other factors, namely the volatility, the exercise price, and the risk-free interest rate do affect the option's price but they are not allowed to change. By forming a portfolio consisting of a long position in stock and a short position in calls, the risk of the stock is eliminated. This hedged portfolio is obtained by setting the number of shares of stock equal to the approximate change in the call price for a change in the stock price. This mix of stock and calls must be revised continuously, a process known as delta hedging.

Black and Scholes then turn to a little-known result in a specialised field of probability known as stochastic calculus. This result defines how the option price changes in terms of the change in the stock price and time to expiration. They then reason that this hedged combination of options and stock should grow in value at the risk-free rate. The result then is a partial differential equation. The solution is found by forcing a condition called a boundary condition on the model that requires the option price to converge to the exercise value at expiration. The end result is the Black and Scholes model.

16.4 Currency Futures

Globalisation and integration of financial markets, coupled with the progressively increasing cross-border flow of funds, have transformed the intensity of market risk, which, in turn, has made the issues relating to hedging of such risk exposures very critical. The economic agents in India currently have a menu of over-the-counter (OTC) products, such as forwards, swaps and options, available to them for hedging their currency risk and the markets for these are quite deep and liquid. However, in the context of growing integration of the Indian economy with the rest of the world, as also the continued development of financial markets, a need has been felt to make available a wider choice of hedging instruments to the market participants to enable them to cope better with their currency risk exposures.

16.4.1 The Origin: The origin of futures can be traced back to 1851 when the Chicago Board of Trade (CBOT) introduced standardized forward contracts which were being traded in non-standard bilateral form for the preceding three years. In comparison, the birth of currency futures is of a recent origin and was a sequel to the breakdown of the Bretton Woods system. The resultant currency volatility provided a business opportunity for launching futures contracts in foreign currencies. The Chicago Mercantile Exchange (CME) first conceived the idea of a currency futures exchange and it launched the same in 1972 amidst considerable scepticism, since traditionally futures market had traded agricultural commodities and not financial instruments. The CME commissioned Professor Milton Friedman to write a paper on currency futures in order to gain credibility in the market. Professor Milton Friedman stated, "Changes in the international financial structure will create a great expansion in the demand for foreign cover. It is highly desirable that this demand be met by as broad, as deep, as resilient a futures market in foreign currencies as possible in order to facilitate foreign trade and investment. Such a wider market is almost certain to develop in response to the demand. The major open question is where. The US is a natural place and it is very much in the interests of the US that it should develop here". The CBOT saw this as a competitive challenge, as also an opportunity to launch other financial futures and proposed trading options and futures on stocks.

16.4.2 The Rationale: The rationale for establishing currency futures market is manifold. Both residents and non-residents are exposed to currency risk when residents purchase foreign currency assets and non-residents purchase domestic currency assets. If the exchange rate remains unchanged from the time of the purchase of the asset to its sale, no gains and losses are made out of currency exposures. But if domestic currency depreciates (appreciates) against the foreign currency, the exposure would result in gain (loss) for residents purchasing foreign assets and loss (gain) for non-residents purchasing domestic asset. In this backdrop, unpredicted movements in exchange rates expose investors to currency risks. Currency futures enable them to hedge these risks. Nominal exchange rates are often random walks with or without drift, while real exchange rates over long-run are mean reverting. As such, it is possible that over a long-run, the incentive to hedge currency risk may not be large.

However, financial planning horizon is much smaller than the long-run, which is typically inter-generational in the context of exchange rates. As such, there is a strong need to hedge currency risk and this need has grown manifold with fast growth in cross-border trade and investments flows. The argument for hedging currency risks appear to be natural in case of assets, and applies equally to trade in goods and services, which result in income flows with leads and lags and get converted into different currencies at the market rates. Empirically, changes in exchange rate are found to have very low correlations with foreign equity and bond returns. This in theory should lower portfolio risk. Therefore, sometimes argument is advanced against the need for hedging currency risks. But there is strong empirical evidence to suggest that hedging reduces the volatility of returns and indeed considering the episodic nature of currency returns, there are strong arguments to use instruments to hedge currency risks.

Currency risks could be hedged mainly through forwards, futures, swaps and options. Each of these instruments has its role in managing the currency risk. The main advantage of currency futures over its closest substitute product, viz., forwards which are traded over-the-counter (OTC) lies in price transparency, elimination of counterparty credit risk and greater reach in terms of easy accessibility to all. Currency futures are expected to bring about better price discovery and also possibly lower transaction costs. Apart from pure hedgers, currency futures also invite arbitrageurs, speculators and noise traders who may take a bet on exchange rate movements without an underlying or an economic exposure as a motivation for trading.

From an economy-wide perspective, currency futures contribute to hedging of risks and help traders and investors in undertaking their economic activity. There is a large body of empirical evidence which suggests that exchange rate volatility has an adverse impact on foreign trade. Since there are first order gains from trade which contribute to output growth and consumer welfare, currency futures can potentially have an important impact on real economy. Gains from international risk sharing through trade in assets could be of relatively smaller magnitude than gains from trade. However, in a dynamic setting these investments could still significantly impact capital formation in an economy and as such currency futures could be seen as a facilitator in promoting investment and aggregate demand in the economy, thus promoting growth.

16.4.3 The Basics: A futures contract is a standardized contract, traded on an exchange, to buy or sell a certain underlying asset or an instrument at a certain date in the future, at a specified price. Where the underlying asset happens to be a commodity, the futures contract is termed as *commodity futures* whereas in cases where the underlying happens to be a financial asset or instrument, the resultant futures contract is referred to as *financial futures*.

A currency futures contract, also called an FX future, is a type of financial futures contract where the underlying is an exchange rate. In other words, it is a futures contract to exchange one currency for another at a specified date in the future at a price (exchange rate) that is fixed on the last trading date. The buyer or seller in a futures market locks into an exchange rate for a specific value date or delivery date. In other words, currency futures are used primarily as a price setting mechanism rather than for physical exchange of currencies. The future date is called the delivery date or final settlement date. The pre-set price is termed as future price, while the price of the underlying asset on the delivery date is termed as the settlement price. The future price normally converges towards the spot price on the settlement date. The futures contract gives the holder the right to buy or sell, in contrast to the option contract which gives the holder the right, but not the obligation to buy or sell the underlying.

Thus, both the parties of the futures contract must fulfil their contractual obligations on the settlement date. However, such contracts do provide options to deliver the underlying asset or settle the difference in cash. The holder of a contract could exit from his commitment prior to the settlement date by either selling a long position or buying back a short position (offset or reverse trade). The futures contracts are exchange traded derivatives and the exchange's clearing house acts as counterparty to all contracts, sets margin requirements etc.

16.5 Forward Markets Commission (FMC)

FMC was merged with SEBI in September 2015. FMC was the chief regulator of forwards and futures markets in India. Headquartered in Mumbai, it was overseen by the Ministry of Consumer Affairs, Food and Public Distribution, Government of India.

Established in 1953 under the provisions of the Forward Contracts (Regulation) Act, 1952, it consisted of 2 to 4 members, all appointed by the Government of India. The Commission allowed commodity trading in 22 exchanges in India, of which 6 were national.

Just at the time the FMC was established, the Government felt that derivative markets increased speculation which led to increased costs and price instabilities.

Therefore, options and futures trading was prohibited altogether in 1953.

The industry was pushed underground and the prohibition meant that development and expansion came to a halt. As futures and options markets began to develop in the rest of the world, Indian derivatives markets were left behind. The apprehensions about the role of speculation, particularly in the conditions of scarcity, prompted the Government to continue the prohibition well into the 1980s.

This left the country with a large number of small and isolated regional futures markets. The futures markets were dispersed and fragmented, with separate trading communities in different regions with little contact with one another. The exchanges generally were yet to embrace modern technology or modern business practices.

Next to the officially approved exchanges, there were many *hawala* markets. Most of these unofficial commodity exchanges operated for many decades. Some unofficial markets traded 20 to 30 times the volume of the *official* futures exchanges. They offered not only futures, but also option contracts. Transaction costs were low, and they attracted many speculators and smaller hedgers. Absence of regulation and proper clearing arrangements, however, meant that these markets were mostly *regulated* by the reputation of the main players.

Responsibilities and functions of Forward Markets Commission (FMC) were as follows:

1. To advise the Central Government in respect of the recognition or the withdrawal of recognition from any association or in respect of any other matter arising out of the administration of the Forward Contracts (Regulation) Act, 1952.
2. To keep forward markets under observation and to take such action in relation to them, as it may consider necessary, in exercise of the powers assigned to it by or under the Act.
3. To collect and, whenever the Commission thinks it necessary, publish information regarding the trading conditions in respect of goods to which any of the provisions of the Act is made applicable, including information regarding supply, demand and prices, and to submit to the Central Government, periodical reports on the working of forward markets relating to such goods.
4. To make recommendations generally with a view to improving the organization and working of forward markets.
5. To undertake the inspection of the accounts and other documents of any recognized association or registered association or any member of such association whenever it considers it necessary.

17

Derivative Instruments in India

India has introduced different equity derivatives in a phased manner. This phased approach was adopted in India with index futures being introduced in June 2000, index options in June 2001 and individual stock options in July 2001.

17.1 L.C. Gupta Committee on Derivatives Trading in India

Securities and Exchange Board of India (SEBI) set up a 24-member committee under the Chairmanship of L.C. Gupta on November 18, 1996 to develop appropriate regulatory framework for derivatives trading in India. The Committee submitted its report on March 17, 1998 prescribing necessary preconditions for introduction of derivatives trading in India. The committee recommended that derivatives should be declared as *securities* so that regulatory framework applicable to trading of *securities* could also govern trading of derivatives. [1]

17.1.1 Regulatory Objectives: The Committee outlined the goals of regulation in Paragraph 3.1 of its Report which is reproduced below.

"The Committee believes that regulation should be designed to achieve specific, well-defined goals. It is inclined towards positive regulation designed to encourage healthy activity and behaviour. It has been guided by the following objectives:

A. Investor Protection: Attention needs to be given to the following four aspects:

1. **Fairness and Transparency:** The trading rules should ensure that trading is conducted in a fair and transparent manner. Experience in other countries shows that in many cases, derivative brokers/dealers failed to disclose potential risk to the clients. In this context, sales practices adopted by dealers for derivatives would require specific regulation. In some of the most widely reported mishaps in the derivatives market elsewhere, the underlying reason was inadequate internal control system at the user-firm itself so that overall exposure was not controlled and the use of derivatives was for speculation rather than for risk hedging. These experiences provide useful lessons for us for designing regulations.
2. **Safeguard for Clients' Moneys:** Moneys and securities deposited by clients with the trading members should not only be kept in a separate clients' account but should also not be attachable for meeting the broker's own debts. It should be ensured that trading by dealers on own account is totally segregated from that for clients.
3. **Competent and Honest Service:** The eligibility criteria for trading members should be designed to encourage competent and qualified personnel so that investors/clients are served well. This makes it necessary to prescribe qualification for derivatives brokers/dealers and the sales persons appointed by them in terms of a knowledge base.

4. **Market Integrity:** The trading system should ensure that the market's integrity is safeguarded by minimising the possibility of defaults. This requires framing appropriate rules about capital adequacy, margins, clearing corporation etc.

B. Quality of Markets: The concept of *quality of markets* goes well beyond market integrity and aims at enhancing important market qualities, such as cost-efficiency, price-continuity, and price-discovery. This is a much broader objective than market integrity.

C. Innovation: While curbing any undesirable tendencies, the regulatory framework should not stifle innovation which is the source of all economic progress, more so because financial derivatives represent a new rapidly developing area, aided by advancements in information technology".

17.1.2 Derivative Products:

A. Interest and Currency Futures: The Committee stated in Paragraph 1.24: "There are inter-connections among the various kinds of financial futures [equity, interest rate and currency], because the various financial markets are closely inter-linked, as the recent financial market turmoil in East and South-East Asian countries has shown. The basic principles underlying the running of future markets and their regulation are the same. Having a common trading infrastructure will have important advantages. The Committee, therefore, feels that the attempt should be to develop an integrated market structure".

B. Single Stock Derivatives: The Committee advocated a phased introduction of different equity derivatives in India in Paragraph 2.17 of its report: "The consensus in the Committee was that stock index futures would be the best starting point for equity derivatives in India. The Committee has arrived at this conclusion after careful examination of all aspects of the problem, including the survey findings and regulatory preparedness. The Committee would favour the introduction of other types of equity derivatives also, as the derivatives market grows and the market players acquire familiarity with its operations. Other equity derivatives include options on stock index or on individual stocks. There may also be room for more than one stock index futures. It is bound to be a gradual process, shaped by market forces under the over-all supervision of SEBI".

The Committee was not much inclined towards the fourth type of equity derivatives (individual stock futures) given its then limited popularity globally: "The fourth type, viz. individual stock futures, was favoured much less. It is pertinent to note that the US does not permit individual stock futures. Only one or two countries in the world are known to have futures on individual stocks". (Paragraph 2.3)

17.1.3 Use of Derivatives by Mutual Funds: The Committee recommended that mutual funds should be permitted to use derivatives for hedging and portfolio rebalancing: "Mutual funds should be allowed to use financial derivatives for hedging purposes (including anticipated hedging) and portfolio re-balancing within a policy framework and rules laid down by their Board of Trustees who should specify what derivatives are allowed to be used, within what limits, for what purposes, for which schemes, and also the authorisation procedure". (Paragraph 7.10)

17.1.4 SEBI Related Issues: The Committee very rightly emphasised the need for

SEBI to build competencies in the area of derivatives: "SEBI should immediately create a special Derivatives Cell because derivatives demand special knowledge. It should encourage its staff members to undergo training in derivatives and also recruit some specialised personnel.

A Derivatives Advisory Council may also be created to tap the outside expertise for independent advice on many problems which are bound to arise from time to time in regard to derivatives". (Paragraph 4.11[b])

17.2 Amendment of Securities Contract Regulation Act (SCRA)

In pursuance of the recommendations of the L.C. Gupta Committee, SCRA was amended in December 1999 to include derivatives within the ambit of *securities* and the regulatory framework was developed for governing derivatives trading. The Act also made it clear that derivatives shall be legal and valid only if such contracts are traded on a recognised stock exchange, thus precluding OTC derivatives. The government also rescinded in March 2000, the three-decade old notification, which prohibited forward trading in securities.

Derivatives trading commenced in India in June 2000 after SEBI granted the final approval to this effect in May 2000. SEBI permitted the derivatives segments of two stock exchanges NSE and BSE, and their clearing house/corporation to commence trading and settlement in approved derivative contracts. To begin with, SEBI approved trading in index future contracts based on S&P CNX Nifty and BSE-30 (Sensex) index. This was followed by approval for trading in options which commenced in June 2001 and the trading in options on individual securities commenced in July 2001. Future contracts on individual stocks were launched in November 2001. Trading and settlement in derivative contracts is done in accordance with the rules, by-laws, and regulations of the respective exchanges and their clearing house/corporation duly approved by SEBI and notified in the official gazette.

17.3 Measures to Protect the Rights of Investors in the Derivatives Market

Investors' money has to be kept separate at all levels and is permitted to be used only against the liability of the investor and is not available to the trading member or clearing member or even any other investor.

A trading member is required to provide every investor with a risk disclosure document which will disclose the risks associated with the derivatives trading so that investors can take a conscious decision to trade in derivatives.

Investors get the contract note duly time stamped for receipt of the order and execution of the order. The order is executed with the identity of the client and without client ID order is not accepted by the system. The investors can demand the trade confirmation slip with their respective ID in support of the contract note. This protects them from the risk of price favours, if any, extended by the Member.

In the derivatives market all money paid by the investors towards margins on all open positions is kept in trust with the clearing house/clearing corporation and in the event of default of the trading or clearing member the amounts paid by the client towards margins are segregated and not utilized towards the default of the member. However, in the event of default of a member, losses suffered by the investors, if any, on settled/closed out position are compensated from the investors' protection fund, as per the rules, by-laws and regulations of the derivative segment of the exchanges.

17.4 Recent Developments in the Derivatives Market

The derivatives market got a shot in the arm with the Government deciding to treat income from derivatives trading as a non-speculative income.

The decision to treat income from derivative trading as a non-speculative income will contribute to an increase in trading volume in the derivative market since it provides for setting off of derivative income/loss against normal income/loss.

FIIs are permitted to submit appropriate collateral, in cash or otherwise when trading in domestic derivatives. According to market players, this will bring about flexibility and encourage FIIs to take greater exposure through the derivative contracts.

Local players already had the flexibility of submitting collaterals, such as bank guarantee or shares or deposit receipt, in place of cash or along with cash, for meeting their margin obligations.

17.5 Credit Derivatives

Credit derivatives are gaining increasing popularity in many countries. Since the early 1990s, there has been proliferation of different types of credit derivatives in several countries.

A credit derivative is a contract (derivative) to transfer the risk of the total return on a credit asset falling below an agreed level, without transfer of the underlying asset. This is usually achieved by transferring risk on a credit reference asset. Early forms of credit derivatives were financial guarantees. Credit derivatives are designed to allow independent trading/hedging of credit risk. It is also possible to transfer and/or transform credit risk through securitisation. Credit derivative is a logical extension of two of the most significant developments in financial markets, viz., securitisation and derivatives.

17.5.1 Forms of Credit Derivatives: Credit derivatives are instruments that transfer a part or all of the credit risk of an obligation (or a pool of obligations), without transferring the ownership of the underlying asset(s). This is usually achieved by transferring risk on a credit reference asset. Three common forms of credit derivatives are credit default swap (CDS), total return swap (TRS) and credit linked note (CLN).

A. Credit Default Swap (CDS): A CDS consists of swapping, usually on an ongoing basis, the risk premium inherent in an interest rate on a bond or a loan in return for a cash payment that is made in the event of default by the debtor. The CDS has become the main driver of the credit derivatives market, offering liquid price discovery and trading on which the rest of the market is based. It is an agreement between a protection buyer and a protection seller, whereby the buyer pays a periodic fee in return for a contingent payment by the seller upon a credit event happening in the reference entity. The contingent payment usually replicates the loss incurred by creditor of the reference entity in the event of its default. It covers only the credit risk embedded in the asset, risks arising from other factors, such as interest rate movements, remain with the buyer.

B. Total Return Swap (TRS): A TRS (also known as total rate of return swap) is a contract between two counterparties, whereby they swap periodic payments for the period of the contract. Typically, one party receives the total return (interest payments plus any capital gains or losses for the payment period) from a specified reference asset, while the other receives a specified fixed or floating cash flow that is not related to the creditworthiness of the reference asset, as with a vanilla interest rate swap. The payments are based upon the same notional amount. The reference asset may be any asset, index or basket of assets. The TRS is simply a mechanism that allows one party to derive the economic benefit of owning an asset without use of the balance sheet, and which allows the other to effectively buy protection against loss in value due to ownership of a credit asset.

While the CDS provides protection against specific credit events, the TRS protects against the loss of value irrespective of cause, whether default and widening of credit spreads, among others.

C. Credit Linked Note (CLN): A CLN is an instrument whose cash flow depends upon a credit event, which can be a default, credit spread, or rating change. The definition of the relevant credit events must be negotiated by the parties to the note. A CLN, in effect, combines a credit-default swap with a regular note (with coupon, maturity, redemption). Given its regular-note features, a CLN is an on-balance sheet asset, unlike a CDS.

17.5.2 Significance of Credit Derivatives: Credit derivative markets are most active where credit quality measurement and rating systems are transparent and have widespread adoption as in North America and Europe. In addition, the demand for structured credit products in Asia and the Middle East has been growing. The rapid pace of growth and widespread participation in the credit derivatives market in several countries has transformed the financial landscape. Credit derivatives have significance for both banks and investors in mitigating credit risk. For instance, a commercial bank can use credit derivatives to manage the risk of its loan portfolio and an investment bank can use credit derivatives to manage the risks it incurs when underwriting securities. Investors—such as an insurance company, asset manager, or hedge fund—can use credit derivatives to align its credit risk exposure with its desired credit risk profile.

Credit derivatives in international markets have effectively helped to enhance the efficiency of the financial system by providing to both bank and non-bank financial institutions access to a broader range of risk-return combinations and a wider pool of underlying risks and enhancing the liquidity of corporate bond markets. The information revealed through credit derivative mechanism is very useful for supervision and market surveillance.

17.5.3 Benefits of Credit Derivatives: Banks and the financial institutions derive at least three main benefits from credit derivatives:

1. Credit derivatives allow banks to transfer credit risk and hence free up capital, which can be used for other productive purposes.

2. Banks can conduct business on existing client relationships in excess of exposure norms and transfer away the risks. For instance, a bank which has hit its exposure limits with a client group may have to turn down a lucrative guarantee deal. However, with credit derivatives, the bank can take up the guarantee and maintain its exposure limits by transferring the credit risk on the guarantee or previous exposures. This allows bank to maintain client relationships.
3. Banks can construct and manage a credit risk portfolio of their own choice and risk appetite unconstrained by funds, distribution and sales effort.

17.5.4 Risks Involved in Credit Derivatives: Credit derivatives pose risk management challenges of their own. Credit derivatives can transform credit risk in intricate ways that may not be easy to understand. Complex credit derivatives rely on complex models, leading to model risk. Credit rating agencies interpret this complexity for investors, but their ratings can be misunderstood, creating rating agency risk. The settlement of a credit derivative contract following a default can have its own complications, creating settlement risk. Apart from these risks, the credit risk remains the core risk in the credit derivative segment. The use of credit derivative instruments has changed the underlying borrower-lender relationship and established new relationships between lenders that become risk shedders and the new risk takers. This new relationship has the potential for market failure due, for instance, to asymmetric information. The growth of hedge funds, particularly credit-oriented hedge funds, has accelerated market development and credit risk dispersion. While credit derivative markets increasingly facilitate the primary transfer of credit risk, secondary market liquidity is still lacking within some segments, creating the potential for market disruptions. As such, these markets are subject to increased attention from supervisors and policymakers and raise some supervisory concerns.

In short, the use of credit derivatives raises the following concerns:

1. Some of the credit derivatives, which are being used, are at their infancy and need to mature. Introduction of such products, therefore, may be potentially destabilising.
2. The measurement and management of credit risk is much more complicated than market risk.
3. Documentation risk is an important aspect of credit derivatives.
4. Certain incentive issues arise with the use of credit derivatives. This is because such instruments typically change the underlying borrower-lender relationship and establish new relationships between lenders that become risk shedders and the new risk takers. This new relationship has the potential for market failure due, for instance, to asymmetric information.

17.5.5 Credit Derivatives and Sub-prime Crisis of 2007: The role that credit derivatives played in the 2007 sub-prime crisis is well-known. The macroeconomic environment with a prolonged period of low interest rates, high liquidity and low volatility led to underestimation of risks by financial institutions, breakdown of credit and risk management practices in many financial institutions, and shortcomings in financial regulation and supervision. Banks, especially in the US, increasingly turned to *originate* *and distribute model* in which they bundled and sold standardised mortgages as securities. Though favourable credit ratings were obtained for most of these bundled securities by carefully structuring their priority in receiving cash flow from servicing of the original portfolio, many of these were in reality sub-prime securities. As housing prices in the US declined, the defaults rose in several leading international banks. The kind of problems witnessed in the US sub-prime mortgage market can also surface in other types of lending such as leveraged loans and consumer credit. Furthermore, such problems may not confine to industrial countries, but can surface in other emerging economies as well where financial institutions take excessive risks in the wake of weak lending practices, and where regulatory and supervisory frameworks are found to be inadequate.

The unbridled proliferation of complex credit derivatives and excessive risk transfer by adoption of the originate-to-distribute model is recognised as one of the root causes of the current financial crisis. The recent credit turmoil has also underscored the importance of liquidity risk arising from off-balance sheet commitments, implicit or explicit, of the credit intermediaries.

While the development of markets for credit derivatives and asset securitization products can play a critical role in furthering economic growth, this requires to be pursued in a gradual manner by sequencing reforms and putting in place appropriate safeguards before introducing such products.

17.6 Credit Derivatives in India

The credit market refers to the market where financial instruments that embrace credit risk are traded. In addition to traditional instruments, such as loans and advances, corporate bonds, and commercial papers the credit market now includes securitised products in which various credit risks have been pooled as well as credit derivatives whose underlying assets encompass credit risks.

As a financial system which is dominated by bank intermediation, credit has traditionally been the main source of funds to various sectors in the Indian economy, and loans and advances continue to be the preferred part of asset books of banks. However, the implementation of risk management guidelines and the requirement for providing a capital charge for credit risk in the balance sheet has given banks an incentive to look for innovative methods of transferring credit risk from their books.

While simple techniques for transferring credit risk, such as financial guarantees, collateral and credit insurance have long been prevalent in the Indian banking industry, the recent innovative instruments in credit risk transfer are yet to make an impact. However, in recent years the risk management architecture of banks in India has strengthened and they are on the way to becoming Basel II compliant, providing adequate comfort level for the introduction of credit derivatives.

The Reserve Bank in its Annual Policy announced in April 2007 mentioned that as part of the gradual process of financial sector liberalization in India, it was considered appropriate to introduce credit derivatives in a calibrated manner. Furthermore, the amendment to the Reserve Bank of India Act, 1934 had provided legality to OTC (over the counter) derivative instruments, including credit derivatives.

Although derivative instruments were introduced in July 1999 in the money/foreign exchange market in the form of forward rate agreements (FRAs) [2] and interest rate swaps (IRS), [3] credit derivatives are yet to be introduced. The RBI's Annual Policy Statement 2007-08 announced the introduction of credit derivatives in India in a calibrated manner. In view of certain adverse developments in the international financial markets, especially credit markets, resulting from recent financial turmoil, it was widely felt that time is not opportune to introduce the credit derivatives in India for the present. As such, the RBI announced on June 19, 2008 its decision to keep in abeyance the issuance of the final guidelines on introduction of credit derivatives in India.

17.7 Traders and Trading System of Derivatives

17.7.1 Traders in Derivatives Market:

A. Hedgers: Hedgers are the traders who wish to eliminate the risk (of price change) to which they are already exposed. They may take a long position on, or short sell, a commodity and would, therefore, stand to lose should the prices move in the adverse direction. The trader can sell future (or forward) contracts with a matching price, to hedge.

Stocks carry two types of risk: company specific and market risk. While company risk can be minimized by diversifying your portfolio, market risk cannot be diversified but has to be hedged.

Hedging involves protecting an existing asset position from future adverse price movements. In order to hedge a position, a market player needs to take an equal and opposite position in the futures market to the one held in the cash market.

How does one measure the market risk? Market risk can be known from Beta which measures the relationship between movement of the index to the movement of the stock. The beta measures the percentage impact on the stock prices for 1 percent change in the index. Therefore, for a portfolio whose value goes down by 11 percent when the index goes down by 10 percent, the beta would be 1.1. When the index increases by 10 percent, the value of the portfolio increases 11 percent. The idea is to make beta of your portfolio zero to nullify your losses.

B. Speculators: If hedgers are the people who wish to avoid the price risk, speculators are those who are willing to take such risk. These are the people who take position in the market and assume risks to profit from fluctuations in prices. In fact, the speculators consume information, make forecasts about the prices and put their money in these forecasts. Depending on their perceptions, they may take long or short positions on futures and/or options, or may hold spread positions (simultaneous long and short positions on the same derivatives).

Speculators are those who do not have any position on which they enter in futures and options market. They only have a particular view on the market, stock, commodity etc. In short, speculators put their money at risk in the hope of earning profit from an anticipated price change. They consider various factors such as demand, supply, market position, open interests, economic fundamentals and other data to take their positions.

C. Arbitrageurs: Arbitrageurs thrive on market imperfections. An arbitrageur profits by trading a given commodity, or other item, that sells for different prices in different markets. This becomes possible by simultaneous purchase of securities in one market where the price is low and sale in another market, where the price is comparatively higher.

This is done when the same securities are being quoted at different prices in the two markets. Arbitrageurs derive advantage from difference in prices of securities prevailing in the two markets.

An arbitrageur is basically risk averse. He enters into those contracts were he can earn riskless profits. When markets are imperfect, buying in one market and simultaneously selling in other market gives riskless profit. Arbitrageurs are always in the look out for such imperfections.

In the futures market one can take advantages of arbitrage opportunities by buying from lower priced market and selling at the higher priced market. In index futures arbitrage is possible between the spot market and the futures market.

17.7.2 Trading System: It is as under:

A. National Exchange for Automated Trading (NEAT-F&O): Futures and options trading system of NSE—called NEAT-F&O trading system—provides a fully automated screen-based trading for index futures and options, stock futures and options and futures on interest rate on a nationwide basis as well as an online monitoring and surveillance mechanism. It supports an order driven market and provides complete transparency of trading operations. It is similar to that of trading of equities in the cash market segment.

The software for the F&O market has been developed to facilitate efficient and transparent trading in futures and options instruments. Keeping in view the familiarity of trading members with the current capital market trading system, modifications have been introduced in the existing capital market trading system so as to make it suitable for trading futures and options.

B. Trading Mechanism: The NEAT-F&O system supports an order driven market, wherein orders match automatically. Order matching is essentially on the basis of security, its price, time and quantity. All quantity fields are in units and price in rupees. The lot size on the futures and options market is 50 for Nifty. The exchange notifies the regular lot size and tick size for each security traded on this segment from time to time. Orders, as and when they are received, are first time stamped and then immediately processed for potential match. When any order enters the trading system, it is an active order. If it finds a match, a trade is generated. If a match is not found, then the orders are stored in different books. Orders are stored in price-time priority in various books in the following sequence: (a) best price, and (b) within price, by time priority.

C. Entities in the Trading System: There are four entities in the trading system:

1. **Trading Members:** Trading members are members of NSE. They can trade either on their own account or on behalf of their clients including participants. The exchange assigns ID to each trading member. Each trading member can have more than one user.

2. **Clearing Members:** Clearing members are members of NSCCL. They carry out risk management activities and confirmation/inquiry of trades through the trading system.
3. **Professional Clearing Members:** Professional clearing members are clearing members who are not trading member. Typically, banks and custodians become professional clearing members and clear and settle for their trading members.
4. **Participants:** A participant is a client of trading members like financial institutions. These clients may trade through multiple trading members but settle through a single clearing member.

D. Corporate Hierarchy: In the F&O trading software, a trading member has the facility of defining a hierarchy amongst users of the system. This hierarchy comprises corporate manager, branch manager and dealer.

1. **Corporate Manager:** The term *corporate manager* is assigned to a user placed at the highest level in a trading firm. Such a user can perform all the functions such as order and trade-related activities, receiving reports for all branches of the trading member firm and also all dealers of the firm. Additionally, a corporate manager can define exposure limits for the branches of the firm. This facility is available only to the corporate manager.
2. **Branch Manager:** The branch manager is a term assigned to a user who is placed under the corporate manager. Such a user can perform and view order and trade-related activities for all dealers under that branch.
3. **Dealer:** Dealer is a user at the lower level of the hierarchy. A dealer can perform trade-related activities only for himself and does not have access to information on other dealers under either the same branch or other branches.

17.7.3 Order Types and Conditions: The system allows the trading members to enter orders with various conditions attached to them as per their requirements. These conditions are broadly divided into the following three categories:

A. Time Conditions:

1. **Day Order:** A day order, as the name suggests, is an order which is valid for the day on which it is entered. If the order is not executed during the day, the system cancels the order automatically at the end of the day.
2. **Immediate or Cancel (IOC):** An IOC order allows the user to buy or sell a contract as soon as the order is released into the system, failing which the order is cancelled from the system. Partial match is possible for the order, and the unmatched portion of the order is cancelled immediately.

B. Price Conditions:

1. **Stop-loss:** This facility allows the user to release an order into the system, after the market price (last traded price) of the security reaches or crosses a threshold price, e.g. if for stop-loss buy order, the trigger is 1027, the limit price is 1030 and the market (last traded) price is 1023, then this order is released into the system once the market price reaches or exceeds 1027. This order is added to the regular lot book with time of triggering as the time stamp, as a limit order of 1030. For the stop-loss sell order, the trigger price has to be greater than the limit price.

C. Other Conditions:

1. **Market Price:** Market orders are orders for which no price is specified at the time the order is entered (i.e. price is market price). For such orders, the system determines the price.
2. **Limit Price:** Price of the order after triggering from stop loss book.
3. **Pro:** Pro means that the orders are entered on the trading member's own account.
4. **Cli:** Cli means that the trading member enters the orders on behalf of a client.
5. **Trigger Price:** It is the price at which an order gets triggered from stop-loss book. Several combinations of the above are allowed thereby providing enormous flexibility to the users.

17.7.4 Market Watch: The purpose of market watch is to allow continuous monitoring of contracts or securities that are of specific interest to the user. It displays trading information for contracts selected by the user. The user also gets a broadcast of all the cash market securities on the screen. This function is also available if the user selects the relevant securities for display on the market watch screen. Display of trading information related to cash market securities is in *read only* format, i.e. the dealer can only view the information on cash market but cannot trade in them through the system. This is the main window from the dealer's perspective.

The following windows are displayed on a trader's workstation screen.

1. Title bar.
2. Ticker window of futures and options market.
3. Ticker window of underlying (capital) market.
4. Tool bar.
5. Market watch window.
6. Inquiry window.
7. Snap quote.
8. Order/trade window.
9. System message window.

17.7.5 Placing Orders on the Trading System: While entering orders on the trading system—for both futures and the options market—members are required to identify orders as being proprietary or client orders. Proprietary orders should be identified as *Pro* and those of clients should be identified as *Cli*. Apart from this, in the case of *Cli* trades, the client account number should also be provided. The futures and options market is a zero sum game, i.e. the total number of long in contracts always equals the total number of short in contracts. The total number of outstanding contracts (long/short) at any point in time is called the *open interest*. This open interest figure is a good indicator of the liquidity in the contract. Based on studies carried out in international exchanges, it is found that open interest is maximum in near month expiry contracts.

17.7.6 Eligibility Criteria for Securities/Indices Traded in F&O:

A. Eligibility Criteria for Stocks:

1. The stock is chosen from amongst the top 500 stocks in terms of average daily market capitalisation and average daily traded value in the previous 6 months on a rolling basis.

2. A stock's median quarter-sigma order size over the last 6 months should not be less than ₹ 1 lakh. For this purpose, a stock's quarter-sigma order size should mean the order size (in value terms) required to cause a change in the stock price equal to one-quarter of a standard deviation.
3. The market wide position limit in the stock should not be less than ₹ 50 crore. The market wide position limit (number of shares) is valued taking into account the closing prices of stocks in the underlying cash market on the date of expiry of contract in the month. The market wide position limit of open position (in terms of the number of underlying stock) on futures and option contracts on a particular underlying stock should be lower of 20 percent of the number of shares held by non-promoters in the relevant underlying security i.e. free-float holding.

If an existing security fails to meet the eligibility criteria for 3 months consecutively, then no fresh month contract will be issued on that security.

However, the existing unexpired contracts can be permitted to trade till expiry and new strikes can also be introduced in the existing contract months.

For unlisted companies coming out with initial public offering, if the net public offer is ₹ 500 crore or more, then the exchange may consider introducing stock options and stock futures on such stocks at the time of its listing than in cash market.

B. Eligibility Criteria for Indices: The exchange may consider introducing derivative contracts on an index if the stocks contributing to 80 percent weightage of the index are individually eligible for derivative trading. However, no single eligible stock in the index should have a weightage of more than 5 percent in the index. The above criteria is applied every month, if the index fails to meet the eligibility criteria for 3 months consecutively, then no fresh month contract would be issued on that index.

C. Eligibility Criteria for Stocks for Derivatives Trading on Account of Corporate Restructuring: The criteria in this case are as under:

1. All the following conditions shall be met in the case of shares of a company undergoing restructuring through any means for eligibility to reintroduce derivative contracts on that company from the first day of listing of the post- restructured company's stock in the underlying market:

- Futures and options contracts on the stock of the original (pre-restructure) company were traded on any exchange prior to its restructuring.
- Pre-restructured company had a market capitalisation of at least ₹ 1,000 crore prior to its restructuring.
- Post-restructured company would be treated like a new stock and if it is, in the opinion of the exchange, likely to be at least one-third the size of the pre-restructured company in terms of revenues, or assets, or (where appropriate) analyst valuations.
- In the opinion of the exchange, the scheme of restructuring does not suggest that the post-restructured company would have any characteristic (for example extremely low free float) that would render the company ineligible for derivatives trading.

2. If the above conditions are satisfied, then the exchange takes the following course of action in dealing with the existing derivative contracts on the pre-restructured

company and introduction of fresh contracts on the post- restructured company:

- In the contract month in which the post-restructured company begins to trade, the exchange introduces near month, middle month and far month derivative contracts on the stock of the restructured company.
- In subsequent contract months, the normal rules for entry and exit of stocks in terms of eligibility requirements would apply. If these tests are not met, the exchange shall not permit further derivative contracts on this stock and future month series shall not be introduced.

To sum up, financial derivatives are of recent origin in India, barring trade-related forward contracts in the forex market. Over-the-counter (OTC) as well as exchange-traded derivatives have been introduced, marking an important development in the structure of financial markets in India. Forward contracts in the forex market have also been liberalised. OTC derivatives, viz. interest rate swaps (IRS) and forward rate agreements (FRAs) were introduced in July 1999. The IRS and FRA were introduced with a view to deepening the money market as also to enable banks, primary dealers and financial institutions to hedge interest rate risks.

Endnotes

1. SEBI also set up a group in June 1998 under the chairmanship of Professor J.R. Varma, to recommend measures for risk containment in derivatives market in India. The report, which was submitted in October 1998, worked out the operational details of margining system, methodology for charging initial margins, net worth of brokers, deposit requirements and real-time monitoring requirements.
2. The FRA is an off-balance sheet contract between two parties under which one party agrees on the start date for trade and the party that agrees, would lodge a notional deposit with the other for a specified sum of money for a specified period of time (the FRA period) at a specified rate of interest (the contract rate). The party that has agreed to make the notional deposit has, thus, sold the FRA to the other party who has bought it.
3. The IRS is a contract between two counter-parties for exchange interest payment for a specified period based on a notional principal amount. The notional principal is used to calculate interest payments, but is not exchanged. Only interest payments are exchanged.

Part III
Interest Rates

18

Determination of Interest Rates

Interest is defined as a payment made or received for the use of money. It is calculated as a percentage of the principal amount, payable annually. Rate of interest is important because it affects saving and investment decisions of the people in an economy.

18.1 Significance of Interest Rate

The efficacy of monetary policy depends on the magnitude and the speed with which policy rate changes are transmitted to the ultimate objectives of monetary policy, viz., inflation and growth. With the deepening of financial systems and growing sophistication of financial markets, most monetary authorities use interest rate as the key instrument to achieve the ultimate objectives of monetary policy. Adjustments in the policy interest rate, for instance, directly impact short-term money market rates which then transmit the monetary policy impulses across financial markets and maturity spectrum, including banks' deposit and lending rates. These, in turn, influence consumption, saving and investment decisions of firms and households, which ultimately influence aggregate demand, and hence, output and inflation. The interest rate channel of transmission is the leading channel of transmission in several countries, including many emerging market economies.

18.2 Types of Rate of Interest

18.2.1 Gross and Net Rate of Interest: Gross interest means the rate of interest actually charged in the loan market. However, the lender has to spend some money to maintain accounts and collect payment of interest. If the lender is to be compensated for all these administrative expenses, the gross rate will be somewhat above the net rate which is actually available to him. Thus,

Net interest = Gross interest - Administrative costs.

18.2.2 Real and Money Rate of Interest: Money rate of interest is calculated simply in terms of money paid. Real rate of interest pertains to the ratio of the purchasing power of money returned to the purchasing power of money borrowed. This distinction is important in the context of inflationary pressures in the economy. Real rate of interest is the difference between the money rate of interest and the rate of inflation. For example, if the money rate of interest is 15 percent and the inflation rate is 10 percent, the real rate of interest is 5 percent. If inflation rate is 18 percent, the real rate is -3 percent.

Among the various explanations provided by economists for the determination of the rate of interest, the following two are important:

1. Loanable fund theory.
2. Liquidity preference theory.

They are explained below.

18.3 Loanable Fund Theory of the Rate of Interest

Loanable fund theory is attributed to Swedish economist Knut Wicksell (1851-1926) and the British economist Dennis Robertson (1890-1963). According to this theory, the rate of interest is determined by the demand for and the supply of loanable funds in an economy. It is based on the assumption of perfect competition. The demand for loans originates from three types of borrowers, viz. producers, consumers and government. Producers borrow in order to make investment in industrial and commercial activities. Consumers borrow primarily for financing the purchase of durable consumer goods. Government borrows to finance public works (roads, bridges etc.) in peace-time and to meet emergencies like a war.

Adding up the demand for loans by producers, consumers and the government, a combined demand curve for loans is obtained. Like any other demand curve, it slopes downward, signifying that lower the rate of interest, greater the demand for loans and vice versa.

Supply of loans comes from the current savings of households as well as business firms. These savings are channelled through commercial banks, insurance companies and other financial institutions. They are made available to various types of borrowers. Adding up the personal and business savings, a combined supply curve is obtained which, like any other supply curve, slopes upwards, denoting that lower the rate of interest, the lower the supply of loans and vice versa.

By bringing together the demand and supply curves of loanable funds, one can see the determination of the rate of interest at the point where the two curves intersect. In Figure 18.1, this point of intersection (or equilibrium) is represented by E.

Loanable fund theory is a very simplistic explanation of an otherwise complex phenomenon. In real world, rate of interest is influenced by a host of subjective and objective factors.

18.4 Liquidity Preference Theory of the Rate of Interest

According to British economist John Maynard Keynes (1883-1946), rate of interest is a reward for parting with liquidity for a specified period of time. Rate of interest, he believed, is a purely monetary phenomenon determined by the demand for and supply of money (liquidity).

The supply of money is given by the government, and it is an exogenous (or autonomous) factor and accepted as it is. However, the demand for money (or preference for liquidity) varies and hence plays active role in the determination of the rate of interest.

18.4.1 Motives for Holding Cash: Why do people demand money (i.e. liquidity) when they know that holding of cash does not earn them any interest income? If wealth can be held in the form of interest-earning bonds why hold it in the form of cash? Keynes explained public preference for liquidity in terms of the following three motives.

A. Transactions Motive: People prefer to hold some money for meeting current transactions of daily life.

Figure 18.1: Equilibrium Interest Rate (Loanable Fund Theory)

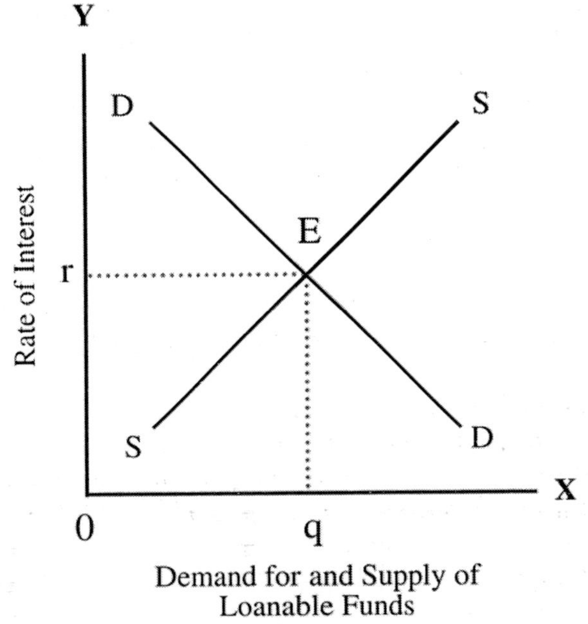

B. Precautionary Motive: People hold liquidity to provide for contingencies requiring sudden expenditure, e.g. accident, illness etc.

According to Keynes, the demand for liquidity for transaction and precautionary motives (labelled L_1) is positively related to the level of income. It is generally a fixed proportion of an individual's income. Thus, $L_1 = kY$.

C. Speculative Motive: People may hold surplus cash over and above what is required to satisfy transaction and precautionary motives. Keynes called this extra demand for liquidity (labelled L_2) as speculative demand for money for speculative motive. It arises due to fluctuations of interest rates and uncertainty about them. Thus, it is a function of the rate of interest, $L_2 = f(r)$.

Let us assume that the normal expected rate of interest is 10 percent and the bonds also carry 10 percent rate of interest. If the actual market rate of interest falls below the normal rate, the bond prices will lie above their normal price because there is inverse relationship between bond prices and interest rates. In such a situation people in general will expect rate of interest to rise (i.e. bond prices to fall) in the near future. Bond holders would like to sell their bonds now at their high price and hold cash with a view to repurchase bonds when their prices fall to normal (i.e. rate of interest rises to normal). In this process they expect to make capital gains. Thus, individuals prefer to hold cash rather than bonds when the rate of interest is low relative to their expectations. The reverse holds when actual rate of interest lies above the normal rate (i.e. bond prices are below their normal price). Thus, Keynesian theory postulates a negative relationship between interest rate and the speculative demand for cash.

Keynsian theory assumes that different people have different expectations about future interest rates (or bond prices). There are two types of speculators in the market, the bulls and the bears. Bulls are those who expect the bond prices to rise in the future while bears are those who anticipate fall in bond prices. Thus, bulls invest all their surplus cash in bonds whereas bears move out of bonds into cash. Therefore, the speculative demand for liquidity arises from bears. These bears accumulate their cash reserves to purchase bonds when either bond prices have fallen as expected or when they start anticipating that bond prices will rise in future.

The demand for money (liquidity) is represented by the downward-sloping curve labelled LP in Figure 18.2.

Figure 18.2: Liquidity Preference Curve

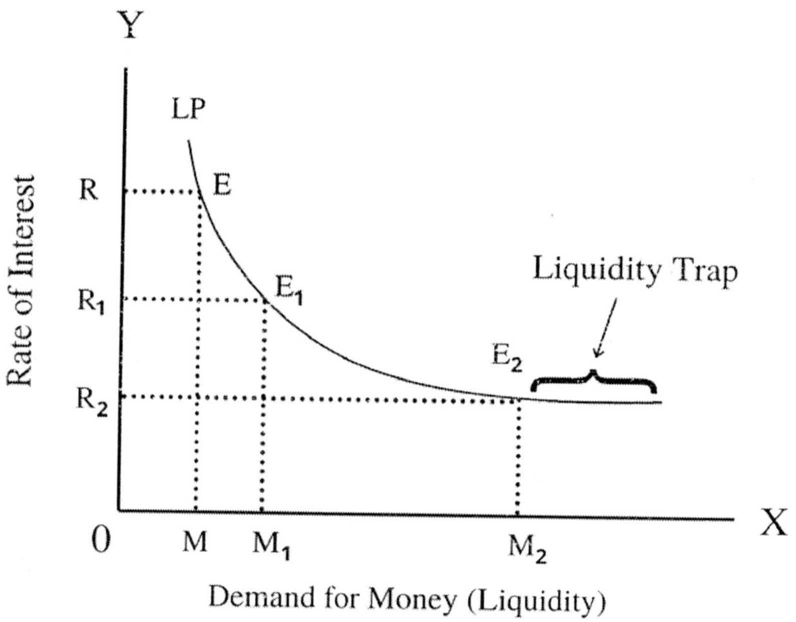

Since money supply is determined by monetary authorities, it can be considered as fixed at a particular time.

The demand curve for liquidity describes an inverse relation between interest rate and the demand for money. The quantity of money demanded declines as interest rate rises because the opportunity cost (interest foregone) of holding money is high. The LP curve comes closer and closer to the vertical axis.

Conversely, at lower interest rates, larger money balances will be held because the cost of holding money (interest foregone) is low. Keynes suggested the possibility of *liquidity trap* which refers to a situation when the demand for liquidity for speculative purpose is very high because the rate of interest is very low. Everybody wants to hold as much cash as possible in expectation of future rise in the rate of interest. Expansion of money supply by the government cannot lower the rate of interest below a certain point. The extra money released by the government is held by the public, i.e. it gets trapped in public hands. The rate of interest R_2 in Figure 18.2 is the minimum below which it cannot fall.

A major criticism of the Keynesian theory of demand for liquidity is that it does not explain how people form their expectations about future normal rate of interest. In order to explain the rate of interest it assumes the existence of a normal rate about which the actual rate gravitates. Thus, the theory assumes what it intends to explain.

19

Causes of Interest Rate Differentials

Borrowers pay interest because they must pay a price for gaining the ability to spend now, instead of having to wait years to save up enough money. For example, a person or family may take out a mortgage for a house for which they cannot presently pay in full, but the loan allows them to become homeowners now instead of far into the future.

Businesses also borrow for future profit. They may borrow now to buy equipment so they can begin earning those revenues today. Banks borrow to increase their activities, whether lending or investing and pay interest to clients for this service.

Interest can thus be considered a cost for one entity and income for another. It can represent the lost opportunity or opportunity cost of keeping money as cash in almira as opposed to lending it.

As interest rates are a significant factor of the income one can earn by lending money, it is important that one understand how prevailing interest rates change. Interest rates change primarily by the forces of supply and demand, which are also affected by inflation and monetary policy.

19.1 How Are Interest Rates Determined?

Interest rate levels are a factor of the supply and demand of credit. An increase in the demand for money or credit will raise interest rates, while a decrease in the demand for credit will decrease them. Conversely, an increase in the supply of credit will reduce interest rates while a decrease in the supply of credit will increase them.

An increase in the amount of money made available to borrowers increases the supply of credit. For example, when you open a bank account, you are lending money to the bank. Depending on the kind of account you open, the bank can use that money for its business and investment activities. In other words, the bank can lend out that money to other customers. The more banks can lend, the more credit is available to the economy. And as the supply of credit increases, the price of borrowing (interest) decreases.

Credit available to the economy decreases as lenders decide to defer the repayment of their loans. For instance, when you choose to postpone paying this month's credit card bill until next month or even later, you are not only increasing the amount of interest you will have to pay but also decreasing the amount of credit available in the market. This, in turn, will increase the interest rates in the economy.

Supply and demand are the primary forces behind interest rate levels. The interest rate for each different type of loan, however, depends on the credit risk, time, tax considerations.

For details, see chapter 18 of this book.

19.2 What is an Interest Rate Differential?

An interest rate is the cost of borrowing money. Or, on the other side of the coin, it is the compensation for the service and risk of lending money. In both cases it keeps the economy moving by encouraging people to borrow, to lend, and to spend. But prevailing interest rates are always changing, and different types of loans offer different interest rates. A lender or a borrower must understand the reasons for these changes and differences.

In the real world varying interest rates prevail at the same time in a country. Thus, individual borrowers pay a higher rate of interest than corporate bonds just like corporate bonds carry a higher interest rate than government bonds.

Interest rate differentials pertain mainly to gross interest (or market rate of interest) though there can be differences in pure rate of interest. Pure rate of interest is defined as the rate received on riskless loan.

In general, an interest rate differential weighs the contrast in interest rates between two similar interest-bearing assets. Interest rate differentials simply measure the difference in interest rates between two securities. If one bond yields 5 percent and another 3 percent, the differential would be 2 percentage points. Such diffetentials are most often used in fixed income trading, forex trading, and lending calculations.

19.3 Causes of Differences in Interest Rates

The important causes of differences in interest rates are the following:

19.3.1 Risk of Default: Rate of interest varies directly with the risk attached to the loan. Thus, lower is the risk, the lower the interest rate and vice versa. Governments can obtain loans at lower rates than private firms. In fact, investment in government bonds is risk-free (gilt-edged investment) and therefore the interest earned is almost pure rate of interest. The higher rate of interest earned from non-government agencies is a premium for risk-taking.

19.3.2 Duration of the Loan: Rate of interest differs with the term (duration) of a loan because duration is related to uncertainty. Thus, the shorter is the term of a loan, the lower the interest rate and vice-versa. Lenders expect a higher rate of interest on long-term loans because the risk element is greater. Also, the face value of a long-term loan, compared to that of a short-term loan, is more vulnerable to the effects of inflation.

Return on risk is a part of gross interest in addition to pure interest. Moreover, a short-term loan is more liquid type of investment and therefore the lender would be willing to charge a lower rate of interest.

Other things being the same, rates of interest also differ according to term to maturity (time-length) of debt. The resulting structure is called the term structure of interest rates and the curve showing the relation between yield and term to maturity is called the *yield curve*.

See yield curve in chapter 20 of this book.

19.3.3 Liquidity of the Security: Liquidity of an asset refers to the degree of ease and certainty with which it can be converted into cash at short notice without any loss.

Creditors generally prefer more liquid to less liquid assets. This means, that, other things being the same, a lender would be willing to charge a lower rate of interest on more liquid debt than on a less liquid debt.

Risk refers to the likelihood of the loan being repaid. A greater chance that the loan will not be repaid leads to higher interest rate levels. If, however, the loan is *secured*, meaning there is some sort of collateral that the lender will acquire in case the loan is not paid back (such as a car or a house), the rate of interest will probably be lower. This is because the risk factor is accounted for by the collateral.

Interest rate varies with the nature of securities offered by the borrowers. Loans against the security of gold or government bonds carry less interest since these securities can easily be converted into cash by the lenders. But loans are also sanctioned by giving securities of immovable properties, like land and house. Rate of interest against those securities will tend to be high since these are not easily converted into cash.

19.3.4 Financial Standing of the Borrower: Rate of interest may vary due to the lender's idea about the financial strength or creditworthiness of the borrower. A borrower with known integrity and reputation can get loans at low rates. The reverse will be the case if the credibility of the borrower is doubtful. Usually, whenever government takes loans from its own citizens, it pays low interest rate as no one casts any doubt on the ability of the government to pay back money in due time.

19.3.5 Market Imperfections: Market imperfections seem to be another reason for the variation in interest rates. There is variety of institutions that carry on money-lending business. For instance, banks, insurance companies, house building bank specialize in different kinds of loans charging different interest rates.

Interest rate may differ due to monopolistic/oligopolistic advantages enjoyed by the lenders. A lending institution in a small town may have no competitors and the loan-seekers there will have to pay higher rate of interest than prevalent in a big city. Moneylenders and pawnbrokers in Indian villages provide good examples of such monopolistic advantage. Because they know each other well and live in the same community, they understand each other's financial circumstances and can offer very flexible, convenient and fast services. These services can also be costly and the choice of financial products limited and very short-term.

Historically, moneylenders have played a significant role in meeting the credit needs of the rural producers. With stringent laws against money lending and the phenomenal growth of the formal credit delivery system, the role of moneylenders has decreased, but they are still in business under several disguises.

Moneylenders usually charge higher rates from poorer borrowers. While moneylenders are often demonized and accused of usury, their services are convenient and fast, and they can be very flexible when borrowers run into problems. Moneylenders are popular because, unlike government agencies, they give credit for every purpose. They are easily approachable by the credit seekers and there are not many formalities in transacting a loan. However, the malpractices adopted by the moneylenders to exploit the needy farmers cannot be overlooked. These malpractices pertain to charging of high rate of interest and adopting unfair means in the maintenance of accounts.

19.3.6 Rate of Inflation: The moneylender takes a risk that the borrower may not pay back the loan. Thus, interest provides a certain compensation for bearing risk. Coupled with the risk of default is the risk of inflation. When one lends money now, the prices of goods and services may go up by the time one is paid back. Therefore, the original purchasing power of money decreases. Thus, interest protects against future rises in inflation.

The higher the inflation rate, the more interest rates are likely to rise. This occurs because lenders will demand higher interest rates as compensation for the decrease in purchasing power of the money they are paid in the future.

19.3.7 Cost of Servicing Loans: Giving a loan often entails a certain cost of keeping records, making collections and sometimes resorting to legal measures to recover the money. These costs differ from borrower to borrower. It is administratively economical for a bank to lend large sum of money to an industrial company than to lend small sums to a large number of individuals. In general, the bigger is the loan with fewer instalments, the lower the cost per rupee of servicing the loan.

19.3.8 Government Policy: The government has a say in how interest rates are affected. In India, Reserve Bank of India (RBI) often makes announcements about how monetary policy will affect interest rates. RBI announces various types of interest rates periodically.

For current interest rate policy of RBI, see section 21.3 of chapter 21 of this book.

19.4 Types of Credit: Based on Repayment and Interest Options

19.4.1 Revolving Line of Credit: Bank decides on the limit up to which a borrower can withdraw from this facility. Flexibility of withdrawal and repayment is provided to the borrower. Interest is charged on the balances either on a monthly basis or on daily basis depending on the agreement. Examples of this type of credit include credit cards and overdraft loans.

19.4.2 Flat Rate Loans: Interest on the loan is charged on the original principal amount disbursed and not on the outstanding loan balance as, for example in the case of personal loans.

19.4.3 Floating Rate Loans: Loan is disbursed at the beginning. The tenure and monthly payments are also fixed. But interest rate is not fixed. If the interest rate undergoes change either monthly payment is revised or tenure is revised. Home loans are good example of this type of loan.

19.4.4 Equated Monthly Instalment (EMI): The entire loan is disbursed at the beginning to the borrower. The monthly repayment amount and the number of payments are fixed in the beginning. The repayment mostly starts one month after disbursal of loan, and sometimes first instalment is taken at the time of disbursal. Car loans and home loans are cases in point.

19.4.5 Loan without Collateral: Some loans like personal loans and credit card loans are given without any collateral or guarantee. Loans which are given without any guarantee attract higher rate of interest.

19.4.6 Loan with Collateral: Loans with lesser interest rate can be availed by giving gold or some other collateral. If the loan is not repaid on time, the lender can auction the collateral and recover the borrowed amount.

19.4.7 Mandatory Interest but Flexible Principal Repayment: The entire loan is disbursed at the beginning. The borrower has to compulsorily pay only interest periodically. The principal repayment can be done by the borrower any time. Examples include loan against LIC policy, gold or securities.

20

Theories of Term Structure of Interest Rates

20.1 What is Term Structure of Interest Rates?

Term structure of interest rates, commonly known as the yield curve, depicts the interest rates of similar quality bonds at different maturities.

Essentially, term structure of interest rates is the relationship between interest rates or bond yields and different terms or maturities. When graphed, the term structure of interest rates is known as a yield curve, and it plays a crucial role in identifying the current state of an economy. The term structure of interest rates reflects expectations of market participants about future changes in interest rates and their assessment of monetary policy conditions.

Generally, yields increase in line with maturity, giving rise to an upward-sloping, or normal, yield curve. The yield curve is primarily used to illustrate the term structure of interest rates for standard government-issued securities. This is important as it is a measure of the debt market's feeling about risk.

Although some financial instruments are issued by the same borrowers and have the same characteristics except for maturities, they have often different interest rates.

20.2 Shapes and Uses of Yield Curve

Yield curve has three primary shapes.

1. **Upward-sloping Curve:** It means long-term yields are higher than short-term yields. This is considered to be the *normal* slope of the yield curve and signals that the economy is in an expansionary mode.
2. **Downward-sloping Curve:** It indicates that short-term yields are higher than long-term yields. Labelled as an *inverted* yield curve, it signifies that the economy is in, or about to enter, a recessive period.
3. **Flat Curve:** It shows very little variation between short- and long-term yields. It signals that the market is unsure about the future direction of the economy.

The term structure of interest rates reflects expectations of market participants about future changes in interest rates and their assessment of monetary policy conditions.

The yield curve is considered the benchmark for the credit market, as it reports the yields of risk-free fixed income investments across a range of maturities. In the credit market, banks and lenders use this benchmark as a gauge for determining lending and savings rates.

Ordinarily, yield curve is upward-sloping. One basic explanation for this phenomenon is that investors demand higher interest rates for longer-term investments as compensation for investing their money in longer-duration investments. Occasionally, long-term yields may fall below short-term yields, creating an inverted yield curve that is generally regarded as a harbinger of recession.

The term structure of interest rates and the direction of the yield curve can be used to judge the overall credit market environment. A flattening of the yield curve means longer-term rates are falling in comparison to short-term rates, which could have implications for a recession. When short-term rates begin to exceed long-term rates, the yield curve is inverted, and a recession is likely occurring or approaching.

When longer-term rates fall below shorter-term rates, the outlook for credit over the long term is weak. This is often consistent with a weak or recessionary economy, which is defined by two consecutive periods of negative growth in the gross domestic product (GDP).

Yield curve is a plot of the interest rates (yield to maturity) for particular types of bonds with different terms of maturity, but the same risk, liquidity, and tax treatments. Yield curves are classified in terms of their shapes and are used to explain the condition in financial markets and the economy. Yield curve may be upward-sloping, flat, downward-sloping or any other shape in-between. Different shapes appear under different economic conditions. They are used to explain or predict an economic condition. A typical yield curve is shown in Figure 20.1. Interest rate is 5 percent on 1-year maturity, 6 percent on 2-year maturity, and 7 percent on 3-year maturity.

Figure 20.1: A Normal Yield Curve

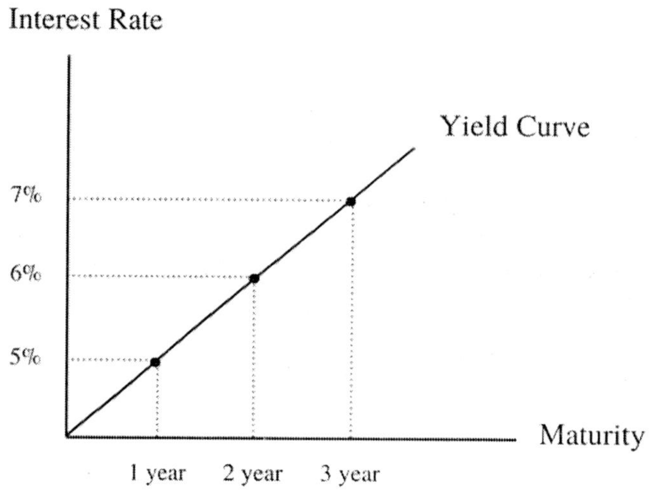

20.3 Three Theories to Explain Yield Curve

Why does a yield curve have different shapes? Why does it change from time to time?

There are three theories for different interest rates among financial instruments with different maturities.

1. Liquidity premium theory.

2. Segmented market theory.
3. Expectations theory.

20.3.1 Liquidity Premium Theory: Normally, the yield curve is upward-sloping. Interest rates on short-term securities are normally lower than interest rates on long-term securities. Securities include shares, scrips, stocks, bonds, debentures, debenture stocks, or other marketable securities of a like nature in or of any incorporated company or other body corporate. Liquidity of an asset means how easily it can be converted into cash and at what loss of its capital value. If an asset cannot be converted into cash easily (i.e. at short notice) or at minimum loss of its value, it is less liquid.

One important difference between short-term securities and long-term securities is their liquidities. In this context, following general rules are noteworthy:

1. Liquidity of short-term securities is higher than liquidity of long-term securities.
2. Even if one cannot sell them, short-term securities will mature sooner than long-term securities and owners of short-term securities will receive full payment sooner.
3. Savers (lenders) prefer liquidity.
4. Demand for short-term securities is higher than demand for long-term securities.
5. Interest rate on short-term securities is lower than interest rates on long-term securities.

Although the liquidity premium theory can explain the yield curve most of the time, it cannot explain why a yield curve becomes sometimes flat, downward-sloping or any shape in-between. Segmented market and expectations theories complement the liquidity premium theory.

20.3.2 Segmented Market Theory: It assumes that the interest rate on each instrument is determined in a separate market with a separate market demand and supply. A short-term interest rate is determined by demand for and supply of short-term securities in the short-term security market. Similarly, a long-term interest rate is determined by demand for and supply of long-term securities in the long-term security market.

In fact, markets of securities can be divided into three different maturities: short-term, mid-term, and long-term. Then, depending on relative demand and supply in each market, a yield curve may have a particular shape.

Although the segmented market theory can explain any shapes of yield curve, based on relative demand and supply of each maturity security, it cannot explain why demands and supplies differ among markets. In reality, demand for each maturity securities is not completely independent of each other. The expectations theory considers this interdependency among securities and provides a reason for different demands.

20.3.3 Expectations Theory: Expectations mean how professional traders and other interested persons in the market anticipate future economic conditions, inflation rate and other macroeconomic variables in an economy. If they expect, for example, the Indian economy to be in an expansion phase of business cycle, then they will expect interest rates to rise in the future. Hence, the yield curve of today should be upward-sloping. Reverse will hold if they expect recessionary tendencies in the future. Similarly, if they expect the inflation rate to rise in the Indian economy, then they will again expect interest rates to rise in the future. So the yield curve of today should again be upward-sloping. Thus, an upward-sloping yield curve of today may indicate expectations of market players of either an expansion or inflation in the Indian economy in the near future.

The three theories of the shape of yield curve explained above are complimentary. While interpreting an actual yield curve, one must apply all the three theories.

21

Interest Rates in India

In India, banks are the main conduits through which monetary impulses are transmitted to the real economy. Hence, it has been the endeavour of RBI to strengthen the monetary transmission by focussing on the design of the lending interest rates of the banking system. It was in keeping with this that Reserve Bank of India (RBI) introduced the base rate system in July 2010, which was replaced by the marginal cost of funds based lending rate (MCLR) system in April 2016.

However, the transmission to lending rates of banks has been impeded by a variety of factors, the major one being the opacity in the process by which the banks set their lending interest rates. To address this concern, RBI has refined the interest rate setting methodology of banks from time-to-time.

21.1 Interest Rate Policy: Pre-reforms Period (Before 1991)

Prior to 1991, given the command and control nature of the economy, the RBI had to resort to direct instruments like interest rate regulations, selective credit control and the cash reserve ratio (CRR) [1] as major monetary policy [2] instruments. These instruments were used intermittently to mitigate the monetary impact of the budgetary operations of the Government.

The administered interest rate regime in the pre-reform period kept the yield rate of the government securities artificially low. The demand for these securities was created through intermittent hikes in the statutory liquidity ratio (SLR). [3] The task before the RBI was, therefore, to develop the markets to prepare the ground for indirect operations. As a first step, yields on government securities were made market-related. At the same time, the RBI helped create an array of other market-related financial products. At the next stage, the interest rate structure was simultaneously rationalised and banks were given the freedom to determine their major rates. As a result of these developments, the RBI could use open market operations (OMO) [4] as an effective instrument for liquidity management, including curb on short-term volatility in the foreign exchange market.

21.2 Interest Rate Policy: Post-reforms Period (i.e. since 1991)

21.2.1 Prime Lending Rate (PLR) System: After the introduction of the financial sector reforms in the early 1990s, RBI initiated various measures to progressively deregulate the interest rates—both deposit and lending rates. In a major initiative in October 1994, RBI deregulated lending rates for credit limits over ₹ 2 lakh. Banks were also required to declare their prime lending rates (PLR), i.e., the interest rate charged for the most creditworthy borrowers. PLR was to be computed taking into account factors such as cost of funds and transaction costs, and was expected to act as a floor for lending above ₹ 2 lakh. The experience with the working of the PLR system, however, was not satisfactory mainly for two reasons: (i) both the PLR and the spread charged over the PLR varied widely across banks and (ii) the PLRs of banks were rigid and inflexible in relation to the overall direction of interest rates in the economy.

21.2.2 Benchmark Prime Lending Rate (BPLR) System: Keeping in view the request from banks that the PLR should be converted into a reference or benchmark rate for banks, RBI advised banks in April 2003 to announce a Benchmark PLR (BPLR) with the approval of their boards.

Banks were required to compute BPLRs taking into account the cost of funds, operational costs, minimum margin to cover regulatory requirements (provisioning and capital charge), and profit margin. The BPLR system also fell short of its original intent of enhancing transparency and serving as the reference rate for pricing of loan products. The transparency aspect, in particular, was hit by the fact that a large part of the lending actually took place at interest rates below the announced BPLRs. The residential housing loans and the consumer durable loans were outside the purview of the BPLR. As such, sub-BPLR lending became a major distortion in terms of cross-subsidisation across borrower categories.

21.2.3 Base Rate System: The drawbacks of the BPLR system called for a further refinement of the lending rate system and the base rate system was introduced in July 2010. Under this framework, each bank was required to announce its base rate, taking into account, *inter alia*, the costs of borrowed funds. The base rate was to be the minimum rate for all loans, except for some specified categories. The actual lending rate charged to the borrowers was to be the base rate plus borrower-specific charges. The base rate system, with a link to the banks' cost of funds, was expected to facilitate better pricing of loans, enhance transparency in lending rates and improve the assessment of the transmission of monetary policy.

In practice, flexibility accorded to banks in the determination of cost of funds—average, marginal or blended cost—caused opacity in the determination of lending rates by banks and clouded an accurate assessment of the speed and strength of the transmission. Moreover, the discrimination in the pricing of credit between the new and old customers continued, as banks often adjusted the spread over the base rate to benefit the new borrowers.

21.2.4 Marginal Cost of Funds Based Lending Rate (MCLR) System: The weaknesses and rigidities observed with the transmission under the base rate system were intended to be addressed through MCLR system for new loans, effective April 1, 2016. The base rate system, however, was expected to be in operation concomitantly for the loans already contracted, pending their maturity or a shift to the MCLR system at mutually agreeable terms between the bank and the borrower. The parallel operation of the MCLR and the base rate systems has considerably impacted the transmission in respect of the outstanding loans linked to the base rate.

MCLR consists of four components:

1. Marginal cost of funds [marginal cost of borrowings (comprising deposits and other borrowings) and return on net worth].
2. Negative carry on account of cash reserve ratio (CRR).
3. Operating costs.
4. Term premium.

Under the MCLR system, banks are required to determine their benchmark lending rates linked to their marginal cost of funds [unlike the base rate system where banks had the discretion to choose between the average cost or the marginal cost (or blended cost) of funds]. As such, lending rates were expected to be more sensitive to the changes in the policy rate under the MCLR system vis-à-vis its predecessor (the base rate). The MCLR plus spread is the actual lending rate charged to a borrower. The spread comprises only two components, viz. business strategy and credit risk premium.

The experience with the MCLR system has not been satisfactory, even though it has been an improvement over the base rate system. The transmission has remained uneven in terms of its pace and magnitude: (i) across the sectors of the economy, (ii) between deposit and lending rates and (iii) between fresh rupee loans and outstanding rupee loans. The base rates of different banks, in particular, have remained rigid since introduction of the MCLR. While the extent of change in base rate may not necessarily mirror the changes in the MCLR, the rigidity of the base rate is a matter of concern for efficient transmission of monetary policy to the real economy. Also, a large portfolio of banks' loans continues at the base rate and does not show the expected sensitivity to changes in the policy rate of the RBI.

21.3 Current Interest Rate Policy of RBI

21.3.1 Policy Rates: These are as under:

A. Repo Rate: In simple terms, repo rate is the rate at which RBI lends money to the banks against the collateral of government and other approved securities. Repo rate, along with other instruments of monetary policy, is used to balance growth (more spending) and inflation.

A major point in favour of the policy repo rate as a benchmark is that it is robust and reliable as it is decided by the Monetary Policy Committee (MPC) [5] keeping in view the macroeconomic conditions. It is also transparent, simple and easy to understand by the general public. Another major advantage is that the transmission from the repo rate to lending rates is direct, quick and strong.

RBI keeps repo rate changing according to changing macroeconomic factors. Whenever RBI modifies the rates, it impacts every sector of the economy, although in different ways. Some segments gain as a result of the rate hike while others may suffer losses.

Following an increase in repo rate, commercial banks usually raise the rates at which they extend loans to borrowers. For consumers, it translates into higher cost of homes, automobiles and personal loans at higher equated monthly instalments (EMIs).

A lower repo rate means loans from banks become cheaper for corporate borrowers as well as individuals for funding houses, cars, vacations and other purposes. To ensure that lower rates are passed on to the borrowers, RBI has asked banks to link their lending rates to an external benchmark like the repo rate, which has been chosen by most banks.

RBI cuts interest rates only when price level is comfortable. It may increase interest rate (making credit costlier) if inflation threatens to breach permissible limits. Since inflation is a politically-sensitive issue, RBI takes no chances to overlook it.

Repo rate is fixed by the MPC.

As on June 15, 2020 repo rate was 4.00 percent (Table 21.1).

B. Reverse Repo Rate: It is the (fixed) interest rate at which the RBI absorbs short-term liquidity, generally on an overnight basis, from banks against the collateral of government and other approved securities under the Liquidity Adjustment Facility (LAF). [6] The RBI also conducts variable interest rate reverse repo auctions, as necessary.

As on June 15, 2020 reverse repo rate was 3.35 percent (Table 21.1).

C. Marginal Standing Facility (MSF) Rate: MSF is a facility under which scheduled commercial banks can borrow additional amount of overnight money from the RBI by dipping into their SLR portfolio up to a limit (currently two percent of their net demand and time liabilities deposits) at a penal rate of interest, currently 50 basis points (half percent) above the repo rate. This provides a safety valve against unanticipated liquidity shocks to the banking system. MSF rate and reverse repo rate determine the corridor for the daily movement in the weighted average call money rate.

As on June 15, 2020 MSF rate was 4.25 percent (Table 21.1).

D. Bank Rate: As the lender-of-the-last-resort, RBI helps commercial banks in temporary need of cash when other sources of raising cash are exhausted. Bank rate is the rate at which RBI is ready to buy or rediscount bills of exchange or other commercial papers. Bank rate is a traditional weapon to control money supply. An increase in the bank rate would discourage commercial banks to borrow from the RBI and a corresponding increase in the lending rate of commercial banks to general public would decrease public borrowings from the banks.

The bank rate is published under Section 49 of the Reserve Bank of India Act, 1934. This rate has been aligned to the MSF rate and, therefore, changes automatically as and when the MSF rate changes alongside policy repo rate changes.

As on June 15, 2020 bank rate was 4.25 percent (Table 21.1).

21.3.2 Lending/Deposit Rates: These are as under:

A. Base Rate: It is the minimum rate for all loans, except for some specified categories. As on June 15, 2020 base rate ranged from 8.15 to 9.00 percent (Table 21.1).

B. MCLR (Overnight): It is benchmark lending rate linked to marginal cost of funds of a bank. As on June 15, 2020 MCLR ranged from 6.95 to 7.45 percent (Table 21.1).

C. Saving Deposit Rate: Savings account in a bank has the following features:

1. Can be opened by one person or jointly.
2. Nominal interest is paid on balance in the account.
3. Some accounts may require maintenance of minimum balance.

As on June 15, 2020 saving deposit rate ranged from 2.70 to 3.50 percent (Table 21.1).

D. Term Deposit Rate: Term deposit in a bank has the following features:

1. It is opened for a particular period, ranging from 7 days to 10 years.
2. Rate of interest depends on the amount and the term of the deposit.
3. Interest is usually paid as a lump sum at the end of the term.
4. There are also options to receive interest at periodic intervals.
5. Deposits can be withdrawn prematurely provided the account holder has opted for it.

As on June 15, 2020 term deposit rate > 1 year ranged from 6.20 to 6.40 percent (Table 21.1).

Table 21.1: Policy Rates and Lending/Deposit Rates of Reserve Bank of India (RBI) (As on June 15, 2020)

Policy Rates	
1. Policy repo rate	4.00 percent
2. Reverse repo rate	3.35 percent
3. Marginal standing facility rate	4.25 percent
4. Bank rate	4.25 percent
Lending/Deposit Rates	
1. Base rate	8.15 to 9.00 percent
2. MCLR (overnight)	6.95 to 7.45 percent
3. Saving deposit rate	2.70 to 3.50 percent
4. Term deposit rate > 1 year	5.10 to 5.75 percent

Source: RBI website.

21.4 Competitive Financial Saving Rates

Small savings by the government compete directly with bank deposits. Although the government has been periodically adjusting downwards the interest rates on these instruments since April 2016, these still remain well above those being offered by the banking system. The tax adjusted rate of return on select small savings schemes (viz., 5-year time deposits, public provident fund, national savings certificates and senior citizen's savings scheme) are even higher. A large interest rate differential in favour of small savings can lead to a significant migration of deposits away from banks, with an adverse impact on banks' lending capacity. Hence, this appears to have constrained banks from reducing their deposit interest rates in consonance with the changes in the monetary policy rate, especially during the easing phase of monetary policy.

Mutual funds have recently emerged as a major source of competition to the banks for financial savings. Assets under management (AUM) of mutual funds have grown rapidly in recent years. Funds mobilised under debt-oriented schemes have also increased sharply. The investor base of mutual funds is also becoming more broad-based

Banks face competition from mutual funds mainly from debt-oriented and liquid schemes, especially because such schemes carry tax benefits. In the case of bank deposits (savings or fixed), interest income gets taxed at the applicable marginal slab tax rate of the depositor (the peak rate is 30 percent at present). On the other hand, returns from the long-term debt funds (held for more than three years) are taxable at 20 percent with indexation benefit and 10 percent without indexation (again well below the peak marginal income tax rate of 30 percent).

Investments in banks' fixed deposits with a lock-in period of 5 years as well as in the equity linked saving schemes (ELSS) of mutual funds enjoy tax benefits under Section 80C of the Income Tax Act. However, the overall tax benefits are loaded in favour of mutual funds. First, the lock-in period associated with the ELSS is lower (3 years) than that of bank deposits (5 years). Second, ELSS returns are tax free, while interest income on deposits is taxable at the applicable tax slab in the hands of the depositor.

In the case of fixed deposits, there is a penalty associated with premature withdrawal. Mutual funds, on the other hand, offer higher liquidity and exit load is typically charged only for withdrawal under a year (most liquid funds do not charge an exit load). Thus, mutual fund schemes are also liquid like bank deposits.

Falling interest rates on bank deposits and tax benefits in favour of mutual funds have made mutual fund investments highly attractive relative to bank deposits. This appears to have constrained banks from reducing their interest rates on fresh deposits.

A level-playing field for all the competing financial saving instruments is necessary for enhanced monetary transmission. Any tax benefit in favour of a particular saving instrument distorts the risk-return perception of a saver, which is not conducive for developing a balanced and diversified financial system.

To sum up, the country has moved towards liberalised credit allocation mechanism and reduced direct control over interest rates by the monetary authorities. The purpose of deregulation is to promote healthy competition among the banks and encourage their operational efficiency.

Endnotes

1. CRR is the average daily balance that a bank is required to maintain with the RBI as a share of such percent of its net demand and time liabilities (NDTL) that the RBI may notify from time-to-time in the Gazette of India. Increase/decrease in CRR is used by the RBI as an instrument of monetary control, particularly to mop up excess increases in the supply of money. This power was given to RBI in 1956.
2. Monetary policy refers to the policy of the central bank with regard to the use of instruments under its control to achieve the specified goals. In India, RBI is vested with the responsibility of conducting monetary policy with the primary objective of maintaining price stability while keeping in mind the objective of growth. This responsibility is explicitly mandated under the Reserve Bank of India Act, as amended in 2016 and notified in the official Gazette on May 14, 2016. Like other central banks, the core function of the RBI is to formulate and administer monetary policy to maintain the stability of the rupee.
3. Banks in India are subject to statutory liquidity requirement. SLR is the share of net demand and time liabilities (NDTL) that a bank is required to maintain in safe and liquid assets, such as, unencumbered government securities, cash and gold. Changes in SLR often influence the availability of resources in the banking system for lending to the private sector. All the commercial banks in India are required to maintain SLR as per Section 24 and Section 56 of

the Banking Regulation Act, 1949. The underlying philosophy of this provision is to allocate total bank credit between the government and the rest of the economy. The assurance of a certain minimum share of bank credit to the government affects the borrowings of the government from the RBI and hence serves as a tool of quantitative monetary control.

4. Open market operations (OMOs) are conducted by the RBI via outright sale/purchase of government securities to/from the market with the primary aim of modulating rupee liquidity conditions in the market. OMOs are an effective quantitative policy tool in the armoury of the RBI, but are constrained by the stock of government securities available with it at a point in time.
5. RBI Act provides for the creation of a six-member Monetary Policy Committee (MPC) chaired by the RBI governor, who has a casting vote in the event of a tie. Of the six, three are from RBI—the governor, a deputy governor and another officer. The other three members are appointed by the Central Government on the recommendations of a search-cum-selection committee. They are chosen from experts in economics, banking, finance and monetary policy. Government notified the constitution of the MPC on September 29, 2016. MPC is entrusted with the task of fixing the benchmark policy rate (repo rate) required to contain inflation within the specified target level. Under the RBI Act, the Central Government, in consultation with the RBI, determines the inflation target in terms of the Consumer Price Index (CPI), once in every five years. This target is notified in the Official Gazette.
6. As part of the financial sector reforms in 1998, Liquidity Adjustment Facility (LAF) was introduced on the recommendations of the Committee on Banking Sector Reforms (Narasimham Committee II). Under LAF, the RBI conducts auctions on all working days and even several times a day depending on the evolving liquidity conditions. Depending on the stance of the monetary policy, the RBI sets its repo rate, which is the policy rate.

Part IV
Banking System

22

Meaning, Importance and Functions of a Commercial Bank

22.1 Meaning and Importance of Commercial Banks

A commercial bank is a financial intermediary which accepts deposits of money from the public and lends them with a view to make profits. A post office may accept deposits but it cannot be called a bank because it does not perform the other essential function of a bank, i.e. lending money. Similarly, some other institutions like Unit Trust of India (UTI) may be lending to others but since they do not accept chequable deposits, they cannot be termed as banks. They are non-banking financial institutions.

The banking system forms the core of the financial sector of an economy. The role of commercial banks is particularly important in underdeveloped countries. Through mobilisation of resources and their better allocation, commercial banks play an important role in the development process of underdeveloped countries. By offering attractive saving schemes and ensuring safety of deposits, commercial banks encourage willingness to save among the people. By reaching out to people in rural areas, they help convert idle savings into effective ones. Commercial banks improve the allocation of resources by lending money to priority sectors of the economy. These banks provide a meeting ground for the savers and the investors. Savers may not invest either because of inadequate savings and/or lack of risk-taking spirit.

The banking industry all over the world has undergone transformation since the early 1980s under the impact of deregulation, advances in information technology and globalisation. These forces have increased competitive pressures which have: (a) unleashed the strong forces of restructuring and consolidation with the number of banks declining all over the world, and (b) prompted banks to seek new sources of revenue beyond traditional products. These, in turn, have led to the blurring of distinctions among providers of various financial services and emergence of financial conglomerates. Although these developments have made institutions more efficient by lowering transaction costs, they have also challenged the traditional regulatory arrangements based on institutions. Also, heightened competitive pressures, by squeezing profit margins of institutions, could lead them to pursue riskier strategies, raising the possibility of failure. Financial instability can also impinge on a country's ability to pursue a prudent macroeconomic policy. The safety and soundness of financial institutions, therefore, have come to occupy a centre-stage in the policy making.

Under the forces of liberalisation and globalisation, many banking institutions have expanded beyond their home countries and traditional lines of business leading to emergence of large international banks. Many product innovations and new ways of doing business have also emerged that have led to widespread use of securitisation, derivatives and other financial products linking traditional banking functions to the operations of capital markets, whereas these developments have led to some degree of efficiency in financial intermediation, new issues have emerged over the past year that merit attention. Most, if not all of these large banks have become financial conglomerates operating in all the different segments of the financial sector. This movement has been enabled both by technological developments leading to faster transmission of financial transactions and financial innovations, and by falling national barriers allowing cross border capital flows.

22.2 Functions of a Commercial Bank

A bank can generate revenue in a variety of different ways including interest, transaction fees and financial advice. The main method is via charging interest on the capital it lends out to customers. The bank profits from the difference between the level of interest it pays for deposits and other sources of funds, and the level of interest it charges in its lending activities. This difference is referred to as the spread between the cost of funds and the loan interest rate. Historically, profitability from lending activities has been cyclical and dependent on the needs and strengths of loan customers and the stage of the economic cycle. Fees and financial advice constitute a more stable revenue stream and banks have therefore placed more emphasis on these revenue lines to smooth their financial performance.

A commercial bank generally performs the following functions.

1. It accepts deposits which are of various types like current, savings, recurring and fixed deposits.
2. It grants credit in various forms such as loans and advances, discounting of bills and investment in open market securities.
3. It collects cheques, drafts, bills and other instruments for its depositors.
4. It provides remittance facilities through drafts and telegraphic transfers.
5. It renders investment services such as underwriter and banker for new issues of securities to the public.
6. It provides such agency services as purchase and sale of foreign exchange, acceptance of tax payments, electricity bills etc.
7. It provides facilities like travellers' cheques, gift cheques and safe deposit vaults to its customers.

22.3 Deposits and Loans

Banks are financial institutions which accept deposits and provide loans.

22.3.1 Savings and Current Accounts: These accounts provide facilities like cheque book, funds transfer, debit card, and unified payments facility.

A. Savings Account: It has the following features:

1. Can be opened by one person or jointly.
2. Nominal interest is paid on balance in the account.
3. Some accounts may require maintenance of minimum balance.

B. Current Account: It has the following features:

1. Meant for business entities such as proprietorships, partnership firms, public and private companies, trusts, association of persons etc.
2. No restrictions on the number and amount of deposits and withdrawals as long as the account holder has funds in the bank.
3. No interest is paid on the account balance.

22.3.2 Deposits: There are two main types of deposit:

A. Recurring Deposit: It is popularly known as RD with the following features:

1. A certain fixed amount is accepted every month for a specified period and the total amount is repaid with interest at the end of the period.
2. Deposits can be opened for periods ranging from 6 months to 120 months.
3. RDs are suitable for those who do not have a large amount of savings, but are ready to save small amounts every month.
4. No withdrawals are allowed.
5. Bank may allow the account to be closed before the maturity period.
6. Any default in payment within the month attracts a small penalty.

B. Fixed Deposit: Also called FD, it has the following features:

1. It is opened for a particular period, ranging from 7 days to 10 years.
2. Rate of interest depends on the amount and the term of the deposit.
3. Interest is usually paid as a lump sum at the end of the term.
4. There are also options to receive interest at periodic intervals.
5. Deposits can be withdrawn prematurely provided the account holder has opted for it.

22.3.3 Loans: Loans from the bank are of various types:

A. Personal Loan: This type of loan can be used for any purpose. It is usually taken for emergencies like medical expenses, marriage expenses etc. The interest rate is higher on such loans.

B. Vehicle Loan: This type of loan is provided for the purpose of buying a vehicle. The vehicle is hypothecated to the bank and in case of default of the loan, the bank may take possession of the vehicle.

C. Home Loan: Everyone dreams of having his own home, but buying a home requires a large amount of money, which many people cannot afford. To fill this gap, banks provide home loans.

D. Education Loan: Banks offer education loans to students who want to pursue higher studies. Once the student completes his/her course and starts earning, he/she can repay the loan.

E. Agricultural Loan: To cater to the needs of farmers, banks offer various types of loans. Using this loan, farmers can buy seeds, insecticides, tractors and other equipment needed for agriculture.

In the banking industry, it is fast changing the way products are conceived, designed and delivered across channels and market segments. Today, technology enabled business models are disrupting the entire supply chain be it retail, corporate or government business. The emergence of third party aggregators for loans, personal finance management, rural banking products/services, payments etc. are making significant impact to our traditional business processes or models. With increasing adoption of technologies like mobility, cloud, social media, electronically transferable database etc., technology will continue to be critical in responding to customer expectations across identified market segments and creating the agility needed to respond to opportunities. In order to derive a competitive advantage, banks must therefore effectively leverage technology to deliver on fast-changing customer expectations, align with regulatory controls and compliances, and attract the tech-savvy Generation Y.

It is, therefore, critical for banks to increase their IT investments to align with new innovations in technology to meet their objectives. In this context, technology initiatives in the banking industry coupled with continued innovations by technology vendors will define a new growth path for the industry. In addition to IT innovations and applications, banks are also leveraging social media to reach out to the next generation.

23

Balance Sheet and Portfolio Management of a Bank

23.1 Balance Sheet of a Bank

Balance sheet of a bank is a statement of liabilities and assets of a bank at a point of time. It reflects the policies, size and soundness of the operations of a bank. The liabilities indicate the sources of its funds. The assets show the nature of its investments. To understand the conflict between liquidity and profitability and how it is resolved, the study of the balance sheet of a bank is necessary.

It is pertinent to note that a commercial bank has to satisfy the interests of three distinct groups.

1. Depositors whose withdrawal needs it must meet without delay.
2. Shareholders for whom it must earn profits.
3. Central bank under the control and supervision of which it has to work and abide by its various directives.

It is indeed a tightrope walking for the bank. How it tries to satisfy the three masters simultaneously will become clear with an understanding of its balance sheet.

23.1.1 Liabilities of a Bank: The liabilities of a bank are mainly composed of the following items.

1. **Paid up Capital and Reserves:** Paid up capital means the amount of share capital actually contributed by the shareholders. Reserves are retained earnings or undistributed profits of the banks. These two items put together constitute the owned funds of the bank.
2. **Deposits:** Deposits from the public are the main source of funds for a commercial bank. Therefore, these deposits constitute the main liability of a bank. These deposits are of various types like current, savings and fixed deposits.
3. **Borrowings:** Commercial banks borrow from each other as well as from non-banking financial institutions like LIC, GIC and the UTI.
4. **Miscellaneous:** Liabilities like bills payable.

23.1.2 Assets of a Bank: The asset portfolio of a bank is of crucial importance. It strikes a balance between liquidity and profitability of a bank. A commercial bank has to earn profit for its shareholders and at the same time satisfy the withdrawal needs of its customers. A bank tries to achieve the twin conflicting objectives by selecting a diversified and balanced asset portfolio within the framework of the regulations of the central bank. The various items of its assets described below will show that some are more liquid than others. The more liquid the asset, the less profitable it is.

1. **Cash:** Cash-in-hand (also called vault cash) is held to meet the withdrawal needs of the depositors. Commercial banks also hold cash balances with the RBI. These balances are held with the RBI under the statutory cash reserve ratio.

2. **Money at Call/Short Notice:** Commercial banks lend their surplus cash to each other and also to other financial institutions for short periods of time. This type of lending earns interest for the banks while maintaining liquidity at the same time.
3. **Investment in Securities:** Banks are required statutorily to invest a part of their assets in Government securities. These securities carry a low rate of interest but banks can borrow from the RBI against these securities. Thus, they provide return as well as liquidity to the bank.
4. **Loans and Advances:** Loans and advances constitute the main item of a bank's assets. They are also the main source of income for the banks. Loans are given in the form of overdrafts, term loans, and demand loans.

Thus, we see that a bank holds its assets in such a way that the requirements of liquidity and profitability are balanced. Liabilities are shown on the left side and assets on the right side of a balance sheet.

23.2 Portfolio Management

A portfolio can be defined as different investments tools namely stocks, shares, mutual funds, bonds, cash all combined together depending specifically on the investor's income, budget, risk appetite and the holding period. It is formed in such a way that it stabilizes the risk of non-performance of different pools of investments.

23.2.1 Portfolio Management and Portfolio Manager: Portfolio Management is the art and science of making decisions about investment mix and policy, matching investments to objectives, asset allocation for individuals and institutions, and balancing risk against performance. Portfolio management includes a range of professional services to manage an individual's and company's securities, such as stocks and bonds, and other assets, such as real estate.

Portfolio management refers to managing an individual's investments in the form of bonds, shares, cash, mutual funds etc so that he earns the maximum profits within the stipulated time frame. It is the art of managing the money of an individual under the expert guidance of portfolio managers.

A portfolio manager is a professional responsible for making investment decisions and carrying out investment activities on behalf of vested individuals or institutions.

Portfolio managers are primarily responsible for creating and managing investment allocations for private clients. A portfolio manager determines a client's appropriate level of risk based on the client's time horizon, risk preferences, return expectations and market conditions.

The investors invest their money into the portfolio manager's investment policy for future fund growth such as a retirement fund, endowment fund, education fund, or for other purposes. Portfolio managers work with a team of analysts and researchers, and are responsible for establishing an investment strategy, selecting appropriate investments, and allocating each investment properly towards an investment fund or asset management vehicle. Services of portfolio managers are meant for those who want to invest their funds but have limited knowledge of financial dealings. Similarly, people who are from a different work profile and do not have time may also avail the services of portfolio managers.

23.2.2 Types of Portfolio Management: There are mainly four types of portfolio management methods:

1. **Discretionary Portfolio Management**: In this form, the individual authorizes the portfolio manager to take care of his financial needs on his behalf.
2. **Non-discretionary Portfolio Management**: Here, the portfolio manager can merely advise the client what is good or bad, correct/incorrect for him, but the client reserves the full right to take his own decisions.
3. **Passive Portfolio Management:** It is the form which involves only tracking the index.
4. **Active Portfolio Management:** This includes a team of members who take active decisions based on hard core research before investing the corpus into any investment avenue (e.g. close ended funds). The aim of the active portfolio manager is to make better returns than what the market dictates.

23.2.3 Objectives of Portfolio Management: These are as under:

1. It ensures customization of the investment needs of the investors.
2. It helps in providing the best options for investments to individuals as per the defined criterions of their income, budget, age, holding period and risk taking capacity.
3. It is done by portfolio managers who understand an investor's financial needs and accordingly suggest the investment policy that would bring maximum returns with minimum risks involved.
4. Some of the portfolio management schemes are also done for tax saving purposes.
5. It helps the investors maintain the purchasing power.

23.2.4 Techniques of Portfolio Management: These are as follows:

1. Potential investors who lack financial literacy and awareness approach portfolio managers for their financial services.
2. An agreement is reached between an investor and a portfolio manager regarding fee, time frame, risk exposure etc.
3. Portfolio manager carries out a market survey in terms of different schemes and their performance in the past.
4. He uses his experiences and accordingly selects the funds in which money should be invested.
5. The portfolio is structured on the basis of the agreed terms.
6. The report of the performance of the portfolio is periodically sent to the investors.
7. The fund manager takes decisions on the basis of the hardcore research related to financial markets.

In the current scenario where there are competitive and complex financial instruments, portfolio management is indeed a preferred method of making investments. With the range of products available across different schemes, there is something to offer for every individual as per the different criterions defined. Portfolio managers understand the financial needs of their clients design a suitable investment plan as per their income and risk-taking abilities. After understanding the financial goals and objectives of an investor, the portfolio manager provides the appropriate investment solution. The role played by the portfolio manager is indeed a challenging, responsible and answerable one.

With the increasing integration of various segments of financial markets, the distinctions between banks and other financial intermediaries are also getting increasingly blurred. There is increased participation of financial institutions, especially banks, in the capital market. These factors have led to increased inter-linkages across financial institutions and markets. While increased inter-linkages are expected to lead to increased efficiency in the resource allocation process and the effectiveness of monetary policy, they also increase the risk of contagion from one segment to another with implications for overall financial stability. This would call for appropriate policy responses during times of crisis. Increased inter-linkages also raise the issue of appropriate supervisory framework.

24

Structure and Changing Role of Banks in India

24.1 Post-Independence History and Developments

24.1.1 Phase I: Early Years of Independence (1947-69): As in several other developing countries, the financial system in India has traditionally been dominated by financial intermediaries, especially banking institutions. Banking in India has a long history and it has evolved over the years passing through various phases. At the time of Independence, the Indian banking system was weak. The entire banking sector was in the private sector and the credit requirements of agriculture and other needy sectors were ignored.

The period soon after Independence posed several challenges to the Indian economy including the virtual absence of institutional credit facilities in the vast rural areas of the country. Further, the non-availability of adequate assets made it difficult for people to approach banks. In 1951, India launched its First Five Year Plan (1951-56) which accorded high priority to the development of rural India, particularly agriculture. The All India Rural Credit Survey Committee recommended the creation of a State-partnered and State-sponsored bank by taking over the Imperial Bank of India and integrating with it the former State-owned or State-associated banks. Accordingly, an Act was passed in the Parliament in May 1955 and the State Bank of India was constituted on July 1, 1955. Later, the State Bank of India (Subsidiary Banks) Act was passed in 1959 enabling the State Bank of India to take over eight former State-associated banks as its subsidiaries.

During this period, the industrial sector claimed the lion's share in bank credit. Within the industry, the large-scale sector cornered the bulk of credit and the share of small-scale industries was marginal. There were many reasons for the dominance of large industrial companies in the banking sector. Firstly, many commercial banks were under the ownership/control of big industrial houses. Secondly, through common directors (called interlocking of directorship), many commercial banks were connected with industrial and business houses, facilitating the flow of credit to large industries. Thirdly, the established industrial houses could obtain industrial licenses easily and on that basis, appropriate long-term bank credit.

A disturbing feature of the banking policy during this period was the negligible share of agricultural sector in bank credit. This share hovered around 2 percent of total commercial bank credit. The privately-owned commercial banks were neither interested nor geared to meet the risky and small credit requirements of the farmers. Similarly, the share of other non-industrial sectors in bank credit was also low. Since the commercial banks were under the control of big industrialists, the lendable funds of the banks were sometimes used to finance socially undesirable activities like hoarding of essential commodities.

24.1.2 Phase II: From Nationalisation of Banks till Initiation of Banking Sector Reforms (1969-91): With a view to better aligning the banking system to the needs of planning and economic policy, the policy of social control over the banking sector began in 1967. The year 1969 was a landmark in the history of commercial banking in India. In July of that year, the government nationalised 14 major commercial banks of the country. In April 1980, government nationalised 6 more commercial banks. Leading commercial banks of the country were nationalised with the following objectives in view.

1. To break the ownership and control of banks by a few business families.
2. To prevent concentration of wealth and economic power.
3. To mobilise savings of the masses from every nook and corner of the country.
4. To pay greater attention to the credit needs of the priority sectors like agriculture and small industries.

With the nationalisation of these banks, the major segment of the banking sector came under the control of the Government. Massive expansion of the branch network that followed the nationalisation of banks resulted in large deposit mobilisation by banks, which helped in stepping up the overall savings rate of the economy. However, during this period, a major portion of resources of the banks were pre-empted at below market rates by way of directed credit and directed investments. Profitability of the banking sector was, therefore, affected. Banks were also saddled with large non-performing assets. Their capital base also became weak.

The nationalisation of banks was an attempt to use the scarce resources of the banking system for the purpose of planned development. The task of maintaining a large number of small accounts was not profitable for the banks as a result of which they had limited lending in the rural sector. The problem of lopsided distribution of banks and the lack of explicit articulation of the need to channel credit to certain priority sectors was sought to be achieved through nationalisation policy. The Lead Bank Scheme provided the blueprint of further bank branch expansion.

The course of evolution of the banking sector in India since 1969 has been dominated by the nationalisation of banks. This period was characterised by rapid branch expansion that helped to draw the channels of monetary transmission far and wide across the country. The share of unorganised credit fell sharply and the economy seemed to come out of low level equilibrium trap. However, the stipulations that made this possible and helped spread institutional credit and nurture the financial system, also led to distortions in the process. The administered interest rates and the burden of directed lending constrained the banking sector significantly. There was very little operational flexibility for the commercial banks. Profitability occupied a back seat. Banks also suffered from poor governance. Fortunately, for the Indian economy, quick action was taken to address these issues.

The biggest achievement of nationalisation was the reallocation of sectoral credit in favour of agriculture, small industries and exports which formed the core of the priority sector. Within agriculture, credit for the procurement of food grains (food credit) was a major item. Other agricultural activities preferred for credit included poultry farming, dairy, and piggeries. Certain other sectors of the economy which also received attention for credit allocation were: professionals and self-employed persons, artisans and weaker sections of society. Conversely, there was a sharp fall in bank credit to large-scale industries. However, the share of small-scale industry registered an upward trend.

Nationalisation of commercial banks was a mixed blessing. After nationalisation there was a shift of emphasis from industry to agriculture. The country witnessed rapid expansion in bank branches, even in rural areas. Branch expansion programme led to mobilisation of savings from all parts of the country. Nationalised banks were able to pay attention to the credit needs of weaker sections, artisans and self-employed. However, bank nationalisation created its own problems like excessive bureaucratisation, red-tapism and disruptive tactics of trade unions of bank employees.

24.1.3 Phase III: Banking Sector Reforms since 1991: The period beginning from the early 1990s witnessed the transformation of the banking sector as a result of financial sector reforms that were introduced as a part of structural reforms initiated in 1991.

For details on banking sector reforms, see chapter 25 of this book.

24.2 Classification of Commercial Banks in India

Commercial banks in India can be classified in the following ways:

24.2.1 Scheduled and Non-scheduled Banks: A scheduled bank is one which is included in the second schedule of the Reserve Bank of India Act, 1934. Certain conditions are to be satisfied to be eligible for this as, for example, a bank must be a corporation and not a partnership or a single-owner firm. Scheduled banks enjoy certain facilities like borrowings from the RBI. In return, they have to meet certain obligations of RBI such as maintaining a part of their cash reserves with the RBI. Non-scheduled banks are disappearing from the banking scene and hence they are not important.

24.2.2 Indian and Foreign Banks: Indian banks are those which are incorporated in India and have their head offices in India. Some big Indian banks have their branches in foreign countries. Foreign banks are incorporated in foreign countries with their head offices outside India. They are scheduled banks and generally specialise in the field of foreign exchange.

24.2.3 Public Sector and Private Sector Banks: The Central Government entered the banking business with the nationalisation of the Imperial Bank of India (now the State Bank of India) in 1955. In 1969, 14 large banks were nationalised and again in 1980, 6 more banks were taken over by the Government. These nationalised banks are called public sector banks. The others are private sector banks.

24.3 Legal Framework for Banking Sector in India

Banking is a Central Government subject as per Entry 45 of List I (Union List) of the Seventh Schedule of the Constitution of India.

The legal framework for banking in India is provided by a set of enactments, mainly the Banking Regulations Act, 1949 and the Reserve Bank of India Act, 1934. Broadly, no entity can function as a bank in India without obtaining a license from Reserve Bank of India under Banking Regulations Act, 1949. Different types of activities which a bank may undertake and other prudential requirements are provided under this Act. Accepting of deposit from public by a non-bank attracts regulatory provisions under Reserve Bank of India Act, 1934.

24.3.1 Banking Law (Amendments) Act, 2012: As already noted, Banking Regulation Act, 1949 is the principal legislation for regulating banking companies and introducing governance in the management of banks in India. Reserve Bank of India (RBI) is the prime regulator and statutory watch dog of banks and banking companies. With the advent of private sector banking companies, the role played by RBI has become very important.

Banking Law (Amendments Act), 2012 made certain important amendments to the Banking Regulation Act, 1949. The said Amendment Act amended the Banking Regulation Act, 1949, the Banking Companies (Acquisition and Transfer of Undertakings) Act, 1970, the Banking Companies (Acquisition and Transfer of Undertakings) Act, 1980 and also made consequential amendments to certain other enactments including the Indian Stamp Act, 1899 and the Indian Contract Act, 1972.

RBI has advised that the amendments will be binding on private sector banks notwithstanding any clauses to the contrary contained in the memorandum of association (MoA) and articles of association (AoA) of such private sector banks.

24.3.2 Laws Related to Banking Operations: Apart from the Banking Regulation Act, 1949 which governs all the scheduled commercial banks, there are various other legislations governing different bank groups. The nationalised banks are governed by two Acts, viz. Banking Companies (Acquisition and Transfer of Undertakings) Act, 1970 and Banking Companies (Acquisition and Transfer of Undertakings) Act, 1980. The State Bank of India and its subsidiaries are governed by two legislations, viz. State Bank of India Act, 1955 and State Bank of India (Subsidiary Banks) Act, 1959, respectively. IDBI Bank is governed by the Industrial Development Bank (Transfer of Undertaking and Repeal) Act, 2003. The private sector banks come under the purview of the Companies Act, 1956. The overall regulation of the banking sector is governed by the Banking Regulation Act, 1949.

The Multi-state Co-operative Societies Act, 2002, which came into force with effect from August 2002, in replacement of the Act of 1984, empowers the Central Government to give directions to the multi-state co-operative societies in the public interest or to supersede their board only with respect to those multi-state co-operative societies in which not less than 51 percent of the paid-up share capital or of the total shares is held by the Central Government.

Reserve Bank of India (Amendment) Act, 2006 provides flexibility to the RBI in prescribing reserve requirements for scheduled banks as also comprehensive powers to regulate the money and government securities market. Accordingly, these amendments: (i) empower the RBI to determine the cash reserve ratio (CRR) for scheduled banks without any floor or ceiling, (ii) empower the RBI to deal in derivatives, to lend or borrow securities and to undertake repo or reverse repo transactions, (iii) remove the ambiguity regarding the legal validity of derivatives, and (iv) empower the RBI to determine the policy relating to interest rates or interest rate products and give directions in that behalf to all agencies dealing in securities, money market instruments, foreign exchange, derivatives and to inspect such agencies etc.

Banking Companies (Amendment) Act, 2007 under which the RBI has been conferred with the power to specify statutory liquidity ratio (SLR) without any floor (i.e. removing the existing floor of 25 percent while retaining the ceiling of 40 percent).

Banking Regulation (Acquisition and Transfer of Undertakings) and Financial Institutions Laws (Amendment) Act, 2006 provides for: (a) increase in number of whole-time directors of the nationalised banks from 2 to 4, (b) the director to be nominated by the Government on the recommendation of the RBI to be a person possessing necessary experience and expertise in regulation or supervision of commercial bank, (c) removal of the provision for nominee directors from amongst the officials of SEBI/NABARD/Public Financial Institutions, (d) nomination of up to 3 shareholder directors on the board of nationalised banks on the basis of percentage of shareholding, (e) elected directors to be persons having *fit and proper* status as per the criteria notified by the RBI from time to time, and (f) the RBI to appoint one or more additional directors, if necessary, in the interest of banking policy/public interests/interest of the bank or the depositors.

The salient features of the State Bank of India (Subsidiary Banks Laws) Amendment Act, 2007 include: (a) increasing the authorised capital of subsidiary banks to ₹ 500 crore and divide the authorised capital into shares of ₹ 100 each, or of such denomination as may be decided by the subsidiary banks, with the approval of State Bank of India (SBI), (b) allowing the subsidiary banks to issue share certificates of such denominations as may be prescribed by regulations made by SBI with approval of the RBI to existing shareholders, (c) allowing the subsidiary banks to raise issued capital through preferential allotment or private placement or public issue in accordance with relevant procedures, (d) allowing reduction of SBI's shareholding in subsidiary banks to 51 percent from 55 percent, (e) removing the restriction on individual shareholdings in excess of 200 shares and increase the percentage of voting rights of shareholders (other than SBI) from 1 percent to 10 percent of the issued capital of the concerned banks, and (f) conferring power on the RBI to supersede the board of directors of subsidiary banks in public/depositors interests.

24.3.3 Laws Relating to Debt Recovery and Enforcement of Security: In the area of dispute settlement, the Legal Services Authority Act, 1987 has conferred statutory basis on the *Lok Adalats* (people's courts). The Reserve Bank of India (RBI) has consequently issued guidelines to commercial banks and financial institutions to make increasing use of the forum of *Lok Adalats*. As per the earlier guidelines, banks could settle disputes involving amounts up to ₹ 5 lakh through the forum of *Lok Adalats*. This was enhanced to ₹ 20 lakh in August 2004. Further, banks have also been advised by the RBI to participate in the *Lok Adalats* convened by various debt recovery tribunals (DRTs) and/or debt recovery appelate tribunals (DRATs) for resolving cases involving ₹ 10 lakh and above to reduce the stock of NPAs.

The Securitisation and Reconstruction of Financial Assets and Enforcement of Security Interest (SARFAESI) Act, 2002, effective from June 21, 2002, was extended to cover co-operative banks by a notification dated January 28, 2003. The Enforcement of Security Interest and Recovery Debts Laws (Amendment) Act, 2004 amended the SARFAESI Act, Recovery of Debts Due to Banks and Financial Institutions Act, 1993 and the Companies Act, 1956. By this amendment, the SARFAESI Act was amended, *inter alia*, to: (a) enable the borrower to make an application before the debt recovery tribunal against the measures taken by the secured creditor without depositing any portion of the money due, (b) provide that the debt recovery tribunal shall dispose of the application as expeditiously as possible within a period of 60 days from the date of application, and (c) enable any person aggrieved by the order by the debt recovery tribunal to file an appeal before the debt recovery appellate tribunal after depositing with the appellate tribunal 50 percent of the amount of debt due to him as claimed by the secured creditor or as determined by the debt recovery tribunal, whichever is less.

24.3.4 Laws Relating to Payment Systems: The Negotiable Instruments (Amendments and Miscellaneous Provisions) Act, 2002, effective from February 6, 2003, introduces the concepts of *electronic cheque* and *cheque truncation* by expanding the definition of *cheque* as provided in the Negotiable Instruments Act, 1881. It also enhances the punishment for dishonour of cheques from one year to two years, excludes the nominee directors from prosecution and provides for speedy and time-bound disposal of criminal complaints by summary trial, day-to-day hearing and complainant's evidence through affidavit.

The Payments and Settlement Systems Act 2007, designates the RBI as the authority to regulate payment and settlement systems. The Payment and Settlement Systems Act, 2007 has received the assent of the President on the December 20, 2007, and has been notified in the Official Gazette. Under this Act, the Reserve Bank has been given wide regulatory and supervisory powers in respect of payment systems. The Act provides for: (i) authorisation by the Reserve Bank to commence or operate payment systems; (ii) empowering the Reserve Bank to audit and inspect by entering the premises where payment systems are being operated; (iii) empowering the Reserve Bank to issue directions; and (iv) finality of settlements (including netting) and their irrevocability in the event of insolvency, overriding other laws. According to sub-section (3) of Section 1 of the said Act, its provisions shall come into force on such date as the Central Government may by notification in the Official Gazette appoint, and different dates may be appointed for different provisions of the Act. The provisions of the Act have been brought into force by the Central Government with effect from August 12, 2008. The Reserve Bank is empowered, under the Act, to make regulations to operationalise the provisions of the Act. Accordingly, the regulations, viz.: (i) Board for Regulation and Supervision of Payment and Settlement Systems Regulations, 2008, and (ii) Payment and Settlement Systems Regulations, 2008 have been framed by the Reserve Bank.

24.3.5 Competition Act, 2002: Implications for the Banking Sector: India has been aware of the need for a competition policy for several years. Competition Act,

2002, enacted in January 2003 is designed to uphold competition in the Indian economy. The Competition (Amendment) Act, 2007 passed by the Parliament in September 2007 incorporated some changes in the Competition Act, 2002. While serving an important national purpose, it nevertheless has certain provisions that could adversely impact the financial sector. For example, every person or enterprise proposing to enter into a combination via a merger or an amalgamation is required to give notice to the Commission before entering into a combination. The applicant then has to wait for a maximum period of 210 days.

While reasonable in several cases, this provision—when applied to the proposal for the voluntary amalgamation of banks under Section 44A of the Banking Regulation Act, 1949—could become a problem as the wait of 210 days may defeat the purpose of the proposed combination. The RBI can give its sanction to the amalgamation only thereafter which would delay the whole process and is also likely to raise regulatory conflicts. Similar would be the case with amalgamations under the schemes made by the Central Government in the exercise of its powers under Section 9(2) of the two Nationalisation Acts, viz. Banking Companies (Acquisition and Transfer of Undertakings) Act, 1970 and Banking Companies (Acquisition and Transfer of Undertakings) Act, 1980. There is, therefore, a need to re-examine the whole issue and, if necessary, the Central Government may grant the necessary exemption under Section 54 of the Competition Act.

24.3.6 Other Laws: The Credit Information Companies (Regulation) Act, 2005 is aimed at providing for regulation of credit information companies and to facilitate efficient distribution of credit. The Act provides for establishment, supervision and regulation of credit information companies that can undertake the functions of collecting, processing and collating information on trade, credit and financial standing of the borrowers of credit institutions which are members of the credit information company. This enactment will now enable the introduction of credit information bureaus in India within a suitable regulatory framework.

The Government Securities Act, 2006 provides for: (a) empowering the RBI to prescribe the form for transferring government securities; (b) holding of government promissory notes by trusts; (c) simplifying the procedure for recognising title to government securities up to ₹ 1 lakh with enabling power to the Central Government to enhance the said limit up to Rupees one crore; (d) allow micro films, facsimile copies of documents, magnetic tapes and computer print outs to be admissible as evidence; and (e) suspension of holders of subsidiary general ledger account in the event of misuse of the said facility.

The Securities Contract Regulation (Amendment) Act, 2007 has amended the Securities Contract Regulation Act, 1956 so as to provide a legal framework for trading in securitised debt, including mortgage-backed debt.

In order to combat the menace of crime-related money, the Prevention of Money Laundering Act, 2002 (PMLA) was enacted to provide the enabling legal framework. It may be mentioned that the provisions of PMLA and the Rules notified thereunder by the Central Government, cast certain obligations on the banking companies and financial institutions with regard to preservation of records of transactions and reporting of certain cash transactions and suspicious transactions to the Financial Intelligence Unit (FIU-IND).

Under the Foreign Exchange Management Act 1999, no Indian resident can lend, open a foreign currency account or borrow from a non-resident, including non-resident banks, except under certain circumstances provided in law.

The banks have continued to be managed by different legislations due to historical reasons and the Government has been considering at various points of time to bring in a single banking legislation.

24.4 Ownership and Governance of Commercial Banks in India

Banks are special for several reasons. They accept and deploy large amount of uncollateralised public funds and leverage such funds through credit creation. Banks also administer the payment mechanism. Accordingly, ownership and governance of banks assume special significance. Legal prescriptions relating to ownership and governance laid down in the Banking Regulation Act, 1949 have, therefore, been supplemented by regulatory prescriptions issued by the RBI from time to time. The existing legal framework and significant current practices cover the following aspects.

1. Composition of boards of directors.
2. Guidelines on corporate governance.
3. Guidelines for acknowledgement of transfer/allotment of shares in private sector banks issued as on February 3, 2004.
4. Foreign investment in the banking sector.

24.4.1 Public Sector Banks: Public sector banks (PSBs) are statute-based banks. They are regulated by their respective statutes of Parliament in addition to some important provisions of Banking Regulation Act, 1949 as enunciated in Section 51 thereof. Primarily, public sector banks constitute the following:

1. State Bank of India regulated by State Bank of India Act, 1955.
2. Subsidiary banks of State Bank of India regulated by State Bank of India (Subsidiary Banks) Act, 1959.
3. Nationalised banks regulated by Banking Companies (Acquisition and Transfer of Undertakings) Act, 1970 and 1980.

As per the provisions of their respective statutes, the Central Government is mandated to hold a minimum percentage of shareholding which is 51 percent in case of nationalised banks and 55 percent in case of the State Bank of India. In case of the subsidiary banks, the shareholding of the State Bank of India cannot go below the minimum of 51 percent of the total shareholding in those banks. Foreign investment in any form cannot exceed 20 percent of the total paid-up capital of the PSBs. The PSBs are permitted to divest their holdings subject to minimum holding by Central Government as stated above.

24.4..2 Private Sector Banks: The RBI, in consultation with the Government of India, laid down a comprehensive policy framework for ownership and governance in private sector banks on February 28, 2005. The broad principles underlying the framework ensure the following.

1. Ultimate ownership and control is well diversified.
2. Important shareholders are *fit and proper* (as per the guidelines of February 3, 2004 on acknowledgement for allotment and transfer of shares).
3. Directors and CEO are 'fit and proper' and observe sound corporate governance principles.
4. Private sector banks maintain minimum capital (initially ₹ 200 crore, with a commitment to increase to ₹ 300 crore within three years)/net worth (₹ 300 crore at all times) for optimal operations and for systemic stability.
5. Policy and processes are transparent and fair.

In order to attain a well-diversified ownership structure, it is to be ensured that no single entity or a group of related entities has shareholding or control, directly or indirectly, in excess of 10 percent of the paid-up capital of a private sector bank. Where any existing shareholding by any individual entity/group of related entities is in excess of 10 percent, the bank will be required to indicate a timetable for reduction of holding to the permissible level. Any bank having shareholding in excess of 5 percent in any other bank in India will be required to indicate a time bound plan for reduction of such holding to the permissible limit of 5 percent. The parent of any foreign bank having presence in India having shareholding directly or indirectly through any other entity in the banking group in excess of 5 percent in any other bank in India will be similarly required to indicate a time bound plan for reduction of such holding to 5 percent. In the case of restructuring of problem/weak banks or in the interest of consolidation in the banking sector, the RBI could permit a higher level of shareholding, including by a bank.

As per the FDI Policy effective April 17, 2014, the aggregate foreign investment in private banks from all sources (foreign direct investment, foreign institutional investment, investment by non-resident Indians etc.) cannot exceed 74 percent. At all times, at least 26 percent of the paid-up capital of the private sector banks will have to be held by resident Indians. Currently, there is a limit of 10 percent for individual foreign institutional investors with the aggregate limit for all foreign institutional investors restricted to 24 percent which can be raised to 49 percent with the approval of board/general body. Similarly, there is a limit of 5 percent for individual portfolio investment by non-resident Indians with the aggregate limit for all non-resident Indians restricted to 10 percent which can be raised to 24 percent with the approval of board/general body.

24.4.3 Foreign Banks in India: With a view to delineate the direction and pace of reform process in this area and to operationalise the extant guidelines of March 4, 2004 in a phased manner, the RBI, on February 28, 2005, released the road map for presence of foreign banks in India. The roadmap was divided into two phases.

A. Phase I: March 2005 to March 2009: During the first phase, foreign banks were permitted to establish presence by way of setting up a wholly-owned banking subsidiary (WOS) or conversion of the existing branches into a WOS. The guidelines covered, *inter alia*, the eligibility criteria of the applicant foreign banks such as ownership pattern, financial soundness, supervisory rating and the international ranking. The WOS was required to have a minimum capital requirement of ₹ 300 crore and maintain a capital adequacy ratio of 10 percent or as was prescribed from time to time on a continuous basis, from the commencement of its operations. The WOS was treated on par with the existing branches of foreign banks for branch expansion with flexibility to go beyond the existing WTO commitments of 12 branches in a year and preference for branch expansion in under-banked areas. During this phase, permission for acquisition of share holding in Indian private sector banks by eligible foreign banks was limited to banks identified by the RBI for restructuring. The RBI—if it was satisfied that such investment by the foreign bank concerned was in the long-term interest of all the stakeholders in the investee bank—permitted such acquisition. Where such acquisition was by a foreign bank having presence in India, a maximum period of 6 months was given for conforming to the *one form of presence* concept.

B. Phase II: April 2009 onward: Phase II commenced in April 2009 after a review of the experience gained and after due consultation with all the stakeholders in the banking sector. The review examined issues concerning extension of national treatment to WOS, dilution of stake and permitting mergers/acquisitions of any private sector banks in India by a foreign bank in Phase II.

The parent foreign bank will continue to hold 100 percent equity in the Indian subsidiary for a minimum prescribed period of operation. The composition of the Board of directors should, *inter alia*, meet the following requirements: (a) not less than 50 percent of the directors should be Indian nationals resident in India, and (b) not less than 50 percent of the directors should be non-executive directors.

Foreign banks which commenced banking business in India before August 2010 shall have the option to continue their banking business through the branch mode. However, they will be incentivised to convert into WOS. To prevent domination by foreign banks, restrictions would be placed on further entry of new WOSs of foreign banks/capital infusion, when the capital and reserves of the WOSs and foreign bank branches in India exceed 20 percent of the capital and reserves of the banking system. The initial minimum paid-up voting equity capital for a WOS shall be ₹ 5 billion for new entrants.

Table 24.1 provides a list of top 10 foreign banks in India as on September 30, 2019.

24.5 Deposit Insurance System

India was the second country to institute a Deposit Insurance Scheme way back in 1961 in the wake of failure of a few banks. The deposit insurance system is designed to provide protection to small depositors who lack adequate financial skills and do not have the wherewithal to monitor their banks. The scheme is in the nature of a pay-box system in the case of: (a) liquidation, and (b) reconstruction/amalgamation of an insured bank.

Deposit Insurance and Credit Guarantee Corporation (DICGC) which operates the scheme is governed by the DICGC Act, 1961. However, where there are no specific provisions, the DICGC Board may make regulations, consistent with the DICGC Act, with the approval of the RBI. Thus, the RBI has the powers conferred by the DICGC Act to make regulations for DICGC. The Corporation is a wholly-owned subsidiary of the

RBI. The authorised capital of the Corporation is ₹ 50 crore which is entirely issued and subscribed by the RBI. The management of the DICGC vests in a board of directors constituted as per the provisions of the DICGC Act, 1961.

Table 24.1: Top 10 Foreign Banks in India and their Branches (as on September 30, 2019)

S. No.	Name of the Bank	Number of Branches in India
1.	Standard Chartered Bank	100
2.	Citibank N.A.	35
3.	HSBC Ltd.	26
4.	Deutsche Bank	17
5.	BNP Paribas	8
6.	Barclays Bank PLC	6
7.	Shinhan Bank	6
8.	Credit Agricole Corporate & Investment Bank	5
9.	Mizuho Bank Ltd.	5
10.	MUFJ Bank Ltd.	5

Source: Reserve Bank of India.

In India, deposit insurance is compulsory for all banks. However, under the DICGC Act, the Corporation has the power to cancel the registration of an insured bank if it fails to pay the premium for three consecutive half-year periods. All deposits—with the exception of deposits of foreign governments, deposits of State/Central Governments, inter-bank deposits, and deposits held abroad—are insured by the DICGC. The insurance cover is provided to deposits held in the same capacity and in the same right and presently the limit is ₹ 1,00,000. Banks are charged premium on total assessable deposits (10 paise/₹ 100 of assessable deposit). With the existing limit, there is a high degree of protection available to small depositors. The Deposit Insurance Fund (DIF) is mainly built out of the premium received from the insured banks and the coupon income received from investment in the Central Government securities.

The Corporation's liability to the depositors of an insured bank arises in the event of the liquidation of that bank or its amalgamation with another bank or its reconstruction, and the claim payment needs to be made before the expiry of two months from the receipt of the claim.

With a view to educating the small depositors, DICGC has taken steps to increase public awareness of the deposit insurance scheme by sending relevant written materials to the insured banks for them to display in all branches at all places where depositor interaction is involved. DICGC has also hosted its own website (www.dicgc.org.in) for providing information to the public.

25

Banking Sector Reforms in India Since 1991

The period beginning from the early 1990s witnessed the transformation of the banking sector as a result of financial sector reforms that were introduced as a part of structural reforms initiated in 1991. The reform process in the financial sector was undertaken with the prime objective of having a strong and resilient banking system. The progress achieved in the areas of strengthening the regulatory and supervisory norms has ushered in greater accountability and market discipline amongst the participants. The RBI has made sustained efforts towards adoption of international benchmarks in a gradual manner, as appropriate to the Indian conditions, in various areas such as prudential norms, risk management, supervision, corporate governance and transparency and disclosures. The reform process has helped in taking the management of the banking sector to the level, where the RBI ceased to micro-manage commercial banks and focused largely on the macro goals. The focus on deregulation and liberalisation coupled with enhanced responsibilities for banks made the banking sector resilient and capable of facing several newer global challenges.

25.1 Backdrop of Banking Sector Reforms

Until the early 1990s, the banking sector suffered from lack of competition, low capital base, low productivity and high intermediation cost. Commenting on the performance of the nationalised banks, the Reserve Bank of India observed, "After the nationalisation of large banks in 1969 and 1980, the Government-owned banks have dominated the banking sector. The role of technology was minimal and the quality of service was not given adequate importance. Banks also did not follow proper risk management systems and the prudential standards were weak. All these resulted in poor asset quality and low profitability". [1]

Prior to reforms, the Indian Government determined the quantum, allocation and the price of credit, a situation referred to as *financial repression* by some experts.

It was in this backdrop, that wide-ranging banking sector reforms in India were introduced as an integral part of the economic reforms initiated in the early 1990s. Reforms in the commercial banking sector had two distinct phases.

The first phase of reforms—implemented subsequent to the release of the Report of the Committee on Financial System (Chairman: M. Narasimham), 1992 (or Narasimham Committee I)—focussed mainly on enabling and strengthening measures. The Committee was guided by the fundamental assumption that the resources of the banks come from the general public and held by the banks in trust. These resources have to be deployed for maximum benefit of their owners, i.e. the depositors. This assumption automatically implies that even the Government has no business to endanger the solvency, health and efficiency of the nationalised banks. According to the Committee, the poor financial shape and low efficiency of public sector banks was due to: (a) extensive degree of central direction of their operations, particularly in terms of investment, credit allocation and branch expansion, and (b) excessive political interference, resulting into failure of commercial banks to operate on the basis of their commercial judgement and in the framework of internal economy. Despite opposition from trade unions and some political parties, the Government accepted all the major recommendations of the Committee some of which have already been implemented.

The second phase of reforms—implemented subsequent to the recommendations of the Committee on Banking Sector Reforms (Chairman: M. Narasimham), 1998 (or Narasimham Committee II)—placed greater emphasis on structural measures and improvement in standards of disclosure and levels of transparency in order to align the Indian standards with international best practices.

25.2 Objectives of Banking Sector Reforms

The key objective of reforms in the banking sector in India has been to enhance the stability and efficiency of banks. To achieve this objective, various reform measures were initiated that could be categorised broadly into three main groups: (a) enabling measures, (b) strengthening measures, and (c) institutional measures.

Enabling measures were designed to create an environment where banks could respond optimally to market signals on the basis of commercial considerations. Salient among these included reduction in statutory pre-emptions so as to release greater funds for commercial lending, interest rate deregulation to enable price discovery, granting of operational autonomy to banks and liberalisation of the entry norms for financial intermediaries.

The strengthening measures aimed at reducing the vulnerability of banks in the face of fluctuations in the economic environment. These included, *inter alia*, capital adequacy, income recognition, asset classification and provisioning norms, exposure norms, improved levels of transparency, and disclosure standards.

Institutional framework conducive to development of banks needs to be developed. Salient among these include reforms in the legal framework pertaining to banks and creation of new institutions.

25.3 Contents of Banking Sector Reforms

With a view to overcoming several weaknesses that had crept into the system over the years and with a view to creating a strong, competitive and vibrant banking system, several measures, including the following, were initiated beginning the early 1990s. Banking sector reforms since 1991 have included, among others, the following.

1. Granting operational autonomy to banks.
2. Reduction in statutory pre-emptions so as to release greater funds for commercial lending.
3. Deregulation of interest rates.
4. Relaxation in investment norms for banks.
5. Easing of restrictions in respect of banks' foreign currency investments.

6. Withdrawal of reserve requirements on inter-bank borrowings.
7. Introduction of prudential norms in line with international best practices.
8. Allowing entry of new private sector banks and enhanced presence of foreign banks.
9. Allowing public sector banks to access the capital market and providing to them operational flexibility and functional autonomy.
10. Revamping of supervisory system for creating a sound banking system.
11. Strengthening corporate governance practices and disclosure standards of banks.

As a result of above measures, the size and structure of the banking sector has undergone a significant change. Financial repression has eased substantially with the deregulation of interest rates and substantial removal of credit allocation.

25.3.1 Deregulation of Deposit and Lending Interest Rates: Narasimham Committee I had recommended that the level and structure of interest rates in the country should be broadly determined by market forces. All controls and regulations on interest rates should be removed.

The process of deregulation of domestic deposit rates began when banks were allowed to set interest rates for maturities between 15 days and up to 1 year subject to a ceiling of 8 percent effective April 1985. However, this freedom was withdrawn by end-May 1985 in the face of an ensuing price war. The process of deregulation was resumed in April 1992 by replacing the existing maturity-wise prescriptions by a single ceiling rate of 13 percent for all deposits above 46 days. The ceiling rate was brought down to 10 percent in November 1994, but was raised to 12 percent in April 1995. Banks were allowed to fix the interest rates on deposits with maturity of over 2 years in October 1995 which was further relaxed to maturity of over one year in July 1996.

In October 1997, the deposit rates were fully deregulated. Consequently, the RBI gave the freedom to commercial banks to fix their own interest rates on domestic term deposits of various maturities with the prior approval of their respective boards of directors/Asset Liability Management Committee. Banks were permitted to determine their own penal interest rates for premature withdrawal of domestic term deposits and the restrictions on banks that they must offer the same rate on deposits of the same maturity irrespective of the size of deposits was removed in respect of deposits of ₹ 15 lakh and above in April 1998 with the laying down of policy in this regard by the board of the bank. Presently, banks have complete freedom in fixing their domestic deposit rates, except interest rate on savings deposits which continues to be regulated.

Prime lending rates of banks for commercial credit are now entirely within the purview of the banks and are not set by the RBI. The country has moved towards liberalised credit allocation mechanism and reduced direct control over interest rates by the monetary authorities. The purpose of deregulation is to promote healthy competition among the banks and encourage their operational efficiency.

25.3.2 Organisation of Banking Structure: Narasimham Committee I proposed a substantial reduction in the number of public sector banks through mergers and acquisitions. The broad pattern should consist of the following.

1. 3 or 4 large banks which could become international in character.

2. 8 or 10 national banks with a network of branches throughout the country.
3. Local banks whose operations would be generally confined to a specific region.
4. Rural banks whose operations will be confined to rural areas.

Significantly, Narasimham Committee I recommended that RBI should permit the setting up of new banks in the private sector. It wanted a positive declaration from the Government that there would be no more nationalisation of banks. It further recommended that there should not be any difference in treatment between the public sector banks and the private sector banks.

It recommended that RBI should follow a more liberal policy in respect of allowing the foreign banks to open branches in India and they should be subjected to the same requirements as are applicable to the Indian banks.

In January 1993, RBI had issued guidelines for licensing of new banks in the private sector. It had granted licenses to 10 banks which are presently in business. Based on a review of experience gained on the functioning of new private sector banks, revised guidelines were issued in January 2000. Following are the major revised provisions.

1. Initial minimum paid-up capital shall be ₹ 200 crore which will be raised to ₹ 300 crore within three years of commencement of business.
2. Contribution of promoters shall be a minimum of 40 percent of the paid-up capital of the bank at any point of time. This contribution of 40 percent shall be locked in for five years from the date of licensing of the bank.
3. While augmenting capital to ₹ 300 crore within three years, promoters shall bring in at least 40 percent of the fresh capital which will also be locked in for five years.
4. NRI participation in the primary equity of a new bank shall be to the maximum extent of 40 percent.

25.3.3 Duality of Control: Narasimham Committee I recommended removal of duality of control over the banking system by the banking department of the Finance Ministry on the one hand, and by the RBI on the other hand. The Committee desired the RBI to assume full responsibility of overseeing the functioning of the banking system.

25.3.4 Abolition of Selective Credit Controls (SCCs): SCCs, introduced in India in 1956, pertain to regulation of credit for specific purposes. The techniques of SCCs used by the RBI include fixing minimum margins for lending against securities, ceiling on maximum advances to individual borrowers against stocks of certain commodities, and minimum discriminatory rates of interest prescribed for certain kinds of advances. SCCs have been used mainly to prevent the speculative holding of essential commodities like foodgrains to prevent price rise.

Selective credit controls have been abolished in the post-liberalisation period.

25.3.5 Managerial Autonomy for Public Sector Banks: Competition among the commercial banks has increased with the entry of private sector banks, permission to foreign banks to open up to 12 branches a year with effect from 1998-99 and relaxation of various restrictions on public sector banks which, *inter alia,* are now allowed to access the capital market to raise funds. This will dilute the shareholding of the Government.

Commenting on the emerging scenario, the RBI of India's *Report on Currency and*

Finance, (1999-2000) observed, "The competition in the banking sector has so evolved in the recent years that the market structure of the banking sector has tended to be oligopolistic. While the number of banks is reasonably large, the dominance of public sector banks, and especially of a few large banks continues. Such banks accounting for large share of deposits and advances as market leaders are able to influence decisions about liquidity and rate variables in the system. But, even such banks may face challenges in the future and face tougher competition, given the gradual upgradation of skills and technologies in competing banks and the restructuring and re-engineering processes being attempted by both foreign and private sector banks". [2]

In the changed scenario, public sector banks will have to improve their efficiency. The highly regulated and directed banking system is now transforming itself into one characterised by openness, competition and prudence. This development conforms to the liberalisation and globalisation needs of the Indian economy.

The Government of India issued a managerial autonomy package for the public sector banks on February 22, 2005 with a view to providing them a level playing field with the private sector banks in India. Under the new framework, the Boards of public sector banks would enjoy more freedom to carry out their functions efficiently without any impediment. The functions, however, have to be in sync with the extant statutory requirements, government policy prescription and regulatory guidelines issued by the RBI from time to time. The revised guidelines allow the following to public sector banks.

1. Pursue new lines of business.
2. Make suitable acquisitions of companies or businesses.
3. Close/merge unviable branches.
4. Open overseas offices.
5. Set up subsidiaries.
6. Exit a line of business.

Similarly, these banks have been allowed to decide human resource issues, including staffing pattern, recruitment, placement, transfer, training, promotions and pensions as well as visits to foreign countries to interact with investors, depositors and other stakeholders. Besides, the Boards of Directors of stronger banks would have additional autonomy for framing their own human resource (HR) policies. Prescription of standards for categorisation of branches, based on volume of business and other relevant factors, have been left to the banks to decide. Public sector banks have been permitted to lay down policy of accountability and responsibility of bank officials.

The public sector banks (PSBs) continued to be a dominant part of the banking system. A unique feature of the reform of the public sector banks was the process of their financial restructuring. The banks were recapitalised by the government to meet prudential norms through recapitalisation bonds. Divestment of equity and offer to private shareholders was undertaken through a public offer and not by sale to strategic investors. Thus, all the PSBs which issued shares to private shareholders, have been listed on the exchanges and are subject to the same disclosure and market discipline standards as other listed entities. To address the problem of distressed assets, a mechanism has been developed to allow sale of these assets to asset reconstruction companies which operate as independent commercial entities.

It needs to be noted that the turnaround in the financial performance of the public sector banks, pursuant to the banking sector reforms, has resulted in the market valuation of government holdings in these banks far exceeding the initial recapitalisation cost—which is something unique to the Indian banking system. Thus, the recapitalisation of banks by the government has not been merely a *holding out* operation by the majority owner of the banks. The Indian experience has shown that a strong, pragmatic and non-discriminatory regulatory framework coupled with the market discipline effected through the listing of the equity shares and operational autonomy provided to the banks, can have a significant positive impact on the functioning of the public sector banks.

25.3.6 Other Measures: Credit restrictions for purchase of consumer durables have been removed/relaxed. Similarly, coverage of priority sector has been enlarged by the inclusion of software, agro-processing industries and venture capital. These measures have given the banks the much-needed flexibility to manage their asset portfolios.

In response to reforms, the Indian banking sector has undergone radical transformation during the 1990s. Reforms have altered the organizational structure, ownership pattern and domain of operations of institutions and infused competition in the financial sector. The competition has forced the institutions to reposition themselves in order to survive and grow. The extensive progress in technology has enabled markets to graduate from outdated systems to modern market design, thus, bringing about a significant reduction in the speed of execution of trades and transaction costs.

In terms of the average capital adequacy ratio for the scheduled commercial banks, which was around 2 percent in 1997, had increased to 13.08 percent as on March 31, 2008. The improvement in the capital adequacy ratio has come about despite significant growth in the aggregate assets of the banking system. This level of capital ratio in the Indian banking system compares quite well with the banking system in many other countries.

In regard to the asset quality also, the gross NPAs of the scheduled commercial banks, which were as high as 15.7 percent at end-March 1997, declined significantly to 2.4 percent as at end-March 2008. The net NPAs of these banks during the same period declined from 8.1 percent to 1.08 percent. These figures too compare favourably with the international trends and have been driven by the improvements in loan loss provisioning by the banks, certain institutional measures, as also by the improved recovery climate enabled by the legislative environment.

The reform measures also resulted in an improvement in the profitability of banks. The return on assets (RoA) of scheduled commercial banks increased from 0.4 percent in the year 1991-92 to 0.99 percent in 2007-08. The Indian banks would appear well placed in this regard too vis-à-vis the broad range of RoA for the international banks.

The banking sector reforms also emphasised the need to improve productivity of the banks through appropriate rationalisation measures so as to reduce the operating cost and improve the profitability. A variety of initiatives were taken by the banks, including adoption of modern technology, which has resulted in improved productivity. The business per employee (BPE), as a measure of productivity, for the public sector banks has registered considerable improvement.

The Indian experience has shown that a strong, pragmatic and non-discriminatory regulatory framework coupled with the market discipline effected through the listing of the equity shares and operational autonomy provided to the banks, can have a significant positive impact on the functioning of the public sector banks.

Commenting on the success of banking sector reforms, the Reserve Bank of India observed, "There is evidence to suggest that competition in the banking industry has intensified. Significant improvement was also discernible in the various parameters of efficiency, especially intermediation costs, which declined significantly. Profitability of commercial banks, on the whole, improved significantly despite a decline in spread and higher provisioning following the introduction and subsequent tightening of prudential norms". [3]

25.4 Challenges for the Banking Sector

Banking system in India has undergone significant transformation following financial sector reforms since the early 1990s. The thrust of the banking sector reforms was on increasing operational efficiency, strengthening the prudential and supervisory norms, removing external constraints, creating competitive conditions and developing the technological and institutional infrastructure. The impact of the reform measures is reflected in an improvement in profitability, financial health, soundness and overall efficiency of the banking sector. Banks have been able to maintain or increase their capital adequacy ratio, despite the sharp increase in their risk-weighted assets.

The Indian banking system is currently passing through a crucial phase. Although the banking sector has become strong, competitive, dynamic and resilient, it is faced with several newer challenges as a result of macroeconomic and financial sector developments, both domestic and global. The major issues/challenges faced by the Indian banking sector could be identified as follows:

1. Emergence of financial conglomerates, which has raised the issue of appropriate regulatory structure/arrangement.
2. Emergence of complex financial products, which pose several supervisory challenges.
3. Need to extend financial services to the large number of people who continue to remain outside the banking system.
4. Mobilising resources to sustain and even accelerate the current economic growth momentum.
5. Issues involved in allowing increased presence of foreign banks in India as the roadmap for foreign banks.
6. Progressive move towards fuller capital account convertibility, which will expose the banking system to greater risks and would require addressing certain issues in banking, including some regulatory and supervisory aspects.

To sum up, the process of financial development in independent India has hinged effectively on the development of banking system. Financing of emerging trade and industrial activities during the 1950s and the 1960s reflected the dominance of banking as the critical source. Functionally, banks catered to the needs of the organised industrial and trading sectors. The primary sector consisting of agriculture, forestry, and fishing had to depend largely on their own financing and on sources outside the commercial banks.

It is against this backdrop that the process of banking development was given impetus with the adoption of the policy of social control over banks in 1967, reinforced in 1969 by the nationalisation of 14 major scheduled commercial banks. Since then, the banking system has formed the core of the Indian financial system. Driven largely by public sector initiative and policy activism, commercial banks have a dominant share in total financial assets and are the main source of financing for the private corporate sector. They also channel a sizeable share of household savings to the public sector. Besides, in recent years, they have been performing most of the payment system functions. With increased diversification in recent years, banks in both public and private sectors have been providing a wide range of financial services.

Prior to reforms, the banking sector suffered from lack of competition, low capital base, inefficiency and high intermediation costs. Ever since the bank nationalisation of 1969, the banking sector had been dominated by the public sector along with a high degree of financial repression characterised by administered interest rates and allocated credit. Over the reforms period, the banking system has experienced tremendous growth in the sophistication and size of non-bank intermediation.

Banking sector reforms, introduced in the early 1990s in a gradual and sequenced manner, were directed at the removal of various deficiencies from which the system was suffering. The basic objectives of reforms were to make the system more stable and efficient so that it could contribute in accelerating the growth process. Banking sector reforms have supported the transition of the Indian economy to a higher growth path, while significantly improving the stability of the financial system. In comparison of the pre-reforms period, the Indian banking system today is more stable and efficient. However, the gains of the past decade have to be consolidated, so that these could be translated to drive the institutions, markets and practices into a mature financial system that can meet the challenges of sustaining India on a higher growth trajectory. The banks would need to reassess their core banking business to view how best they could undertake maturity transformation to step up the lendable resources in support of real economic activity.

Endnotes

1. Reserve Bank of India, *Report on Currency and Finance*, 2001-2002, p. VI-1.
2. Reserve Bank of India, *Report on Currency and Finance*, 1999-2000, p. IV-2.
3. Reserve Bank of India, *Report on Currency and Finance*, 2001-2002, p. VI-16.

26

Digital Technology in Banking Sector

India has a rich diversity of digital payment options. Due to steps taken by the Reserve Bank of India (RBI) to encourage electronic transactions, paper-based systems (cheque, demand draft, banker's cheque, payment order, traveller's cheque, interest warrant, dividend warrants, and money order) constitute a miniscule portion of retail payments. The number of clearing houses has also declined.

26.1 Digitization in Banking Sector

Information technology (IT) has transformed the functioning of businesses, the world over. It has: (a) bridged the gaps in terms of the reach and the coverage of systems (b) enabled better decision-making based on latest and accurate information, (c) reduced costs and (d) improved overall improvement in efficiency. In the Indian context, the financial sector, especially the banking sector, has been a major beneficiary from the inroads made by IT. Many new processes, products and services offered by banks and other financial intermediaries are now IT-centred.

Banks have traditionally been in the forefront of harnessing technology to improve their products, services and efficiency. They have, over a long time, been using electronic and telecommunication networks for delivering a wide range of value added products and services. The delivery channels include, inter alia, direct dial-up connections, private networks, public networks and the devices including telephone, personal computers (PCs), automated teller machines (ATMs), networking of ATMs in the form of shared payment networks, and core banking solutions.

With the popularity of PCs, easy access to internet and World Wide Web (WWW), internet is increasingly used by banks as a channel for receiving instructions and delivering their products and services to their customers. This form of banking is generally referred to as internet banking, although the range of products and services offered by different banks vary widely both in their content and sophistication. Effective integration of technology with sound business practices requires business process re-engineering and banks in India need to follow up on the beginnings made in this regard.

Reserve Bank of India (RBI) has played a proactive role in the implementation of IT in the banking sector. IT-based initiatives are focused on meeting the three-pronged objective of better house keeping, improved customer service and overall systemic efficiency.

26.1.1 What is Digital Payment? According to RBI's Ombudsman Scheme for digital transactions, "*Digital transaction* means a payment transaction in a seamless system effected without the need for cash at least in one of the two legs, if not in both. This includes transactions made through digital/electronic modes wherein both the originator and the beneficiary use digital/electronic medium to send or receive money". [1]

26.2 Benefits of Digital Payments

These are as under:

26.2.1 Common Man:

1. Reduced cash and hence more safety.
2. Faster payment.
3. Reduced number of visits to bank.
4. Interest earning on money in the bank.

26.2.2 Vendors:

1. Transactions settled quickly.
2. Getting rid of coins and change.
3. Larger transactions made easy.
4. Improved accounting and book keeping.
5. No need to keep large amounts of cash.

26.3 Card-based Electronic Payment Systems

Cards are well understood products at the global level, and find acceptance at stores, as well as for online payments. Cards have played an important role in the spread of digital payments. Cards are also used to withdraw money from ATMs, and hence have been issued to most account holders. India has had the presence of international players in the payments space for many years. Recently, an Indian player–National Payments Corporation of India (NPCI)–has also introduced card payments through the RuPay scheme.

Cards are usually issued by banks and can be classified on the basis of their issuance, usage and payment by the card holder. There are three types of cards:

1. Pre-paid cards.
2. Debit cards.
3. Credit cards.

26.3.1 Pre-paid Cards: These are pre-loaded from a customer's bank account and are equivalent to cash. These can be used for limited amount of transaction and can be recharged several times like mobile recharge. Such cards are safe to use. Pre-paid instruments are payment instruments that facilitate purchase of goods and services against the value stored on these instruments. The value stored on such instruments represents the value paid for by the holders by cash, by debit to a bank account, or by credit card. The pre-paid payment instruments can be issued in the form of smart cards, magnetic stripe cards, internet accounts, internet wallets, mobile accounts, mobile wallets, paper vouchers etc. Pre-paid cards can be used at any point-of-sale (PoS).

Subsequent to the notification of the Payment and Settlement Systems (PSS) Act, 2007, policy guidelines for issuance and operation of pre-paid instruments in India were issued in the public interest to regulate the issue of pre-paid payment instruments in the country.

The use of pre-paid payment instruments for cross border transactions has not been permitted, except for the payment instruments approved under Foreign Exchange Management Act (FEMA), 1999.

26.3.2 Debit Cards: A debit card is a plastic payment card that can be used instead of cash when making purchases. Debit card is issued by the bank where a client has an account. Linked to the bank account, debit cards are issued to account holders and any expenditure made is immediately debited to user's account. User can use this card to withdraw cash up to the limit prescribed by the bank. Debit cards can be used only for domestic fund transfer from one person to another.

To complete transaction via debit/credit card, the card is swiped at the card reader (PoS), amount is entered followed by a PIN to be manually punched in by the card holder. Upon authentication the receipt is generated and payment completed.

26.3.3 Credit Cards: A credit card is a payment card issued to users (cardholders) to enable the cardholder to pay a merchant for goods and services, based on the cardholder's promise to the card issuer to pay them for the amounts so paid plus other agreed charges. The card issuer (usually a bank) creates a revolving account and grants a line of credit to the cardholder, from which the cardholder can borrow money for payment to a merchant or as a cash advance.

26.3.4 RuPay: RuPay is an Indian domestic card payment scheme conceived and launched by National Corporation of India (NPCI). It aims to fulfil RBI's vision to offer a domestic, open-loop, multilateral system which will allow all Indian banks and financial institutions in India to participate in electronic payments.

"RuPay", the word itself has a sense of nationality in it. "RuPay" is the coinage of two terms Rupee and payment. The RuPay visual identity is a modern and dynamic unit. The orange and green arrows indicate a nation on the move and a service that matches its pace. The colour blue stands for the feeling of tranquillity which is the people must get while owning a card of the brand 'RuPay'. The bold and unique typeface grants solidity to the whole unit and symbolizes a stable entity.

RuPay was created to fulfil the RBI's desire to have a domestic, open loop, and multilateral system of payments in India. In India, 90 percent of credit card transactions and almost all debit card transactions are domestic. However, the cost of transactions was high due to monopoly of foreign gateways like Visa and MasterCard. In recent years, the usage of credit and debit cards (called plastic money) has increased manifold. It was thought that if this process of transactions is made India-centric, cost can come down drastically. RuPay facilitates electronic payment at all Indian banks and financial institutions, and competes with MasterCard and Visa in India. NPCI maintains ties with Discover Financial to enable the card scheme to gain international acceptance.

RuPay card was launched on March 26, 2012. NPCI entered into a strategic partnership with Discover Financial Services (DFS) for RuPay Card, enabling the acceptance of RuPay Global Cards on Discover's global payment network outside of India.

RuPay cards are accepted at all ATMs across India under National Financial Switch, and under the NPCI's agreement with DFS, RuPay cards are accepted on the international Discover network. All Point of Sale (PoS) terminals in India are under the RuPay platform. To enable this, RuPay has certified major banks in India to accept the RuPay card at their respective PoS terminals located at different merchant locations. In addition to the ATMs and PoS terminals, RuPay cards are accepted online on e-commerce websites.

26.4 Non-card Electronic Payment Systems

In recent years advancements in banking technology, progress in mobile banking and innovative technologies to facilitate digital payments have enabled large number of small denomination transactions to be handled smoothly in electronic mode. The Government of India has taken policy decisions to encourage cashless/electronic transactions. In its endeavour on moving towards electronic payments, the Central Government has announced a number of incentives.

26.4.1 Real Time Gross Settlement (RTGS): RTGS is a funds transfer systems where transfer of money takes place from one bank to another on a *real time* and on *gross* basis. Settlement in *real time* means payment transaction is not subjected to any waiting period. *Gross settlement* means the transaction is settled on one-to-one basis without bunching or netting with any other transaction. Once processed, payments are final and irrevocable. This was introduced in 2004 and settles all inter-bank payments and customer transactions above ₹ 2 lakh.

The system started operations with four banks and settled only inter-bank transactions. Subsequently, the system was opened for settlement of customer transactions. It was operationalised for settlement of multilateral net settlement batch (MNSB) files from September 2006.

26.4.2 National Electronic Funds Transfer (NEFT): NEFT is a nation-wide payments system facilitating one-to-one fund transfer up to ₹ 2 lakh, usually on the same day. NEFT is more secure, nation-wide retail electronic payment system to facilitate funds transfer by the bank customers, between the networked bank branches in the country. This has facilitated the availability of electronic payment modes at more centres. There are 23 daily settlements during weekdays.

The banks are to credit the accounts of the customers for the first four settlements on the same day and for the fifth and sixth settlements, the customers' accounts are to be credited not later than T+1 (next working day).

In its latest notification dated June 11, 2019, the RBI decided that with effect from July 1, 2019, processing charges and time varying charges levied on banks by RBI for outward transactions undertaken using the RTGS system, as also the processing charges levied by RBI for transactions processed in NEFT system will be waived by the RBI. The RBI also advised the banks to pass on this benefit to customers using RTGS and NEFT with effect from July 1, 2019.

It is expected that now even more customers would prefer to transfer funds via NEFT or RTGS as the method is faster compared to offline alternatives such as cheque payments or demand drafts.

26.4.3 Immediate Payment Services (IMPS): IMPS is a non-card retail payment service operated by NPCI in collaboration with member banks and is available 24x7. Under this, beneficiary gets funds on a real time basis with the settlement between banks happening on a deferred net basis.

IMPS has been used for remittances and its use has gone up steadily over the past few years. Recently, IMPS has been allowed for receiving foreign inward remittances.

26.4.4 Unified Payments Interface (UPI): UPI is a system that powers multiple bank accounts into a single mobile application (of any participating bank), merging several banking features, seamless fund routing and merchant payments into one hood.

It is a system for instant electronic payment through user's smart phone. It is an advanced version of Immediate Payment Service (IMPS) which is used to transfer money between bank accounts. Like IMPS, UPI facilitates round-the-clock funds transfer service. It authenticates the identity of the user like a debit card, using the phone as a tool instead of a separate card. It works 24x7 and for 365 days.

One needs a smart phone with UPI application (app) and a bank account.

26.4.5 Unstructured Supplementary Service Data (USSD): It is a service which aims to take banking services to every common man in the country. The service allows every customer to access banking services with a single number irrespective of the telecom service provider, make of the mobile handset or the region. It is offered through a National Unified USSD Platform (NUUP) on a short code *99#. The service can be used for payments up to ₹ 5,000 per day per customer.

26.4.6 Aadhaar-enabled Payment System (AEPS): AEPS is a payment service offered by the National Payments Corporation of India (NPCI) to banks, financial institutions using Aadhaar.

AEPS is a bank-led model, which allows online financial inclusion transaction at Micro-ATM through the business correspondent (BC) of any bank using the Aadhaar authentication. This system is designed to handle both ON-US (intra-bank) and OFF-US (inter-bank) requests seamlessly in an effective way by enabling authentication gateway for all Aadhaar-linked account holders.

It is a payment service empowering a bank customer to use Aadhaar as his identity to access his respective Aadhaar-enabled bank account and perform basic banking transactions. It allows bank-to-bank transaction at PoS (MicroATM). The user has to link his account with his Aadhar number at the bank. User can do as many transactions at any AEPS point without any PIN or password. This service is meant to speed track financial inclusion in the country.

26.4.7 Aadhaar Payment Bridge System (APBS): It is a unique payment system implemented by National Payments Corporation of India (NPCI), which uses Aadhaar number as a central key for electronically channelizing the Government subsidies and benefits in the Aadhaar-enabled Bank Accounts (AEBA) of the intended beneficiaries. It is a payment system based on Aadhaar numbers issued by UIDAI and Issuer Identification Number (IIN) issued by NPCI. APBS is used by the Government departments and agencies for the transfer of benefits and subsidies under Direct Benefit Transfer (DBT) scheme launched by Government of India.

The APBS sub-serves the goal of financial inclusion and provides an opportunity to the Government to attempt financial re-engineering of its subsidy management programme. The implementation of APBS has also lead to electronification of a large number of retail payment transactions which were predominantly either in cash or cheque.

APBS eliminates inordinate delays, multiple channels and paperwork involved in the existing system and transfers benefits and subsidies in a seamless and timely manner and directly into the Aadhaar-enabled bank account. In case of change in bank account, customer is not required to convey the bank account detailsത or change in bank details to the Government department or agency. Customer is also not required to open multiple bank accounts for receiving benefits and subsidies of various social welfare schemes. A customer just needs to open one account and seed his/her Aadhaar number in the bank account to start receiving benefits and subsidies directly into his/her Aadhaar-enabled bank account.

26.4.8 Bharat Interface for Money (BHIM): BHIM is a national system for account-to-account transfers. It is a one app for all users from all banks. It ensures direct transactions from and to your bank account.

It is a mobile app developed by NPCI based on the unified payment interface (UPI). It was launched by Prime Minister Shri Narendra Modi in New Delhi on December 30, 2016. Named after Dr. Bhimrao Ambedkar, it is intended to facilitate e-payments directly through banks and as a part of the drive towards cashless transactions in the wake of demonetization of high value currency notes in November 2016.

This UPI app supports all Indian banks which use that platform, which is built over the *immediate payment service* infrastructure and allows the user to instantly transfer money between the bank accounts of any two parties. It can be used on all mobile devices. It has the potential to revolutionize the mobile payments arena. The customers can provide just a registered virtual address for making or receiving payments.

26.4.9 BHIM Aadhaar (Only for Merchants): BHIM Aadhaar enables the merchants to accept payments from customers using their Aadhaar number and biometric authentication of transactions.

It is an Aadhaar-based system for merchants facilitating account-to-account transfers. Customers can pay without the need of card/phone. A merchant can accept payment through his mobile phone using a fingerprint scanner.

This mode of payment has the following features:

1. Direct credit transactions from customer's bank account to merchant's bank account.
2. Instantaneous transfer.
3. Authentication by customer's fingerprint and hence highly secure.

Following are the requirements for registration on BHIM Aadhaar:

1. Smart phone with internet facility.
2. Fingerprint scanner attached to smart phone.
3. Aadhaar number seeded to bank account.
4. Merchant on-boarded by his bank.

26.4.10 Digital Wallet or Electronic Wallet (E-Wallet): Digital wallet is essentially digital versions of traditional wallet that someone would carry in his pocket. It is a type of electronic card which is used for transactions made online through a computer or a smart phone. The utility of digital wallet is the same as that of a credit or debit card. A digital wallet needs to be linked with the individual's bank account to make payments. This can include purchasing items online from a store. An individual's bank account can also be linked to the digital wallet. He may also have his driving license, health card, loyalty card(s) and other ID documents stored on the phone. The credentials can be passed to a merchant's terminal wirelessly via near field communication (NFC).

Increasingly, digital wallets are being made not just for basic financial transactions but to also authenticate the holder's credentials. For example, a digital wallet could potentially verify the age of the buyer to the store while purchasing alcohol. The system has already gained popularity in Japan, where digital wallets are known as *wallet mobiles*.

26.5 Cyber Security Concerns

Cyber space is a complex environment consisting of interactions among people, software services, devices, networks and worldwide distribution of information and communication technology (ICT). Owing to the numerous benefits brought about by technological advancements, the cyber space is a common pool used by citizens, businesses, critical information infrastructure, military and governments in a manner that makes it difficult to draw clear boundaries among these different groups. The cyber space is expected to be more complex in the foreseeable future, with many-fold increase in networks and devices connected to it.

One of the biggest attractions of cyber space, as an electronic medium, is its openness and freedom. It is a public domain and there is no restriction on who can use it as long as one adheres to its technical parameters. This has also given rise to concerns over the security of data and information and privacy.

However, cyber space is vulnerable to a wide variety of incidents, whether intentional or accidental, man-made or natural, and the data exchanged in the cyber space can be exploited for nefarious purposes by both nation-states and non-state actors.

The only way to protect ourselves from such activities is to be vigilant about our data and protect the data from getting into the hands of scamsters and fraudsters.

Endnote

1. RBI Ombudsman Scheme for Digital Payments.
https://rbidocs.rbi.org.in/rdocs/Content/PDFs/OSDT31012019.pdf

Part V
Central Banking and Monetary Policy

27

History, Objectives and Functions of Central Bank

Central bank of a country is usually a government owned and operated institution that controls the banking system and money supply in the economy. It has, *inter alia*, the following responsibilities.

1. Issuing currency.
2. Managing money supply.
3. Administering rate of interest.
4. Monitoring borrowing and lending policies of commercial banks.
5. Undertaking governmental banking activities
6. Maintaining foreign exchange reserves, external value of money and a country's balance of payments.

Central banks of the leading Western nations (Federal Reserve System in the United States, Deutsche Bundesbank in West Germany, Bank of Japan, and Bank of England) generally work closely to improve the global monetary system and to conduct varying degrees of co-ordinated currency support actions in times of severe exchange or other financial problems.

27.1 History of Central Banks

Central banks have evolved worldwide on a continuous basis in response to changing political and economic forces around them. Beginning in the late 17th century in Sweden and England, central banks spread rather slowly in different parts of the world over the 18th century. In the 19th century, however, several countries in Europe such as France, Finland, the Netherlands, Austria, Norway, Denmark, Portugal, Belgium, Spain, Germany, Italy, and Japan in Asia established the central banks (Table 27.1).

The first central bank, the *Sveriges Riksbank,* was established in Sweden in 1668; and the second was the Bank of England (BoE), set up in 1694 under a Royal Charter. Most of the bigger European central banks were established in the 19th century, while the German *Bundesbank* and the U.S. Federal Reserve System in the 20th century. There were only 18 central banks at the beginning of the 20th century. The early central banks were established primarily to finance commerce, foster growth of the financial system and to bring uniformity in note issue. The Bank of England initially functioned as the banker and debt manager to the government. As a commercial bank, BoE also took deposits and issued notes. With the renewal of BoE's charter in 1781, it was described as *the public exchequer* and acted as the bankers' bank as well. In the 19th century, the BoE undertook the role of lender-of-the-last-resort, providing stability during several financial crises. The BoE was nationalised in 1946 and it remained the Treasury's adviser, agent and debt manager.

Table 27.1: Establishment of Central Banks in Different Countries of the World

Country	Year of Establishment	Country	Year of Establishment
Sweden	1668	Denmark	1818
England	1694	Portugal	1846
France	1800	Belgium	1850
Finland	1811	Spain	1874
Netherlands	1814	Germany	1876
Austria	1816	Italy	1893
Norway	1816	Japan	1882

Source: Reserve Bank of India, *Report on Currency and Finance*, 2004-05, p. 1.

The *Banque de France* was set up in 1800 to restore confidence in the French banking system after the financial upheavals of the revolutionary period. The *Banco de Portugal*, which was established as a public limited company in 1846, was a note issuing commercial bank, whose main job was maintaining convertibility of its notes and making a profit for its shareholders.

In Germany, the *Bundesbank* was set up in 1957 by the *Bundesbank* Law. It had a predecessor known as the *Reichsbank* that was operational from 1876 to 1945. Unlike some of the other European countries where central banks were set up in the 17th and early 18th century, central banking *per se* came late to Germany, as a stable state came into existence only in 1871. One of the rationales for setting up a central bank in Germany was the desire to have a uniform system of coinage, weights and measures. The *Bundesbank* was a federal central bank that gradually helped to integrate its separate units. It was expected that the *Bundesbank* would reduce the multiple setting and integrate existing regulations across Germany. The *Bundesbank* accordingly created a fairly transparent monetary regime, provided an adequate base for dynamic economic growth and integrated the separate entities financially.

The Bank of Italy was founded in 1893 as part of the reorganisation of the Italian banking and monetary system that had reached the state of near collapse at the beginning of the 1890s. The fundamental task of the bank was to free itself from the problems inherited, primarily by cleaning the balance sheet and restoring a capital base. A far reaching objective of the reorganisation of the Italian monetary and credit system was to create a set of uniform rules and institutions that would place the Italian currency on a sound footing and prevent recurrence of crises.

27.2 Changing Objectives of Central Banks

Central banks which began with the need for institutions that could serve as lender-of-the-last resort to commercial banks and lender to the government, were later entrusted with the tasks of management of internal and external value of currency. Typically, central banks are now set up as entities that regulate financial institutions, maintain low inflation, a stable exchange rate and promote economic growth. They have helped economies to tide over business downturns, provided confidence to depositors and helped in avoiding banking crises. They have also bridged information gaps, undertaken policy-oriented research, built databases, disseminated data and information regarding monetary policy and the economy as a whole. Indeed, central banks have taken over a whole range of functions, becoming multi-tasking institutions that conduct monetary policy, regulate and supervise the banking system and perform a crucial role in the payment system.

The primary impulses for establishing and strengthening of central banking activity in many parts of the world in the 20th century emanated from exigency of war financing. Economic historians assign war finance as prime consideration for constitution of many of the early central banks. Further, war financing led to nationalisation of many central banks, which till then were functioning as private entities. Once the spectre of war receded, the role of central banking was increasingly focused in mobilising resources for planned development and at the same time in tackling high inflation.

With the emergence of a number of nation states with the weakening of colonial regimes, central bank mandates in the developing countries, including that in India, went well beyond typical central banking functions so as to encompass a wide range of developmental pursuits. Consequently, central banks in the developing countries envisaged broadening of their mandate beyond the traditional functions of issuing currency and managing the government debt towards facilitating economic recovery and growth. The seeds of the twin and oft divergent objectives of central banking in emerging markets were thus planted. While this transition entrusted the central banks with greater responsibility in national development, they also became exposed to the threat of fiscal dominance, where developmental objectives restrained the growth of financial markets and consequently, the efficient conduct of monetary policy.

The core of modern central banking also consisted of development of financial markets, financial regulation and supervision, management of government debt, administration of payment and settlement systems and maintenance of the external value of currency. Several variants of instruments and targets emerged in different central banks. Though many of the central banks have adopted inflation targeting as the core objective and recorded a fair degree of success, the consensus on inflation targeting as an exclusive central banking mandate remains elusive. Further, with a view to strengthening the operating procedures of central banking in order to achieve the desired objectives, the issues of autonomy, transparency, accounting standards and risk management have assumed importance. With a vision to deal with increasing complexities in operational procedures, research activities have been given considerable importance in analysing the economic environment and devising suitable strategies. The challenges of globalisation leading to free flow of capital, trade and information across the borders have necessitated redefining the statutes of central banking, both in developed and developing countries.

While each country has had a unique experience in the evolution of its central bank, there are some common features: whenever central banks were set up to tackle similar problems, their institutional structures were observed to be similar. Notwithstanding the diversity, there were certain developments affecting the functions, objectives and instruments of monetary policy of central banks all over the world. With the onset of the First World War, paper money issued by central banks replaced the full value metal coin money.

As notes became legal tender and ceased to be convertible into gold, the power of central banks over money supply increased and stabilisation policies became feasible. After the First World War, the role of central banks became even more important. Their role of supervising the business of private commercial banks was extended and lender-of-the-last-resort function to stabilise the banking system during financial panics was strengthened. The First World War also led to the central banks' increasing involvement in extending credit to their governments. In order to handle their new role as brokers for government debt, central banks were allowed to trade government paper in the open market and were entitled to develop open market policy instruments for fine-tuning of interest rates and for credit and money supply expansion. This gave rise to more discretionary powers to central banks to conduct their operations.

As financial systems developed, central banks had to reorient their policies and strengthen their roles in order to cope with the new challenges. During global crises such as the Great Depression of the 1930s, the mandate given to most central banks included monetary stability, promotion of full employment and maximisation of growth. The role of central banks was thus enhanced successively after every crisis.

Similarly, the developing countries that emerged out of shackles of colonialism entrusted their central banks with the objective of economic growth along with price stability. In the late 20th century, development of global financial markets and proliferation of financial instruments coupled with episodes of financial crises brought to the fore central banks' concern for price stability, financial stability and risk management. The journey of central banking, seen through history, has indeed been quite remarkable.

27.3 Functions of a Central Bank

Central bank functions have evolved over time, especially after the economies encountered difficult periods or crises. These functions vary in nature and with the stage of economic development of the country where the central bank is situated. The functions of a central bank can be broadly categorised as follows.

1. Monetary policy functions.
2. Banker to the banks.
3. Banker to the government.
4. Developmental functions.

The functions of note issuance, maintenance of internal and external value of currency evolved as the key objectives of monetary policy. The task of promotion of growth was subsequently added to it. This set of functions became the core monetary policy functions. With the development of the financial sector, lender-of-the-last-resort function grew to encompass the role of a regulator and supervisor. It has assumed wider objective of financial stability in recent years and includes allied activities pertaining to adoption of technology in banking. Many central banks were established predominantly to finance the activities of their governments. This function has been reviewed and many central banks have ceased to finance their governments in recent years. Central banks have assumed many new functions that focus on development of markets, institutions and communication policies.

27.3.1 Monetary Policy Functions: Monetary policy functions form the core of central banking operations and constitute the key functions of almost all central banks. Of these functions, currency management and maintenance of external value of currency were the predominant concerns of central banks in the early years of central banking. The explicit concern for price stability is of relatively later origin.

A. Currency Issue and Management: Currency management is one of the most important traditional functions of central banks in most countries. Until the evolution of central banks, private banks issued their own currency and there were often numerous currencies with varying degrees of acceptability. The task of currency issue was entrusted to the central bank so as to bring uniformity in note issue across the country and facilitate exchange. Central banks have continued to perform this function over the years. Currency issue was nationalised in many countries. This function grew in scope and the present task of currency management includes functions such as estimating the demand for currency, currency design, printing, storage, distribution and disposal of unfit notes.

B. Maintaining Internal Value of the Currency: Instituting a medium of exchange is one of the oldest functions assigned to central banks. Arising from this core function is the monetary policy function of keeping inflation low in order to maintain the value of the medium of exchange over time. This function is still very relevant to modern central banks as can be seen from the widespread adoption of inflation targeting framework.

Central bank of a country uses various instruments to control and regulate the supply of money and credit in the economy in order to maintain price stability.

C. Maintaining External Value of the Currency: Central banks in many economies consider exchange rate management as a crucial function. Through the 1990s, the reform process has transformed many economies into vibrant and open ones. The free determination of the exchange rate is becoming increasingly complex for the emerging market economies. The matter is further complicated by the possibility of capital flows as a result of integration of global markets. The structural changes that have been undertaken in a number of these countries make it feasible to consider exchange rate flexibility.

27.3.2 Banker to the Government: Most central banks such as Bank of England evolved from the need to have an institution that would look after the finances of their governments, lend to it or manage its public debt. Such central banks were entrusted with a variety of fiscal responsibilities and consequently evolved institutional structures to take care of all the associated requirements. In the initial years of central banking in developed countries and even now in developing countries, most central banks provided liquidity to their respective governments to smoothen the temporary mismatches between their revenues and expenditure, against government paper, on an *ad hoc* basis.

Traditionally, debt management of the government was handled by the central bank because of the complementary nature of monetary policy and public debt management. Government securities are useful in providing the central bank a tool for conduct of open market operations and a backing for its note issues.

Interestingly, the management of public debt has changed over the years. Starting from a situation where some governments were initially financed by private bankers, many central banks were established for performing the function of manager of public debt. Now, there is a move for central banks to desist from financing the government due to the widespread recognition of its inflationary implications. Besides this, managing government debt involves large coordination between fiscal and monetary policy and also requires sufficient independence on part of the central bank to deny the government the additional borrowings. The experience of many countries supports separation of the debt management function from the monetary policy function.

27.3.3 Banker to the Banks: Central banks were set up in many countries to perform the function of maintaining financial stability. The financial system in the early days was essentially a bank-dominated system; hence financial stability was focussed on the stability of banks. Lender-of-the-last-resort function was the first financial stability function that central banks performed. This function was fairly limited in its scope, with central bank operations limited merely to the function of crisis management.

The role of central banks has expanded; it now covers oversight of other financial institutions as well as the entire payment system. The potential of any crisis to proliferate has increased several folds. For example, a bank level problem can attain dangerous proportions if depositors lose faith in banks in general after some bank failure, thereby precipitating large-scale withdrawals from sound institutions. Growing globalisation of banking means that such effects may spread across national boundaries. As time has progressed, the duties of central banks have not remained confined only to ensuring soundness of commercial banks but have extended to cover the financial system as a whole.

A. Lender-of-the-last-resort: This function of the central bank is important during a banking crisis. A banking crisis is an event in which many or even all banks in the banking system face sudden demand from their creditors. Given the multiple credit creation principle, it is not possible for any bank to handle such a run. At such times of crisis, apart from providing the routine liquidity to commercial banks through the discount window, the central bank may also bail out illiquid but not insolvent banks so as to avoid a generalised banking crisis. A banking crisis cannot be averted without an agency working as lender-of-the-last-resort. In fact, many central banks were established specifically to take care of banking crises.

The term 'lender of last resort' (LoLR) refers to a function of a central bank whereby it lends money to support a financial institution facing temporary liquidity stress even after exhausting recourse to the market and whose failure is likely to have systemic implications. The classical LoLR doctrine asserts that during periods of liquidity crisis faced by a *solvent but illiquid* bank, the central bank in its role as LoLR may support it by lending to it against good collateral, valued at pre-crisis levels, and at a penal rate.

The central bank, as the only institution able to create liquidity in the banking system, has an important role to play as LoLR, particularly if the liquidity problem threatens systemic stability.

However, the role of LoLR entails significant moral hazard because the central bank might be seen as too willing to underwrite the banking system and bail out banks that are not as well run as others, thereby indirectly encouraging imprudent practices.

27.3.4 Developmental Functions: Developmental functions are undertaken by the central bank, while not ignoring their traditional tasks. This makes the functions and goals before a developing country central banker much broader and challenging.

In systems where markets are imperfect, differential interest rates are often set by the central banks for various purposes and according to the needs of borrowers and policies of governments. Aligning the central banks' policies to the governments' developmental goals is crucial in a developing country. For this purpose, central banks often take over developmental and promotional activities. Selective credit policies such as micro allocation of credit, credit subsidies to preferred sectors are undertaken in order to support the governments' growth initiatives. This approach to economic management leads to crowding out of private enterprise as increasing share of credit flows are mopped up by the government and public enterprises.

Given dependence of monetary policy on the financial structure of the economy, central banks in developing countries are concerned about macroeconomic management of the cost and supply of money and credit. In order to address the problems of the financial system, central banks in developing countries make specific efforts to replace informal credit by spreading the umbrella of organized credit. Expansion of commercial banks network is very useful in the mobilisation of savings and the availability of adequate formal credit. The deposit insurance and credit guarantee schemes are introduced to address the issue of market failure that is often encountered in a developing economy. Central banks in developing countries are required to strive hard for the efficient functioning of the financial sector. They are often involved in the designing of the financial infrastructure and making appropriate regulation for ensuring market discipline. They need to put in place *the rules of the game* or an appropriate regulatory and supervisory framework, and upgrade it periodically with improvement in the financial sector.

28

Balance Sheet of Central Bank

Balance sheet of a central bank summarizes its financial position, and is made up of assets and liabilities. In other words, balance sheet of a central bank, like most balance sheets, is divided into assets and liabilities. In contrast to a commercial bank or a company, currency in circulation (cash) is a liability for a central bank.

28.1 Significance of the Balance Sheet of Central Bank

Since changes in the supply of money are revealed in the central bank's balance sheet, the balance sheet is the most important item that the central bank discloses. Most central banks publish their balance sheets weekly as a way to maintain transparency. When a central bank fails to publish its balance sheet, it often indicates trouble.

The central bank's balance sheet plays a critical role in the functioning of the economy. The main liabilities of the central bank (banknotes and commercial bank reserves) form the ultimate means of settlement for all transactions in the economy.

Although most central banks have moved from quantitative targets for monetary policy operations to price targets, where the domestic interest rate and/or the exchange rate are the operational target for monetary policy, the central bank's balance sheet remains the best place to understand policy implementation.

Whenever a central bank transacts with the rest of the world—that is when it issues currency, conducts foreign exchange operations, invests its own funds, engages in emergency liquidity assistance, and, last but not least conducts monetary policy operations—all of these operations affect its balance sheet. Therefore, the balance sheet of the central bank is critical to everything the central bank does.

The structure and evolution of a central bank's balance sheet remains a crucial tool in understanding the policy goals that the central bank is aiming to achieve and its effectiveness in doing so.

To understand the role that the balance sheet of central bank plays in an economy it is important to understand the role of money. The central bank's balance sheet is important as its main liabilities—banknotes and commercial bank reserves—are both a form of money in a modern economy and in fact underpin nearly all other forms of money.

Only a central bank can control its balance sheet at will because only a central bank can create or destroy money. Due to the relationship between the supply of money and the bank's balance sheet, the creation of money is sometimes referred to as *expanding the balance sheet of the central bank*, because both its assets and liabilities increase. Similarly, the destruction of money causes the *contraction of the balance sheet of the central bank*.

28.2 Frequency and Format of Balance Sheet

While central banks publish their balance sheets in a wide range of publications on a regular basis, there is no agreed frequency or standard format. The most common place for a central bank to publish its balance sheet is in its annual report. However, such reports by their very nature appear only on an annual basis and often at a significant lag. In addition, many central banks separately publish their balance sheets on their websites and in other publications at a higher frequency. Some central banks, such as the Bank of England and the Federal Reserve of USA, publish their balance sheets (or parts of their balance sheet) on a weekly basis with minimal lag. Others, such as the national central banks within the euro system and the Hong Kong Monetary Authority publish their balance sheet monthly, again with a minimal lag.

The format and breakdown of the central bank balance sheet also varies across countries. Often these variations are down to accounting practices and local needs. In particular, the importance of certain balance sheet items varies across countries. For example, for central banks that permit a fully floating exchange rate, the breakdown of foreign exchange reserves may be more concise than for central banks that fix their exchange rate, as they are likely to hold a smaller amount of such assets.

28.3 Components of the Balance Sheet

28.3.1 Liabilities of a Central Bank: Liabilities of a central bank, *inter alia*, include the following:

A. Capital: In many ways central banks are structured like private corporations. They 'are incorporated within similar legal structures and utilise similar accounting principles. Like private sector institutions central banks carry capital on their balance sheets and like private institutions the capital buffer becomes the channel through which the central bank absorbs losses.

Unlike private financial institutions central banks are not subject to regulatory capital requirements. Commercial banks and other financial institutions are mandated by international and domestic regulations to hold capital buffers directly proportional to the size and riskiness of their lending activities. No such regulations exist for central banks. In addition, if a private institution wishes to increase the amount of capital it wishes to hold then it can either retain earnings or go to financial markets to raise additional funds. The ability of the central bank to do this is limited. More often than not the central bank is wholly owned by the government and such choices have wider fiscal implications.

B. Notes in Circulation: This element covers banknotes issued by the central bank that are *in circulation*, either being held by commercial bank in vaults or automatic teller machines (ATMs) or by the people. In most economies, banknotes enter circulation through commercial banks. The process involves commercial banks drawing down banknotes in exchange for reserve balances held at the central bank. People then obtain banknotes either through direct withdrawals from commercial banks or from other agents. Most central banks targeting price targets will supply banknotes on demand to commercial banks.

C. Reserves Held by Commercial Banks at the Central Bank: Reserves are overnight balances that banks hold in an account at the central bank. As such, they are a claim on the central bank. Together with banknotes, reserves are the most liquid, risk-free asset in the economy. Moreover, they are the ultimate asset for settling payments. Banking transactions between customers of different banks are either directly or indirectly settled through transfers between reserves accounts at the central bank. Reserves can be thought of a current account balances held by commercial banks at the central bank in the same way that individuals hold such accounts at commercial banks.

(a) Required versus Free Reserves: Many central banks impose reserve requirements on commercial banks that hold reserve accounts with them. This requires commercial banks to hold a certain balance on their reserve account, either at all times, at a specific point in time or on average over a period. The justification for imposing such requirements has changed. There can be following five potential roles for reserve requirements:

1. Monetary policy purposes.
2. Liquidity management purposes.
3. Structural liquidity purposes.
4. Central bank revenue purposes.
5. Sectorial behaviour purposes.

(b) Voluntary versus Excess Free Reserves: In addition to required reserves commercial banks may also hold free reserves at the central bank. Free reserves are any reserves that do not contribute to the fulfilment of reserve requirements. It must be stressed that the presence of free reserves at a system-wide level is the result of central bank actions. While an individual commercial bank may look to hold free reserves, if the central bank does not provide or allow the extra reserves in the system then these holdings must come at the expense of another commercial bank being unable to meet its reserve requirement. Free reserves can be further broken down into two separate categories: voluntary free reserves, which commercial banks are happy to hold and excess free reserves, which commercial banks do not wish to hold and will look to trade away.

D. Deposits of Central and State Governments: In addition to maintaining balances for commercial banks, in many countries the central bank also acts as banker for the government. Where government deposits funds at the central bank these appear as liabilities. Fundamentally such accounts are identical to reserve accounts, although they may be treated differently within the central banks operational framework, i.e. they may not be subject to reserve requirement or remunerated in the same way. Balances held on such accounts are reserves.

E. Other Liabilities and Provisions: These include bills payable, contingency fund and miscellaneous items. Also, a central bank may hold accounts for other institutions, in addition to reserve accounts for commercial banks and government, for example foreign central banks.

28.3.2 Assets of a Central Bank: Assets of a central bank, *inter alia*, include the following:

A. Gold Coins and Bullion: In India, the aggregate value of gold coins, gold bullion and foreign securities held as assets in the Issue Department of Reserve Bank of India (RBI) shall not at any time be less than ₹ 200 crore. Of this, the aggregate value of gold coins and gold bullion shall not be less than ₹ 115 crore.

B. Foreign Exchange Reserves: Foreign assets are those denominated in a non-domestic currency. The main form of foreign assets held by central banks is foreign exchange reserves. Central banks hold foreign exchange reserves for a variety of purposes including intervention, the need to meet external obligations on foreign currency debt and to cover trade balances.

Foreign exchange reserves are also a prerequisite for a central bank being able to intervene to offset depreciation in the domestic currency. The central bank will intervene by selling foreign assets in exchange for domestic currency denominated assets. This has the joint impact of increasing the supply of foreign assets and reducing the supply of domestic assets, which should offset depreciation pressure.

C. Investments: Like individuals and institutions, a central bank can also make investments in foreign countries and domestically.

D. Bills Purchased and Discounted: RBI holds internal bills of exchange and commercial papers eligible for purchase as a cover for notes issued.

F. Loans and Advances: RBI gives loans and advances to the Central and State Governments, commercial and co-operative banks and others in terms of Sections 17 and 18 of the Reserve Bank of India Act, 1934.

G. Other Items: These, *inter alia*, include investment portfolios and property of the central bank in foreign countries.

The distinction between liabilities and assets driven balance sheets is not just a technical one, it has the ability to influence the effectiveness of monetary policy, the central bank's interaction with commercial banks and the central bank's income. The structure and evolution of the central bank's balance sheet is crucial in determining the level of central bank income.

28.4 Balance Sheet of the Reserve Bank of India (RBI)

The balance sheet of RBI (Table 28.1) plays a critical role in the functioning of the country's economy largely reflecting the activities carried out in pursuance of its currency issue function as well as monetary policy and reserve management objectives.

The balance sheet of RBI is largely a reflection of the activities carried out in pursuance of its currency issue function as well as monetary policy and reserve management objectives. On the recommendations of Technical Committee I constituted in 2012-13 to review the Form of Presentation of the Balance Sheet and Profit & Loss Account (Chairman: Y.H. Malegam), Government of India notified the new format of weekly accounts of RBI on July 15, 2015. Accordingly, the accounts of RBI from the year 2014-15 have been drawn up in the new format resulting in the merger of the Balance Sheets of Issue Department and Banking Department wherein each item of asset and liability is shown as line items supported by schedules.

Table 28.1: Balance Sheet of Reserve Bank of India (RBI): As on June 30, 2019

(₹ billion)

Liabilities		**Assets**	
Capital	0.05	Assets of Banking Department (BD)	
Reserve fund	65.00	Notes, Rupee coins, small coins	0.09
Other reserves	2.30	Gold coins and bullion	882.98
Deposits	7,649.22	Investments-Foreign-BD	6,964.53
Other liabilities and provisions	11,624.51	Investments-Domestic-BD	9,898.77
Liabilities of Issue Department		Bills purchased and discounted	0.00
Notes issued	21,687.97	Loans and advances	931.87
Total liabilities	41,029.05	Investment in subsidiaries	19.64
		Other assets	643.20
		Assets of Issue Department (ID)	
		Gold coins and bullion (as backing for note issue)	792.04
		Rupee coins	8.28
		Investments-Foreign-ID	20,887.65
		Investments-Domestic-ID	0.00
		Domestic bills of exchange and other commercial papers	0.00
		Total assets	41,029.05

Source: Reserve Bank of India, *Annual Report, 2018-19*.

To sum up, balance sheet of a central bank is critical to the functioning of the economy as its main liabilities, banknotes and commercial bank reserves, provide the ultimate means of settlement for transactions. Central banks exploit this role when achieving their policy goals by adjusting both the availability and the terms of access to such liabilities in order to achieve their desired targets.

The central bank's balance sheet can reveal a significant amount of information about its policies. However, to truly understand the effectiveness of a central bank in achieving its policy goals one needs to look at how the balance sheet evolves over time.

29

Instruments of Monetary Control

29.1 Enhanced Need for Monetary Control

The increasing volume of cross-border trade in goods and services, along with that of financial flows, has enhanced inter-dependence in monetary policy formulation across countries. Sharp swings in capital flows and volatile exchange rate movements have emerged as key concerns in monetary management in the emerging market economies. Fluctuations in capital movements have important bearing on the conduct of monetary policy.

The operation of monetary policy has to take into account the risks that greater interest rate or exchange rate volatility entails for a wide range of participants in the economy. Financial innovations have also induced significant transformation in the operating procedures of monetary management.

In a world of generalised uncertainty, the conduct of monetary policy has become increasingly complex. Therefore, all central banks are paying greater attention to financial stability considerations in their overall design of monetary policy formulation.

Instituting a medium of exchange is one of the oldest functions assigned to central banks. Arising from this core function is the monetary policy function of keeping inflation low in order to maintain the value of the medium of exchange over time. This function is still very relevant to modern central banks as can be seen from the widespread adoption of inflation targeting framework.

Domestic policy objectives have been centred on price stability goals for years and even today have remained the main pre-occupation of central banks. In the developing world, central banks have an additional task as the governments expect central banks to use their tools to garner resources for faster development. Hence, central banks have to manage very high levels of public debt [1] and often use inflation tax that undermines their price stability objective.

Central banks have increasingly modified the definitions of money as a result of financial innovations and technological progress. Commercial banks create deposit money, plastic money as well as e-cash and e-money [2] with multiplicity of products. With this, the task of managing currency and maintaining the price level has become increasingly difficult. This task is undertaken by the central banks, by proactively estimating the demand for money, given the projected changes in income and interest rates. These relationships, however, are known to vary over time and sometimes become unstable for countries experiencing rapid transformation of their financial sector, thus posing greater challenges for central bankers.

Central bank of a country uses various instruments to control and regulate the supply of money and credit in the economy in order to achieve price stability and other objectives.

Over the years central banks have increasingly sharpened their tools. Since monetary policy is always conducted in anticipation of various outcomes regarding output and prices, the forecasts of these are of great value to monetary policy makers. These forecasts are based on various types of models. Some central banks use specialised tools or models that forecast the performance of their intermediate targets like money growth or the exchange rate to guide their policy decisions. Central bank tools work by increasing or decreasing total liquidity, i.e. the amount of capital available to invest or lend.

29.2 Bank Rate Policy

Bank rate is the rate at which central bank is ready to buy or rediscount bills of exchange or other commercial papers. As lender of the last resort, the central bank helps the commercial banks in temporary need of cash when other sources of raising cash are exhausted. An increase in the bank rate would discourage commercial banks to borrow from the central bank and a corresponding increase in the lending rate of commercial banks to general public would decrease public borrowings from the banks.

Banks use this facility only when they cannot borrow funds from other banks. Using the bank rate window has a stigma attached to it. The financial community assumes that any bank that uses the bank rate window is in financial trouble. In other words, only a desperate bank that has been rejected by others would use the bank rate facility.

29.3 Cash Reserve Ratio (CRR)

In most countries, commercial banks are required statutorily to hold cash reserves with the central bank. Apart from required reserves, banks also hold excess reserves of cash. A large proportion of these excess reserves are held in the form of cash-in-hand or vault cash to meet the withdrawal needs of the depositors and the remaining part with the central bank to meet the net loss of cash due to the cross-clearing of cheques among the banks.

A low CRR requirement allows banks to lend more of their deposits. It is expansionary because it creates credit. A high CRR requirement is contractionary. It gives banks less money to lend. It is especially hard for small banks since they do not have as much to lend in the first place. That is why most central banks do not impose CRR requirement on small banks. Central banks rarely change the CRR requirement because it is difficult for member banks to modify their procedures.

Central banks are more likely to adjust the targeted lending rate than CRR requirement. It achieves the same result with less disruption. If a bank cannot meet CRR requirement, it borrows from another bank that has excess cash.

CRR remains a powerful instrument of monetary policy in developing economies. It not only impounds liquidity at the first instance but also directly impacts banks' cost of raising funds since a portion of deposit mobilisation is continuously impounded by the central bank. Reserve requirements are especially effective in developing countries as their financial markets are not mature enough for open market operations (discussed on next page).

The principal drawback of CRR requirement is that it imposes an indirect tax on the banking system as an across-the-board levy, which does not take into consideration the relative liquidity position of the players in the credit markets.

Most central banks have, therefore, gradually de-emphasised the use of CRR requirement and preferred open market operations as a tool of monetary policy. This allows them to adjust market liquidity and impact on the interest rate structure at varying tenors through an auction mechanism in which market players are able to bid their preferences. For such market operations to be effective, the secondary markets need to be deep and liquid. At the same time, the central bank must have a sufficient stock of eligible securities to undertake market operations.

29.4 Open Market Operations

The central bank can enter the money market for the purpose of purchase or sale of government securities on its own account. Every open market purchase by the central bank increases primary money by equal amount. When the central bank buys securities, it adds cash to the reserves of the banks. That gives them more money to lend. When the central bank sells the securities, it reduces cash holdings of banks. The banks have now has less to lend. A central bank buys securities when it wants expansionary monetary policy. It sells them when it executes contractionary monetary policy.

As regards their advantages, open market operations are highly flexible, easily reversible in time, their effect on money supply is immediate, and they do not carry *announcement effects* as in the case of changes in the bank rate. Open market operations, considered very effective in developed countries, are not of much importance in developing countries due to underdeveloped nature of money and capital markets

29.5 Moral Suasions

Through moral suasions, the central bank can influence the investment and credit policies of the commercial banks. For example, it can ask the commercial banks to invest a larger proportion, than required, of their assets in government securities. Similarly, it can advise them regarding the allocation of credit to the private sector.

29.6 Macro Prudential Policy

The global financial crisis showed that countries need to contain risks to the financial system as a whole with dedicated financial policies. Many central banks that also have a mandate to promote financial stability have upgraded their financial stability functions, including by establishing macro prudential policy frameworks. Macro prudential policy needs a strong institutional foundation to work effectively. Central banks are well placed to conduct macro prudential policy because they have the capacity to analyze systemic risk. In addition, they are often relatively independent and autonomous. In many countries, legislators have assigned the macro prudential mandate to the central bank or to a dedicated committee within the central bank.

Regardless of the model used to implement macro prudential policy, the institutional setup should be strong enough to counter opposition from the financial industry and political pressures and to establish the legitimacy and accountability of macro prudential policy. It needs to ensure that policymakers are given clear objectives and the necessary legal powers, and to foster cooperation on the part of other supervisory and regulatory agencies. A dedicated policy process and is needed to operationalize this new policy function, by mapping an analysis of systemic vulnerabilities into macro prudential policy action.

29.7 Additional Tools of Monetary Management in India

Apart from the instruments of monetary management described above, the Reserve Bank of India (RBI) has several other tools at its command for monetary control. These are listed below:

1. Repo Rate.
2. Reverse Repo Rate.
3. Liquidity Adjustment Facility (LAF).
4. Marginal Standing Facility (MSF).
5. Statutory Liquidity Ratio (SLR).
6. Market Stabilisation Scheme (MSS).
7. Refinance Facilities.
8. Standing Deposit Facility (SDF).

For details, see chapter 32 of this book.

To sum up, central banks play a crucial role in ensuring economic and financial stability. They conduct monetary policy to achieve low and stable inflation. In the wake of the global financial crisis, central banks have expanded their toolkits to deal with risks to financial stability and to manage volatile exchange rates. Central banks need clear policy frameworks to achieve their objectives. Operational processes tailored to each country's circumstances enhance the effectiveness of the central banks' policies.

Since 1990s, there has been an increasing shift from direct to indirect instruments of monetary policy. This is in consonance with the consistent preference for market-based instruments of monetary policy. The process has been reinforced by a switch, within the group of indirect instruments, from relatively less market-oriented instruments such as CRR requirements to relatively more market-oriented instruments such as open market operations.

Endnotes

1. Central banks in developing countries are typically required to facilitate large borrowing programmes of their governments. For this, they may impose high reserve requirements on the banking system to ensure that it remains a captive buyer of government securities, even if the interest rates on these borrowings are at sub-market levels. After some initial level of development, these central banks may take steps to ensure that this dependence of the government borrowing programme on the banking sector is reduced. In this direction, several steps need to be taken such as free market determination of interest rates on government securities and market-based procedures for monetary policy.
2. E-money is monetary value units stored in electronic form on a device held by the consumers. Since e-money has all the features of traditional forms of money, it is an instrument like a cheque or a demand draft, which facilitates transactions actually denominated in the currency.

30

Monetary Management in an Open Economy

30.1 Closed versus Open Economy

A country which has no economic relations with other countries of the world is a closed economy. All other countries except the one under consideration are grouped into one category called the rest of the world.

A country which has economic relations with the rest of the world is an open economy. These economic relations consist of the following:

1. Selling goods and services to foreigners (exports).
2. Buying goods and services from the foreigners (imports).
3. Buying shares, bonds, debentures from foreigners (acquiring foreign assets).
4. Selling shares, bonds debentures etc. to foreigners (incurring foreign liabilities).
5. Lending to foreigners and borrowing from foreigners.
6. Sending gifts to foreigners and receiving gifts from them.
7. Residents of a country going abroad to work there and foreign residents coming and working in the domestic territory of the country.

30.2 Monetary Transmission Mechanism in the Open Economy

No country can exist alone in the world economy. World economies are inter-dependent and inter-linked.

30.2.1 Rejection of Decoupling Hypothesis: Prior to the initiation of globalisation process in the 1990s and the establishment of WTO in 1995, countries around the world, particularly emerging market economies, enjoyed considerable leverage to shape their own national policies and policy-making mechanisms.

The decoupling hypothesis held that even if advanced economies went into a downturn, emerging economies will remain unscathed because of their substantial foreign exchange reserves, improved policy framework, robust corporate balance sheets and relatively healthy banking sector. In a rapidly globalizing world, the decoupling hypothesis was never totally persuasive.

With globalization and anti-protection rules of WTO, domestic economic policies of countries have increasingly come under the influence of international agencies and processes or by big private corporations and economic/financial players. This has led to the narrowed ability of governments and people to make choices from options in economic and even social policies.

Decoupling hypothesis stood completely invalidated after the sub-prime crisis that emerged in the U.S. housing mortgage market in the second half of 2007, and snowballed into a global financial and economic crisis. What started off as a sub-prime crisis turned successively into a global banking crisis, global financial crisis and then a global economic crisis (recession). It was billed by experts as the worst since the Great Depression of late 1920s and early 1930s that originated in the advanced economies and rapidly engulfed the whole world.

30.2.2 Key Elements in the Monetary Transmission Mechanism: Monetary policy has international implications as well. Changes in interest rates lead to changes in supply and demand in the foreign exchange market. In turn, changes in exchange rates affect exports and imports and influence the overall demand for goods and services. Among other things, this means that the monetary policy of other countries will have an effect on the domestic economy. Thus, actions of the Federal Reserve System (Fed) of USA can affect Indian economy. Conversely, actions of Reserve Bank of India (RBI) can affect financial decisions of foreigners.

The ability of the central bank to influence the real interest rate is an important component of the monetary transmission mechanism. Changes in real interest rates lead to changes in spending on durable goods, which are a component of aggregate expenditures. But there is also another channel of influence. If the Fed cuts interest rates, for example, then the demand for dollars to invest in US asset markets will be reduced. If nothing else happens, this decrease in Fed interest rates gives rise to an arbitrage opportunity. Investors in USA may move funds to India to take advantage of the higher interest rates. There is an increased demand for Indian assets and hence an increased demand for rupee. Rupee will appreciate in value as against dollar. Higher value of the rupee leads to fewer exports from India and more imports into India. Fed is a big player in world financial markets. Its actions move world interest rates and world currency markets.

30.3 Recent Challenges in Monetary Management

The 1990s witnessed growing integration of goods and financial markets across the globe. With growth in global trade in goods and services outpacing growth in world output, the share of external trade in output has increased further. Opening up of the services to international trade and remittances flows have accelerated the integration process. The opening up of the economy has implications for the conduct of monetary policy as well as the monetary transmission mechanism. In particular, it has rendered economies vulnerable to external demand and exchange rate shocks. This, in turn, has enhanced the possibility of significant changes in trade and other current account flows in a short span of time.

30.3.1 Globalization: The 1990s witnessed a paradigm shift towards market-oriented economic policies and a careful dismantling of obstacles in its wake. Globalisation implies widening and deepening integration with the *globe*, i.e. with people and processes abroad. The trend towards the evolution of a global society is generally thought of in economic terms and in terms of the consequences of the revolution in communication technologies. There is undoubtedly much greater economic integration among the nations of the world today. Globalisation is widely seen as the most important factor that could influence economies of nations the world over in the new millennium. The rapid advancement in information technology and communications has made it not just possible but absolutely essential for economies of the world to adapt or fall by the wayside. More changes can be expected in the business scenario specifically in terms of openness, adaptiveness and responsiveness.

Globalization has resulted in the growing concentration and monopolisation of economic resources and power by transnational corporations and by global financial firms and funds. This process has been termed transnationalisation, in which fewer and fewer transnational corporations are gaining a large and rapidly increasing proportion of world economic resources, production and market shares. Where a multinational company used to dominate the market of a single product, a big transnational company (TNC) now typically produces or trades in an increasing multitude of products, services and sectors. Through mergers and acquisitions, fewer and fewer of these TNCs now control a larger and larger share of the global market, whether in commodities, manufactures or services.

Globalisation process has led to globalisation of national policies and policy-making mechanism. National policies (including economic, social, cultural and technological) that until recently were determined by the States and people within a country have increasingly come under the influence of international agencies and processes or by big private corporations and economic/financial players. This has led to the narrowed ability of governments and people to make choices from options in economic, social and cultural policies.

Most developing countries have seen their independent policy-making mechanism capacity eroded, and have to adopt policies influenced by other entities, which may on balance be detrimental to the countries concerned. The developed countries, where the major economic players reside, and which also control the processes and policies of international economic agencies, are better able to maintain control over their own national policies as well as determine the policies and practices of international institutions and the global system. However, it is also true that the large corporations have taken over a large part of decision-making even in the developed countries, at the expense of the power of the state or political and social leaders.

In short, globalization has transformed the environment in which monetary policy operates, throwing up a number of challenges. The foremost challenge is the progressive loss of discretion in the conduct of monetary policy.

30.3.2 World Trade Organization (WTO) and Trade Openness: Created by Uruguay Round of Negotiations (1986-94), WTO was established on January 1, 1995 with headquarters in Geneva, Switzerland. As on June 15, 2020, 164 countries of the world were members of WTO. WTO's creation in 1995 marked the biggest reform of international trade since 1948. During those 47 years, international commerce was regulated under General Agreement on Tariffs and Trade (GATT) which helped establish a prosperous multilateral trading system.

WTO is the only international body dealing with the rules of trade between nations. At its heart are the WTO agreements, the legal ground rules for international commerce and for trade policy. The agreements have three main objectives: (a) to help trade flow as freely as possible, (b) to achieve further liberalisation gradually through negotiations and (c) to set up an impartial means of settling disputes.

A number of simple, fundamental principles run throughout all the WTO agreements. They are the foundation of the multilateral trading system. They include: non-discrimination, freer trade, predictable policies, encouragement to competition and extra provisions for less developed countries.

Establishment of WTO has led to substantial increases in international trade as well as financial flows. An issue in this context is whether increased integration has led to a larger degree of synchronisation of business cycles across countries. A global shock—say an increase in global oil prices—will affect all countries simultaneously. As regards country-specific shocks, a number of forces are at work, some tend to increase co-movement while others reduce co-movement. For countries quite open to external trade, economic developments in their partner countries can get transmitted through exports and imports and this is expected to increase the co-movement of output across countries. Enhanced financial integration, on the other hand, allows countries to smoothen their consumption through borrowing and lending in international markets.

30.3.3 Capital Movements: A more serious challenge to conduct of monetary policy emerges from the capital account. A distinctive feature of capital flows is the greater volatility *vis-à-vis* the trade flows. Capital flows in gross terms are much higher than those in net terms. Global capital flows impact the conduct of monetary policy on a daily basis, imparting volatility to monetary conditions. Along with the explosion in financial innovations and the information technology revolution, this has led to the swift transmission of market impulses across countries and a structural change in the process of financial intermediation. All this has fundamentally altered not only the environment of monetary policy formulation but also its instrumentality and operating framework. Monetary policy formulation has become much more interdependent than before across economies and has to factor in the developments in the global economic situation, the international inflationary situation, interest rates, exchange rate movements and capital flows. A stylised fact in regard to many, if not most, emerging market economies (EMEs) is that their external borrowings are usually denominated in foreign currency.

Furthermore, a more recent challenge in monetary management in EMEs has emanated from a significant increase in capital flows coupled with current account surpluses which have led to large overall balance of payments surpluses in these economies. In their efforts to maintain external competitiveness and financial stability, the central banks in EMEs have absorbed the market surpluses. Consequently, the foreign exchange reserves of the EMEs have increased in the recent past.

The absorption of excess supplies by the central banks has, however, implications for monetary expansion and the objective of price stability. The central banks, therefore, face a trade-off: by preventing nominal appreciation, they may ultimately endanger their primary objective of price stability. Typically, central banks attempt to overcome the policy dilemma by undertaking a variety of operations such as open market sales of government/own bonds to neutralise the expansionary monetary effect arising out of their market purchases. Such sterilisation operations, in turn, have their own limitations and involve costs, especially if external flows are persistent.

30.4 India's Monetary Management in the Globalized World

Like other EMEs, India too has witnessed a progressive opening up of the economy. External sector reforms were a key aspect of the structural reforms initiated in the early 1990s. While current account convertibility was achieved in 1994, the Indian approach towards capital account liberalisation has been one of caution. Trade openness of the economy has increased significantly. There has been a sustained increase in capital flows and the balance of payments has recorded large surpluses. Since 1993-94, balance of payments developments have thus come to play a dominant role in the conduct of monetary policy. Net capital inflows to India have been largely stable, reflecting a prudent approach to capital account liberalisation with a focus on attracting stable capital flows. Nonetheless, there have been brief episodes of volatility in capital flows and these periods have been associated with volatility in the foreign exchange market. Overall, however, the recent past has seen a significant increase in capital flows and the balance of payments has posted surpluses. External developments have thus been a key driver of money supply.

While encouraging foreign investment flows, especially direct investment inflows, Government has adopted a more cautious approach in regard to debt flows. Debt flows in the form of external commercial borrowings are subject to ceilings and some end-use restrictions, which are modulated from time-to-time taking into account evolving macroeconomic and monetary conditions. Similarly, portfolio investment in government securities and corporate bonds are also subject to macro ceilings, which are also modulated from time-to-time. Prudential policies have attempted to prevent excessive recourse to foreign borrowings and dollarisation of the economy. In regard to capital outflows, the policy framework has been progressively liberalised to enable the non-financial corporate sector to invest abroad and to acquire companies in the overseas market. Resident individuals are also permitted outflows subject to reasonable limits.

India is in a different economic milieu today than it was two decades ago. India is virtually part of the world of globalised finance and is learning to walk, negotiating the strong currents, both positive and negative, generated by the forces of financial globalisation.

To sum up, the behaviour of the capital flows reveals that these flows can increase rapidly but can be highly volatile. Surges in capital flows and the associated volatility have implications for the conduct of monetary, exchange rate and foreign exchange reserve policies. Emerging market economies, thus, need to be equipped to deal with such volatility in order to ensure monetary and financial stability.

Monetary authorities, therefore, need to decide as to whether capital flows are durable or reversible. In case, flows are perceived to be reversible, authorities need to be prepared through building up foreign exchange reserves.

31

Reserve Bank of India

There is only one central bank in a country whose main function is to control the operations of the rest of the banking system. [1] Reserve Bank of India (RBI), the central bank of India, is the apex institution responsible for managing and supervising the monetary and financial system of the economy.

31.1 Establishment and Early History of RBI

The Imperial Bank of India, which emerged as a consequence of the amalgamation of three Presidency Banks of Bengal, Bombay and Madras in 1921, assumed certain central banking functions except currency management. The control of currency management continued to be with the Government of India in order to ensure that the central banking entity did not appropriate powers greater than those mandated by the political authority. The Reserve Bank of India Act was placed on the statute book on March 6, 1934. The RBI commenced operations on April 1, 1935 and was nationalised on January 1, 1949. The head office of the Bank is in Mumbai and its executive head is called the Governor.

The objective of establishing the RBI, as stated in the preamble to the RBI Act 1934, was to "regulate the issue of bank notes and the keeping of the reserves with a view to securing monetary stability in India and generally to operate the currency and credit system of the country to its advantage". The Bank's functions as laid down in the statutes were: (a) issue of currency (b) banker to Government; and (c) banker to other banks. Except in the sphere of agriculture, the Bank was not entrusted with any great promotional role and that too on a limited scale.

Central banks occupy a pivotal position in the institutional fabric of an economy. The functions of a modern central bank are vastly different from what was expected from the early central banks founded in Europe in the 17th century. The evolution of central banking in the Indian context has its own specificity. The RBI, while discharging its statutory responsibilities, has played a crucial role in the nation building process, particularly in the development of the financial sector. In fact, institution building constitutes a distinguishing feature of central banking in India.

31.2 Pre-Independence Activities of RBI

During most of the pre-Independence period, RBI was a private bank, though formed under a statute and overseen by the then colonial government. The functions of the RBI during this phase were confined essentially to traditional central banking, *i.e.* note issue authority and banker to the Government. During the war and post-war years, its major preoccupation was facilitation of war finance, repatriation of sterling debt and planning and administration of exchange control.

The initial phase of RBI was marked by several war and post-War developments including the separation of Burma (modern Myanmar) in 1937, partition of the country in 1947 and nationalisation of the RBI, which altered the area of operations of the RBI. After the separation of Burma, the RBI acted as currency authority of that country till 1942 and as banker to the Burmese Government till March 1947. Upon the partition of the country in 1947, the RBI rendered central banking services to the Dominion of Pakistan until June 1948. In terms of the Pakistan Monetary System and Reserve Bank (Amendment) Order, 1948, the RBI ceased to function as central bank for Pakistan from July 1, 1948.

31.3 Functions of Reserve Bank of India (RBI)

RBI performs all the major functions of a central bank and these are discussed below.

31.3.1 Sole Currency Issuing Authority: The management of currency is one of the core functions of a central bank which commands a high degree of public visibility. This is especially so in a country like India where people have a marked preference for cash transactions. The fact that there are many inaccessible pockets in the country adds to the already formidable challenges in managing currency in India.

Presently, barring coins, RBI is the sole authority for the issue of currency in India. Coins are issued by the Central Government which supplies them to the RBI on demand. RBI puts the coins into circulation on behalf of the Central Government. According to Section 6 of Coinage Act, 2011 only coins issued under this section can be legal tender.

A. Printing of Currency Notes and Minting of Coins: Four printing presses print and supply banknotes. These are as under:

1. Bharatiya Reserve Bank Note Mudran Private Limited, Salboni, West Bengal.
2. Bharatiya Reserve Bank Note Mudran Private Limited, Mysore, Karnataka.
3. Currency Note Press, Nashik, Maharashtra.
4. Bank Note Press, Dewas, Madhya Pradesh

Coins are minted by the Government of India. The Reserve Bank is the agent of the Government for distribution, issue and handling of coins. Following four mints are in operation:

1. Indian Government Mint, NOIDA, Uttar Pradesh.
2. Indian Government Mint, Mumbai.
3. Indian Government Mint, Hyderabad.
4. Indian Government Mint, Kolkata.

As a step for easing the pressure on the distribution channels, coin distribution has been outsourced to private transport operators and the practice of RBI staff and police personnel accompanying coin remittances has been done away with.

B. Denominations of Notes and Coins in Circulation:

Notes in circulation: ₹ 5, 10, 20, 50,100, 500 and 2000.

Coins in circulation: 50 paise; ₹ 1, 2, 5 and 10.

In short, focus continues to be on ensuring availability of clean notes and on strengthening the security features of bank notes. Given the volumes involved and costs incurred in the printing, transport, storage and removal of unfit/soiled notes, RBI is evaluating ways to extend the life of bank notes, particularly in lower denominations. It is considering issue of ₹ 10 banknotes in plastic.

31.3.2 Banker and Debt Manager to Governments: Managing banking transactions of the governments is a key RBI role. Like individuals, businesses and banks, governments need a banker to carry out their financial transactions in an efficient and effective manner, including the raising of resources from the public. Since its inception, the Reserve Bank of India has undertaken the traditional central banking function of managing banking transactions of the governments.

As the banker to the Central Government and to the State Governments by virtue of agreements entered into with them, the RBI provides a range of banking services for these Governments such as acceptance of money on government account payment/withdrawals of funds and collection and transfer of funds through different means. Sections 20, 21 and 21A of the RBI Act provide the statutory basis for these functions. The terms and conditions on which the RBI acts as banker to the Central and State Governments are set out in separate agreements, which the RBI entered into with these Governments.

RBI provides all those banking services to the Central and State Governments which a commercial bank ordinarily offers to its customers. The Governments keep their cash balances on current account deposit with the RBI and the latter carries out banking business involving receipts and payments of money on behalf of the Governments.

Another function of the RBI as the Government's banker is the management of public debt. RBI manages public debt on behalf of the Central and the State Governments.

RBI manages all new issues of Government loans, servicing the public debt outstanding, and prepares the market for Government securities. Various measures are taken to ensure success of Government's borrowing for mobilising resources.

It involves issue of new rupee loans, payment of interest and repayment of these loans and other operational matters such as debt certificates and their registration. To formulate borrowing programme for the year, a number of other factors are also taken into account, such as, the amount of Central and State loans maturing during the year, the estimated available resources, market appetite and the absorptive capacity of the market.

31.3.3 Banker to the Banks and Lender of Last Resort: Under the Reserve Bank of India Act, 1934 and the Banking Regulation Act, 1949, the RBI is vested with extensive powers of supervision, regulation, and control over commercial and co-operative banks. The regulatory functions of the RBI pertain to licensing, branch expansion, and amalgamation of commercial banks. The RBI calls for returns and other information from the commercial banks and periodically inspects their working.

Banks are required to maintain a portion of their demand and time liabilities as cash reserves with RBI. These are compulsory reserves of banks with the RBI and are not available to them for meeting inter-bank clearing claims. The underlying philosophy of this statutory reserve requirement is that by varying it within limits, the RBI can use it as a weapon of monetary-credit control.

For this purpose, they need to maintain accounts with RBI. They also need to keep accounts with RBI for settling inter-bank obligations such as clearing transactions of individual bank customers who have their accounts with different banks or clearing money market transactions between two banks, buying and selling securities and foreign currencies.

In order to facilitate a smooth inter-bank transfer of funds, or to make payments and to receive funds on their behalf, banks need a common banker. By providing the facility of opening accounts for banks, RBI becomes this common banker, known as *banker to banks* function.

As banker to banks, RBI provides short-term loans and advances to select banks, when necessary, to facilitate lending to specific sectors and for specific purposes. These loans are provided against promissory notes and other collateral given by the banks.

A. Lender of Last Resort: As banker to banks, RBI also acts as *lender of last resort*. It can come to the rescue of a bank that is solvent but faces temporary liquidity problems by supplying it with much needed liquidity when no one else is willing to extend credit to that bank. RBI extends this facility to protect the interest of the depositors of the bank and to prevent possible failure of the bank which, in turn, may also affect other banks and institutions and can have an adverse impact on financial stability and thus on the economy.

31.3.4 Controller of Money and Credit: An important function of RBI is to control money and credit in the country. The RBI has multiple instruments at its command such as repo and reverse repo rates, cash reserve ratio (CRR), statutory liquidity ratio (SLR), open market operations, including the market stabilisation scheme (MSS) and the liquidity adjustment facility (LAF), special market operations, and sector-specific liquidity facilities. In addition, the RBI also uses prudential tools to modulate flow of credit to certain sectors consistent with financial stability. The availability of multiple instruments and flexible use of these instruments in the implementation of monetary policy has enabled the RBI to modulate the liquidity and interest rate conditions amidst uncertain global macroeconomic conditions.

For details, see chapter 32 of this book.

31.3.5 Controller of Foreign Exchange: The RBI is the custodian of the foreign exchange reserves of India. It manages exchange control and the external value of the rupee. The history of exchange control in India dates back to the outbreak of Second World War in 1939. The exchange control is operated in a manner so that the demand for foreign exchange is contained within the limits of its available supplies. In other words, the available foreign exchange is allocated among competing demands in such a way as to make its optimum use. The need for this control and planned use arises in view of the general shortage of foreign exchange reserves in most developing countries. All foreign exchange transactions made by the RBI are at the official rates of exchange.

The RBI has delegated considerable powers to the authorised dealers to release foreign exchange for a variety of purposes and has been focusing on the development of the foreign exchange market. In order to deepen the foreign exchange market, a large number of products have been introduced and the entry of newer players has been allowed. Additional hedging instruments, such as, foreign currency-rupee options have been introduced and authorised dealers have been permitted to use innovative products like cross-currency options, interest rate and currency swaps, caps/collars and forward rate agreements (FRAs) in the international forex market.

31.3.6 Source of Economic Information: RBI's economic research work is designed to:

1. Provide reliable, data-driven information for policy and decision-making.
2. Supply accurate and timely data for academic research as well as to the general public.
3. Provide support for collaborative research to research institutions/universities.
4. Develop and maintain statistical data reporting systems.
5. Conduct forward-looking surveys for monetary policy.
6. Educate the public.

RBI's economic research focuses on study and analysis of domestic and international macroeconomic issues.

RBI has over time established a sound and rich tradition of policy-oriented research and an effective mechanism for disseminating data and information. Like other major central banks, RBI has also developed its own research capabilities in the field of economics, finance and statistics, which contribute to a better understanding of the functioning of the economy and the ongoing changes in the policy transmission mechanism.

The research undertaken at RBI revolves around issues and problems arising in the current environment at national and international levels, which have critical implications for the Indian economy. The primary data compiled by RBI becomes an important source of information for further research by the outside world. RBI also disseminates data and information regularly in the form of several publications and through its website.

RBI has made focussed efforts to provide quality data to the public, which has emanated from its internal economic research and robust statistical system, established and strengthened over the years. It endeavours to provide credible statistics and information to users across the spectrum of market participants, businesses, the media, professionals and the academics. This is done through various tools such as website, press releases, and weekly, monthly, quarterly and annual publications.

The RBI provides, through its publications, useful data and information on various aspects of the economy, particularly monetary and banking activities. Three important and regular publications of the RBI are: (a) Reserve Bank of India *Bulletin* (Monthly), (b) *Report on Currency and Finance* (Annual) and (c) *Handbook of Statistics on Indian Economy.*

31.3.7 RBI as Institution Builder: After Independence, a major task thrust upon the RBI was to put in place the necessary institutional mechanism to complement the planning efforts. This was crucial especially in the context of the weak financial system with an underdeveloped and evolving commercial banking set up. Organised credit institutions had a negligible presence in rural India. In this backdrop, building up a sound and adequate institutional structure for rural banking and credit was paramount.

Apart from performing the customary functions of a central bank, the RBI has played an important role in building, consolidating, and strengthening the financial infrastructure of India. It has also played an effective role in influencing the allocation of credit in favour of priority sectors. Commercial banking facilities have been extended to small towns and rural areas as a result of the policies of the RBI.

The RBI has paid special attention to the credit needs of the rural (agricultural) sector. The National Bank for Agriculture and Rural Development (NABARD) is an example of the promotional role of the RBI in the agricultural sector. Similarly, the RBI promoted the cause of industrial finance by actively associating itself with such public sector undertakings as erstwhile Industrial Development Bank of India (IDBI). In the area of credit allocation, RBI has followed the policy of special consideration for priority sectors, like agriculture and small-scale industries, at concessional rates of interest and lenient collateral requirements. Similarly, Deposit Insurance Corporation (DIC) is a wholly-owned subsidiary of the RBI.

31.3.8 Consumer Education and Protection: RBI's approach to customer service focuses on protection of customers' rights, enhancing the quality of customer services, spreading awareness and strengthening the grievance redressal mechanism in banks.

RBI's initiatives in the field of consumer protection include the setting up of a Customer Redressal Cell, creation of a Customer Service Department in 2006 which was recently rechristened as Consumer Education and Protection Department. Further, the setting up of the Banking Codes and Standards Board of India (BCSBI), an autonomous body for promoting adherence to self-imposed codes by banks for committed customer services.

In order to strengthen the institutional mechanism for dispute resolution, RBI in the year 1995 introduced the Banking Ombudsman (BO) scheme. The BO is an Alternate Dispute Redressal Mechanism for resolution of disputes between a bank and its customers. There are 22 Banking Ombudsman offices in the country at present. The scheme covers grievances of the customers against commercial banks, scheduled primary Co-operative banks and regional rural banks (RRBs). In 2006, RBI revised the BO scheme. Under the revised scheme, BO and the staff in the offices of the BO are drawn from the serving employees of RBI. The new scheme is fully funded by RBI and virtually covers all banking transactions related grievances except their business decisions like sanctioning of credit etc.

Effective from July 1, 2017 the scope of Banking Ombudsman Scheme 2006 was widened to include, inter alia, deficiencies arising out of sale of insurance/mutual fund/ other third party investment products by banks and non-adherence to RBI instructions with regard to mobile banking/electronic banking as grounds of complaint.

All public sector banks and select private sector and foreign banks are mandated to appoint the Internal Ombudsman for final examination of all rejected/partially accepted complaints before conveying the final decision to the complainant.

A. Recent Initiatives for Consumer Education and Protection: RBI has formulated a "Charter of Customer Rights" for banks based on global best practices in the area of consumer protection. The Charter enshrines broad, overarching principles for protection of bank customers and enunciates the following five basic rights of bank customers.

1. Right to fair treatment.
2. Right to transparency, fair and honest dealing.
3. Right to suitability.
4. Right to privacy.
5. Right to grievances redress and compensation.

Banks are required to prepare their own Board-approved policy, incorporating the five rights of the Charter, or suitably integrate their existing customer service policy with the model customer rights policy formulated by IBA/BCSBI.

31.4 Changing Role of RBI in the Financial Sector

Since the setting up of the Reserve Bank of India in 1935, its role in the financial sector and financial market development has undergone significant changes. Emerging primarily as a bank-based financial system, the development of financial structure in India has been to finance the planned development efforts. To this end, institutional development received considerable attention of the RBI. The broad-based development of the banking sector to meet short-term financing needs was supplemented by the setting up of specialised development finance institutions by the RBI to cater to long-term financing needs. Since the early 1990s, the introduction of financial sector reforms has provided a strong impetus to the development of financial markets. The introduction of market-based monetary policy instruments, the liberalisation of capital controls and integration of the Indian economy with global markets have exposed the country to potentially volatile capital inflows, posing new challenges and dilemmas for the RBI in monetary and exchange rate management.

The RBI has been suitably reorienting the regulatory and supervisory framework so as to meet the challenges of a new environment. It has been the endeavour of the RBI to develop a competitive, strong and dynamic banking system so that it plays an effective role in supporting the growth process of the economy. The emphasis has been on safeguarding the financial stability of the overall system through increased emphasis on prudential guidelines and effective monitoring, improving institutional soundness, strengthening the regulatory and supervisory processes by aligning with international best practices and by developing the necessary technological and legal infrastructure. While the approach towards the reforms has essentially been gradual and relevant to the context, consultative processes and appropriate timing and sequencing of measures have succeeded in aiding growth, enhancing efficiency, avoiding crises and imparting resilience to the financial system.

31.5 RBI's Vision Documents for Payments

31.5.1 Vision Document for Payment Systems, 2005-08: In the recent period, the RBI has taken a number of initiatives to strengthen the institutional, technological and procedural framework for the payment and settlement systems. To carry forward these initiatives in an integrated and cohesive manner, a Vision Document for 2005-08 was prepared after taking into consideration the feedback from the various stakeholders such as banks, technology solution providers, members of public and other experts in the field. The Vision Document set out the roadmap for implementing the vision for payment and settlement systems within the next three years. The key themes of the action plans identified in the Vision Document were safety, security, soundness and efficiency (Triple-S and E). While safety in payment and settlement systems related to risk reduction measures, security implied confidence in the integrity of the payment systems. All payment systems were envisaged to be on a sound footing with adequate legal backing for operational procedures and transparency norms. Efficiency enhancements were envisaged by leveraging the benefits of technology for cost effective solutions.

31.5.2 Vision Document for Payment Systems, 2012-15: The main focus of the Vision Document for Payments Systems, 2012-15 was to provide a thrust to modern electronic payments that are safe, simple and low-cost for use by all. The document aimed at increasing the share of electronic payment transactions and taking measures towards moving to a less cash society and customer convenience.

The focus of cheque clearing operations in the coming years would be consolidation, rationalisation, centralisation, through the implementation of grid-based CTS solution (which is Information Technology Act compliant) across the country by NPCI. The grid-based CTS will usher in a standardised cheque clearing scenario across the country. The issuance of CTS 2010 compliant cheques will facilitate this process. Introduction of user/customer friendly features and increasing the number of settlement cycles in NEFT would be further examined.

31.5.3 Payment and Settlement Systems in India: Vision 2018: The *Vision 2018 for Payment and Settlement Systems in India* reiterated the commitment of the RBI to encourage greater use of electronic payments by all sections of society so as to achieve a *less-cash* society. The objective was to facilitate provision of a payment system for the future that combines the much-valued attributes of safety, security and universal reach with technological solutions which enable faster processing, enhanced convenience, and the extraction and use of valuable information that accompanies payments.

31.5.4 Payment and Settlement Systems in India: Vision 2019-21: RBI's Vision Document on Payment and Settlement Systems, released on May 15, 2019, has the core theme of Empowering Exceptional (E) Payment Experience.

Vision 2021 concentrates on a two-pronged approach of: (a) exceptional customer experience; and (b) enabling an eco-system which will result in this customer experience.

With this in view, the Vision aims towards,

1. Enhancing the experience of customers.
2. Empowering payment system operators and service providers.
3. Enabling the eco-system and infrastructure.
4. Putting in place a forward-looking regulation.
5. Supported by a risk-focussed supervision.

To achieve the above, the Vision envisages four goalposts (4Cs): competition, cost, convenience and confidence.

To sum up, several steps have been taken by the RBI in recent years to improve customer service of commercial banks. In the context of the rapidly evolving financial landscape, RBI has also been suitably reorienting its regulatory and supervisory framework to meet the needs of the common man. It has also been the endeavour of RBI to improve credit delivery and customer service by banks. RBI has simultaneously focussed on financial inclusion and extension of banking services to the unbanked areas of the economy. RBI has taken a host of measures in recent years aimed at providing customer service at reasonable cost. These measures include enhancing customer protection and disclosures, code of ethics and grievance redressal, among others. RBI's broad approach to financial inclusion aims at *connecting people* with the banking system and not just credit dispensation; giving people access to the payments system; and portraying financial inclusion as a viable business model and opportunity. RBI has been initiating measures to improve the outreach of banks and their services, and promote financial inclusion in less developed states and union territories.

Endnote

1. For history, objectives and functions of central banks, see chapter 27 of this book.

32

Monetary Policy of India

32.1 Meaning of Monetary Policy

Monetary policy refers to the use of monetary instruments under the control of the central bank to regulate magnitudes such as interest rates, money supply and availability of credit with a view to achieving the ultimate objective of economic policy. In India, the Reserve Bank of India (RBI) is vested with the responsibility of conducting monetary policy. This responsibility is explicitly mandated under the Reserve Bank of India Act, 1934. The conduct of monetary policy has been changing in response to the process of financial liberalisation.

The operating procedure of monetary policy changed dramatically with the opening up of the Indian economy in the 1990s. It was driven by the following: (a) the need for a market-oriented policy mix of open market operations and interest rate signals consistent with the process of price discovery; (b) the need to manage capital flows following the opening up and (c) the need for swift policy reactions to maintain orderly conditions in the financial markets.

32.2 Objectives of Monetary Policy

The objectives of monetary policy are drawn from the Reserve Bank of India Act, 1934. Prior to its amendment in 2016, this Act set out the RBI's objective as "to regulate the issue of bank notes and keeping of reserves with a view to securing monetary stability and generally to operate the currency and credit system of the country to its advantage". Securing monetary stability was the predominant objective of the RBI which was set up essentially as a monetary authority.

Although there was no explicit mandate, the major objectives of monetary policy in India, as evolved over the years through policy statements, were those of maintaining price stability and ensuring adequate flow of credit to the productive sectors of the economy. The growth objective was subsumed in the credit objective.

The RBI has multiple objectives. Apart from pursuing monetary policy goals, financial stability is one of the overriding concerns of the RBI. Similarly, the RBI acts as a banking regulator, public debt manager, government debt market regulator and currency issuer. It is thus faced with such multiple tasks and complex mandates.

With economic liberalisation, the objective of financial stability gained importance. The relative emphasis between the objectives depended on the underlying economic conditions, and was spelt out from time-to-time. Compared to many other developing economies, India has been able to maintain a moderate level of inflation over the years. Inflation rates in India have rarely touched double-digit levels.

The primary objective of monetary policy is to maintain price stability while keeping in mind the objective of growth. Price stability is a necessary precondition to sustainable growth.

In May 2016, the Reserve Bank of India (RBI) Act, 1934 was amended to provide a statutory basis for the implementation of the flexible inflation targeting framework.

See chapter 33 of this book for inflation targeting framework.

32.3 Monetary Policy Framework

The amended RBI Act explicitly provides the legislative mandate to RBI to operate the monetary policy framework of the country. The framework aims at setting the policy (repo) rate based on an assessment of the current and evolving macroeconomic situation; and modulation of liquidity conditions to anchor money market rates at or around the repo rate. Repo rate changes transmit through the money market to the entire the financial system, which, in turn, influences aggregate demand—a key determinant of inflation and growth.

Once the repo rate is announced, the operating framework designed by RBI envisages liquidity management on a day-to-day basis through appropriate actions, which aim at anchoring the operating target—the weighted average call rate (WACR) — around the repo rate.

The operating framework is fine-tuned and revised depending on the evolving financial market and monetary conditions, while ensuring consistency with the monetary policy stance. The liquidity management framework was last revised significantly in April 2016.

32.4 Monetary Policy Process

Section 45ZB of the amended RBI Act, 1934 provides for an empowered six-member monetary policy committee (MPC) to be constituted by the Central Government by notification in the Official Gazette. Accordingly, the Central Government constituted the MPC in September 2016.

The Governor, one Deputy Governor and one officer of the RBI are ex-officio members of the MPC. The other three members are appointed by the Central Government as per the procedure laid down in the amended RBI Act.

MPC determines the policy interest rate (repo rate) required to achieve the inflation target. The first meeting of the MPC was held on October 3 and 4, 2016 in the run up to the Fourth Bi-monthly Monetary Policy Statement, 2016-17.

RBI's Monetary Policy Department (MPD) assists the Governor in formulating the monetary policy. Views of key stakeholders in the economy and analytical work of the RBI contribute to the process for arriving at the decision on the policy repo rate.

The Financial Markets Operations Department (FMOD) operationalises the monetary policy, mainly through day-to-day liquidity management operations. The Financial Markets Committee (FMC) meets daily to review the liquidity conditions so as to ensure that the operating target of the weighted average call money rate (WACR).

Before the constitution of the MPC, a Technical Advisory Committee (TAC) on monetary policy with experts from monetary economics, central banking, financial markets and public finance advised the Reserve Bank on the stance of monetary policy. However, its role was only advisory in nature. With the formation of MPC, the TAC on Monetary Policy ceased to exist.

32.5 Monetary Transmission Mechanism

The monetary transmission mechanism refers to the process through which changes in monetary policy instruments (such as monetary aggregates or short-term policy interest rates) affect the rest of the economy and, in particular, output and inflation. Monetary policy impulses transmit through various channels, affecting different variables and different markets, and at various speeds and intensities. For monetary policy to be effective, it is, therefore, essential to have a broad understanding of these channels and the associated lags. Monetary policy affects output and prices through its influence on key financial variables such as interest rates, exchange rates, asset prices, credit and monetary aggregates. At the same time, changes in the structure of the economy tend to alter the effects of a given monetary policy measure. This requires central banks to continuously reinterpret monetary transmission channels.

With the initiation of financial sector reforms, monetary management in India has been increasingly relying on the use of indirect instruments like open market operations and fine-tuning of liquidity conditions through the liquidity adjustment facility. Modulations in policy interest rates have emerged as a principal instrument of signalling monetary policy stance.

Based on the recommendations of the *Working Group on Operating Procedure of Monetary Policy,* the operating framework of monetary policy was refined effective May 3, 2011. The repo rate was made the only independently varying policy rate. A new marginal standing facility (MSF) was instituted, under which scheduled commercial banks (SCBs) are allowed to borrow overnight at their discretion, up to 1 percent of their respective net demand and time liabilities (NDTL), at 100 bps (1 percent) above the repo rate. The revised MSF reverse repo corridor was defined with a fixed width of 200 bps (2 percent) with the repo rate placed in the middle of the corridor.

The stance of monetary policy and the rationale are communicated in a variety of ways, the most important being the annual monetary policy statement of the Governor of RBI in April and the mid-term review in October. Quarterly reviews of January and July were introduced in 2005, with a pre-announcement of dates. The statements, though technically extra-statutory in nature, have become over time more analytical and elaborate giving a comprehensive assessment of the economy in all its dimensions, as a backdrop to the policy stance. These statements are accompanied by a detailed macroeconomic review of the economy as a supplement. Monetary measures are undertaken as and when the circumstances warrant, but the rationale for such measures is given in the press releases and also in statements made by the Governor and Deputy Governors. The means of communicating the policy stance include several statutory and non-statutory publications, speeches and press releases.

Of late, the RBI's website has become a very effective medium of communication and is rated by experts as one of the best among central bank websites in content, presentation and timeliness. The RBI's communication strategy and provision of information have facilitated greater transparency in the conduct of policy in an increasingly market-oriented environment.

32.6 Operating Procedures of Monetary Policy

The conduct of contemporary monetary policy in the Indian economy is based on a carefully crafted strategy. The strategy aims to balance the linkages between monetary policy, credit policy and the regulatory regime in a dynamic environment of structural transformation.

Monetary policy now simultaneously pursues the objectives of price stability, provision of appropriate credit for growth and increasingly, financial stability. While there are complementarities between the objectives, especially in the long- run, it cannot be denied that there are certain trade-offs, particularly in the short-run. The RBI has always had to address the monetary policy dilemma of providing adequate credit to the Government and the commercial sector, without fuelling inflationary pressures. With the deregulation of interest rates, an added dimension is to balance the interest cost of public debt with the price of commercial credit. Besides, with the opening up of the economy, there are times when it is necessary to tighten monetary conditions to ward off speculative pressures on the exchange rate, although the growth objective presages a softer interest rate regime. Finally, the imperatives of price stability have to be increasingly balanced with the impact of monetary policy actions on balance sheets of the banking system.

In order to achieve these objectives, the RBI has, at its disposal, three instruments, viz. monetary policy, credit policy and regulatory policies. At the same time, it is, however, not possible to compartmentalise the policy actions, especially as the instruments are also used interchangeably to serve different objectives. Changes in the policy interest rates, for example, not only transmit a monetary policy signal but also change the price of credit and impact asset prices. This, in turn, requires some other complementary measures to manage the short-run trade-offs, especially in the context of the transitional problems and transactional costs of an economy in transition.

The operating procedures of monetary policy in India have undergone a significant shift. In particular, short-term interest rates have emerged as instruments to signal the stance of monetary policy. In order to stabilise short-term interest rates, the RBI now modulates market liquidity to steer monetary conditions to the desired trajectory. This is achieved by a mix of policy instruments including changes in reserve requirements and standing facilities and open market (including repo) operations which affect the quantum of marginal liquidity and changes in policy rates, such as the Bank Rate and reverse repo/repo rates, which impact the price of liquidity.

32.7 Constituents of Monetary Reforms

Monetary policy reforms in India since 1991 have hinged on easing the fiscal constraint. The first important step was introduction of an auction system for the Central Government's market borrowings in June 1992. This enabled an increasing proportion of the fiscal deficit to be financed by borrowings at market-related rates of interest. This, in turn, enabled the RBI to scale down the statutory liquidity ratio (SLR) to the targeted statutory minimum level of 25 percent by October 1997.

32.7.1 Treasury Bills Replaced by Ways and Means Advances (WMA): Following an agreement between the Government and the RBI in September 1994, the automatic monetisation of the Centre's fiscal deficit was eliminated by gradually phasing out ad hocs by April 1997. A system of WMA to the Central Government subject to mutually agreed limits at market-related rates, was put in place instead to meet mismatches in cash flows. Since the RBI reserves the right to trigger floatation of fresh government loans as and when the actual utilisation crosses 75 percent of the limit, the WMA does not acquire the cumulative character of ad hocs. This enables the RBI to accommodate the Government at its discretion and helps impose a market discipline on fiscal activism.

32.7.2 Reactivation of the Bank Rate: Another major step towards a market-based monetary policy was the reactivation of the Bank Rate. In April 1997, the interest rate on the majority of the accommodation extended by the RBI was initially linked to the Bank Rate. As the price of primary money is now increasingly market-determined, essentially at rates emerging out of the Liquidity Adjustment Facility (LAF) auctions, the Bank Rate is now used, more or less, as a signalling instrument of monetary policy in line with the evolving macroeconomic and liquidity conditions.

32.7.3 Deregulation of Interest Rate: Deregulation of interest rates was central to the new market-oriented monetary strategy in terms of rejuvenating the price discovery process. The process of interest rate liberalisation began in September 1991 with the discontinuation of sector-specific and programme-specific prescriptions excepting for a few areas like agriculture, and small industries. Loans above ₹ 2 lakh were freed from various prescriptions, subject to the minimum lending rate prescribed by the RBI. The process of deregulation was carried forward with the withdrawal of the minimum lending rate in October 1994, thereby providing banks full freedom to determine lending rates for loans above ₹ 2 lakh.

32.7.4 Deregulation of Credit: The reforms in credit regulation which began in the mid-1980s, intensified in the 1990s with a shift in focus from micro-regulation towards macro-management of credit. These included a scaling down of pre-emptions in the form of statutory stipulations to expand the pool of lendable resources, rationalisation of priority sector requirements, phasing out of directed credit programmes and relaxation of balance sheet restrictions to improve the credit delivery system.

32.8 Instruments of Monetary Policy

Monetary policy refers to the policy of the central bank with regard to the use of instruments under its control to achieve the specified goals. In India, RBI is vested with the responsibility of conducting monetary policy with the primary objective of maintaining price stability while keeping in mind the objective of growth. This responsibility is explicitly mandated under the Reserve Bank of India Act, as amended in 2016 and notified in the official Gazette on May 14, 2016. Like other central banks, the core function of the RBI is to formulate and administer monetary policy to maintain the stability of the rupee.

Prior to 1991, given the command and control nature of the economy, the RBI had to resort to direct instruments like interest rate regulations, selective credit control and the CRR as major monetary policy instruments. These instruments were used intermittently to mitigate the monetary impact of the budgetary operations of the Government.

The RBI has multiple instruments at its command such as repo and reverse repo rates, cash reserve ratio (CRR), statutory liquidity ratio (SLR), open market operations, including the market stabilisation scheme (MSS) and the liquidity adjustment facility (LAF), special market operations, and sector-specific liquidity facilities. In addition, the RBI also uses prudential tools to modulate flow of credit to certain sectors consistent with financial stability. The availability of multiple instruments and flexible use of these instruments in the implementation of monetary policy has enabled the RBI to modulate the liquidity and interest rate conditions amidst uncertain global macroeconomic conditions.

32.8.1 Repo Rate: The (fixed) interest rate at which the RBI provides short-term (overnight) liquidity to banks against the collateral of government and other approved securities under the liquidity adjustment facility (LAF). The LAF consists of overnight and term repo auctions. Progressively, the RBI has increased the proportion of liquidity injected in the LAF through term-repos (of up to 56 days) at variable rates. The aim of term repo is to help develop inter-bank term money market, which, in turn, can set market based benchmarks for pricing of loans and deposits, and through that improve transmission of monetary policy.

RBI keeps changing the repo rate and reverse repo rate according to changing macroeconomic factors. Whenever RBI modifies the rates, it impacts every sector of the economy; although in different ways. Some segments gain as a result of the rate hike while others may suffer losses.

In simple terms, repo rate is the rate at which RBI lends money to the banks against the collateral of government and other approved securities. Repo rate, along with other instruments of monetary policy, is used to balance growth (more spending) and inflation.

Following an increase in repo rate, commercial banks usually raise the rates at which they extend loans to borrowers. For consumers, it translates into higher cost of homes, automobiles and personal loans at higher equated monthly instalments (EMIs).

A lower repo rate means loans from banks become cheaper for corporate borrowers as well as individuals for funding houses, cars, vacations and other purposes. To ensure that lower rates are passed on to the borrowers, RBI has asked banks to link their lending rates to an external benchmark like the repo rate, which has been chosen by most banks.

RBI cuts interest rates only when price level is comfortable. It may increase interest rate (making credit costlier) if inflation threatens to breach permissible limits. Since inflation is a politically-sensitive issue, RBI takes no chances to overlook it.

32.8.2 Reverse Repo Rate: The (fixed) interest rate at which the RBI absorbs short-term liquidity, generally on an overnight basis, from banks against the collateral of government and other approved securities under the LAF. The RBI also conducts variable interest rate reverse repo auctions, as necessary.

32.8.3 Liquidity Adjustment Facility (LAF): The LAF consists of overnight as well as term repo auctions. Progressively, the RBI has increased the proportion of liquidity injected under fine-tuning variable rate repo auctions of range of tenors. The aim of term repo is to help develop the inter-bank term money market, which in turn can set market based benchmarks for pricing of loans and deposits, and hence improve transmission of monetary policy. RBI also conducts variable interest rate reverse repo auctions, as necessitated under the market conditions.

32.8.4 Marginal Standing Facility (MSF): It is a facility under which scheduled commercial banks can borrow additional amount of overnight money from the RBI by dipping into their SLR portfolio up to a limit at a penal rate of interest. This provides a safety valve against unanticipated liquidity shocks to the banking system. MSF rate and reverse repo rate determine the corridor for the daily movement in the weighted average call money rate.

32.8.5 Corridor: The MSF rate and reverse repo rate determine the corridor for the daily movement in the weighted average call money rate.

32.8.6 Bank Rate: As the lender-of-the-last-resort, the RBI helps the commercial banks in temporary need of cash when other sources of raising cash are exhausted. Bank rate is the rate at which RBI is ready to buy or rediscount bills of exchange or other commercial papers. Bank rate is a traditional weapon to control money supply. An increase in the bank rate would discourage commercial banks to borrow from the RBI and a corresponding increase in the lending rate of commercial banks to general public would decrease public borrowings from the banks.

The Bank Rate is published under Section 49 of the Reserve Bank of India Act, 1934. This rate has been aligned to the MSF rate and, therefore, changes automatically as and when the MSF rate changes alongside policy repo rate changes.

32.8.7 Cash Reserve Ratio (CRR): CRR is the average daily balance that a bank is required to maintain with the RBI as a share of such percent of its net demand and time liabilities (NDTL) that the RBI may notify from time-to-time in the Gazette of India. Increase/decrease in CRR is used by the RBI as an instrument of monetary control, particularly to mop up excess increases in the supply of money. This power was given to RBI in 1956.

Commercial banks in India have been traditionally subject to two types of reserve requirements, *viz.* the CRR and the SLR. While the former is a stipulation under Section 42 of the Reserve Bank of India Act, 1934, the latter is specified in Section 24 of the Banking Regulation Act, 1949 under which all banking companies are required to hold a minimum stipulated proportion of their demand and time liabilities in India in the form of cash, gold, balances with RBI, current account balances with other banks, money at call and short notice and unencumbered Government and other approved securities. The primary objective of the stipulation of liquidity ratio was to ensure that banks hold sufficient liquid reserves to meet any unexpected drain. Thus, it sought to impose financial discipline on banks and provide some protection to depositors.

Cash maintained with RBI for the purpose of meeting CRR requirement formed part of the overall liquidity ratio until 1962. This enabled banks to liquidate their Government security holdings whenever the marginal reserve requirement was raised, thereby blunting the effectiveness of this instrument. The Banking Regulation Act was, therefore, amended in 1962, raising the minimum SLR of banks from 20 percent to 25 percent of their demand and time liabilities in India. The SLR to be maintained was made exclusive of balances maintained for the purpose of meeting cash reserve ratio requirements. Any balances in excess of the prevailing CRR requirements could, however, be included in the computation of SLR. This amendment ensured that with every increase in CRR, the overall liquidity obligations were correspondingly raised. Banks were required to comply with this requirement from September 16, 1964. The amendment of the Banking Regulation Act in 1983 empowered the Reserve Bank to increase SLR of banks up to 40 percent.

32.8.8 Statutory Liquidity Ratio (SLR): Apart from the CRR, banks in India are also subject to statutory liquidity requirement. SLR is the share of NDTL that a bank is required to maintain in safe and liquid assets, such as, unencumbered government securities, cash and gold. Changes in SLR often influence the availability of resources in the banking system for lending to the private sector. All the commercial banks in India are required to maintain SLR as per Section 24 and Section 56 of the Banking Regulation Act, 1949.

The underlying philosophy of this provision is to allocate total bank credit between the government and the rest of the economy. The assurance of a certain minimum share of bank credit to the government affects the borrowings of the government from the RBI and hence serves as a tool of quantitative monetary control.

A. How does SLR Work? In India, the RBI is responsible for regulating the supply of money and stability of prices in order to ensure a progressive economy. It uses the monetary policy for achieving these objectives. Amongst other tools, SLR happens to be one of the important instruments of the monetary policy aimed at ensuring the solvency of the banks and money flow in the economy.

At the close of every business day, every bank is required to maintain a minimum portion of their Net Demand and Time Liabilities (NDTL) in the form of gold, cash, or any liquid asset form. The ratio of these liquid assets to the demand and time liabilities is referred to as SLR. RBI has the authority to increase this ratio up to 40 percent. The increase in this ratio constricts the ability of the bank to inject money into the economy.

B. Components of SLR: These are as under:

(a) Liquid Assets: These are assets that can be easily converted into cash. These include gold and cash reserve, treasury bills, the government approved securities, government bonds. Additionally, it also consists of securities which are eligible under Market Stabilisation Schemes and those falling under the market borrowing programmes.

(b) Net Demand and Time Liabilities (NDTL): NDTL refers to the total demand

and time liabilities (deposits) that is held by the banks of public and with other banks. Demand deposits consist of all liabilities which the bank needs to pay on demand like current deposits, demand drafts, balances in overdue fixed deposits and demand liabilities portion of savings bank deposits.

Time deposits consist of deposits that need to repay on maturity and where the depositor cannot withdraw money immediately. Instead, he is required to wait a certain time period to access the funds. It includes fixed deposits, time liabilities portion of savings bank deposits and staff security deposits. The liabilities of a bank include call money market borrowings, certificate of deposits etc.

(c) SLR Limit: The SLR has an upper limit of 40 percent and a lower limit of 23 percent.

C. Objectives of SLR: The prime objective of SLR is to curtail the commercial banks from liquidating their liquid assets when the Cash Reserve Ratio is raised. This ratio is determined and used by RBI to have control over the bank credit. It helps to ensure that there is solvency in commercial banks and assures that banks invest in government securities.

The flow of bank credit can be increased or decreased in the economy by means of altering the SLR. RBI raises the SLR to control the bank credit during the time of inflation and inversely it decreases the SLR during the time of recession to increase the bank credit.

D. Impact of SLR on the Investor: In order to determine the base rate, SLR acts as one of the reference rates. Base rate means the minimum lending rate which is determined by RBI and no bank is allowed to lend funds below this rate. This rate is fixed to ensure transparency with respect to borrowing and lending in the credit market. The base rate also helps the banks to cut down on their cost of lending so as to be able to extend affordable loans.

When a reserve requirement is imposed on banks, it ensures that a certain portion of the deposits are safe and are always available to be redeemed by the customers. But this condition also restricts the banks capacity for lending. In order to keep the demand in control, the lending rates have to be increased.

E. Consequences of not Maintaining SLR: Every bank including scheduled commercial bank, state cooperative bank, central cooperative banks, and primary co-operative banks have to maintain SLR according to RBI's mandate. For computation and maintenance of SLR, the net demand and time liabilities are calculated and reported every fortnight Friday by banks.

If any commercial bank fails to maintain the required SLR, it is fined a penalty of 3 percent per annum over the bank rate. If the bank continues to default on the following working day as well, then it is penalized 5 percent per annum over the bank rate. RBI does this to make sure that commercial banks do not fail to have ready cash available when customers demand them.

F. Difference between CRR and SLR: Both CRR and SLR are the components of the monetary policy. However, there are a few dissimilarities between them (Table 32.1).

Table 32.1: Dissimilarities between CRR and SLR

Cash Reserve Ratio (CRR)	Statutory Liquidity Ratio (SLR)
CRR requires banks to have only cash reserves with the RBI.	In case of SLR, banks are asked to have reserves of liquid assets which include both cash and gold.
Banks do not earn returns on money parked as CRR.	Banks earn returns on money parked as SLR.
RBI controls the liquidity in the banking system through CRR.	SLR is used to control the bank's leverage for credit expansion.
Under CRR, cash reserve is maintained by the banks with RBI.	Under SLR, the securities are kept with the banks themselves which they need to maintain in the form of liquid assets.

SLR provision has created a captive market for government securities which increases automatically with the growth in the liabilities of the banks. Moreover, it has kept the cost of the debt to the government low in view of the generally low rate of interest on government securities.

Although SLR was initially conceived as a measure of securing the liquidity of banks, it also had implication for their ability to expand credit to the private sector. In the light of the monetary expansion triggered by RBI's unbridled accommodation of the Government and the need to restrain the pace of expansion of bank credit, SLR instrument became a tool for mobilising greater resources for the Government from the banks. SLR was raised gradually from 25 percent in 1970 to 38.5 percent in 1990. This served to increase the captive investor base for Government securities, thereby reducing the pressure on RBI to absorb these securities. However, the incidence of macroeconomic crisis in the early 1990s and the emphasis of the role of SLR as a prudential instrument rather than as an instrument for accommodating fiscal deficit led to scaling down of the SLR back to the statutory minimum of 25 percent in October 1997 and further down to 24 percent in November 2008 in view of the global financial crisis and its impact on India.

32.8.9 Open Market Operations (OMOs): OMOs are conducted by the RBI via outright sale/purchase of government securities to/from the market with the primary aim of modulating rupee liquidity conditions in the market. OMOs are an effective quantitative policy tool in the armoury of the RBI, but are constrained by the stock of government securities available with it at a point in time.

The RBI can enter the money market for the purpose of purchase or sale of Government securities on its own account. Every open market purchase by the RBI increases primary money by equal amount while every sale decreases it. As regards their advantages, open market operations are highly flexible, easily reversible in time, their effect on money supply is immediate, and they do not carry *announcement effects* as in the case of changes in the bank rate.

Open market operations, considered very effective in developed countries, are not of much importance in India in view of the captive nature of the market for Government bonds. For example, the Treasury bill market is limited largely to the RBI itself and scheduled commercial banks which are required under law to invest a certain minimum proportion of their total liabilities in Government securities. The private dealers in Government securities are few and far between.

32.8.10 Market Stabilisation Scheme (MSS): This instrument for monetary management was introduced in 2004. Surplus liquidity of a more enduring nature arising from large capital inflows is absorbed through sale of short-dated government securities and treasury bills. The mobilised cash is held in a separate Government account with the RBI.

32.8.11 Refinance Facilities: Sector-specific refinance facilities aim at achieving sector- specific objectives through provision of liquidity at a cost linked to the policy repo rate. The RBI has, however, been progressively de-emphasising sector specific-policies as they interfere with the transmission mechanism.

32.8.12 Standing Deposit Facility (SDF): The Union Budget 2018-19 paved the way for the introduction of a new Standing Deposit Facility (SDF), which would serve as an additional tool for the RBI to absorb excess liquidity. Accordingly, the RBI Act, 1934 has been amended for introduction of an uncollateralised deposit scheme. The SDF is generally an unlimited, fixed rate and on-tap deposit facility offered by a central bank. Its introduction would enable the Reserve Bank to suck out liquidity without offering any collateral. Hitherto, in times of large liquidity surpluses with the banking system, the Reserve Bank often faced a shortage of collateral in the form of G-securities in its portfolio which hobbled reverse repo operations and necessitated reliance on the government for the supply of Government securities under the market stabilisation scheme (MSS).

32.8.13 Moral Suasions: Through moral suasions (discussions, suggestions and advice), the RBI can influence the investment and credit policies of the commercial banks. For example, it can ask the commercial banks to invest a larger proportion, than required, of their assets in Government securities. Similarly, it can advise them regarding the allocation of credit to the private sector.

32.9 Monetary Policy Assessment

The evolving international situation as also domestic contingencies in the early 1990s called for changes in the formulation and conduct of monetary policy in India. Accordingly, monetary policy evolved with increasing current and capital account liberalisation, liberalisation of the financial sector, changing pattern of credit requirements from the real sector and rapid changes in the world economic scenario. The operating procedure of monetary policy in terms of targets and instruments, therefore, saw substantial changes.

The twin objectives of monetary policy viz., maintaining price stability and ensuring availability of adequate credit to productive sectors of the economy to support growth have remained unchanged, though their relative emphasis varied depending on the circumstances. In line with this, in recent years, a preference emerged for a soft and flexible interest rate environment within the framework of macroeconomic stability. At the same time, the large inflows of external capital have contributed to the liquidity conditions remaining very comfortable. Consequently, the emphasis of monetary policy within the broad objectives of price stability and growth has been on liquidity management so as to ensure orderly conditions in financial markets without impeding the legitimate credit needs of industry.

In India, the conduct of monetary policy since early 1990s has been shaped by wide-ranging structural reforms. This necessitated significant changes in the monetary policy framework in terms of objectives, instruments and targets. The changes had to be dovetailed with a simultaneous process of evolution of financial markets in consonance with the aim of enhancing allocative efficiency through the process of price discovery. At the heart of monetary reforms lay the containment of the fiscal dominance of monetary policy. In contrast, with the opening up of the economy, monetary management had to contend increasingly with challenges emanating from the large volume and sudden switches in capital flows and episodes of volatility in the financial markets. In this milieu, while price stability and credit availability remained twin objectives of monetary policy, financial stability has gradually emerged as a key consideration in the conduct of monetary policy.

An overall assessment of the conduct of monetary policy in India indicates that the RBI has been successful in maintaining price and financial stability, even in an environment characterised by repeated shocks, both domestic and external. Efforts to improve credit delivery mechanism have also started yielding dividend in recent years.

To sum up, in tune with the national economic objectives, RBI has followed a monetary policy usually called the policy of *controlled expansion*. The money supply has expanded sufficiently to meet the growing needs of industry and trade. However, it has been ensured that the expansion is not reckless. Broadly speaking, the expansion of money supply has been somewhat more than the increase in output thereby allowing a reasonable increase in the price level.

33

Inflation Targeting in India

33.1 What is Inflation (Price Rise)?

A significant rise in the general price level in a country over a long period of time is called price rise or inflation. It is the opposite of price stability. In economics, price stability is not used in a rigid sense to mean price fixity. A modest increase of 2 to 3 percent per annum in the price level is compatible, sometimes even desirable, in the context of economic development. However, when the general price rise is appreciable (say in double-digit figure) and experienced over a long period of time, it gets the dreaded name inflation.

What should be the tolerable limit of price rise? There is no cut and dried answer to this question because it all depends upon the economic circumstances prevailing in a country at a particular time. The Indian Committee to Review the Working of the Monetary System (Chairman: S. Chakravarty) [1] recommended, as a general guideline, an increase in price level of no more than 4 percent.

Some price rise (say of 3 or 4 percent) is not only desirable but also necessary to give incentive to the farmers and the manufacturers to produce more. This is particularly true in a dynamic economy like India. The impact of even a moderate price rise is neutralized because of institutional and other arrangements.

Thus, salaries and pensions of the organized sector are linked with consumer price index (CPI). Similarly, subsidies, pensions, scholarships and other benefits to the poor people in the unorganized sector are enhanced if there is a price rise. Subsidy amount increases if the price of LPG cylinder increases.

33.2 Measurement and Reporting of Inflation

Changes in the level of prices are measured by means of index numbers. The index of prices includes a wide variety of goods and services which are essential for life. Since the relative importance of different goods in the family budget is not the same therefore each commodity included in the index is assigned a weight in accordance with the proportion of family expenditure on that commodity. The prices of different commodities multiplied by their respective weights give the aggregate for the year chosen as the base. This is then compared with the similar aggregate of prices in some subsequent year for purposes of comparison. The base year is changed from time-to-time to accommodate new products and reflect current economic conditions.

In India, there are two main indicators of the rate of inflation:

1. Wholesale Price Index (WPI).
2. Consumer Price Index (CPI).

Apart from the above two, there are the following two other indicators:

1. Consumer Price Index for Industrial Workers [CPI (IW)].
2. Consumer Price Index for Agricultural Labourers [CPI (AL)].

33.2.1 Wholesale Price Index (WPI): WPI is the weighted index of commodities transacted at the wholesale level in the country. It includes price quotations on several commodities, divided into three broad categories: (a) primary articles, (b) fuel, power, light, and lubricants and (c) manufactured products. The series is revised periodically to account for the changing pattern of the commodities transacted.

WPI for all of the commodities is released on 14th of every month (the next working day, if 14th of the month is a national holiday). The base year for the WPI was revised from the earlier 2004-2005 to 2011-12 to better capture changes in the economy.

While earlier the Reserve Bank of India (RBI) used WPI inflation to manage monetary policy expectations, it is now the CPI inflation which is taken into account. The RBI highlights its inflation expectations based on the CPI inflation data that comes in.

33.2.2 Consumer Price Index (CPI): CPI is a statistical estimate constructed by using a sample of representative items whose prices are collected periodically. The annual percentage change in CPI is used as a measure of inflation.

All-India CPIs (Rural, Urban, and Combined) are compiled and calculated on a monthly basis by National Statistical Office (NSO), a wing of the Ministry of Statistics and Programme Implementation. [2] The indices are released, through a press note, every month at 5.30 p.m. on 12th day of the following month. If it is a holiday, then they are released on the next working day. The press note also announces the date of the next release of CPI numbers.

The current base for CPI numbers is 2012 = 100. All-India inflation rate is defined as percentage change in the CPI on point-to-point basis, i.e. current month over same month of last year (e.g. September 2020 over September 2019).

33.2.3 Consumer Price Index for Industrial Workers CPI (IW): This index is the oldest among the CPI indices as its dissemination started as early as in 1946. The history of compilation and maintenance of CPI (IW) owes its origin to the deteriorating economic condition of the workers post-First World War which resulted in sharp increase in prices. As a consequence of rise in prices and cost of living, the provincial governments started compiling consumer price index. The estimates were however not satisfactory. In pursuance of the recommendation of Rau Court of Enquiry, the work of compilation and maintenance was taken over by Government in 1943. Presently, the compilation of CPI (IW) is done by Labour Bureau, an attached office under Ministry of Labour and Employment.

33.2.4 Consumer Price Index for Agricultural Labourers [CPI (AL)]: This index is also compiled by Labour Bureau.

The above two indices are occupation-specific and centre-specific. This means that these index numbers measure changes in the retail price of the basket of goods and services consumed by the specific occupational groups in the specific centres.

33.3 Price Stability as an Objective of Monetary Policy in India

The preamble of the Reserve Bank of India Act, 1934 enjoins it "...to regulate the issue of Bank Notes and keeping of reserves with a view to securing monetary stability in India and generally to operate the currency and credit system of the country to its advantage...".

Within this broad mandate, the monetary policy of RBI pursues the twin objectives of price stability and ensuring the availability of credit to the productive sectors in the Indian economy. The emphasis between the twin objectives of price stability and growth has, however, varied over time depending on the evolving price-output situation.

33.3.1 Amendment of the Reserve Bank of India Act, 1934: The Government amended the Reserve Bank of India Act, 1934 through the Finance Act, 2016. The amended Act provides for inflation target to be set by the Government, in consultation with RBI, once in every five years. This target is notified in the Official Gazette. It further provides for a statutory basis for the constitution of an empowered Monetary Policy Committee (MPC). Thus, the earlier agreement, in the form of a memorandum of understanding, was given statutory backing.

The preamble in the RBI Act, as amended by the Finance Act, 2016, now provides that the primary objective of the monetary policy is to maintain price stability, while keeping in mind the objective of growth, and to meet the challenge of an increasingly complex economy. Thus, now there is a statutory basis for a monetary policy framework and MPC.

33.4 What is Inflation Targeting?

In India, the dominant objective of monetary policy is price stability and it is through price stability that it plays a role in growth augmentation. Low rate of inflation creates room for a reduction in interest rates to boost growth and vice versa.

Central banks have the power to print *fiat* money. Unlike money backed by metals such as silver or gold in the pre-World War II era, fiat money gets its value from a legal decree. Every fiat money needs a nominal anchor to tie down the price level. A nominal anchor can take various forms such as money supply, nominal gross domestic product (GDP), value of domestic currency relative to a foreign currency or a price measure such as the consumer price index (CPI). Since the collapse of the gold standard, central banks have tried all kinds of nominal anchors but with limited success. The world has increasingly moved towards inflation targeting where the nominal anchor is the CPI.

Inflation targeting requires a central bank to adjust its monetary policy instruments in response to the gap between the forecast inflation rate and a pre-announced target rate. Most countries today follow a *flexible inflation targeting framework*. This gives the central bank discretion to respond to shocks such as a growth slowdown in the short-run and meet the inflation target in the medium-run.

Inflation targeting is a monetary policy strategy used by central banks for maintaining price level at a certain level or within a range. It indicates the primacy of price stability as the key objective of monetary policy. The argument for price stability stems from the fact that rising prices create uncertainties in decision making, adversely affecting savings and encouraging speculative investments. Inflation targeting brings in more predictability and transparency in deciding monetary policy. If the central banks could ensure price stability, households and companies can plan ahead, negotiating wages on the basis of expecting low and stable inflation.

A unique and at the same time a controversial feature of inflation targeting is that the central bank sidelines all other objectives of monetary policy to ensure that the single goal of price stability is realized.

There is a conflict or trade-off between the objective of price stability and economic growth, the latter requiring lower interest rates and hence augmented money supply which, in turn, can put pressure on prices.

A negative side of inflation targeting as a philosophy is that it openly accepts reduction of economic growth as a way to achieve price stability. However, growth is as important as price stability.

33.5 Origin of Inflation Targeting

Inflation targeting was first adopted by the Reserve Bank of New Zealand in 1989. Since then, the number of countries using it as a framework to conduct their monetary policy has steadily gone up. The US Federal Reserve, European Central Bank and Bank of England all have inflation targets, as do the central banks of Thailand, Indonesia and the Philippines.

Various advanced economies including United States, Canada and Australia have been using inflation targeting as a strategy in their monetary policy framework. The case for inflation targeting has been made in India as the country has been experiencing a high level of inflation till recently.

33.6 Need for Inflation Targeting

Inflation targeting anchors the inflation expectations of the private sector. It imposes discipline on monetary policy. Before the adoption of inflation targeting, monetary policy in India was conducted in an ad hoc manner. RBI would target multiple indicators ranging from inflation and growth to exchange rate and trade balance. There was no clarity about the primary objective of monetary policy. The lack of accountability, clarity and transparency in monetary policy introduced uncertainty. In the absence of a specific mandate to target inflation, monetary policy in India was often used to achieve objectives unrelated to price stability. Uncertainty about the monetary policy objectives of RBI was a risk factor for the Indian economy.

Balancing growth with price stability had previously led to conflict between RBI and the Central Government, which usually wants lower interest rates that can provide a lift to the economy. The Government tried to bolster growth at the expense of the inflation focus.

33.7 Fixing of Inflation Target

RBI officially adopted inflation targeting as a monetary policy strategy in February 2015. RBI and Government of India signed a Monetary Policy Framework Agreement on February 20, 2015. As per terms of the agreement, the objective of monetary policy framework is primarily to maintain price stability, while keeping in mind the objective of growth.

In view of the powers conferred by Section 45ZA of the RBI Act, 1934, the Central Government, in consultation with RBI, notified on August 5, 2016 the inflation target beginning from August 5, 2016 and ending on March 31, 2021.

The Government fixed the inflation target of 4 percent with tolerance level of +/-2 percent for the period stated above. More specifically, the target and tolerance levels are as under:

- Inflation Target: 4 percent.
- Upper tolerance level: 6 percent.
- Lower tolerance level: 2 percent.

The move placed the Government and RBI on the same page. It also sent out a strong signal of stability with respect to the country's macroeconomic policies—something that had come into question in recent years.

While setting the above target, the government elaborated that inflation targeting in India will consider the growth dimensions also. Consumer inflation target of 4 percent for next five years is in line with the Centre's focus on macroeconomic stability to boost growth while keeping prices in check. The announcement also prepared the ground for setting up MPC that will set rates (previously set by the RBI) in keeping with this target. Fixation of an inflation target while giving due emphasis to the objective of growth and challenges of an increasingly complex economy was widely appreciated as an important monetary policy reform.

The advantage of having a band (range) is that it allows the MPC to recognise the short-run trade-offs between inflation and growth but enables it to rein in prices in the long-run and over the course of business cycles. The range also accommodates data limitations, projection errors, short-run supply gaps and instability in agriculture production, an important factor for CPI inflation. Food articles account for a major weight in the inflation index.

Now that the government has acknowledged 4 percent as the inflation target, it should give full freedom to RBI to set the interest rates. There should not be any interference.

As per the new policy, if retail inflation is more than 6 percent for three consecutive quarters from 2015-16 and less than 2 percent for three consecutive quarters from 2016-17, then it will be treated as the failure of the RBI's monetary policy. Counteractive measures should be initiated in such a scenario. The new policy also prescribes the procedure to be followed by the RBI if the target is missed. Where RBI fails to meet the inflation target, it shall set out a report to the Central Government stating: (a) the reasons for failure to achieve the inflation target, (b) remedial actions proposed to be taken by RBI and (c) an estimate of the time-period within which the inflation target shall be achieved pursuant to timely implementation of proposed remedial actions. RBI will publish the operating targets as well as operating procedure for the monetary policy though which the target for the monetary policy will be achieved. The RBI will also be required to bring a document every six months to explain the sources of inflation and forecast for inflation for next 6-18 months.

33.8 Monetary Policy Committee (MPC)

The amendment to the RBI Act provides for the creation of a six-member MPC chaired by the RBI governor, who has a casting vote in the event of a tie. Of the six, three are from RBI—the governor, a deputy governor and another officer. The other three members are appointed by the Central Government on the recommendations of a search-cum-selection committee. They are chosen from experts in economics, banking, finance and monetary policy. Government notified the constitution of the MPC on September 29, 2016.

MPC is entrusted with the task of fixing the benchmark policy rate (repo rate) required to contain inflation within the specified target level. Under the RBI Act, the Central Government, in consultation with the RBI, determines the inflation target in terms of the Consumer Price Index (CPI), once in every five years. This target is notified in the Official Gazette.

In short, inflation hurts everyone in the country from households to firms. Even moderately high inflation is bad for growth as is inflation volatility. The primary objective of monetary policy should be to ensure low and stable inflation. Inflation targeting offers a framework to achieve this objective in a credible and sustainable manner. The adoption of inflation targeting by the RBI is a significant step in the right direction. RBI should stick to this framework and put in place the operating procedure needed to implement it.

To sum up, it is now widely agreed that monetary policy can contribute to sustainable growth by maintaining price stability. High inflation has an adverse effect on growth due to a number of factors: distortion of relative prices which lowers economic efficiency; redistribution of wealth between debtors and creditors; aversion to long-term contracts and excessive resources are devoted to hedging inflation risks. In developing economies, in particular, an additional cost of high inflation emanates from its adverse effects on the poor population. Maintenance of low and stable inflation has thus emerged as a key objective of monetary policy.

Endnotes

1. Reserve Bank of India, *Report of the Committee to Review the Working of the Monetary System in India* (Chairman: Sukhamoy Chakravarty), 1985.
2. Ministry of Statistics and Programme Implementation (MoSPI) came into existence as an Independent Ministry on October 15, 1999 after the merger of the Department of Statistics and the Department of Programme Implementation. The Ministry has two wings, one relating to Statistics and the other Programme Implementation.

   The Statistics Wing called the National Statistical Office (NSO) consists of the Central Statistical Office (CSO), the Computer Centre and the National Sample Survey Office (NSSO).

   The Programme Implementation Wing has three Divisions, namely: (i) Twenty-point Programme, (ii) Infrastructure Monitoring and Project Monitoring and (iii) Member of Parliament Local Area Development Scheme.

   Besides these two wings, there is National Statistical Commission created through a Resolution of Government of India and one autonomous institute, viz. Indian Statistical Institute declared as an institute of national importance by an Act of Parliament.

Bibliography

Bibliography

Armendariz Beatrize and Jonathan Morduch (2007), "Economics of Micro Finance", Prentice Hall of India Pvt. Ltd., New Delhi.

Bimal Jalan (2002), "Strengthening Indian Banking and Finance: Progress and Prospects", Speech delivered at the Bank Economists' Conference in Bangalore.

C.K.G. Nair (2012), "Financial Sector Reforms: Refining the Architecture", in R. Malhotra (ed.), 'A Critical Decade: Policies for India's Development', Oxford University Press, New Delhi.

European Central Bank (2000), "Issues Arising from the Emergence of Electronic Money", *Monthly Bulletin*, November.

F.J. Fabozzi, F. Modigliani, F.J. Jones and M.G. Ferri (2009), "Foundations of Financial Markets and Institutions", Pearson Education, third edition.

F.S. Mishkin and S.G. Eakins (2009), "Financial Markets and Institutions", Pearson Education, sixth edition.

Fitzgerald Valpy (2006), "Financial Development and Economic Growth: A Critical View", Background Paper for World Economic and Social Survey, Oxford University, U.K.

Government of India, Ministry of Finance, *Budget Papers* (various years).

—Ministry of Finance, "Economic Survey" (various issues).

—Ministry of Finance (2013), "Report of the Financial Sector Legislative Reforms Commission", Chairman: B.N. Srikrishna, Volume I.

—Ministry of Law, Justice, and Company Affairs, "Constitution of India".

—Planning Commission (2008), "Report of the Committee on Financial Inclusion", Chairman: C. Rangarajan.

L.M. Bhole and J. Mahukud (2011), "Financial Institutions and Markets", Tata McGraw-Hill, New Delhi.

M.Y. Khan (2011), "Indian Financial System", Tata McGraw-Hill, New Delhi.

Narendra Jadhav (2003), "Central Bank Strategies, Credibility and Independence: Global Evolution and the Indian Experience", RBI Occasional Papers.

Narendra Jadhav, Partha Ray, D. Bose and Indrani Sen Gupta (2003), "The Reserve Bank of India's Balance Sheet: Analytics and Dynamics of Evolution", RBI Occasional Papers.

Priya Basu (2005), "A Financial System for India's Poor", *Economic and Political Weekly*, No. 37.

R.C. Merton (2005), "Financial Innovation and Economic Performance", *Journal of Applied Corporate Finance*, Volume 4, Issue 4.

R.N. Malhotra (1990), "Evolution of Financial System", Nineteenth Frank Moraes Memorial Lecture, Chennai, September.

Raghuram Rajan (2009), "A Hundred Small Steps: Report of the Committee on Financial Sector Reforms", Planning Commission, Government of India, Sage Publications, New Delhi.

Rakesh Mohan (2011), "Growth with Financial Stability: Central Banking in an

Emerging Market", Oxford University Press, New Delhi.

Reserve Bank of India (2013), "Banking Structure in India: The Way Forward", Discussion Paper.

—(2019), "Report of the High-Level Committee on Deepening of Digital Payments", Chairman: Nandan Nilekani, May.

S.K. Chattopadhyay (2010), "RBI Working Paper on Financial Inclusion in India: A Case Study of West Bengal", Working Paper Series, September, RBI.

Sanjeev Kumar Gupta (2011), "Financial Inclusion: IT as Enabler", Reserve Bank of India Occasional Paper 31, No. 2.

T.A. Bhavani and N.R. Bhanumurthy (2012), "Financial Access in Post-Reform India", Oxford University Press, New Delhi.

World Bank Group (2019), "Electronic Payments Acceptance", World Bank-NITI Aayog Roundtable, January.

—(2018), "Payment Systems Worldwide: A Snapshot", September.

Y.S.P. Thorat (2011), "Report of the Working Group on Outreach of Institutional Finance, Co-operatives, and Risk Management", Planning Commission, Government of India.

Y.V. Reddy (1997), "Financial Sector Reforms and RBI's Balance Sheet Management", RBI Bulletin, December.

Index

Index

A

Aadhaar Payment Bridge System (APBS), 210
Aadhaar-enabled Payment System (AEPS), 210
Adverse Selection in Capital Market, 58
Amendment of Securities Contract Regulation Act (SCRA), 141
Appeals against SEBI Judgements, 91
Arbitrageurs, 120
Asian Clearing Union (ACU), 52
Asian Financial Crisis, 1997, 62
Assets of a Bank, 183

B

Balance Sheet of a Bank, 183
Balance Sheet of the Reserve Bank of India (RBI), 225
Bank Rate Policy, 228
Bank Rate, 172, 251
Banking Crisis, 61
Banking Law (Amendments) Act, 2012, 190
Bankruptcy Law Reforms Committee (BLRC), 101
Base Rate System, 170
Benchmark Prime Lending Rate (BPLR) System, 170
Benefits and Risks of Financial Integration, 45
Benefits of Demat, 113
Benefits of Digital Payments, 207
Benefits of E-money, 4
Bharat Interface for Money (BHIM), 211
Black-Scholes Formulae, 134
Bombay Stock Exchange (BSE) Ltd., 105
Book-building, 88
Broad Money, 14

C

Call Money Market, 70
Call Options, 131
Capital Market in the Pre-reforms Period, 81
Capital Market Reforms since 1991, 82
Capital Market, 38, 81
Card-based Electronic Payment Systems, 207
Cash Reserve Ratio (CRR), 14, 228, 251
Certificates of Deposit (CDs), 74
Chiang Mai Initiative, 53
Chicago Board of Trade, 121
Classification of Commercial Banks in India, 189
Classification of Financial Institutions in India, 28
Clearing Corporation of India Ltd. (CCIL), 50
Collateralised Borrowing and Lending Obligation (CBLO), 77
Commercial Banks, 32
Commercial Paper (CP), 73
Companies Act, 2013, 96
Competition Act, 2002, 192
Competitive Financial Saving Rates, 173
Consumer Price Index (CPI), 258
Consumer Price Index for Agricultural Labourers [CPI (AL)], 258
Consumer Price Index for Industrial Workers CPI (IW), 258
Corporate Social Responsibility, 98
Credit Cards, 208
Credit Default Swap (CDS), 142
Credit Derivatives in India, 145

Credit Derivatives, 142
Crypto Currency, 7
Currency Crisis, 61
Currency Derivatives, 108
Currency Futures, 135

D

Debit Cards, 207
Debt Market, 108
Dematerialisation (Demat), 112
Demutualisation and Corporatisation of Stock Exchanges, 110
Dennis Robertson, 156
Deposit Insurance System, 196
Depositories Act, 1996, 93
Depository System, 112
Derivative Contracts, 118
Determinants of Access to Financial Services, 23
Determinants of Money Supply, 14
Development Finance Institutions (DFIs), 34
Developments in the Money Market since 1991, 69
Digital Money, 7
Digital Wallet, 211
Digitization in Banking Sector, 206
Dimensions of Financial Market Integration, 44
Domestic Financial Integration, 45

E

Economic Role of Derivatives, 120
Electronic Money (E-Money), 3
E-Money in India, 6
Equated Monthly Instalment (EMI), 163
Equation of Exchange, 11
Equity Derivatives, 108
European Central Bank (ECB), 10
Expectations Theory, 167

F

Fiduciary Money, 3
Financial (Sub-prime) Crisis, 2007-08, 62
Financial Activism, 24
Financial Globalisation, 25
Financial Literacy, 87, 108
Financial Neutrality, 24
Financial Stability, 25
Financial Volatility, 25
Fiscal Deficits, 15
Fiscal Responsibility and Budget Management (FRBM) Act, 2003, 16
Flat Rate Loans, 163
Floating Rate Loans, 163
Foreign Banks in India, 195
Forward Contracts, 118, 125
Forward Markets Commission (FMC), 137
Four Measures of Money Supply, 12
Free Pricing, 48
Functions of a Central Bank, 218
Functions of a Commercial Bank, 180
Functions of Money, 9
Functions of Reserve Bank of India (RBI), 237
Functions of SEBI, 89
Future Contracts, 118, 127

G

Global Financial Integration, 45
Gross and Net Rate of Interest, 155

H

Hedgers, 120
Heterogeneous Nature of Financial Markets, 44
High Powered Money and Money Multiplier, 15
History of Central Banks, 215
History of Derivatives, 121
History of Futures, 129

I

Immediate Payment Services (IMPS), 209
Implications of E-money for the Central Bank, 5
Importance of Financial Markets, 37
Index Futures, 130
Insolvency and Bankruptcy Board of India (IBBI), 103
Insolvency and Bankruptcy Code (IBC), 2016, 99, 101
Instruments of Monetary Policy, 249
Insurance Organisations, 36
Insurance Regulatory and Development Authority (IRDA), 36
Integration of Financial Markets, 43
Integration of the Credit Market, 51
Integration of the Foreign Exchange Market, 51
Integration of the Government Securities Market, 51
Interest Rate Futures, 108
International Experience of Derivatives, 123
International Financial Integration, 53
International Monetary Fund (IMF), 62
Introduction of Free Pricing, 83
Introduction of Futures in India, 129
Investor Protection Fund, 86
Investor Protection in Derivatives Market, 87

J

John Maynard Keynes, 64, 156

K

Kinds of E-Money, 4
Knut Wicksell, 156
Kumar Mangalam Birla Committee, 111

L

L.C. Gupta Committee on Derivatives Trading in India, 139
L.C. Gupta, 92
Legal Framework for Banking Sector in India, 189
Liabilities of a Bank, 183
Limitations of Stock Market, 104
Limited Liability Partnership (LLP) Act, 2008, 98
Liquidity Adjustment Facility (LAF), 251
Liquidity Preference Theory of the Rate of Interest, 156
Liquidity Premium Theory, 167
Loanable Fund Theory of the Rate of Interest, 156
Lok Adalats, 191

M

M. Narasimham, 69
Macro Prudential Policy, 229
Manmohan Singh, 107
Marginal Cost of Funds Based Lending Rate (MCLR) System, 170
Marginal Standing Facility (MSF) Rate, 172
Marginal Standing Facility (MSF), 251
Meaning of Derivatives, 117
Measurement and Reporting of Inflation, 257
Measures of Money Supply in India, 17
Metallic Money, 3
Model Listing Agreement, 91
Monetary Policy Committee (MPC), 261
Monetary Transmission Mechanism, 247
Money Market, 38, 65
Money Supply in Open Economy, 17
Money Supply, 11
Moral Hazard in Insurance Industry, 59
Moral Hazard, 59
Moral Hazards in Financial Transactions, 59

Moral Suasions, 229
Mortgage-Backed Securities (MBS), 116
Motives for Holding Cash, 156
Mutual Funds, 35

N

Narrow Money, 13
National Electronic Funds Transfer (NEFT), 209
National Exchange for Automated Trading (NEAT-F&O), 147
National Securities Clearing Corporation Ltd (NSCCL), 114
National Securities Depository Limited (NSDL), 113
National Stock Exchange (NSE) of India Ltd., 106
Need for Inflation Targeting, 260
Non-banking Financial Companies (NBFCs), 34
Non-card Electronic Payment Systems, 209

O

Objectives of Banking Sector Reforms, 199
Objectives of SEBI, 89
Open Market Operations (OMOs), 14, 229
Operating Procedures of Monetary Policy, 248
Options in Historical Perspective, 132
Options, 119, 131
Organisation of Banking Structure, 200
Origin of Inflation Targeting, 260

P

P.V. Narasimha Rao, 107
Paper Money, 3
Pension Funds, 35
Portfolio Management, 184
Powers of SEBI, 90
Prime Lending Rate (PLR) System, 169
Private Sector Banks, 194
Protection of Investors, 86
Public Sector Banks, 194
Put Options, 131

R

RBI's Vision Documents for Payments, 242
Real and Money Rate of Interest, 155
Real Time Gross Settlement (RTGS), 209
Reasons for the Popularity of Derivatives, 117
Recurring Deposit, 181
Reforms in the Financial Markets, 39
Regional Financial Integration, 45
Regional Rural Banks (RRBs), 33
Regulation and Supervision of Financial Institutions in India, 29
Regulation and Supervision of Financial Markets in India, 38
Regulation and Supervision of Financial System, 23
Rejection of Decoupling Hypothesis, 231
Rematerialisation (Remat), 113
Repo Rate, 171, 250
Report of the Technical Group on Money Market, 77
Reverse Repo Rate, 172, 251
Revolving Line of Credit, 163
Risk of Default, 161
RuPay, 208
Rural Co-operative Credit Institutions, 33

S

S.S. Tarapore, 42
Saving Deposit Rate, 172
Securities and Exchange Board of India (SEBI) Act, 1992, 89